Understanding India's Maoists
Select Documents

Understanding India's Maoists

Select Documents

P V Ramana

INSTITUTE FOR DEFENCE STUDIES & ANALYSES
NEW DELHI

PENTAGON PRESS

The Cover shows the Peace Memorial, unveiled on July 30, 2005, in memory of victims of Naxalite/Maoist violence, in Beerpur Village, Karimnagar District, Telangana. Beerpur is the native place of Muppala Lakshman Rao alias Ganapathy, General Secretary of CPI (Maoist).

Photograph courtesy: Mr K.M. Daya Shankar, Principal Correspondent, *The Hindu.*

Understanding India's Maoists: Select Documents / *PV Ramana*

First Published in 2014

ISBN 978-81-8274-801-9

Published by
PENTAGON PRESS
206, Peacock Lane, Shahpur Jat
New Delhi-110049
Phones: 011-64706243, 26491568
Telefax: 011-26490600
email: rajan@pentagonpress.in
website: www.pentagonpress.in

Branch:
Prime Arcade
Office #11
1154 Saifee Street
Opp. M.G.Road, Camp
Pune-411001
Email: pentagonpresspune@gmail.com

In association with
Institute for Defence Studies and Analyses
No. 1, Development Enclave,
New Delhi-110010
Phone: +91-11-26717983
Website: www.idsa.in

Maps: Geographic Information Systems (GIS) Lab, IDSA.
Printed at Aegean Offset Printers, Greater Noida, U.P.

To Krishna, my father, and Krishna, my son

CONTENTS

Author's Note

The proscribed Communist Party of India (Maoist), Maoists in short, also knownin India as Naxalites, is the most lethal and largest of all such groups. Its ultimate aim is to capture/seize political/state power through protracted people's war (PPW), on the lines propounded by Mao Tse Tung.

This volume is a modest attempt to understand the thought process of the Communist Party of India (Maoist). In this wake, some of the more important documents of the Maoists have been edited and compiled in this volume. These have been classified under various heads viz. Organisational Aspects; Interviews; Unity Congress; Central Committee/Politburo Circulars/Statements; Synchronised/Large Scale Attacks; and Statements on other Organisations.

The Introduction presents a profile of the Maoists and attempts to summarise the outfit's thought process. Thereafter, the Maoists' documents are presented. Each of it is prefaced with a summary and a background to its preparation by the Maoists. These documents, unless otherwise stated, have been collected from a variety of sources during field-visits over the past nine years. However, it needs to be mentioned here that most, if not all, of these are available now on the Internet. Besides, I have used the spelling 'Ganapathy' while referring to the general secretary of the CPI (Maoist), while retaining the spellings 'Ganapathy' and 'Ganapathi' as mentioned variously in the original in different documents.

I gratefully acknowledge the support and encouragement of Dr Arvind Gupta, Director General, IDSA, at whose suggestion this project has been undertaken. He was immensely patient and always smilingly nudged me to increase the pace of work. I thank all members of the Internal Security Centre, past and present, for their kind support. I am also thankful to my colleague Vivek Kaushik—for his support in the production process.

I am grateful to the two anonymous referees for their kind suggestions that helped improve the contents of this volume.

I am grateful to my friend, Mr K Srinivas Reddy, Resident Editor, *The Hindu*, at Hyderabad, who has always been a source of inspiration, support and encouragement. I also thank my numerous friends in various States, who wish to remain anonymous, for their help whenever I approached them.

I thank Mr Rajan Arya and Mr Virender Negi of Pentagon Press for publishing this volume.

My parents, wife and son, and brother have been my strongest pillars of support in all my endeavours.

New Delhi **P V Ramana**

Introduction

INDIA'S MAOISTS: PROFILE AND THOUGHT PROCESS

SECTION I: PROFILE

ORGANISATION[1]

The CPI (Maoist) is headed by its general secretary, Muppala Lakshmana Rao alias Ganapathy[2]. The outfit's organisational structure is hierarchical. At the apex is the all-powerful Central Committee (CC). As in January 2014, it is believed that the CC consists of 17 members. A smaller core group of seven people constitute the Politburo (PB) that runs the affairs of the outfit on a day-to-day basis. The Regional Bureau (RB)—a conglomerate of areas in different States—reports to the CC. The State Committee (SC) and its equivalent Special Zone Committee (SZC) reports to the RB. Each State/SZC is responsible for all activities of the outfit within its jurisdiction. Each State is further divided into zones and sub-zones, below which are District/Division Committees (DC/DVC). Below the District/Division level, there are Squad Area Committees (SAC), which are responsible for activities within a cluster of villages in which the guerrilla squad operates. A village/town cell is at the bottom of the hierarchy.

A seven-member Central Military Commission (CMC) is at the apex of the Maoist military machine, the People's Liberation Guerrilla Army (PLGA). There exists a Military Commission corresponding to each of the committees mentioned above. Besides, there is an overlap between the political and military structures of the CPI (Maoist), i.e., while there are separate political and military structures, their membership is common in the largest measure. In other words, at each level a large number of members are common to both the various committees and commissions.

The Maoist propaganda machinery is guided by the Central Propaganda Bureau (CPB), whose members are also members of the CC. The CPB is responsible for dissemination of all internal circulars of the CPI (Maoist), as well as distribution of its periodicals with varied publication schedules, such as monthly, half-yearly or annual.

All the major decisions are taken by the CC after a careful assessment of their pros and cons. The CC then leaves it to the individual field-level commanders to plan and execute the decisions. After every major action—an attack on a police station, looting an armoury or killing of an important public person or a well-protected security official—a detailed de-briefing is conducted to assess strengths, mistakes and weaknesses and, thus, learn lessons for future tactics.

The CPI (Maoist) gathers intelligence in pursuit of its activities, and has a dedicated intelliegence wing, which was once headed by Patel Sudhakar Reddy and later by Sakhamuri Appa Rao, both of whom were killed in separate encounters with the Andhra Pradesh police. Also, there is enough indication that, sooner than later, there are plans to institute a Disciplinary Committee.[3]

Recruitement and Cadre Strength

According to Bimal, a Central Committee member, the Maoists have "a party controlled mechanism under which we receive proposals from the locals. After obtaining the consent of the parents of applicants, we forward the proposals to one of our committees. It vets them and takes a final call on whether or not to recruit, based on the person's antecedents, class and disposition towards others in his or her village".[4]

Last known, the armed, underground strength of the CPI (Maoist) was approximately 13,000 fighters, both men and women, as illustrated in Table 1 and Table 2. Besides, there are an estimated 50,000 over-ground supporters/ sympathisers.[5]

Table 1: Strength of the State Committees of CPI (Maoist)

Sl. No.	*Party Committee*	*Cadre strength (Approximately)*
1	Dandakaranya Special Zonal Committee (DKSZC)	2500
2	Andhra - Orissa Border Special Zonal Committee (AOBSZC)	175
3	North Telangana Special Zonal Committee (NTSZC)	78
4	Bihar - Jharkhand North Chhattisgarh - Special Area Committee (BJNCSAC)	1900
5	Chhattisgarh-Odisha Border Special Zonal Committee (COBSZC)	104
6	West Bengal State Committee (WBSC)	100
7	Punjab State Committee (PJSC)	25
8	Maharashtra State Committee (MRSC)	45
9	Karnataka State Committee (KASC)	40
10	Tamilnadu State Committee (TNSC)	00
11	Uttar Pradesh State Organising Committee (UPSOC)	20
12	Orissa State Organising Committee (ORSOC)	
13	Kerala State Organising Committee (KLSOC)	30
14	Uttarakhand Zonal Committee (UKZC)	21
15	Assam Zonal Committee (ASZC)	50
16	Delhi Leading Team (DLT)	18
17	Haryana Leading Team (HLT)	8
18	Jammu & Kashmir Leading Team (JKLT)	10
Total		5184

Source: Headquarters, Andhra Pradesh Police. Data on 31.12.2013.

Table 2: Strength of Military and Militia Platoons

SC/SAC/SOC/SZC	*No. of Platoons*	*No. of militia Platoons*
DKSZC	26	60
AOBSZC	6	1
MRSC	-	-
WBSC	2	-
BJNCSAC	10	21
ORSOC	-	-
NTSZC	1 (SGS)	1
Total	45	83

Source: Headquarters, Andhra Pradesh Police. Data as on 31.12.2013.

The cadre comprises of people from various backgrounds—caste, economic and professional. Thus, the guerrillas include those from Scheduled Tribes (STs) or *adivasis*, Scheduled Castes (SCs) or *dalits*, Backward Castes (BCs), and Forward Castes (FC). According to the Constitution of the CPI (Maoist),[6] there are prescribed norms for granting membership to cadres. People belonging to the working class and agriculture labourers would be put on observation, which in Maoist parlance is known as 'Candidature Period', for six months before being granted membership. The observation period for middle peasants, petty bourgeoise and urban middle class is one year, where as those belonging to the other classes have to wait for two years.[7] Also, according to the Constitution, rich and upper caste persons would not be taken into the rebel fold until they handed over all their property to the outfit.[8]

According to an arrested senior and top leader of the CPI (Maoist), women comprise 40 per cent of the total cadre strength of the Maoists.[9] The cadre composition would depend upon the demography of a State, and is largely representative of the caste composition of that State. Thus, it can be noticed that while BCs form the majority of the cadres in Andhra Pradesh, STs would form the majority in a significantly tribal-inhabited State like Chhattisgarh or Jharkhand.

Besides, there have been infrequent reports of children being members of the underground. Though their exact numbers are not known, it is believed that children in Andhra Pradesh, Bihar, Jharkhand, Orissa and Chhattisgarh are involved in the outfit's activities. Largely, they are used for intelligence collection. Known as *Bala Sangham* or *Bal Sangham*, which is a banned organisation in States such as Chhattisgarh and Orissa, its members are not fielded in the fight against the security forces until they reach the age of 17, though they could be admitted upon attaining the age of 16 and accorded "full time" membership.[10]

Figure 1: Economic Background of Cadres of the Erstwhile PW, 2001

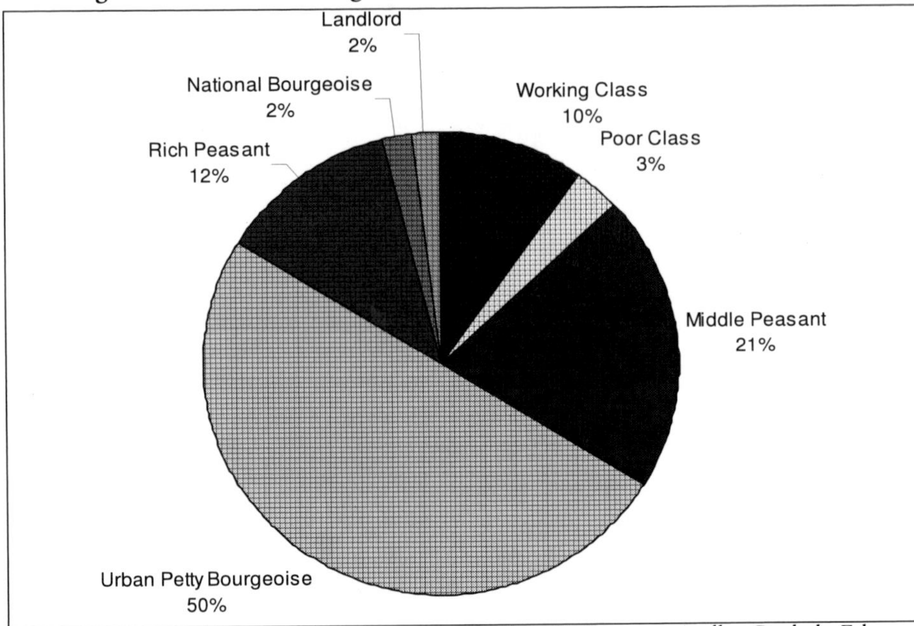

Source: Interview with a Senior Superintendent of Police, Karimnagar, Andhra Pradesh, February 2002.

Figure 2: Professional Background of Cadres of the Erstwhile PW, 2001

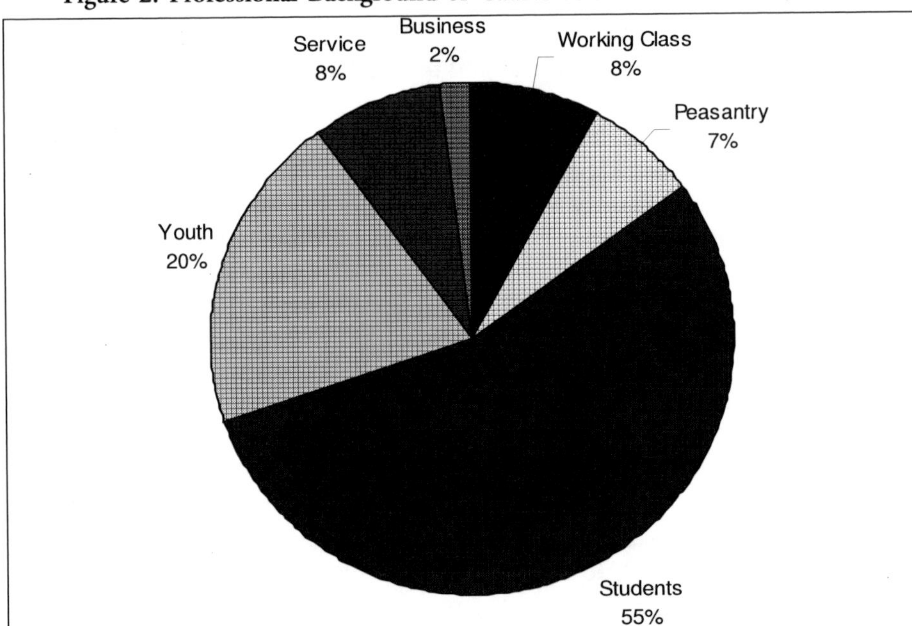

Source: Interview with a Senior Superintendent of Police, Karimnagar, Andhra Pradesh, February 2002.

While there have been reports of conscription in the Bastar region of Chhattisgarh,[11] largely, recruitment into the rebel fold has been voluntary. Men and women join the underground cadre for a number of reasons. For instance, Suneetha, then of an 'impressionable age', who this author interviewed,[12] joined the group because she was inspired by a moving song—*O veera vanitha*!—that was sung by a visiting squad in her village. Besides, she was also influenced by her uncle who was a squad member. Also, it is not uncommon for villagers, especially the youth, to get stirred into joining the group after listening to fiery speeches made by local-level squad commanders and leaders against exploitation and oppression by the rich, high-caste landlords, or neglect by the government.

Another squad member, Sudhakar, a college dropout, who this author spoke to,[13] had an interesting tale to narrate. Some unknown persons had burnt down the *tendu* (also known in some areas as *kendu*, similar to *beedi* leaf) crop on a tiny patch of land behind his humble dwelling. Police suspected it to be the handiwork of the rebels, and pestered him to come out with details. This "harassment" continued for months at end. One day, a District Committee member of the rebels accosted him and advised him to join the underground and save himself from being harassed by the police. A few days later, Sudhakar went underground.

Bharati, the wife of Polem Sudarshan Reddy, former Warangal District Committee Secretary (DCS) of the rebels and later DCS of Nizamabad,[14] simply followed her husband's footsteps. After her husband was killed in an encounter with the police, she surrendered in 2003. Similarly, the wife of Anupuram Komaraiah, member of the flagship North Telengana Special Zone Committee (NTSZC), too, followed her husband a few years after he went underground. She, too, later surrendered to the police after Komaraiah was killed in a police encounter.[15]

Thus, as there are various reasons for different individuals joining the rebel fold, similarly there are a variety of reasons for their quitting the outfit. For instance, in the case of Sudhakar mentioned above, he decided to quit the underground after he was taken seriously ill following malaria attack. He was frustrated as the rebel leadership did not provide him with proper medical treatment, and he was rendered immobile. He had joined with a cause, inspired in good measure by the ideology of the outfit, but soon felt 'useless'. This prodded him to leave the underground, after spending 20 years in rebel ranks, complete his studies, get married and settle down to a peaceful life.

In the case of Bharati and the other woman cadre, they got disillusioned with the outfit and its ideology after their husbands were killed in encounters with the police. So, they decided to quit the underground. Also, in a good number of cases, the male cadre (husband) is constantly persuaded by the female cadre (wife) that they should come over-ground and lead a normal life. Explaining this fact to this researcher, a senior police officer, who has an uncanny knack of having his finger exactly on the pulse of Maoist cadres and leaders, said "... in general, after marriage Indian women turn quite sentimental, and would prefer to lead a normal life, rather than spend the rest of their lives braving risk to life and leading a harsh life in the underground.[16] With some, it could also be the case that one of the two (husband, or wife) has taken ill and, therefore, the two would come over ground together to receive better medical attention".

LEADERSHIP

The leadership of the CPI (Maoist) largely hails from the Forward Castes. However, some of the leaders also belong to the Backward Castes, Scheduled Castes and Scheduled Tribes. Presently, ther is no woman member in the Central Committee of the CPI (Maoist). Earlier, Sheela Marandi and Sangeeta Ghandy were members of the Central Committee. While the former is the wife of Prasanth Bose alias Kishanji, the No. 2 in the outfit and general secretary of the erstwhile MCCI, the latter, now deceased, was the wife of Kobad Ghandy alias Rajan, who headed the Central Propaganda Bureau (CPB) until he was arrested in September 2009 in Delhi.

In fact, the Central Committee, as already mentioned, is headed by Muppala Lakshmana Rao alias Ganapathy, a *Velama* by caste. Ironically, at that time the then PW—the precursor to the present day CPI (Maoist)—gained popularity because it fought and put to an end the inhumane oppression of the *Velama* landlords *(doras)*. On the other hand, the Maoist military machine is headed by Nambala Kesava Rao alias Basava Raju.

The Maoist leadership has consistently denounced parliamentary politics as a sham, and is unflinchingly committed to waging an armed revolution to capture political power. At the same time, the leadership consistently opposes American "imperialism", Indian hegemony in the South Asian region, and the policies of the US-led Brettonwood Institutions. It contends that LPG (liberalisation-privatisation-globalisation) has been detrimental to the interests of Indian agrarian economy.

The sheer commitment of the leadership, the hard underground life they lead under constant fear of death and the visible, unimaginable successes they have achieved inspire people's confidence in them and win their support. Two of the most notable achievements of the rebels need to be mentioned. In North Telengana, their flagship guerrilla zone, they had totally reversed social relations by eliminating a few people who were from the high castes and notorious for their atrocities and exploitation. And, thus, permanently put to an end their high-handedness and atrocities. Among the tribal population the rebel leaders had earned enormous goodwill by securing better wages for them, which was unimaginable for the tribals till the the rebels came on to the scene.[17]

The CPI (Maoist) leadership is quite authoritarian and takes a serious view of lack of professionalism, indiscipline and loose behavior/moral conduct. There have been a number of instances when cadres were reprimanded, punished, or demoted, while even high ranking leaders were demoted.

Noted folk singer Gummadi Vithal Rao alias Gaddar[18] is one of the most important over-ground supporters of the outfit. He represented the organisation during talks with the government, and frequently submits memoranda, or demands action by the government through the print and visual media. He was kept at arms length by the rebels for a long time because he lent his voice to a few *Telugu* film songs. Eventually, he tendered an apology and promised never to repeat the mistake after which he was allowed to associate himself with the rebels.

The leadership has not always been cohesive. Ideological differences leading to dissent, personality clashes, professional deficiency and personal weakness are some of the issues that plague/plagued the leadership. Especially, cohesiveness has not always been easy to achieve. Over 20 months after the merger of the PWG and MCCI,[19] the Politburo of the CPI (Maoist) advised leaders and commanders to achieve complete unity within the ranks and desist from displaying tendencies of being supportive to/favouring comrades of their respective erstwhile organisations[20]—PWG or MCCI, as the case may be.

In 2003, Manik, the then West Bengal State Committee Secretary of the erstwhile PWG, quit the organisation owing to differences on the line to be adopted by the outfit. In 2006, there was a vertical split in the Karnataka State Unit of the CPI (Maoist), with a majority of the urban cadres, under the leadership of State Committee Secretary Sundaramurthy, quitting the outfit insisting that the emphasis should be on building the urban movement, rather than focusing on rural areas.[21]

Further, in August 2012, Sabyasachi Panda alias Sunil Das, secretary of the Orissa State Organising Committee (OSOC) wrote a scathing letter criticising the highest leadship while resigning from his post and membership of the outfit.

Moreover, the founder of the PWG, Kondapalli Seetharamaiah, was expelled from the organisation[22] as he failed to provide strong leadership and indulged in notorious activities. His wife, Koteswaramma, in an interview[23] to *Hans India*, Hyderabad, bluntly stated that he deserted her for the wife of a guerrilla squad member who was killed in an encounter with the security forces.

On January 2, 2008, Lanka Papi Reddy alias Lachanna, a native of Warangal district, Andhra Pradesh, Central Committee Member, surrendered to the authorities in Andhra Pradesh. Lachanna was earlier Secretary of the Dandakaranya Special Zone Committee (DKSZC) which is the fiercest guerrilla zone in the country at present. Lachanna surrendered claiming that he was unwell and was disillusioned with the outfit as it was not adhering to the ideological line and principles of the founding fathers. On the other hand, in a scathing attack through a press release,[24] the Central Committee accused Papi Reddy of being individualistic, lacking in discipline and character and mis-behaving with a female comrade.

The CPI (Maoist), understandably, detests renegades and keeps a careful watch on them. If the renegades were found harming the interests of the organisation, or particularly if they were found assisting the police, then the outfit would not hesitate to kill them in the most inhuman and barbaric manner. Also, the organisation has victimised and terrorised common people who have openly fought against it. The case of Baddam Satyanarayana Reddy is moving.[25]

FINANCES

The Maoists finance their activities, in overwhelming measure, through extortion. Practically, anyone who has ill-gotten wealth, and who they could target, contributes to Maoist coffers. These include corrupt government officials, rich landlords, businesses, including big industrial houses, etc. According to a Director General of Police, the Maoists annually extort a sum of rupees 1,500 crore.[26] He further told this researcher that Andhra Pradesh, Bihar and Jharkhand contribute the largest sum to Maoist coffers.

Besides, supporters and sympathisers make contributions, while card members pay an annual subscription. According to the 'Constitution'[27] of the CPI (Maoist), "Membership fees are Rs 10 per annum. [The] [c]oncerned unit after assessing the economic situation of the party member will fix monthly party levy."[28] It is believed that a total of 10 per cent of the funds collected across the country is made available to the Politburo and Central Committee to meet the expenses of its members; 25-30 per cent of the annual extortion is spent on Research and Developmnt (R&D) to manufacture weapons and fabricate ammunition.[29]

The Maoists also spend funds on intelligence gathering and in undertaking development works in their areas of control, though there are no precise estimates about how much this would account for. It is also said that approximately five to 10 per cent of the extorted amount is siphoned-off.

ARSENAL

The Maoist arsenal is largely indigenous and, indeed, ingenious; outright purchase of arms in the grey arms market is only in 'fits and bouts'. Their ingenuity in the manufacture of weapons is noteworthy. For example, there have been instances when the Maoists uprooted telephone poles, cut them into two pieces, filled them with explosive material and used them as cannons.[30] The rebels maintain production units in all areas of their operations, and a dedicated team undertakes the repair and fabrication of weapons.

Notably, they have been using towns and cities with some degree of impunity to manufacture arms. On January 10, 2007, police in Bhopal unearthed an arms making-cum-R&D unit and seized 25 books on arms published by international publishing houses, detailed drawings of cross-sections of rocket launchers, etc.[31]

ROCKET LAUCHER PROGRAMME[32]

On September 7 and 8, 2007, police in Andhra Pradesh, in two separate raids, recovered a huge quantity of empty rockets shells and rocket launchers. The investigations brought to light an elaborate network that originated in Ambattur industrial estate, Chennai, and spread across Andhra Pradesh, Maharashtra, Madhya Pradesh and Chhattisgarh.

The story of the Maoists' rocket launcher programme is interesting and, perhaps, merits some description. In 2002, under the guidance of Sande Rajamouli alias Krishna, Member, Central Military Commission (CMC), Akkiraju Hara Gopal alias Srinivas, Central Committee Member (CCM), Sakhamuri Appa Rao alias Ravi, Andhra Pradesh State Military Commission Secretary (APSMCS), Matta Ravi Kumar alias Sreedhar, Member of the Andhra Pradesh State Committee (APSCM), a Technical Team was formed to design rockets and rocket launchers. Thota Kumara Swamy alias Tech Madhu alias Raghu was tasked with it.

Tech Madhu developed the initial version in Malkangiri Camp, Orissa, in 2003. Subsequently, he was sent to Chennai in 2003 to get separate parts of these manufactured in different industrial units there in two phases viz. "Rocket Launchers – I and Rocket Launchers – II".

"Rocket Launcher – I" was a pilot project, as part of which 25 rockets with a launcher were developed at a cost of Rs. 950 per rocket; these were thereafter tested in the presence of some important Maoist leaders. "Rocket Launcher – II" was a project for developing shoulder–fired launchers and rockets. These were tested in 2004 and it was opined that "even though they were not effective they had good nuisance value". At this stage, Tech Madhu was directed to return to Chennai to get manufactured 1,600 rockets and 40 launchers at a cost of approximately Rs. 35 lakh. However, only 1,550 rockets and 40 launchers were manufactured and dispatched to different parts of the country.

The police in Andhra Pradesh caught wind of these developments and seized part of the consignment in Mahabubnagar and Prakasam districts on September 7 and 8, 2006, respectively. Subsequent raids in industrial units in Ambattur, an industrial suburb of Chennai, revealed an elaborate network that stretched across five States viz. Tamil Nadu, Andhra Pradesh, Madhya Pradesh, Chhattisgarh and Orissa.

The guerrillas have come a long way from fielding traditional farm implements such as crowbars, sickles and spears to fielding a melange of weapons, including country made weapons, single barrel breach guns (SBBLs), double barrel breach guns (DBBLs), light machine guns (LMGs), self-loading rifles (SLRs), AK series rifles, INSAS rifles and crude rocket launchers. At the official level, there are no precise estimates of the total weapons-holding of the Maoists. In 2006, the Annual Report of the Ministry of Home Affairs stated that the Maoists have 6,500 weapons of various make.[33]

Besides, they have also acquired proficiency in setting-off explosives. These include a variety of improvised explosive devices (IEDs)—bucket bombs, tiffin bombs, claymore mines, pressure mines[34] and the like. According to a former Director of the Intelligence Bureau, KP Singh, the Maoists set-off approximately "100 land mine explosions every year. [T]he Naxalites use the wire-controlled method. These are more difficult to neutralise because they are immune to electronic interference."[35]

The adeptness of the Maoists in meticulously planning and finely executing landmine explosions can be gauged by a few spectacular attacks. On October 1, 2003, the then Chief Minister of Andhra Pradesh, N Chandra Babu Naidu, had a miraculous escape because he was travelling in a bullet proof vehicle and a mere eight out of 17 mines exploded. His ministerial colleague, A Madhava Reddy, former Home Minister of the State, was not as lucky. He was killed in a similar attack on March 7, 2000. In another incident, 24 security force personnel—travelling in a mine proof vehicle (MPV)—were killed when the rebels set-off an 80 kg mine in the Bastar region of Chhattisgarh, on September 5, 2005. Also, on September 7, 2007, N Janardhan Reddy, former Chief Minister of Andhra Pradesh, had a close shave with death in his native Nellore district.

Further, the Maoists are fielding pressure mines which do not distinguish between a security force personnel, innocent civilian or cattle.

LINKAGES

The CPI (Maoist) has formed a web of linkages[36] with both fraternal groups as well as non-fraternal outfits.[37] In fact, the Maoists have ties with 22 fraternal groups across the globe.[38] Some of these include:

- Unified Communist Party of Nepal (Maoist)
- Shining Path of Peru
- Workers Party of Belgium
- Turkey Communist Party (Marxist-Leninist)
- Communist Party of Philippines
- Revolutionary Communist Party, USA
- Purba Banglar Sarbahara Party - Bangladesh
- Communist Party of Bhutan (Marxist-Leninist-Maoist)
- Communist Party of Ceylon (Maoist) - Sri Lanka
- Communist Mazdoor Kisan Party - Pakistan
- Maoist Communist Party - Italy
- Marxist Leninist Communist Organisation - Tunisia
- Revolutionary Communist Group – Colombia
- Workers Party of New Zealand (WPNZ)
- Communist Party of Afghanistan
- Communist Party of Iran (Marxist-Leninist-Maoist)

The non-fraternal ties were entirely opportunistic, and ideological compatibility was never a factor. These linkages exist within the country, within the region and stretch across continents. While speaking in the Lok Sabha, Bandaru Dattatreya, former Union Minister of State for Railways, said on December 10, 1991, that the then PW had acquired 60 AKs and 20 sten guns from the now defunct Liberation Tigers of Tamil Eelam (LTTE). He was quoting the then Home Minister of Andhra Pradesh as having said so on the floor of the State Legislature on August 20, 1991. On another occasion, two video cassettes containing LTTE's training modules were recovered in December 2001, from an arms dump of the erstwhile PW in Visakhapatnam district. Further, reports of late-December 2002 indicated that the PW and the LTTE had some months earlier struck an arms deal, but the modalities (pricing) had to be finalised.

Besides, in the aftermath of the failed October 1, 2003 assassination attempt on the then Andhra Pradesh Chief Minister, and as landmines acquired focus as a cheap and lethal form of weapon, the then Deputy Prime Minister, L K Advani, said that the erstwhile PW has links with the LTTE. It had received expertise in using Improvised Explosive Devices (IEDs) from the LTTE.

Alluding to such links when questioned about LTTE instructors conducting training camps for erstwhile PW squads 'Ganapathy' said during an interview in 1998, "They were not LTTE. They were ex-LTTE. What happened was that these people came to India after leaving their organisation and formed communist groups. The PW had relations with these groups. As part of that, they held training camps for us." Even as the denial was unconvincing, Ganapathy added, "We have had no relations with the LTTE till now. But we are not against having relations with them. We will certainly have links with them if an opportunity arises. We feel that such a relation would be conducive to the revolutionary movement."

In fact, a senior police officer from Andhra Pradesh told this researcher that a leader of the erstwhile PW had visited Dhaka and met with leaders of the Indian terrorist outfit, the United Liberation Front of Asom (ULFA) and inquired of them the fate of the money they paid to ULFA (some where to the tune of rupees 10 million) for purchase of sophisticated arms. The ULFA's links with the ISI are by now well-known, and are well-documented.

Lately, the Moists' linkages with the People's Liberation Army (PLA) of Manipur have come to light. A few years back the CPI (Moist) signed a MoU with the PLA.[39] The unstated objective in forming this linkage is to procure weapons with the assistance of PLA which has access to the grey arms market and gun-runners.

Strategy and Tactics

The Maoists follow the principle of 'one step forward, four steps backward'. There are in no hurry. They are clinically aware that their numbers are few and that it is not an easy task to face the might of the Indian state, with its large reservoir of arms and a few million State police, paramilitary forces and the Army. Thus the PLGA—the Maoist guerrilla army—follows the dictum laid out by Mao: 'You fight your way and we'll fight our way. We fight when we can win and we retreat when we cannot'.

The rebels' aim is to prolong the war and wear out the security forces. They have repeatedly attacked the security forces at the least unexpected place and in the weakest point. In fighting the security forces they follow the principle of stealth and speed—lightening speed. The Maoist belief is that numerically strong and well-equipped police forces can be defeated by numerically small guerrilla forces, which are politically motivated and are committed.[40] Again, as Mao said, 'they strike at the enemy's communication lines, harass him constantly, render his forces lame, lost, thirsty. The guerrilla forces hope that as the SF's morale dips they (the guerrillas) gain in strength and the morale strengthens'.

Sometime in 2007, a CD was seized from Chaitanya Natya Mandali (CNM) —a Maoist cultural affiliate—activists in Haryana.[41] Apparently, they were screening it among villagers to propagate their ideology. The CD contained detailed visuals of Maoist training procedures, tough drills, which an Indian Army Brigadier told this researcher even the jawans would find difficult to perform.[42] Moreover, the CD contained visuals of the rehearsal conducted by the guerrillas ahead of looting the National Mineral Development Corporation (NMDC) godown in Chhattisgarh and emptying all 20 tonnes of explosives stored there; and the rehearsal for an attack on an Armed Outpost in Bastar of Chhattisgarh. In fact, the contents of the press release issued after Operation Jehanabad, give the impression that it was a good rehearsal for the people's militia.

In the November 14, 2007 press release the Maoists also held:

> The Jehanabad politico-military campaign, like the Koraput campaign in February last year in which over 500 arms were captured from ten different locations in the district, show the superiority of guerrilla tactics based on the military line enunciated by Com. Mao for waging war in situations where the enemy has a vastly superior force.

Broadly, the guerrillas operate on the following "important" tactical principles:

- Protracted people's war is arduous and tortuous
- The spirit of prolonged self-endurance should be upheld
- In campaign and battles the PLGA should prefer and firmly adhere to the principle of using large numbers to defeat a relatively fewer number of security forces stationed at the targeted place
- The PLGA guerrillas should rely upon its members and the masses (people's militia) in order to confront and defeat the strong security forces
- Thus, the PLGA should firmly integrate itself with the people

The centrality of the masses, which would also include the people's militia, to the Maoist scheme of things comes out clearly in the words of Mao. He said:

> We must mobilise the people to support our armed forces enthusiastically and to fight the enemy together with them. The people are the eyes and ears of the army; they feed and keep our soldiers. It is they who help the army in sabotage and in battle. The people are the water and our army the fish.

Further, the important tactical principles include:

- Relying on the actions and attacks to enhance fighting capacity (Thus, each action and attack is a learning exercise for the guerrillas)
- Loot/snatch arms for the security forces
- Increase patience and tide-over, establish production units to manufacture weapons
- Endeavour to carry on the people's war even in the most difficult times

The rebels have an elaborate and well-knit informant network. Some of their daring and spectacular attacks are enough evidence for this. For instance, they were aware to the finest detail the exact position of the vehicle in the convoy in which Madhava Reddy, Panchayat Raj Minister and earlier Home Minister, was travelling when it was blown-up in a landmine blast. Similarly, they were aware of the vehicle in which Chandra Babu Naidu and Janardhan Reddy, both Chief Ministers of Andhra Pradesh during different periods in time, were travelling (in a convoy) when they made failed assassination attempts on them. Similarly, on numerous occasions they escaped the security forces when pursued because they were tipped-off, in different States. In fact, the deployment of UAVs in the Bastar region was of little use earlier, because the rebels knew in advance the direction in which the UAV would fly on a particular day, and they religiously avoided that area.[43] As a result UAVs were withdrawn. However, the deployment of UAVs has been resumed, once again, as also that of the portable *Nethra* drone.

SECTION II: UNDERSTANDING THE MAOISTS

Internal documents of the CPI (Maoist) indicate that the rebels hope to take their so-called people's war to the next higher level in their areas of operation——as a consequence of which violence is bound to increase. They plan to induct larger numbers of people into their armed movement in order to transform their People's Liberation Guerrilla Army (PLGA) into a People's Liberation Army (PLA), spread their influence to newer areas, and co-opt various sections of the society into their movement by targeting urban areas.

The Maoist challenge had, for the first time in recent years, engaged the attention of the Union Government in 1998 when it constituted a Coordination Centre headed by the Union Home Secretary involving some of the affected States to deal with the issue. Nevertheless, little was achieved and, meanwhile, the Maoists expanded their presence to the present levels. Besides, over time, the number of States represented in this Coordination Centre has increased.

In 2009, after the United Progressive Alliance (UPA) was elected to office for a second consecutive term, the Union Government began to display a sense of urgency in 'squarely' dealing with the Maoist challenge. The government unveiled a 'new' Naxal strategy in October, and initiated preparations to pursue a 'two-pronged' approach to deal with the rebels—of ensuring security and bringing-in rapid socio economic development in the affected areas. In this wake, the massive security build-up envisaged by the Union Government received more publicity in media coverage—of the proposed deployment of 99,000 para-miliatry personnel (CRPF 82 Bns; BSF 11 Bns; and ITBP 6 Bns) in the worst-affected areas across the country in States such as Jharkhand, Chhattisgarh, Orissa, Maharashtra. The objective of the security response is to simultaneously engage the guerrillas in armed operations in different parts of the country.

The founding documents of the CPI (Maoist) carefully analysed the political and socio-economic conditions in the country and devised a programme of action as also outlined the broad contours of their strategy and tactics. The rebels declared that their immediate objective was to 'capture state power' and to 'transform the PLGA into the PLA'.

IDEOLOGY[44]

The CPI (Maoist) describes India as backward, semi-colonial and semi-feudal. It is committed to Marxism-Leninism-Maoism. Its objective is to wage protracted people's war (PPW) on the lines propounded by Mao, seize/capture state/political power and herald a New Democratic Revolution (NDR), under the leadership of the agrarian class. This NDR would be conducted through guerrilla warfare by establishing base areas in the villages and then encircling the towns and cities, before the final Long March to capture political power.

In the perception of the CPI (Maoist), the comprador bureaucratic capitalist (CBC) classes of India are 'tools' in the hands of the imperialists, and the comprador big bourgeoisie (CBB) classes tailor the policies of the country to suit the interests of the imperialists. It contends that this has become more brazen and visible after 1990 with the introduction of liberalisation, privatisation, globalisation (LPG). The CPI (Maoist) considers that neither the Congress (I) nor the BJP is better than the other. Moreover, it contends: "The ... support of the so-called Left parties to the present Congress government with the fake posture of opposing its economic policies is a new fraud (on) the Indian people". It argues that the imperialist dictated LPG policies followed by both the Union and various State governments "have not only greatly deteriorated the overall Indian economy but also the living conditions of the Indian people..., particularly the peasantry".

In the opinion of the CPI (Maoist), "The overall crises are so deep that the ruling classes are no longer in the position of providing even the minimum relief by accepting the mostly minimum just demands". According to the Maoists, in these circumstances, only under the leadership of the Maoist party, the working class will be more forcefully able to mobilise and channelise all the struggles of the various sections of the people, particularly the struggles of the peasantry against imperialism and feudalism and leading towards establishing a new democratic India by smashing old India, and thereby advancing towards building socialism and communism on a world scale. That is, by advancing, strengthening and expanding the flames of the already ongoing protracted people's war in various parts of the country under the leadership of the Maoist party.

The CPI (Maoist) considers the Indian caste system as "obnoxious" and holds that the Dalits are "victims of untouchability, caste discrimination and upper caste chauvinism". The CPI (Maoist) argues that "Dalit question is essentially a class question. Hence, the Maoist forces should carry on the struggle against caste oppression as a part of the NDR and also fight for their equal place in the society in all spheres by abolishing the caste system. They should also fight for equal rights and special privileges, including, reservations for Dalits and other backward castes, while exposing the hollowness of the ruling class politics in this regard. The struggle against casteism and untouchability should also be carried on in the ideological, political and cultural spheres".

In order to advance the already ongoing revolution, the CPI (Maoist) has identified the principal and immediate tasks before the party. These include:

- Intensification and advancing of people's war to establish people's political power;
- Building a mighty mass movement against the imperialist the policies of LPG inspired by them;
- Exposing, isolating and defeating Hindu fascist forces, besides exposing all other fundamentalist forces;
- Resisting and defeating state repression and demanding the repeal of all black laws; and
- Fighting US and Indian expansionism and hegemony.

IMMEDIATE OBJECTIVE, 2009-PRESENT

In the wake of the country-wide offensive launched by the various state governments to fight the Maoists, the objective of the rebels is 'self-preservation'. Their goal is two-fold: to create public opinion against the offensives and protect guerrilla bases in Dandakaranya and Bihar-Jharkhand, even as they would seek to advance their struggle in the other areas of their operation.

Towards this end, in a document entitled 'Post-Election Situation: Our Tasks', the rebels have identified various tasks that they would undertake. These include:

- ➢ Launch a fresh series of TCOCs against the security forces with the involvement of the people's militia and also 'target kill' identified persons
- ➢ Unleash propaganda to create public opinion against the offensives and form alliances (United Front) with all manner of people and organisations that oppose the state on one issue or the other through showcasing the success of the rebel attacks on security forces
- ➢ Prevent leadership losses, and ensure avoidable killing of armed cadres

- Fresh recruitment and training, including for leadership roles
- Organisational/internal revamp
- Conduct dispersed attacks through expanding the geographical area of armed activity, i.e. carry out attacks in newer areas, each far removed spatially from the other, and launch attacks at places in strongholds
- Scrupulously desist from killing innocent persons and damaging public property which would likely erode public support
- Project the encirclement of, and advance into, Abuz Maad—the Maoist command centre in Bastar—as an onslaught on the indigenous tribal population and with the intent to gain control over the mineral wealth of the region.

Unity Congress

In January 2007, the CPI (Maoist) conducted its first Congress following the merger of the Communist Party of India—Marxist-Leninist (People's War) and the Maoist Communist Centre of India, in the Beembundh forests of Mungher district in Bihar, which was believed to have been attended by 100 delegates from different parts of the country. This Congress is known as the Unity Congress and also the 9th Congress.

According to CPI (Maoist) General Secretary Ganapathy, the Unity Congress was significant for many reasons. It marked the 'near total unification' of Maoist forces in the country; brought about consolidation of the political line; created a unified leadership; and a single directing centre for the Indian revolution. The unification also meant that the two erstwhile outfits would now be able to pool together their military strategies and men and material, besides bury wars of turf control. At the same time, it had also created the ground for the amalgamation of smaller Naxalite groups with the CPI (Maoist). At the Unity Congress, the rebels passed resolutions on a number of issues. These indicated the types of struggles they would take-up and or support.

Tactical Counter Offensive Campaign (TCOC)

Mindful of the losses they have suffered in security force offensives and aware of the fact that the state was likely to gain an upper hand, the Maoists have conducted Tactical Counter Offensive Campaigns (TCOC), from time-to-time. Typically, a TCOC has no specific time-frame and could last for a few weeks, or for a few months. These campaigns are intended to strike at the morale of the security forces and to bleed the state white.

Thus, the Maoists have conducted a number of TCOCs for putting the state on a back-foot, even if temporarily. At a meeting of its Politburo in December 2007, the CPI (Maoist) decided to launch a TCOC in 2008 and extend it until September of that year. However, as elections to the Lok Sabha and a few State Legislative Assemblies were due in May-June 2009, the rebels subsequently decided to extend the TCOC in the run-up to and during the elections.

The Central Committee of the CPI (Maoist), in one of its documents, enumerated the losses the guerrillas had inflicted on the security forces during this period. Thus, as the general secretary of the CPI (Maoist), Ganapathy said in an October 2009-interview: "...our forces have been able to carry put a series of tactical counter-offensive operations against the enemy in our guerrilla zones in the past few years.... In fact, in the past three years (2007, 2008 and 2009), the enemy forces suffered more casualties than we did". His claim was not incorrect. The rebels suffered casualties of 141, 199 and 217 in 2007, 2008 and 2009, respectively, while 236, 231 and 317 security forces were killed during the corresponding years.

Nevertheless, the CPI (Maoist) also admits that it is in a state of strategic defence vis-à-vis the state, i.e., when viewed from a larger perspective, and at the pan-India level, the government enjoys the upper hand. According to classical understanding, there are three stages in a 'people's war'—strategic defence, strategic equilibrium (or stalemate, in which the state and the guerrilla are said to be on an equal footing) and strategic offensive (in which the guerrilla has an upper hand while the state is running for cover). But, the rebels are unwilling to hazard a guess on when they would be able to move on to the next stage. Thus, Ganapathy said: "It is difficult to predict how long it will take to pass this stage." Much would depend upon realizing the objective of enlarging the PLGA and transforming it into the PLA and the progress of the people's war to the next higher stage in the various areas that rebel activity is currently on. The policies and actions of the government, the Maoists want to believe, would catalyse this process.

The Maoists' involvement in the struggles against land acquisition, and the consequent displacement, for establishing big industries is one such example. Thus, the Maoists supported struggles against allotting land to the Tatas for establishing a car manufacturing plant in Singur, West Bengal, Nandigram, also in West Bengal, and the allotment of land to Korean steel major POSCO for establishing a plant and rights to mine iron ore to supply raw material to the steel plant, in Orissa, and in Kalinganagar, Orissa. The Maoists' opposition to the establishment of Special Economic Zones (SEZs) in these places is two-fold. One, the peasants are being dispossessed because their fertile land is being acquired by the government and two, these lands are being allotted to big businesses 'for unhindered ruthless exploitation' to earn vast amounts of profit.

Special Economic Zones

Land has been allotted to businesses in differet parts of the coutry as part of an initiative to establish SEZs, which would provide employment and give a fillip to trade. However, in some cases, the earmarked land is fertile and aerable.

According to a widely-recognised authority on the Maoists, "At the 9th/Unity Congress, the Maoists resolved to oppose and resist the formation of 300 SEZs. They said these were akin to forming *de facto* foreign enclaves, which would, eventually, result in foreign and local sharks grabing prime agricultural lands."[45] Thus, the Maoists' involvment in agitations against land allotment in Singur, POSCO and Kalinganagar might be viewed in this light.

Lalgarh Movement

On the other hand, the movement in Lalgarh, West Bengal, and the Maoists' involvement with it is of a different nature. The tribal population rose in protest against the alleged high-handedness of the police. Thereafter, led by the Maoists the people had formed a committee known as People's Committee against Police Atrocities (PCPA) and had dug up roads to prevent the entry of state forces. Central para-military forces had to be deployed on a large scale in June 2009 to re-establish state-authority in the area—comprising 17 villages in four revenue blocks in West Medinipore district. The Maoists consider the Lalgarh movement as 'New Naxalbari which has emerged as a new model of mass movement in the country'.

Further, because of its wider participation, the Maoists consider the Lalgarh movement as 'a more widespread and more sustained mass political movement that has spurned the leadership of all parliamentary political parties', of which the rebels have gained control of. It is, thus, possible, that the Maoists would seek to replicate the Lalgarh model in other potential parts of the country. Through this method the rebels would seek to transform a mass resentment against the state into a mass political-militant opposition and then inject armed guerrilla squads to fight the state forces.

Negotiations[46]

In the past, the CPI (Maoist) sent its emmisarries, VaraVara Rao and Gaddar, to discuss the modalities and agenda for talks with the Andhra Pradesh government in the aborted peace process in 2002. Later in 2004, the Maoists, in the second peace process, participated in the historic direct talks with the Andhra Pradesh Government which reached a stalemate down the line and the peace process was aborted. Also, another attempt was made in West Bengal in 2011 to conduct negotiations with the Moists, but it was still-born.

At different points in time, the Maoists have unambiguously stated their stand on conducting negotiations with an elected government. For the Maoists, talks have always been 'war by other means', and 'talks are a tactic'.

A few months after the 2004 peace process was trashed in Andhra Pradesh, the Central Regional Bureau (CRB) of the CPI (Maoist), under whose jurisdiction all the three committees of Andhra Pradesh fall *viz.* AP State Committee, NTSZC and AOBSZC, deliberated in great detail on a number of issues pertaining to its jurisdiction and passed 11 resolutions on these various issues. On the issue of talks the CRB recollected its "bitter experience" in AP and noted that there should be no talks with any future government in AP. It said:[47]

> Regarding talks with the Naxalites, the actual nature of it is already exposed in the first round of talks last October [2004 direct talks]. Congress made a lot of promises that the Naxalite problem is a socio economic problem, that it is not possible to solve it through encounters that it is against fake encounters and that it would conduct judicial enquiry on the fake encounters that took place in Chandrababu's rule. But it broke all the promises. It started obstructing the meetings of the revolutionaries since November. It started encounters from January. After a gap of eight months the YSR government started direct war... Like during the rule of Chandrababu Naidu, the state of AP has turned to be a police state.

In November 2009, the Maoist Central Committee had this to say on the Union Government's proposal for talks:

> The CC, CPI (Maoist) unequivocally asserts that the government's proposal for peace talks is only a propaganda ploy that in no way differs from the peace proposals of Hitler prior to World War II... We appeal to all democratic and peace-loving forces to expose the hypocrisy and double-speak of [Dr] Manmohan [Singh], [Mr] Chidambaram, [Mr] Raman Singh, [Mr] Buddhadeb [Bhattacharjee] and others and oppose their war preparations against the oppressed downtrodden people of our country who are waging a struggle for land, livelihood and liberation from cruel feudal and imperialist exploitation.

In an interview published in a Maoist mouth-piece, general secretary Ganapathy ruled out any talks with the government. He said:[48]

> The fact is that the government doesn't feel any actual need for holding talks. If the peace wished by intellectuals, democrats and the people is to be established, then the most meaningless thing would be to demand that the counter-violence by people should be stopped while the government continues with its killing spree. When Chidambaram announced that Maoists should stop violence for 72 hours and Kishenji responded by giving a time of 72 days, Chidambaram's answer was to target Kishenji...

In the same interview, Ganapathy also said, "It is crystal clear that there [does not exist] a conducive atmosphere for talks. In spite of this we request the people and democrats to demand the government to prove its commitment towards the process of talks by coming forward to implement the following steps.... We want to make it clear once again that any questions regarding talks should be put to the government first and not to us."[49]

In the foreseeable future, it is unlikely that the Maoists shall be willing to sit at the negotiating table with the government. All their statements and protestations are mere positioning and rhetoric. In any case, for the Maoists, 'talks are a tactic and talks are war by other means'.[50] He also said, "...the party would continue the 'protracted people's war' and the talks process would help in taking the movement forward."[51]

During the period the Maoists stayed over-ground for the talks and camped at the Manjeera State Guest House in Hyderabad, several people met with the

Maoists and submitted as many as 836 petitions to 'Ramakrishna'. However, the Maoists can not run a kangaroo court in public, as they can in their strongholds. As a result they could not solve any of the problems brought to their notice. This caused confusion. The people began to lose faith in the Maoists and the Maoists, too, experienced first-hand their helplessness, and thus, the futility of their ideology.[52]

In fact, during the 2004 peace process and the duration of the direct talks with the Andhra Pradesh government, "The Maoists openly propagated their ideology in villages and towns and had even organised a huge public meeting in Hyderabad. For them it was a propaganda exercise both in 2002 and 2004."[53]

ANDHRA PRADESH: SET-BACK

For some time the CPI (Maoist) leadership intensely debated its prevailing position in Andhra Pradesh. In 2006, the leadership quibbled over whether it was a 'loss' or a 'set-back'. Eventually, it conceded that the outfit suffered a set-back. Nonetheless, since then, General Secretary Ganapathy frequently used the two terms inter-changeably. In an interview he noted with concern, "I agree that the losses in the [S]tate of Andhra Pradesh are quite serious. They certainly have a considerable impact on the revolutionary movement in the country as a whole".

While proffering various reasons for this turn of events, Ganapathy also sought to explain that 'there was a shift in the focus of the Maoist movement towards Dandakaranya and Bihar-Jharkhand' to establish liberated zones/base areas. At the same time, he grudgingly acknowledged the counter-operations of the State police, especially the elite Special Intelligence Branch and the Greyhounds. The success of the Andhra Pradesh government in containing the rebels and turning them, largely, away from the State is a result of a number of factors. In a nut-shell, political consensus, intelligence-based operations, attractive surrender and rehabilitation policy, victim re-assurance and development initiatives had vastly helped the Andhra Pradesh government to wrest the initiative from the rebels and had contributed to their declining influence.

However, the Maoists are of the view that tide and ebb are 'natural' to their movement and they would rise like the 'proverbial phoenix' with mass support. "Utilising the excellent international and domestic situation prevailing today we are confident we will be able to come out of the temporary setback in AP", Ganapathy declares in his interview which is reproduced in the succdeding pages of this volume.

CONCLUSION

Whither Maoists?

The Maoist movement is reaching a plateau. The penetration capability of the rebels in the remote, rural and tribal areas is nearly reaching a saturation point. At the same time, their plan to establish a presence in urban centres has met with very limited success. Nevertheless, within the next seven to 10 years, it is difficult to imagine that neither the Maoists, nor their ifluence would wane.

The long trajectory of the movement, determination of the rebels, the planned and systematic way in which they are pursuing their objectives, and importantly, inadequate action by the state, suggests that the various State governments would have to hasten their responses, which they seem to have just about begun. At the same time, the Union government would also need to play a decisive, leading role in addressing the Maoist challenge.

Presently, the leadership is approximately 50 years and plus of age. As new blood reaches to leadership positions, much would depend upon them and the way they envision to chart the course of the movement and its future.

Incontrovertibly, it is possible to defeat to the Maoist challenge. For this, irrespective of the Maoist agenda, the Union government and the various affected States would need to weaken the Maoists' lethal capacities. Moreover, it is essential to ensure that governance is improved; development schemes and programmes are implemented effectively and monitored rigorously, so that those prone to sympathising with, or supporting, the Maoists would, eventually, realize the needlessness and futility of doing so.

NOTES

1. This section is based on the organisational chart of the CPI (Maoist), "Organisational Hierarchy: Communist Party of India (Maoist)", in PV Ramana, ed., *The Naxal Challenge: Causes, Linkages and Policy Options*, New Delhi: Pearson-Longman, 2008, p. 198.
2. Ganapathy is a native of Bheerpur village, Karimnagar district, Andhra Pradesh. A teacher by profession, the bespectacled Ganapthy joined the Naxalite movement in the seventies, and was second-in-command to Kondapalli Seetharamaiah, the founder of Communist Party of India—Marxist-Leninist (People's War), popularly known as PWG, whom he ousted in 1992 and went on to become PWG's leader. In 2004, the PWG merged with the Maoist Communist Center of India (MCCI). The amalgam was christened Communist Party of India (Maoist).
3. An internal document of the CPI (Maoist) read during a field visit to Andhra Pradesh, February 2006.
4. *Mint*, New Delhi, May 29, 2009.
5. Interview with a senior Intelligence officer dealing with the Maoists, Hyderabad, August 2011.
6. "Party Constitution", of the CPI (Maoist), read during a field visit to Hyderabad, February 2005.
7. *Ibid.*
8. *Ibid.*

9. Misir Besra, a Member of the Central Military Commission of the CPI (Maoist), while speaking to media persons.
10. "Party Constitution", n. 5. Also see *Hindustan Times*, New Delhi, March 21, 2008; and P V Ramana, "Child Combatants in the People's War Group", accessible at http://www.ipcs.org/nmt_militaryIndex2.jsp?action=showView&kValue=1058&military=1016& status=article& mod=b
11. Interview with a Senior Superintendent of Police, Chhattisgarh, February 17, 2007.
12. Interview with K Suneetha, Warangal, February 2002.
13. Interview with Sudhakar, Karinmnagar, February, 2002. Incidentally, he joined the outfit at the prodding of Sande Rajamouli, then a District Committee Member. Rajamouli later rose to become a Member of the Polit Bureau, Central Military Commission and Central Committee of the CPI (Maoist). He was later killed in an encounter with the police in Hindupur, Anatapur district, Andhra Pradesh.
14. He was an an accused in 1042 criminal offences and was a member of the North Telengana Special Zone Committee (NTSZC) and secretary of the Karimngar West-Nizamabad division. Earlier he was the Warangal district committee Secretary. He was killed on March 25, 2003, in the forests in Nizamabad district, in a meticulously planned police operation. See *The Hindu*, Chennai, March 26, 2003.
15. He was killed on April 25, 2003, in an encounter with the police in Karimnagar district. Komaraiah was a member of the North Telengana Special Zone Committee (NTSZC). See www.rediff.com/news/2003/apr/26ap.htm
16. Interview with a senior IPS officer, Andhra Pradesh, February 2006.
17. In 1975, a tendu leaf labourer was paid four naya paise for a bundle of 100 leaves, instead of the government stipulated five naya paise. Besides, the labourers were also victims of "corruption and mischief". The Naxalites entered the fray, put an end to the misery of the labourers, and also secured a raise in wages. Ever since, ever year they have been securing increased minimum wages for these hapless labourers. For a lucid description of the misery of the labourers, their mobilisation by the Naxalites and its impact on the consolidation and spread of the movement see K Srinivasulu, *Caste, Class and Social Articulation in Andhra Pradesh: Mapping Differential Regional Trajectories*, Working Paper # 179, Overseas Development Institute, London, September 2002, pp.25-26.
18. Gaddar was twice emissary of the rebels, in 2002 and 2004, along with Vara Vara Rao, in the talks with the Government of Andhra Pradesh.
19. The two outfits merged on September 21, 2004, to found what is now known as the CPIN (Maoist). See the Press Release issued on October 14, 2004, announcing the founding of the outfit. This was later reproduced in *People's March*, Ernakulam, a Maoist mouthpiece. See *People's March*, Vol : 5, Nos. 11-12, November-December 2004.
20. An internal document of the CPI (Maoist) read during a field visit to Andhra Pradesh, September 2006.
21. K Srinivas Reddy, "Karnataka naxal movement splits", *The Hindu*, February 14, 2007. The splinter group termed itself as Maoist Coordination Committee (MCC).
22. He was expelled from the then PWG in 1993 and was subsequently arrested by the police in Andhra Pradesh.
23. See MMA Sarma, "The Eternal Communist", intervire with Kondapalli Koteswaramma, wife of Seetharamaiah, *Hans India*, Hyderabad, November 7, 2012.
24. See the Press Release , in the succeeding pages of this volume, issued on January 4, 2008 by the Central Committee of the CPI (Moist) in which it said: "It is indeed shocking to all Party members and the revolutionary masses to see such degenerate behaviour and extreme political weakness from a member of the highest committee of the Party".
25. Interaction with the victim in Karimnagar, Andhra Pradesh, February 2004. Satyanarayana was an eyewitness to the murder of his friend by the rebels. He gave evidence against them

in a court of law, following which there was an attempt on his life. There were a total of three attempts on his life. When he refused to fall in line and reiterated his testimony, his house was burnt down. He can not cultivate his fields either. He now lives in near total penury.

26. Interview with Mr. Vishwaranjan, the then Director General of Police, Chhattisgarh, Raipur, July 16, 2007. He was earlier Additional Director in the Intelligence Bureau.
27. See the full text of the Constitution of the CPI (Maoist) in the succeeding pages of this volume.
28. See a Maoist document entitled "Party Constitution", read during a field visit to Andhra Pradesh, February 2007.
29. Interview with Mr Vishwaranjan, the then Director General of Police, Chhattisgarh, July 16, 17, 2007.
30. Interview with Mr G P Singh, the then Senior Superintendent of Police, Bastar (Jagdalpur), Chhattisgarh, July 17, 2007.
31. Interview with Mr S K Raut, the then Additional Director General of Police (Intelligence), Madhya Pradesh , who later superannuated as Director General of Police, Bhopal, January 12, 2007.
32. On this aspect, I have borrowed from P V Ramana, "Trends in India's Maoist Movement", in S D Muni, ed., *Asian Strategic Revioew 2008*, New Delhi: Institute for Defence Studies and Analyses—Academic Foundation, pp. 165-87.
33. *Annual Report, 2005-2006, Ministry of Home Affairs, New Delhi.*
34. For a somewhat elaborate discussion on the development of rocket launchers and the lethal impact of pressure mines that the rebels are fielding see P V Ramana, "Rockets and rocket launchers now in Maoist arsenal", originally published by IANS, March 14, 2008, later reproduced by various websites, including http://www.indiaenews.com/india/20080314/104152.htm and "Maoists unleash new terror in the heart of India", reproduced by various websites, including http://www.indiaenews.com/pdf/97158.pdf; also see K Srinivas Reddy, "Where deadly traps take a heavy toll", *The Hindu*, July 23, 2007.
35. See K P Singh, "The Trajectory of the Movement", in PV Ramana (ed), *The Naxal Challenge*, p. 14.
36. This section is based on my chapter "The Maoist Web: An Overview, PV Ramana (ed), *The Naxal Challenge*, pp. 111-35.
37. *Ibid.*
38. Interview with a senior Indian Police Service (IPS) officer of Andhra Pradesh, in New Delhi, October 5, 2012.
39. See the document in the succeeding pages of this volume.
40. See the press release issued by Azad, spokesperson of the Central Committee of CPI (Maoist), on November 14, 2005, a day after Operation Jehanabad.
41. Interviews with two Senior Superintendents of Police in Chhattisgarh, July 2007, and Hyderabad, September 2007.
42. Conversation with an Army officer, on conditions of anonymity, New Delhi, October 2007.
43. Interview with a Senior Superintendent of Police, Chhattisgarh, February 2007.
44. This section draws significantly from an internal document of the CPI (Maoist), prepared at the time of its founding, read during a field visit to Andhra Pradesh, February 2007.
45. Interview in New Delhi, September 28, 2012, with K Srinivas Reddy, Resident Editor (Andhra Pradesh), *The Hindu*, Hyderabad.
46. On this aspect, I have borrowed from P V Ramana, "Negotiaing with Maoists", IDSA Fellow Paper, January 25, 2011.
47. An internal document of the CPI (Maoist) read during a field-visit to Andhra Pradesh in November-December 2009.
48. See the interview with Ganapathy by Jan Myrdal and Gautam Navlakha in the succeeding

pages of this volume, published in *Open*, New Delhi, Ocotber 17, 2009.

49. *Ibid.*
50. This was stated by Akkiraju Haragopal alias Ramakrishna alias Sake at a press conference in Hyderabad, on October 14, 2004, a day ahead of the historic direct talks between the Maoists and the Andhra Pradesh government. See *The Hindu*, October 15, 2004.
51. *Ibid.*
52. Interview with Dr R S Praveen Kumar, the then Joint Commissioner, Special Branch, Hyderabad, December 1, 2010.
53. Interview with Mr M Shashidhar Reddy, MLA, Sanatnagar, and Vice Chairman, National Disaster Management Authority, Hyderabad, December 2, 2010. He was earlier Convenor of the AICC Task Force on Naxal Violence, during 2004-2005. The government wanted him to be a part of the government negotiating team, but he declined the offer.

Documents

SECTION I

ORGANISATIONAL ASPECTS

This section comprises of three documents, *viz.* Constitution, Urban Perspective Plan and *Janatana Sarkar*. While the Constitution gives a fair idea of how the rebels envision organizing themselves and carrying forward their movement, there is no gainsaying that there is an intrinsic link between Urban Perspective Plan and *Janatana Sarkar*. In the Maoist scheme of things, the rebels would establish control over the rural hinterland and from thereon storm the towns and cities.

The second document is a blue-print on how to organize and conduct the movement in urban centres, i.e. towns and cities. The third document is a blue-print on people's government in the rebels' areas of control.

CONSTITUTION OF THE CPI (MAOIST)

The Constitution of the CPI (Maoist) consists of 13 Chapters and 61 Articles. The Constitution unambiguously describes the Maoist agenda and declares: "The ultimate aim ... is to bring about communism by continuing the revolution under the leadership of the proletariat." Members of the outfit are of two types, viz. *Professional Revolutionaries ad Part Timers. The eligibility criterion for the membership of the rebel group is described in good detail in this document.*

Among the duties of the members of the rebel organisation, the Constitution says in Article 19 that every member has to be ready to 'participate in Protracted People's War and other forms of revolutionary mass struggles', i.e. partial struggles. Members are also offered the 'right to dissent', among other things. However, 'democratic centralism' shall be the guiding principle of the outfit. There are also detailed procedures on 'promotions, transfers and re-assignments'.

Besides, the Constitution describes the organisational structure and principles of election to various levels of hierarchy in the outfit. At the apex is the all-powerful Central Committee, while a party cell at the village/town level is at the bottom of the hierarchy, with a number of intermediary committees.

Also, Articles 26, 27 and 28 a, b, c, d, e and f prescribe the modalities of discipline within the organisation. The CPI (Maoist) boasts of "iron discipline". The disciplinary measures mooted against erring party members are mentioned in the Constitution. These include 'warning, serious warning, suspending from party posts, removal from post, suspending or canceling party membership, expelling from the party, etc. In fact, what the document does not mention is that the highest from of disciplinary measure adopted by the outfit is annihilation of people who are perceived to have 'betrayed' the revolutionary cause.

According to the Constitution the Party Congress shall be conducted every five years. Delegates elected from the various areas/regions of operations of the rebel outfit participate in the Congress and these people hold various levels of posts in the rebel hierarchy. The importance of the Congress is that it has to ratify the POR (Political Organizational Report) prepared by the Central Committee, failing which the Central Committee has to resign en masse. *The Congress elects the Central Committee and sets the future direction of the outfit. The last Congress was held in 2007 January. It was attended by 100 delegates from 16 States and had passes nine Resolutions. These are discussed in good detail in the section on '9th/Unity Congress in the present volume.*

Likewise, the Constitution discusses various aspects, including mass organizations, finances, etc.

PARTY CONSTITUTION

FOREWORD

CHAPTER-1: GENERAL PROGRAMME

The Communist Party of India (Maoist) is the consolidated political vanguard of the Indian proletariat. Marxism-Leninism-Maoism is the ideological basis guiding its thinking in all the spheres of its activities. Immediate aim or programme of the Communist Party is to carry on and complete the new democratic revolution in India as a part of the world proletarian revolution by overthrowing the semi-colonial, semi-feudal system under neo- colonial form of indirect rule, exploitation and control and the three targets of our revolution—imperialism, feudalism and comprador bureaucratic big bourgeoisie. The ultimate aim or maximum programme of the party is the establishment of communist society. This New Democratic Revolution will be carried out and completed through armed agrarian revolutionary war i.e. the Protracted People's War with area wise seizure of power remaining as its central task. The Protracted People's War will be carried out by encircling the cities from the countryside and thereby finally capturing them. Hence the countryside as well as the Protracted People's War will remain as the center of gravity of the party's work from the very beginning. During the whole process of this revolution the party, army and the united front will play the role of three magic weapons. In their interrelationship the party will play the primary role, where as the army and the united front will be two important weapons in the hands of the party. Since the armed struggle will remain the main form of struggle and army as the main form of organization of this revolution, the armed struggle will play a decisive role, whereas the united front will be built in the course of advancing armed struggle and for armed struggle. Mass organizations and mass struggles are necessary and indispensable but their purpose is to serve the war. The immediate and most urgent task of the party is to establish full-fledged people's liberation army (PLA) and base areas by developing and transforming the guerilla zones and guerrilla bases.

Just after completing the NDR the party will advance towards establishing socialism without any delay or interception. Because the NDR will already lay the basis for socialism and hence there will be no pause. Thereafter, the party will continue to advance towards realizing communism by continuing the revolution under the dictatorship of the proletariat.

Socialist society covers a considerable long historical period. Throughout this historical period, there will be classes, class contradictions and class struggle. The struggle between socialist road and capitalist road will also continue to exist. Only depending on and carrying forward the theory of continuing the revolution under the dictatorship of the proletariat can correctly resolve all these contradictions. In this context the GPCR initiated and led by Mao Tse-tung was a great political revolution carried out under the conditions of socialism by the proletariat against the bourgeoisie and all other exploiting classes to consolidate the dictatorship of the proletariat and there by fighting against the danger of capitalist restoration.

Party will also continue to hold high the proletarian internationalism and will continue to firmly contribute more forcefully in uniting the genuine M-L-M forces at the international level. The party will also struggle against all forms of revisionism. While uniting the M-L-M forces, it will also establish unity with oppressed people and nations of the whole world and continue its fight together with them in advancing towards completing the world proletarian revolution against imperialism and all reaction, thereby paving the way towards realizing communism on a world scale.

During the whole course the comrades throughout the party must cherish the revolutionary spirit of daring to go against the tide, must adhere to the principles of practicing Marxism and not revisionism, working for unity and not for splits, and being open and aboveboard and not engaging in intrigue and conspiracy, must be good at correctly distinguishing contradictions among the people from those between ourselves and the enemy and thereby correctly handling those, fighting left and right opportunism and non proletariat trend must develop the style of integrating theory with practice, maintaining close ties with the masses and practicing criticism and self-criticism.

The future is certainly bright, though the road is tortuous. All the members of our party will wholeheartedly dedicate their lives in the lofty struggle for communism on a world scale, must be resolute, fear no sacrifice and surmount every difficulty to win victory!

CHAPTER-2: THE PARTY, FLAG, OBJECTIVES

Article - 1: Name of the Party: Communist Party of India (Maoist)

Article - 2: Flag: Party Flag is red in color with hammer and sickle printed in the middle in white colour. The hammer of the sickle will remain towards the side of the pole. The ratio of length and breadth of the flag is 3:2.

Article - 3: (a) The Communist Party of India (Maoist) is the consolidated vanguard of the Indian proletariat. It takes Marxism-Leninism-Maoism as its guiding ideology.

(b) The party will remain underground throughout the period of New Democratic Revolution.

Article - 4: Aims and Objectives:

The immediate aim of the party is to accomplish the New Democratic Revolution in India by overthrowing imperialism, feudalism and comprador bureaucratic capitalism only through the Protracted People's War and establishes the people's democratic dictatorship under the leadership of the proletariat. It will further fight for the establishment of socialism. The ultimate aim of the party is to bring about communism by continuing the revolution under the leadership of the proletariat and, thus, abolishing the system of exploitation of man by man from the face of earth.

The Communist Party of India (Maoist) dedicates itself at the service of the people and revolution, cherishes high affection and respect for the people, relies upon the people and will be sincere in learning from them. The party stands vigilant against all reactionary conspiracies and revisionist maneuvers.

Article - 5: The party will continue to hold high the banner of proletarian internationalism and will put its due share in achieving the unity of the Marxist-Leninist-Maoist forces at international level.

CHAPTER-3: MEMBERSHIP

Article - 6: Any resident of India, who has reached the age of 16 years, who belongs to worker, peasant, toiling masses petty-bourgeoisie classes or any other revolutionaries, accepts Marxism-Leninism-Maoism as his/her guiding ideology in day to day activities, accepts Party Programme and Constitutions, actively participates in party activities under any one of the party unit observing discipline, prepare to face the danger encountered in that course and agree to pay regularly membership fees and levies that are decided by the party unit may become a party member. Party membership will be renewed every year.

Article - 7: Generally party members are admitted as individuals, through a primary party unit. Every applicant for membership must be recommended by two party members; they must have thorough knowledge about him/her and provide all the necessary information to the party. And the applicant for party membership should do so formally.

Article - 8: Concerned primary unit will investigate the applicant and it will be done secretly with in party as well as among masses. Essentially the application must be recommended by concerned party cell/ unit and letter on approved by next higher party committee. The applicant will be admitted into the party as a candidate member. After candidate membership is given, he/she should be observed for a minimum period of six months- for applicants from working class, landless-poor peasants and agricultural laborers; one year for middle peasants, petty-bourgeoisie and urban middle class; and two years for those coming from other classes. From AC to all other higher party committees will also have the right to give new membership, while following the same method.

Article - 9: No one from exploiting classes will be admitted in to the party unless he/she hands over his property to the party and should deeply integrate with the masses.

Article - 10: Proven renegades, enemy agents, careerists, individuals of bad character, degenerates and such alien class-elements will not be admitted into the party

Article - 11: Generally party members will be admitted from activist groups organized for party activity working under the guidance of party unit. They must be involved in party activities as decided by the concerned party unit at least for six months before admitting them as candidate member.

Article - 12: By the end of the candidature period, the concerned party unit after reviewing can give full membership or his/her candidature can be extended for another six months, by explaining the reasons. This decision should be reported to the next higher committee. Higher committees may change or modify the decision taken by the lower committee. Zonal/Dist. committee must approve the new membership. SAC/State Committee will finally approve.

Article - 13: An Indian residing in a foreign country that has all the necessary qualifications for party membership may be given membership; a foreigner residing in India permanently can also be given membership.

If a member of other Marxist-Leninist groups wants to join our party, he/she may be admitted with the approval of the next higher committee. If his/her status is that of primary member in the original party, he/she shall be admitted as full fledged member with the approval of the district/sub-zonal committee. If he/she is an AC member in the original party, he/she shall be admitted with the approval of the state/regional committee. If he/she was of the rank of district or regional level in the original party, he/she shall be admitted by the central committee if he/she was of the rank above regional committee.

If an ordinary member of a bourgeois or revisionist party wants to leave that party and join our party, his/her application shall be recommended by two party members, one of them being a party member at least for two years. His/ Her candidate membership shall have to be accepted by the next higher committee. Similarly, if a member of a bourgeois or revisionist party bearing area level or above responsibilities wants to join our party, his/her application shall have to be recommended by two party members one of them being party members at least for five years. His/her membership shall have to be accepted by the state committee or by the central committees.

Article - 14: Membership fees are Rs.10 per annum. Under the guidance of the State Committee the concerned unit after assessing the economic situation of the party member will fix monthly party levy.

CHAPTER-4: RIGHTS AND DUTIES OF PARTY MEMBERS

The Duties of the Party Members :

Article - 15: He/she shall study and apply Marxism-Leninism-Maoism lively. In the concrete condition of India, he/she must be creative, firm and capable in practice. He/she should try to develop his/her consciousness from the rich experiences of party's ideological, political and organizational line as well as style and method of work.

Article - 16: He/she shall defend and try to develop ideological and political basis of the party and shall consistently wage ideological and political struggle against various types of non proletarian trends, revisionist policies, trends and style of work; 'left' and right opportunism, economism, spontaneity, parliamentarianism, legalism, reformism, liberalism, sectarianism, empiricism, subjectivism, dogmatism and anarchist concepts and trends.

Article - 17: He/she must study party organs, documents and magazines regularly and must take initiative in popularizing party's literature and collecting party fund.

Article - 18: Party members must take part actively and regularly in the day-to-day work of those party units and organizations to which they are attached. They must following party line, programme, policies, principles, directives and decisions.

Article - 19: Every member must be ready to participate and play a vanguard role in class struggle in the form of armed agrarian revolutionary war i.e. Protracted People's War and other forms of revolutionary mass struggles. They must be prepared to take part in war and give leadership in Protracted People's War for seizure of political power.

Article - 20: He/she must subordinate his/her personal interests to the interests of the party and the people. Party members must fight for the interests of the great masses of the people, must integrate with broad masses, learn from them, rely upon them and strengthen the party relations with the broad masses. He/she must be true servant of the people, sacrifice everything for them and must go to the people for taking the solution of their problems i.e. keep to the principle of "from the masses to the masses". He/she must be concerned about the problems of the people, try for their solutions, intimate all those things to the party in time and explain the party line and policies to them. If he/she is coming from other than proletariat class, should declass himself/herself with the proletarian ideology by taking part in the task of agrarian revolution and adopting the life style of proletariat.

Article - 21: He/She must not practice on own will, and should relentlessly fight with a proletarian class outlook against discrimination based on gender, caste, nationality, religion, race, region and tribe, and ruling class policies of divide and rule.

Article - 22: With the aim of helping each other, he/she must develop the method of collective functioning by comradely criticism and self-criticism. He/she must have attitude to work even with those who raise criticism and hold different views and be able at unite with the great majority, including those who have opposed them but are sincerely correcting their mistakes.

Article - 23: He/She must accept firmly in theory and practice -party unity, party committee functioning and party discipline.

He/She must safeguard the secrecy of the party. He/She must defend the party and hold its cause against the onslaught of the enemy. He/she must safeguard the unity of the party against factionalism. He/She must develop professional attitude towards his/her revolutionary work and must develop his/her level of skills, knowledge and proletarian out look.

Article - 24: **The Rights of the Party Members:**

a) The right to elect and to be elected to party committees at the concerned levels.
b) The right to get Party Magazines, documents, circulars, etc., and the right to freely discuss in the party meetings and party organs about the political and organizational line, policies and decisions of the party and about problems arising in implementing them.
c) In case of any disagreement with the decision of the committee/unit, a member of the concerned committee/unit, must remain loyal to carry out the decision, may retain his/her dissenting opinion and demand resettlement of the issue in any subsequent meeting or may even send his/her opinion to higher

committees, including the central committee, for consideration through his/her respective party unit, when the respective committee fails to solve the problem within six months, he/she has the right to send his/her opinion directly and the right to get reply also. It is, however, the discretion of the committee to decide whether to reopen the matter or not.

d) Any member has the right to send criticism against any other party member not in his/her unit to the next higher committee. Any party member has the right to send criticism and suggestions on the decisions taken by any party committee up to Central Committee through the next higher committee.

e) The duties and rights of the candidate members and party members are identical but for one difference. The candidate members have no right to elect or to be elected or to vote.

f) In case of punishment to any unit or party member, detailed explanation and discussion regarding the specific case must be conducted in his/her presence and information regarding decision must be sent to the higher committee in writing.

CHAPTER-5: ORGANISATIONAL PRINCIPLES OF THE PARTY

Article - 25:

a) The organizational principle of the party is democratic centralism. Party structure and internal life is based on this principle. Democratic centralism means centralism based on inner party democracy and inner party democracy under centralized leadership. While discussing open heartedly and being united in party work, such a political atmosphere has to be created where centralism as well as democracy, discipline as well as freedom, unity of will as well as personal ease of mind and liveliness – all these will be present. Only in such an atmosphere the principle of democratic centralism can be implemented successfully.

b) Most important principle of democratic centralism for organizational structure, the leading committees at all levels shall be compulsorily elected on the basis of democratic discussion. Conferences, plenums and elected committee at all levels shall have approval from higher-level committees. Essentially the whole party shall follow the principle that the individual is subordinate to the organization, the minority is subordinate to the majority, the lower level is subordinate to the higher level, and the entire party is subordinate to the Central Committee.

c) Leading committees of the party shall present the organizational report in Congress/Conference or Plenum. These committees will listen to the opinions of people both inside and outside the party and will be answerable to them. Party members shall have the right to criticize and send their opinions/resolutions to the higher committee; even if any party member has a different point of view then he/she can send his views to the higher committee and even up to the central committee.

d) Every member of the leading committee must bear the responsibility to give party leadership to a specified area and a front. They will take direct experience from it and knowledge acquired from this experience can help in guiding other committees, except special responsibility given by higher committees. Any member/members of all the leading committees including central committee can be given any special responsibility by the central committee.

e) The leading committees must regularly send reports to their lower committees and must intimate their decisions promptly. All lower bodies shall likewise be responsible to make regular reports to higher committees about their respective activities.

f) Except those, who are given some special tasks, every party member shall be a member of any one of the party units.

g) Before decisions are taken every party member may freely and fully discuss in the concerned party units. He/She may express his/her opinions on party policies and various problems and some times may abstain from expressing final opinion explaining the reason for it. But, after taking a decision, everybody must strictly abide by them. However, if a member still holds different opinion, he/she has the right to reserve it. It is not permissible to raise discussion on those issues immediately after they were discussed and decisions taken in Congress /conference.

Any member may raise discussion on new issues in the concerned committees. If he/she feels that the issues are concerned with the whole party then he/she may send his/her opinion up to the Central Committee through his/her committees or/and in special circumstances, directly. If one third of the Central Committee members opine so and also want to call plenum for its solution then it will be circulated at least up to the State Committees. In case the majority of the State Committees agree with this demand then the Central Committee will call the plenum. In such special circumstances, the Central Committee will ensure that the democratic method of resolving issues is followed.

h) Keeping in mind the difference between the tactics and method, every unit has the freedom to take initiative in developing new methods of implementation of the party general line and tasks given by higher committees.

i) If a member is arrested, he/she shall be relieved of all responsibilities and the membership will be placed under observation. Depending on his/her behaviour during the period of detention by enemy or in the jail or after coming out his/her membership shall be continued/cancelled. If continued he/she shall be admitted into the party committee which he/she belonged to prior to his/her arrest unless the party decides otherwise.

j) The method of criticism and self-criticism shall be practiced in the party committee at all levels. There must be relentless struggle against bureaucratic, individualistic, liberal, ultra-democratic, Multi-centered factionalist tendencies and trends in the functioning of the committees. The committees should function on the basis of collective leadership and individual responsibility.

k) Comradely relations and mutual co-operation shall be extended in rectifying the mistakes of others. A party member's work has to be reviewed on the basis of his/her overall practice in party life and not on the basis of minor mistakes and some trifle matters.

l) It is only the Central Committee that shall have the right to take decision on domestic and international issues. Decisions on various levels regarding local issues and problems shall be taken by the respective committees, which will not be against the decisions taken by higher committees.

m) When a party member is transferred to another region, she/he shall be recognized as party member of the same level responsibility in that region. While transferring a member from one region to another all details about the member being transferred shall be sent to the concerned unit in writing.

CHAPTER-6: PARTY DISCIPLINE

Article - 26: Party Discipline is must to defend unity of the party, to increase the fighting capacity and to implement the policy of democratic centralism. Without iron discipline, no revolutionary party will be able to give capable leadership to the masses in the war and fulfill the responsibility of revolution. Party discipline is same for all the party members including the leadership.

Article - 27: a) To reject the aims and objective of the party, party programme or organizational structure or to violate them will be tantamount to indiscipline and the member or unit involved in such activities, will be liable to disciplinary action.

b) When party members violate party discipline, the concerned party unit shall take appropriate disciplinary measures warning, serious warning, suspending from party posts, removal from post, suspending or canceling the party membership, expelling from the party etc., subject to the approval of the higher committee. Cancellation and expulsion of party membership shall come into force only after the next higher committees approve them. Time limit shall be specified while suspending a party membership, which should not be more than one year. The next higher committee shall ratify suspension.

c) When any Party unit violates the discipline, the higher committees shall take disciplinary measures such as reprimanding the unit to partially reconstituting the unit. For dissolving the unit, approval of the next higher committee is necessary.

d) When a Central Committee member seriously violates party discipline (acts as enemy agent or indulges in open anti-party activities) the Central Committee shall have the right to remove him/her from his/her rank or to expel him/her from the party. But, such a measure will come into force only when two-thirds of Central Committee members give their approval.

e) The party unit or the party member whom disciplinary measure is taken shall be submitted a charge sheet beforehand. If the unit or the member thinks that such a disciplinary measure was unjustified, then the unit or the member may raise objection, may request for reviewing the decision or may appeal to the higher committee. Such appeals shall be sent to the higher committees by the concerned lower committees without any delay. Every member shall have the right to defend himself/herself in person in his/her committee/unit or to submit his/her written explanation to the higher committee, which takes disciplinary action against him/her.

Article - 28: a) Punishment should be given only if all other options of discussion and convincing to rectify a member or a party unit fails. Even after giving punishment efforts must be made to rectify. Policy of saving the patient and curing disease should be followed. In special circumstances to defend party security and respect, punishment should be given as soon as possible.

b) The lower committee cannot take any disciplinary action on any member of the higher committee. However, in case of dual membership they may send their allegations and suggestions about the members of the higher committees in writing to the concerned committees.

c) In case of gross breach of Party discipline which may cause serious harm to the party, if he/she be allowed to continue his/her membership or post in the party, a member can be summarily suspended from party membership, removed from his/her party post by his/her committee or by higher committees pending framing charge sheet and getting his/her explanation. At the time of taking such disciplinary steps, the concerned committee should specify the period by which a final decision will be taking in the matter.

d) If any party member or candidate member (or a member at any level) does not participate in party activities or does not implement party decisions for six months without showing proper reason; does not renew membership and does not pay membership fee and levy, he/her shall be deemed to have voluntarily withdrawn from the party and his/her membership shall either be suspended or cancelled.

e) The harshest measures among all the disciplinary measures taken by the party are expulsion and cancellation from the party. Hence while taking such decision; concerned party unit shall observe utmost care. Such measures will be taken when all the efforts in rectifying the concerned-member failed .The party members appeal must be carefully examined by the concerned higher committee and the circumstances, under which he/she committed the mistakes, must be thoroughly reviewed. Those members, who are corrupted in economic matters, politically degenerated, becomes characterless or betray the party-secrecy, shall be liable to punishment.

f) If persons whose party membership has been cancelled or have resigned express their willingness again to join the party, the concerned committees, should take a decision after thorough investigation. Membership should give only after testing through practice for a minimum period of six months. Only the state or Central Committee may take members once expelled from the party barring betrayals. Lower committees may, however, forward recommendations in this regard.

CHAPTER-7: PARTY'S ORGANISATIONAL STRUCTURE

Article - 29: a) The party organization shall be formed according to geographical divisions or spheres of production.

b) Party is constituted with two types of membership professionals and part-timers.

Article - 30: The party structure at the various levels shall be as follows:

a) The highest body of the party shall be the Party Congress. Between two Congresses the Central Committee will be the highest body of the party. Below the Central Committee there will be Special Area Committee/Special Zonal Committee/ State Committee; Regional Committee; Zonal Committee/ District/Divisional Committee; Sub-Zonal/Sub-Divisional Committee; Area Committee; local level committees such as village/Basti/Factory/College party committee. The primary unit of the party will be cell. The Town and city committee will be formed and the concerned higher committee will decide the status of the committee.

b) All committees will elect their secretaries. All committees may form secretariats according to the needs of the movement and the size of the committee. The secretaries of all committees and the secretariats are of the same level and will have same rights as the committee of which they are part. However they, secretaries and secretariats, will have special duties and responsibilities.

c) All the leading committees from Area Committee onward will be constituted only with professional revolutionaries.

d) The party congress is the supreme body of the entire party. The Central Committee elected by the congress is the highest authority body in between two congresses.

e) Special Area Committee/Special Zonal Committee/State Committee elected by the SAC/SZC/SC conference is the highest body at the SAC/SZC/State level.

f) Regional committee elected by the regional conference is the highest body at the region level. Regional committee can be formed by dividing the states or with parts of different states according to the requirements of the movement.

g) Similarly, Zonal/District/Divisional and Sub-Zonal/Sub-Divisional Committees will be elected at their respective level conferences. Area Committees are elected at the Area level conference.

h) Town/City Committee elected at the respective level conference.

i) Party cell – it consists of three to five members in a village, or in two or three villages combined, or a factory, or educational institution, or a locality, or two or three localities combined. In mass organisations units, cells may be formed.

j) In the period between two conferences or congresses, the committees elected at the respective levels are the highest bodies.

k) Various sub-committees and commissions under the leadership at different levels may be formed to efficiently carry out the party's work in various spheres.

Basic Unit:

Article - 31:

a) Party cell will be basic unit of the party. Party cell can be formed area-wise, profession-wise or production-wise. Party cells are the nucleus for day-to-day activities. The members in cells will be minimum 3 and maximum 5. Cell members will fulfill their responsibilities and duties as full-fledged party members and they will avail all the rights of party membership (except candidate members). The cell will elect its secretary.

b) Candidate members will also work according to the decisions of the party cell. They shall participate in the discussions and follow the party directives but they will not have voting rights at the time of decision-making.

c) While forming party cells area wise, efforts will be made to form party cells in factories and in mass organizations.

d) If there are two or more cells in an area, a committee below that of AC can be formed i.e. the local level committees (village/basti/factory/college party committees).

e) Party cell is a living link between broad masses of an area and the party. The cell will lead the revolutionary war of broad masses of people with full initiative. It shall make relentless efforts to bring the masses of factory, locality and peasant areas close to the political line and aims of the party. By involving militant activists and party followers in the revolutionary war against autocratic semi-colonial, semi-feudal state system. It will stress from the very beginning to educate the masses to function secretly, illegally and according to the strategy and tactics of the Protracted People's war. By selecting 3-5 party activists and organizing them in a group educating them in party politics and organizing them as members are important responsibilities of party cells.

CHAPTER-8: PARTY CONGRESS

Article - 32: Holding the all India party Congress shall be decided by the central committee. The party Congress shall be held once in five years. Under special circumstances it may either be postponed or preponed. Decision has to be taken by majority of the CC.

Article - 33: The party congress elects a presidium to conduct the congress and discharges the following tasks:

a) It undertakes the political and organizational review of the party since the preceding congress.

b) It adopts and amends the party programme, party constitution and the strategy and tactics, financial policy and formulates other policy matters.

c) Appraises the domestic and international situation and lays down the tasks.

d) Decides the number of central committee members and elects the central committee and alternate CC members.

e) It ratifies the financial statements.

Article - 34: (a) the central committee elects general secretary of the party. It also elects a Politbureau depending on the requirements of the movement, will take political, organizational and military decisions according to the party-line and the decisions of the central committee in between the period of one central committee meeting to the next and will get its decisions ratified in the subsequent central committee meeting. It will also set up regional bureaus, CMC, other commissions and other sub-committees & departments. The General Secretary also acts as the in charge of the Politbureau.

(b) To run its party organs, the central committee appoints editorial boards for each organ. The General Secretary will be the chief editor of the theoretical-ideological organ of the central committee.

Article - 35: The central committee may convene central plenums to deal with special problems in the period between two Congresses. These plenums can discuss and take decisions on problems relating to party line and policies in that period. Similarly election of new members into the central committee or removal of Central Committee members can also be taken up by the central plenums. Whenever it is necessary, the central committee can co-opt members not exceeding one-fourth of its existing strength if two-third of its members agree.

Article - 36: Special Area/Special Zonal/State; Regional; Zonal/District/ Divisional plenums shall be held once in every three years. Under special circumstances they may be held earlier or postponed. However area conferences/plenums should be held once every two years. These conferences/plenums take decisions after holding discussions on problems relating to their respective levels, send their opinions on the party line and polices to higher committees, and elect the respective committees along with alternate members, if necessary.

Article - 37: In the period between above level conferences, if necessary, plenums may be convened, with the approval of the next higher committee. Decisions may be taken after discussion on problems in the areas under the jurisdiction of the various committees in their respective plenum of the respective committee members may either be elected or removed. If plenums of any committee cannot be held due to special circumstances, the concerned committees may co-opt one-fourth of their respective strengths with the approval of the next higher committee.

Article - 38:

a) The number of delegates to the various conferences including the congress shall be decided by the respective committees according to membership strength as per the decisions of different levels of committees and party congress.

b) The respective committees are empowered to specially invite up to ten percent of the strength of delegates attending the congress, and other different level conference. Observes and non-voting delegates may also be invited to the conference of the respective committees.

Article - 39: The Central Committee shall release relevant draft documents to be discussed in the party congress to all party members giving sufficient time as decided by the CC, before the process of the congress starts. All amendments to drafts submitted by the lower level conferences and by members should be sent to the Central Committee, which will place them before the party congress. Delegates to the party congress shall enjoy the right to move amendments to the draft documents. After going through the draft documents, if any committee delegate/delegates want to move alternative document, he/she/they must immediately inform the Central Committee, and the central committee will decide about the time to be given to the concern delegate/delegates committee for drafting the document. The concerned committee delegate/ delegates have to draft the document within a scheduled time as decided by CC, and thus submit it to the Central Committee. The Central Committee deserves the right to circulate it with its own comment.

Article - 40: The out going central committee shall propose to the congress a panel of members of the new central committee to be formed. Any delegate shall have the right to object to any name in the panel, or can even propose a new panel, with the prior approval of the member whose name is proposed. If there are no alternate proposals, the approval to the panel proposed by the out going Central Committee shall be taken by a show of hands, in case of alternate proposal all committees including the Central Committee shall be elected by secret ballot.

Article - 41: The guidelines for the selection of delegates will be given by the Central Committee and the lower committees will apply these guidelines.

CHAPTER-9: RIGHTS AND DUTIES OF CENTRAL COMMITTEE

Article - 42: The Central Committee will be elected by the party congress. In between the two party congresses the Central Committee is the highest leading body of the party. The Central Committee represents the whole party and can take crucial decisions with full authority on behalf of the party. The Central Committee shall meet at least once in a year.

Article - 43: a) Central Committee may form Politburo, Central Military Commission, regional bureaus and various sub-committees for smooth functioning of the party. The PB is of the same level and enjoys the same rights as the CC. However, it has special duties and responsibilities which it will fulfill on behalf of the CC in between two CC meetings.

Article - 44: The Central Committee can take step and remove any Central Committee member for gross breach of discipline, serious anti party activities and heinous factional activities. The punished member has the right to appeal before the congress. Till the matter is not decided or settled, Central Committee's decision will remain standing. If 2/3 of the Central Committee members agree, they can take decision to oust any member of the Central Committee

Article - 45: The Central Committee can co-opt any member in the Central Committee if any post remains vacant or for the need of the movement. Whenever it is necessary the Central Committee can co-opt members not exceeding one fourth of its existing strength, if 2/3 of its members agree. But it is to be ratified in the next congress. Co-option should be made from among alternative members, if there are no alternate members, then cc can co-opt from others.

Article - 46: The CCS will decide the date and time of the Central Committee meeting and will provide the agenda of the meeting beforehand. If 1/3 members of the Central Committee demand a meeting of the Central Committee, the secretary will have to call the meeting.

Article - 47: The Central Committee or Politburo holds the right to send its any member or members to check-up the work of any unit or any area. The Central Committee has the right to disband any committee and thereby form any organizing committee at any level.

Article - 48: If necessary the Central Committee can convene special conferences and plenums in between two congresses. The Central Committee will decide the other members of the different committees who will attend this plenum other than the CCMs.

CHAPTER-10: INTERNAL DEBATES IN THE PARTY

Article - 49: It is very essential to go through deep discussions to unify the whole party ideologically, politically and organizationally and to improve our methods. This is also democratic right of party members. At different levels of party, we should strive to resolve the questions related with the tactics by openhearted and unbridled debates in respective committees. When needed, help and advice of higher committees shall be taken. In the name of democratic rights of party members, endless debates on a particular issue will only harm the party functioning. So, any type of controversial debate or discussion can be permissible only after the consent of the 2/3 members of the concerned committees.

Article - 50: In case any member or committee has different views about the basic line of the party and it demands its circulation in the party, central committee has the right to take final decisions whether to accept or reject this demand.

Article - 51: If any central committee member has different views in regard with all India or International questions and he/she demands to take this idea in the whole party, in that case, the above-said views will be sent to state/regional committees or to any level if accepted by1/3rd members of the central committee. But any committee member cannot send his/her different views to the lower level committees without the permission from the central committee.

Article - 52: If any lower level committee or committee member has different views on the political and organizational line of the central committee, then they can send their views to the central committee according to the party committee functioning. If needed central committee can send these views along with its opinion in the whole party.

Article - 53: All debates in the party under the control of central committee or under its direction shall be sent to special area, state/regional and zonal committees or to all the levels of party.

CHAPTER-11: PARTY FUNCTIONING IN THE PEOPLE'S ARMY

Article - 54: The people's army is the chief instrument of the party. Hence the party will use this instrument in rousing, mobilizing, organizing and arming the people in carrying out the task of the revolution. It will participate in social production also. Only through the Protracted People's War, with people's army as the highest weapon, the Party will carry out the task of seizure of political power by overthrowing the present reactionary state power which represents the interests of imperialism, feudalism and comprador big bourgeoisie and thereby establish a new democratic state. It will protect the country; defend the victory of NDR, with the goal of socialism. Party will educate the army with the weapon of MLM.

Article - 55: The Party will exercise full control over the army from the very beginning. Because the party decides the overall political strategy and tactics of revolution, hence it also decides the functioning and forms of party organizations in the army by keeping the level of development of the Protracted People's War before it. Central Military Commission constituted by the Central Committee will conduct the military affairs according to the military line of the party as well as the policies, directives and decisions of the Central Committee. In this light the Military Commissions and Commands will be constituted at various levels to conduct the military operations. Being the leader and organizer of the People's Army the party ranks at various level will play a leading and front-ranking role in all the affairs of the army.

Article - 56: This People's Army will be constituted of three forces that is the main force, the secondary force and the base force.

Article - 57: In our guerrilla army all the formations from platoon, company and above level will have party committees. The party branch will be constituted with party members. Various squads will have party cells and party branches. Where needed, a party committee will be constituted at that level. Party members and ranks will also remain in the militia and play the leading and front-ranking role there.

Article - 58: All members of military formations will function under the leadership of the respective party committees. The decisions of these party committees will be carried out and implemented by the respective military formations.

Party members in PLGA will be invited to the party conference/ plenums according to their respective level. In general, the party committees in the military formations at and above platoon level will be elected in conferences held at that level.

CHAPTER-12: PARTY FRACTIONS IN MASS ORGANISATIONS

Article - 59: The party fractions shall be formed in the executive committees of mass organizations. Party fractions will guide the executive committees of the mass organizations adopting suitable method in accordance with the correct concrete situation. Fraction will function secretly. The opinions of party committee/ member guiding the fraction shall be considered as final opinion. If fraction committee members have any difference of opinion, they will send their opinions in writing to the concerned party committee/higher committee. The concerned party committees shall guide fraction committees of different mass organizations at their own level.

CHAPTER-13: PARTY FUNDS

Article - 60: The party funds shall be obtained through the membership fees, levies, donations, taxes, penalties, and the wealth confiscated from enemies.

Article - 61: The levy to be paid by party members shall be decided and collected in their respective state committees.

***

STRATEGY AND TACTICS*

At the foundinf of the CPI (Maoist), on September 21, 2004, a doccuent entitled Strategy and Tactics of the Indian Revolution *was adopted by the rebels. In this document, the Maoists present the broad essence of their operational plan, which is, indeed flexible.*

According to the rebels, "The strategy and tactics of the Indian Revolution should be formulated by creatively applying the universal truth of Marxism-Leninism Maoism to the concrete conditions prevailing in our country. This means that the strategy and tactics should be evolved by basing on an objective class analysis of the Indian society; the character of the Indian State; the fundamental contradictions and the principal contradiction; and by taking into account the specific characteristics, the special features as well as the peculiarities of the Indian situation."

*On this theme, I have borrowed from P V Ramana, "Measures to Deal with Left-Wing Extremism, *IDSA Occassional Paper No. 20*, October 2011, pp. 13-16.

Political Strategy

To build their movement, the Maoists aim to develop progressive forces, win over fence-sitters, and isolate staunch opponents, in order to defeat the state. Thus, the political strategy of the Indian Democratic Revolution is to unite, under the leadership of the proletariat, all the above motive forces which constitute the vast majority - almost nine-tenths - of the Indian population to overthrow the three heavy mountains that are weighing down the backs of the Indian people and keeping the country in a semi-colonial and semi-feudal state.

As part of their political strategy, the Maoists hold that "it is the contradiction between feudalism and broad masses of the people at present that is the principal contradiction. Agrarian revolutionary programme and area-wise seizure of power remain primary during the entire period. But if the principal contradiction changes to that between imperialism and the Indian people, accordingly a specific programme to unite all the anti-imperialist forces will have to be drawn up as part of the general programme of the New Democratic Revolution."

Military Strategy

According to the Maoists, "The military strategy has to be formulated basing on the specific characteristics of the revolutionary war in India. These characteristics determine the military strategy to be one of protracted people's war, as enunciated by comrade Mao—of establishing revolutionary base areas first in the countryside where the enemy is relatively weak and then to gradually encircle and capture the cities which are the bastions of the enemy forces."

The Maoists also hold that the strategy and tactics of the revolution in any country cannot be worked out in isolation from the overall international situation. One has to take into account the actual situation both in the world at large and in the given country prevailing at a given point of time in order to formulate the strategy and tactics correctly. This is because in the imperialist epoch the revolution in every country is an integral part of the world proletarian revolution.

In a comprehensive document entitled "Strategy and Tactics" *that was adopted in 2004 at the founding of the CPI (Maoist), the Maoists have identified the major contradictions in the Indian society. They contend that these contradictions are a result of India being a semi-feudal, semicolonial country, under neo-colonial form of indirect rule, exploitation and control. The major contradictions identified by the Maoists are:*

1. *The contradiction between imperialism and the Indian people;*
2. *The contradiction between feudalism and the broad masses;*
3. *The contradiction between capital and labour; and*
4. *The internal contradictions among the ruling classes.*

They further contend that the Maoist movement "in India has to pass through more than one phase and in any of the phases, one of these fundamental contradictions becomes the principal contradiction. However, the principal contradiction cannot remain unchanged throughout the entire process of the New Democratic Revolution;

rather the principal contradiction and the non-principal one among the two fundamental contradictions are bound to change their positions with the changes in the phases of the revolution."

For the Maoists, the "central task of the Indian Revolution is the seizure of political power. To accomplish this, the Indian people will have to be organised in the People's Army and will have to wipe out the Armed Forces of the counter-revolutionary Indian state and establish in its place their own state."

According to the CPI (Maoist), the principle characteristics of the Indian revolutionary war are:

1. *India is a vast semi-colonial and semi-feudal country with uneven political, economic and social development, with favourable terrain for guerrilla warfare that has witnessed a long period of armed struggle by the peasantry and also now witnessing the ongoing agrarian revolutionary guerrilla struggle in which the peasantry is playing a heroic role.*
2. *Our enemy is big and powerful having centralized state machinery and a well-equipped modern army.*
3. *The Communist Party, the guerrilla army and the agrarian revolutionary movement in India are still weak.*
4. *Our country is a prison-house of nationalities where some nationalities are engaged in bitter struggles against the Indian state to achieve their right to self-determination.*

Some other salient aspects of the document include:

- *The strength of the Armed Forces of the reactionaries is quite inadequate in the vast country, and communication system makes it quite inconvenient for the quick movement of the enemy forces.*
- *A large part of the remote countryside, most advantageous for the establishment of Red liberated areas from the geographical and military point of view, is inhabited by the discontented and agitated nationalities and tribes who are engaged in bitter armed confrontation with the Indian state.*
- *It becomes imperative for the enemy's Armed Forces to be deployed in large numbers in even wider areas to contain the armed struggle waged by the various nationalities. Lakhs of enemy Armed Forces have been deployed since long in Kashmir and the North Eastern States.*
- *As a considerable part of the enemy's Armed Forces will inevitably be engaged against the growing tide of struggles by various nationalities, it will be difficult for the Indian ruling classes to mobilize all their Armed Forces against our revolutionary war.*
- *We are presently in the phase of Strategic Self Defence. At present, the revolutionary movement is advancing in a vast belt of people's war encompassing the extensive areas of Dandakaranya, Jharkhand, Andhra, Bihar-Orissa border, North Telangana and Koel-Kaimur. We will be able to build these areas into contiguous areas of armed struggle with each area influencing the other.*

- *The revolutionary situation can become even more favourable for the rapid advance of the people's war due to several factors such as a war with the neighbouring countries.*
- *The exploiting ruling classes will never relinquish or give up power voluntarily. Without smashing the present state machinery and the main constituents of state power, the mercenary Armed Forces, the instruments of the suppression of the people by ruling classes… the Indian people can not establish political power. Hence, in order to completely smash the state machinery, the building up of the People's Army as the organised Armed Force of the masses is indispensable.*
- *When there is a serious enemy offensive in the form of encirclement and suppression campaign, we should not make futile attempts to hold territory. We should disperse in mobile squads and at the same time should carry on attacks from exterior lines, simultaneously with attacks from within the area of encirclement. The tactical counter offensive against the enemy should be carried out in the form of small and big military actions. A 'meal is eaten mouthful by mouthful'. By following the tactics of sudden attack and annihilation it is absolutely possible to defeat the enemy and achieve victory for the people in single battles.*

STRATEGY AND TACTICS OF THE INDIAN REVOLUTION CENTRAL COMMITTEE (P) CPI (MAOIST)

FOREWORD

The present draft document has been finalized by Joint CC of the erstwhile CPI (ML)[PW] and the MCCI in September 2004 after extensive discussions. Five draft documents were prepared after intense discussions in a series of bilateral meetings held between the high-level delegations of the two erstwhile parties between February 2003 and September 2004. The Joint CC meeting deeply studied these five draft documents, freely exchanged the rich experiences acquired through the revolutionary practice during the past three decades and more, and arrived at a common understanding on several vexed questions confronting the Indian revolution in the backdrop of the international developments.

The present document – **Strategy & Tactics** – is the synthesis of all the positive points in the documents of the two erstwhile parties, as well as their experiences in the course of waging the people's war, fighting against revisionism, and right and left opportunist trends in the Indian and international communist movement, and building a stable and consistent revolutionary movement in various parts of our country.

We are placing the present document before the entire rank and file of our new Unified Party for immediate guidance and implementation. At the same time, it should be borne in mind that this is a draft for the forthcoming Congress of the Unified Party. Hence, it has to be enriched further by the participation of all the Party members and suggesting amendments where necessary. Thus, it should become an effective weapon in the hands of the Party for solving the fundamental problems of the Indian revolution and to advance it towards victory.

Central Committee (P)

21-9-2004 Communist Party of India (Maoist)

INTRODUCTION

The aim of Strategy and Tactics will always be to successfully complete a given stage of any revolution based on the programme related to that stage. It is important to bear in mind the guidelines given by Com. Stalin that theory should guide the Programme; Programme should guide the Strategy; and Strategy should guide the Tactics. The strategy can be correctly worked out only by basing itself on the data provided by, and the conclusions drawn from, the theory and programme of MLM.

The Strategy and Tactics of the Indian Revolution should be formulated by creatively applying the universal truth of Marxism-Leninism Maoism to the concrete conditions prevailing in our country. This means that the Strategy and Tactics should be evolved by basing on an objective class analysis of the Indian society; the character of the Indian State; the Fundamental contradictions and the Principal contradiction; and by taking into account the specific characteristics, the special features as well as the peculiarities of the Indian situation.

The strategy of the Indian Revolution in the present stage should thus serve to fulfill the New Democratic programme by successfully completing the New Democratic Revolution. The tactics that are to be formulated in every twist and turn of the movement in the various regions at various times should be subordinated to the strategy and to serve to effectively implement the above strategy. Such is the dialectical relationship between the Programme, Strategy and Tactics of the Indian Revolution.

Regarding Strategy and Tactics Comrade Stalin stated as follows:

"Strategy: is the determination of the direction of the main blow of the proletariat at a given stage of the revolution, the elaborating of the corresponding plan for the disposition of the revolutionary forces (main and secondary reserves), the fight carry out this plan throughout the given stage of the revolution.

"Tactics: Tactics are the determination of the line of conduct of the proletariat

in the comparatively short period of the flow or ebb of the movement, of the rise or decline of the revolution, the fight to carry out this line by means of replacing old forms of struggle and organisation by new ones, by combining these forms etc.

"Tactics deal with the forms of struggle and forms of organisation of the proletariat with their change and combinations. During a given stage of the revolution tactics may change several times, depending on the flow or ebb, the rise or decline, of the revolution."

(Problems of Leninism - pages 80, 82, 84)

However, the above definition of strategy by Com. Stalin should not be followed mechanically in a doctrinaire manner but apply it to the concrete conditions of our country in which our revolution is taking place. We must also keep in mind the caution given by the Communist Party of China in this regard:

"Stalin put forward a formula that in different revolutionary periods, the main blow should be so directed as to isolate the middle-of-the-road social and political forces of the time. This formula of Stalin's should be treated according to circumstances and from a critical, Marxist point of view. In certain circumstances it may be correct to isolate the middle forces, but it is not correct to isolate them under all circumstances." ***(On the Historical Experience of the Dictatorship of the Proletariat, April 5, 1956)***

Thus a policy of *"developing the progressive forces, winning over the middle-of-the-roaders, and isolating the die-hards"* for the purpose of defeating the main enemies will have to be adopted in the concrete conditions of our country.

Regarding strategy, comrade Mao said:

'Strategy is the study of the laws of a war situation as a whole'. He further explained, 'the task of the science of strategy is to study those laws for directing a war that govern a war situation as a whole, the task of the science of campaigns and the science of tactics is to study those laws for directing a war that govern a partial situation'. Regarding the importance of the science of strategy comrade Mao further stated, *'an understanding of the whole facilitates the handling of the part and because the part is subordinate to whole.*

'The view that strategic victory is determined by tactical successes alone is wrong because it overlooks the fact that victory or defeat in a war is far and foremost a question of whether the situation as a whole and its various stages is properly taken into account. If there are serious defects or mistakes in taking the situation as a whole and the various stages into account, the war is sure to be lost.'

The above quotation, though deals with military strategy and tactics, gives us a lucid and dialectical understanding about the concept and interrelationship between strategy and tactics.

We learn from the experiences of the Russian and Chinese revolutions that we have to formulate both the political and military strategy in order to carry out any revolution to victory. In the Chinese revolution the CPC under the leadership of Mao worked out the political and military strategy by first making a concrete class analysis of the Chinese society, an assessment of character of the Chinese society and state, and the stage of revolution.

Political Strategy: The political strategy for the Indian democratic revolution arises from the concrete class analysis of the present-day Indian society. It is the task of political strategy to distinguish real friends from real enemies of the proletariat in the present stage of the Indian Revolution. It identifies the targets that have to be overthrown and motive forces that have to be united in order to successfully complete the revolution.

To distinguish real friends from real enemies, we must make a general analysis of various classes in Indian society from the point of view of their respective socio-economic status and their respective political attitudes towards the revolution.

At present new democratic stage of the Indian Revolution the targets to be overthrown are imperialism, feudalism and comprador bureaucrat capitalism. The basic motive force of this revolution is the proletariat, the peasantry, especially the landless and poor peasants, are the main motive forces and the firmest ally of the proletariat, the urban petty bourgeoisie is a reliable ally, and the national bourgeoisie is an ally in certain periods and to a certain extent.

Thus the political strategy of the Indian democratic revolution is to unite, under the leadership of the proletariat, all the above motive forces which constitute the vast majority—almost nine-tenths—of the Indian population to overthrow the three heavy mountains that are weighing down the backs of the Indian people and keeping the country in a semi-colonial semi-feudal, state.

In the present stage, where no imperialist power is resorting to direct aggression on our country or when our country has not been reduced to the status of neo-colony of any single imperialist power, it is the contradiction between feudalism and broad masses of the people at present that is the principal contradiction. Agrarian revolutionary programme and area-wise seizure of power remain primary during the entire period. But f the principal contradiction changes to that between imperialism and the Indian people, accordingly a specific programme to unite all the anti-imperialist forces will have to be drawn up as part of the general programme of the New Democratic Revolution.

Whereas the Strategy of the Indian Revolution remains the same throughout the country, the uneven economic, political, social and cultural development in the country the fighting zeal and the level of consciousness of the people and the ebb and flow of the movement underscore the need for different tactics, which are obviously subordinate to strategy, to be pursued in different region at any given time. The intensity of class struggle in various regions and the uneven economic, political, social and cultural development should be concretely analysed in the respective areas and basing on that analysis, tactics (i.e., forms of struggle and forms of organisation) should be formulated. Along with these different tactics for different regions, common political tactical slogans for the entire country should also be formulated from time to time to mobilise the entire people of the country on specific issues.

Military Strategy: The military strategy has to be formulated basing on the specific characteristics of the revolutionary war in India. These characteristics determine the military strategy to be one of protracted people's war, as enunciated by comrade Mao—of establishing revolutionary base areas first in the countryside where the enemy is relatively weak and then to gradually encircle and capture the cities which are the bastions of the enemy forces.

The strategy and tactics of the revolution in any country cannot be worked out in isolation from the overall international situation. One has to take into account the actual situation both in the world at large and in the given country prevailing at a given point of time in order to formulate the strategy and tactics correctly. This is because in the imperialist epoch the revolution in every country is an integral part of the world proletarian revolution.

CHAPTER-1

Indian Revolution in the continuous

Process of World Revolution

The history of social development throughout the world since the emergence of class divided society is the history of class struggles itself. In the process of social development the revolutionary struggles of the peoples of different countries proceed through different stages and these struggles will have their peculiar characteristics too; but they are always subordinate to the general laws of development of the history. The motion of development of world history through class struggle is towards the very establishment of a society without class and without exploitation, towards socialism and communism. The revolutionary movement of the Indian people is also advancing through different stages; it has got its own peculiarities too. But it remains within the general laws of development towards socialism and communism.

The world-historic objective of the international proletariat and its vanguard, the Communist Parties of the whole world, is in full conformity with the laws of development of history. The historic goal of the working class of India, as well as of the whole world, is to establish socialism and communism in the world as a whole.

The Great October revolution was nothing but an inevitable outcome of the revolutionary struggles of the international proletariat and the people and the Great Chinese Revolution was the continuation of that process. The Indian Revolution too is an inseparable part of the revolutionary struggles of the international proletariat and the people.

Hence without "*the correct class analysis of the objective conditions of the whole world and of world politics and economics, that is, the correct class analysis on the basis of Marxism-Leninism of the fundamental contradictions of the contemporary world and their mutual relations and influences*", it is impossible to make a correct appraisal of the international situation and of the internal situation of India, it is impossible to formulate the general line determining the main direction of the revolutionary struggles of the working class and the people of all countries or to realise its significance, and it is also impossible to determine in conformity therewith, the correct strategy and tactics of the Indian revolution. The concrete objective condition of India and the question of the Indian revolution should be judged only in the light of the international situation and the revolutionary struggles of the people of the whole world.

In a nutshell, the objective condition of the present day world is manifest in the fundamental contradictions of the present-day world and their interrelations and inter-influences. These fundamental contradictions are:

a) The contradiction between imperialism and oppressed nations and people;
b) The contradiction between the proletariat and the bourgeoisie in the capitalist countries.
c) The contradiction between the various imperialist powers.

The concrete situation of today's world has been clearly revealed on the basis of the above-mentioned fundamental contradictions of the present day world and in their mutual relation and influences.

Another fundamental contradiction-the contradiction between the socialist camp and the imperialist camp-that had characterised the world for almost six decades from the Great October Revolution, went out of existence at present with the restoration of capitalism in the last Socialist Base of the world proletariat, People's Republic of China, after the demise of Com. Mao in 1976.

However, the struggle between socialism and capitalism will continue to exist through out the era of imperialism and proletarian revolution. Today it is manifested chiefly in the ideological, political and cultural spheres and as a struggle between the two contending classes—the proletariat, representing the forces of socialism, and the bourgeoisie, representing capitalism. The victory of revolutions in one or a few countries and the re-emergence of a socialist camp will once again bring the fourth fundamental contradiction into existence.

The contradiction between imperialism and oppressed nations and people is the principal contradiction in the present-day world. The countries of Asia, Africa and Latin America are the storm-centres of the world revolution dealing deadly blows against imperialism. The end of direct colonial rule in the aftermath of the Second World War due to the relative weakening of imperialism and the growing national liberation struggles world-wide, had compelled the imperialists to switch over to new methods of rule and control and exploitation of the former colonies i.e. neo-colonialism, and in this respect they depend on their indigenous agents, selected and trained by them. This neo-colonialism is the more sinister and more pernicious form of colonialism and has extended its stranglehold over the countries of entire Asia, Africa and Latin America. This is an important development that should be taken into consideration when analysing the situation in these countries.

India, a vast country inhabited by 105 crores of people, rich and abundant in natural wealth, is one of the strongest bases of imperialism. And that is why the progress and success of the new democratic revolution of India, directed against imperialism, CBB and feudalism, will not only liberate the Indian people from the ruthless exploitation and oppression of imperialism but will also elevate to a new stage the struggle of the people of the whole world for independence, democracy, socialism and peace. The success of the new democratic revolution of India and the establishment of a people's democratic state in India will play an important role in accelerating the world proletarian revolution and will signify an important historical advancement towards the establishment of a new world free of imperialism, capitalism and the exploitation of man by man.

CHAPTER-2

Character of the present-day Indian Society

The contemporary Indian society is semi-colonial and semi-feudal under neo-colonial form of indirect rule, exploitation, and control.

This fact derives from an objective study of the development of the Indian socio-economic and political system ever since the colonial period to the present day. When the British colonialists conquered India in the second half of the 18th century, capitalism was beginning to develop in the womb of feudal society in our country. The British colonialists arrested the independent development of capitalism and the Indian society was transformed from feudal to colonial and semi-feudal. In 1947 the colonial and semi-feudal society was transformed into a semi-colonial and semi-feudal society. Ever since then, just as in other countries of Asia, Africa and Latin America, in India too, the imperialists have adopted a new form of colonial exploitation, control and rule i.e. neo-colonial form of indirect rule instead of the old form of direct colonial rule. For this, the imperialists depend on the 'Indian' compradors who have been nurtured by them since their very inception in the colonial period.

Why do we call India semi-colonial?

After the British colonialists were compelled to give up their direct rule over our country, the power was transferred to their compradors-the big bourgeoisie and big landlords, on condition that the imperialist capital and their interests are protected. Several imperialist powers took the place of British imperialism in oppressing and exploiting our country. It is these imperialist powers that actually control the politics, economy and culture and decide almost all the vital policies of the ruling classes of India under the sign-board of formal independence that is fake in essence. Thus, as no single imperialist power is in a position to exercise its control and rule over the country as a whole, India is not a neo-colony but continues to be a semi-colony under the indirect rule, exploitation and control of various imperialist powers. Hence we call India as a semi-colonial, semi-feudal country under neo-colonial form of indirect rule, exploitation and control.

Thus after the so-called independence, the imperialist exploitation of the Indian people has not only remained uninterrupted but has also tremendously increased in the past years. In accordance with their neo-colonial policies, methods and tactics throughout the world, the imperialists have, in collaboration with the 'Indian' comprador capitalists, invested capital amounting to thousands of cores of rupees in various industries of the private sector, state sector and trapped the entire Indian economy in their financial web through so-called 'aid' and 'loan'. By appointing their so-called advisers and experts, the imperialists have tightened their stranglehold over the various government departments.

In reality, this bureaucrat capital is in the control of imperialism and their instrument of increasing the profits of the imperialists and their Indian compradors. With the help of their Indian compradors, the imperialists are preserving India as the market for their commodities, source of cheap capital export, and are plundering India's wealth and sucking its blood and retarding its development. In a nutshell, the Indian economy is a semi-colonial one of the neo-colonial form.

The exploitation and control of imperialism, particularly U.S. imperialism, are not confined to the sphere of economy alone; with the help of the weapon of neo-colonialism they have established their own influence, exploitation and control over military policies through various means, such as, military "aid and co-operation", employment of "advisers", etc., and are strengthening their positions day by day through various kinds of military pacts. All these are going on under the various signboards of the "national defence", the "defence of the country", etc., etc. This army is being used not only to suppress the revolutionary movements and national liberation struggles in India but also in other countries.

Creation of Bangladesh, forced annexation of Sikkim, interfering in the internal affairs of the neighbouring courtiers, sending army to Sri Lanka and Maldives etc. are the examples of the expansionist activities of Indian State backed by the super powers during the decade of 1970s and 80s. Today it is pursuing the policies of intervention, blackmail, meddling and subversion in the affairs of Nepal, Pakistan, Bangladesh, Sri Lanka etc., with the same backing of the various imperialist powers, particularly the US superpower.

The imperialists have thus established their influence, exploitation and control over the Indian economics, politics, foreign policy, military policy, state and governmental policies, culture, that is, on every aspect of the social life. In reality at present India is nothing but a semi-colony of the neo-colonial type and India is one of the chief fortresses of the international counter-revolution too. The contradiction between imperialism and the great masses of the Indian people remains as one of the fundamental contradictions of the present day Indian society.

Why do we call India semi-feudal?

Unlike in the West, where capitalism developed by overthrowing feudalism, in India, the British colonialism protected feudalism and used it as its social prop. Introduction of capitalist relations by the British imperialist rulers without basically altering the feudal stranglehold over the vast masses of the peasantry had resulted in semi-feudal production relations. The sem-ifeudal production relations continued even after the end of direct colonial rule. The imperialists used both the comprador bureaucrat capitalism and feudalism as their social props for their neo-colonial control and exploitation. Due to this alliance between these three main enemies of the Indian people land reforms have not altered the basic structure of agrarian class relations; and usurious and mercantile exploitation of the vast masses in the countryside continues unhindered even after more than half-a-century of so-called independence.

Land concentration in the hands of a few landlords and kulaks on the one hand, poor and landless peasantry of the rural population on the other, continues to characterise the rural scene. As a result, the number of landless agricultural labourers is swelling by leaps and bounds. Due to dearth of jobs, they are obliged to do inhuman labour like bonded servants of the landlords and plantation owners. Duo to want of jobs most of them are compelled to live most wretched life, millions of people die or illness caused by starvation and half-starvation.

Another dreadful aspect of the feudal exploitation in India is the usury exploitation that extracts enormous sums of interest from the peasantry. Besides private usurers, various banks and financial companies too exploit the peasantry. Thus rural indebtedness has been increasing by leaps and bounds. Ruthless exploitation by unscrupulous traders is squeezing the vast peasant masses while selling the agricultural produce and buying the agricultural inputs from the market. Servitude and personal subordination of the poor and landless peasant masses, who constitute the overwhelming majority of the peasantry, to the feudal forces in innumerable forms, is perpetuated through ideological institutions and through the coercive arm of the State and even private armies.

The life of the peasant masses is shattered continuously by the exploitation and oppression by the gangs of local tyrants, the evil gentry, intermediaries, the police, the courts and by a long hierarchy of government officials-all of whom act as loyal agents of imperialism, feudalism, and comprador bureaucrat capitalism, and by the feudal dictum of various kinds. All these have made the life of the peasant intolerable. The feudal oppression is not in the countryside alone nor is it confined to the peasant masses. In addition, the semi-feudal mode of production itself oppresses the vast masses of the country through the state machinery and through the ideological, cultural and other super-structural aspects. So it can be doubtlessly be said that not only the peasantry but the vast masses of the population of the country have contradiction with feudalism.

The feudal exploitation and oppression is hindering not only the development of agrarian economy but also the path of the industrial development of India. Feudalism is one of the main obstacles on the way to the economic and social development of India. Feudalism versus the broad masses of the people is one of the fundamental contradictions in India.

Major Contradictions in Indian Society

From the above understanding of the contemporary Indian society we find that there are four major contradictions in the present day Indian Society. These are:

1. The contradiction between imperialism and the Indian people;
2. The contradiction between feudalism and the broad masses;
3. The contradiction between capital and labour;
4. The internal contradictions among the ruling classes.

Out of these four major contradictions the first two are the fundamental contradictions in the present day Indian society. Again, out of these two fundamental contradictions feudalism vs. the broad masses of the people is the principal contradiction at present.

The New Democratic Revolution in India has to pass through more than one phase and in any of the phases, one of these fundamental contradictions becomes the principal contradiction. However, the principal contradiction cannot remain unchanged throughout the entire process of the New Democratic Revolution; rather the principal contradiction and the non-principal one among the two fundamental contradictions are bound to change their positions with the changes in the phases of the revolution.

As the existence and development of the principal contradiction and the struggles emerging there from play a decisive role in the existence and development of other contradictions and the struggles emerging out of those contradictions, so, at any stage of development of the revolution, it is very important to correctly determine which of the contradictions is the principal one and who are the main enemies at that particular stage, so that maximum emphasis can be given on organizing and developing the struggles emerging out of the principal contradiction and all the struggles of the people can be spearheaded against the principal enemies at that stage.

The other two major contradictions also have a bearing on the Strategy and Tactics of the Indian Revolution.

Class character of the Indian State

From a concrete class analysis of the Indian society and state we find that, under the signboard of the so-called Republic and the Parliamentary democracy, India is nothing but a semi-colonial and semi-feudal state under neo-colonial form of indirect rule, exploitation and control.

It is the armed forces, judiciary, prisons, bureaucracy, etc. of the state machinery that execute the actual business of the state and the principal organ of this state machinery is its armed forces. The present Indian state machinery is the instrument of class repression, class exploitation and class rule of the comprador bureaucratic bourgeoisie and big landlords who subserve the imperialists. Thus the state machinery protects the interests of the imperialists, the CBB and the feudal forces; renders them armed protection; and oppresses the working class, the peasantry and other toiling masses. The Indian State is the joint dictatorship of the big bourgeoisie-big landlord classes who serve imperialism; it ensures democracy for this tiny section of the society while exercises dictatorship over the vast masses of the Indian people.

Like any other exploiting State, the Indian State too acts as an instrument for the distribution of the surplus produced by the toiling masses among the various sections of the reactionary ruling classes and the imperialists who are the three main enemies of the Indian people. It clears the way for the uninterrupted and unhindered exploitation of the resources of India by the imperialists and by the big bourgeoisie-big landlord classes. It also acts as an instrument to resolve the contradictions among the ruling classes that inevitably occur while distribution of the surplus.

Targets of the Indian Revolution

The targets in the present people's democratic stage of the Indian Revolution: 1. Imperialism, 2. Comprador bureaucrat capitalism, and 3. Feudalism.

Imperialism plunders the country's land, labour, raw materials, and other natural resources. It earns super-profits through ruthless exploitation by various means. It subjugates the entire economy, polity, military and culture of India; destroys indigenous industry particularly the small and medium industries, throws out millions of workers into the streets and hinders the free and independent development of the national economy.

Comprador bureaucrat capitalism collaborates with imperialism and allies itself with feudalism. It destroys the small and medium industries, oppresses not only the working class, peasantry and other toiling masses but also the national bourgeoisie.

Feudalism acts as fetter on the development of the productive forces by holding down the vast majority of the Indian people under backward relations of production. Economically, it keeps the overwhelming majority of the people in dire poverty and destitution, and depresses their purchasing power. It thereby, restricts the growth of the home market, retards industrial development and leads to massive unemployment and stagnation of the economy. Politically, it suppresses the democratic rights of the masses and in some places, even creates a 'state within a state' i.e. a parallel landlord raj in the rural areas with their own private armies or with the support of state-hired armed mercenaries. It keeps the peasantry in perpetual subjugation and bondage.

These three big mountains that are weighing down the backs of the Indian people should be smashed in order to build the new democratic society.

CHAPTER-3

Class Analysis of the Indian Society

Now let us analyse the various classes of present-day Indian society.

Landlord Class

Those persons who own considerable tracts of land and instruments of production, do not engage in labour themselves, or do so only to a very small extent and live by exploiting the peasants and the labourers (bonded attached and different degrees of unfairness and other wage-labourers), are called landlords. They lease out part or whole of their lands to peasants at exorbitant rates. Extortion of sharecroppers, robbing them of at least 50% of their produce is one of their forms of exploitation. In addition they may engage themselves as usurers, merchants, hoarders, quarry owners, contractors, agro-based traders, or in other business activity. Land being the basis of their exploitation, they enmesh impoverished peasants in various forms of bondage and extract as much surplus as possible from them, which is a modified form of feudal rent.

A section of the landlords possess modern instruments of production, employ agricultural labourers, supervise cultivation, produce for market and reinvest a portion of the surplus in agriculture. This section of the landlords represents capitalism in agriculture. But this capitalism is a distorted one. It helps perpetuate feudal values, retards free and independent development of economy to further deepen imperialist exploitation and opposes democracy and the country's interest. Many landlords, like most of the erstwhile princes, are also comprador industrialists.

The landlords enjoy immense social and political power in the countryside. They grab the lion's share of the institutional loans, modern inputs and other infrastructure facilities supplied by the government. Some landlords maintain private armies and also hire anti-socials, dacoits etc., to ruthlessly oppress the rural masses. Besides, they extract huge amounts as extortion money from contractors and traders. Generally they belong to the upper castes, represent the most backward culture, practice patriarchy to oppress women folk; use the obnoxious caste system to oppress dalits and other backward castes. By acting as a fetter on the development of the productive forces, they are the main social base for imperialist control over India.

A section of landlords also belong to the upper layers of the backward castes and has emerged newly. They serve as a social base of various caste based political parties.

Those who collect land rent on behalf of landlords, administer the properties of landlords and whose income mainly depends upon exploitation of the peasant by the landlords and also whose lifestyle is that of upper-middle class peasant, should be treated as landlords. They are the enemies of the peasantry and Indian people as a whole.

Comprador Bureaucrat Bourgeoisie

In India, within the colonial system itself, the colonial capital has developed to a great extent. After the transfer of power by imperialism to the big bourgeoisie and big landlords the capitalism that is being developed in India by imperialism and comprador bureaucratic bourgeoisie is not independent national capitalism but comprador bureaucrat capitalism that is tied up with imperialism and feudalism has become comprador, feudal, state monopoly capitalism. Such is the economic base of the reactionary ruling classes of India. This bureaucrat capitalism is developing on a semi-feudal base. Closely tied up with, and serving the interests of imperialist capital, this comprador bureaucrat capital monopolises the economic lifelines of the whole country and is a hurdle for the development of independent Indian economy. It protects the semi-feudal production relations in India. This comprador bureaucrat capital oppresses not only the workers and peasants but also the urban petty bourgeoisie, and it injures the national bourgeoisie. The CBB, in its six-decades of rule, has amassed an enormous amount of wealth by using state power. It has prepared ample material conditions for the new democratic revolution. This comprador bureaucrat capital of India is an instrument of increasing the profits of the imperialists and the Compradors.

The comprador bureaucratic bourgeoisie class or the big bourgeois class of India that had emerged within the colonial system has a long history of existence. It was born and brought up under the patronage of British imperialism and has been organically linked to feudalism from the very beginning. It had emerged from the class of comprador merchants, feudal lords, brokers and big usurers, and hence has been comprador in character right from its birth. It began to invest in industries in collaboration with British imperialism in the beginning and with other imperialist powers particularly after so-called independence in 1947. This had become transformed into comprador bureaucratic bourgeoisie (CBB) after assuming state power along with the big landlord class, who are subservient to imperialism.

The comprador big bourgeoisie is a class that serves the capitalists of imperialist countries and is nurtured by them. Countless ties link it closely with the feudal forces in the countryside. Com. Mao further says, "The comprador bourgeoisie is always a running dog of imperialism and a target of the revolution."

('Some Experiences in our Party's history') Serving imperialism is its principal character and fulfilling its own interests, and not the development of capitalism in the interests of the Indian people and the country is its non-principal aspect. Or in other words, subservience to imperialism is principal while maneuverability or bargaining is non-principal.

The imperialist powers have made the feudal landlord class as well as the comprador class the main social props for their control and exploitation of India.

The Indian comprador bureaucrat bourgeoisie class and the big landlord class are the main instruments of imperialist exploitation of India. Together, imperialism, comprador bureaucrat capitalism and feudalism dominate over the entire social and economic life of the whole country. The Indian state is a joint dictatorship of the big bourgeoisie, big landlord classes led by the CBB who are subservient to imperialism.

Being subservient to imperialism, the CBB's rapacious role is not confined to India alone. It has its eyes on the neighbouring countries of South Asia too and quite often intervenes in their political affairs. Backed by imperialist powers, India is playing an expansionist role, which is a great menace to the neighbouring countries of India. Through this aggressive expansionist role, the CBB of India, while serving the imperialists principally, has its own interests also in the region in looting these countries of their capital, market, raw materials etc. Its expansionist character is derived from the fact that in exploiting India, British colonialism also used our country as a platform for its domination of the Indian Ocean region. Hence, the Indian comprador bourgeoisie, from the early days of its inception, was a loyal and trusted comprador and served as a middleman for the British not only in India but also in several countries of Africa and Asia that came under British rule.

In the period of globalisation, liberalization and privatization, which was initiated in 1985 and took a major leap in 1991, the policy of nationalization of the earlier period began to be reversed and vast chunks of the public sector are being sold to the TNCs and comprador big bourgeoisie at throw away prices. With the major leap in the penetration of foreign capital, which is continuing space, vast sectors of the economy have fallen into their direct control. Though the alliance between the comprador big bourgeoisie, statecapital and foreign capital continues, their relative proportions in the enterprises are changing; state capital is being reduced while that of a section of the comprador big bourgeoisie is increasing along with that of foreign capital.

The comprador bureaucrat bourgeoisie stands as one of the major stumbling blocks for our country's progress. Hence the targets to be overthrown in the new democratic revolution are: imperialism, comprador bureaucrat capitalism and feudalism.

To sum up, the growth of the CBB in our country after 1947 cannot be seen in separation from imperialism. Its survival and growth is completely dependent on imperialism. The so-called state sector or nationalized sector or the public sector is part and parcel of the comprador bureaucrat capital and is wholly subservient to imperialism. Politically, the comprador bureaucrat bourgeoisie sells the country's interests to imperialism and maintains the sem-ifeudal relations through its alliance with the landlord class.

Due to the phenomenal growth of the public sector and state machinery after the transfer of power in 1947, a small upper stratum of bureaucrats and politicians of ruling class parties have acquired crores of rupees by embezzling state funds through kickbacks and commissions in nefarious business deals and various other unscrupulous means by virtue of their position of power at various levels. Though they don't exist as a distinct class, these parasitic sections are part of the bureaucrat bourgeoisie.

Those intellectuals and professionals who are in the direct service of the comprador bureaucrat bourgeoisie and imperialism and who justify the latter's exploitation of the Indian people should be considered as belonging to this class.

Motive Forces of the Indian Revolution

1. Proletariat

The proletariat is a class that is dispossessed of all means of production and is compelled to sell its labour power to the capitalist owners of the means of production. It is the most concentrated class in present-day Indian society and has a heroic history of revolutionary class struggle including anti-imperialist struggle. The strength of the Indian proletariat in the organised sectors, both in public and private sectors, is about 2.6 crores. The number of wage earners working in small-scale industries, construction work and as contract and casual labour comes to about four crores. Together their number is roughly around seven crores.

The industrial proletariat of India has all the main characteristics that the proletariat all over the world has, such as being associated with, and concentrated in the developed capitalist economic system, having organisational discipline, lacking means of production etc., Indian proletariat is being subjected to oppression by imperialists, comprador bureaucratic bourgeoisie and big landlord classes. As the majority of the Indian proletariat comes from poor peasant classes, they have natural bonds with the peasant population. The proletariat and peasant classes have strong mutual influences and relations.

Apart from the industrial proletariat, there is also a sizeable rural proletariat. These farm workers mainly work in large plantations and farms like coffee, tea, cocoa, coconut, mango, rubber, areca nut, sugar, fruit and vegetables. They have no means of production of their own and live by selling their labour power to the big pro-capitalist landlords, the comprador bourgeoisie and the imperialists who own plantations.

There is also a small section in the working class, comprising of trade union bureaucrats who get various bribes from the employers. This section is the labour lieutenants of capital and represents the bourgeois ideology within the working class. Though this section, in general opposes the working class struggles, in the period of crisis, some of them may change their role and take part in the working class movements.

The basic motive force in the New Democratic Revolution is the proletariat. But it cannot win victory by solely depending on its own strength. For achieving victory, this class has to give its leadership to all classes, especially the peasantry, and other strata of people that can participate in the revolution. The proletariat plays the role of leadership in the revolution.

2. Landless and poor peasants

Generally the landless peasants, including the agricultural labourers (rural proletariat), do not have land and agricultural tools of their own. They live by either totally or mainly selling their labour power.

Some among the poor peasants own lands nominally or rent in small plots of land. Similarly some have meager agricultural tools. In addition to paying land rent and interest, they sell their own labour power and hence they are exploited in all these forms.

They constitute 65-70% of the rural population. Of all classes that are existing in Indian society, the poor and landless peasants are the basic motive forces and are the firmest ally of the proletariat.

3. The Semi-Proletariat

The major component of the semi-proletariat is the huge mass of poor peasants. Those who own some simple implements like the small handicraftsmen, carpenters, masons, mechanics and the like also form part of the semi-proletariat. There are also those who earn their living working as hawkers, hamalis, rickshaw pullers, autorickshaw drivers, temporary rural construction workers, house servants and engaged in many other similar jobs, earning daily wages. Fishermen also form part of semi-proletariat. They are continuously becoming part of the proletariat.

Those semi-proletarians are an important motive force of the New Democratic Revolution.

4. Middle Peasant

Most of the middle peasants have their own lands. Some others take land on lease in addition to theirs. Generally they own sufficient agricultural tools. The entire income of the middle peasant, or most of it, is derived from their own labour. Generally the middle peasant does not exploit others and also does not sell their labour power and is subjected to exploitation by feudalism, imperialism and comprador bureaucratic capitalism. Some middle peasants exploit to a small extent but it is not their main income. Some of them (well-to-do middle peasants) have surplus land and hire labour occasionally. Some even lend small sums of money at interest.

Oppressed by feudalism, imperialism and comprador bureaucrat capitalism, the middle peasant will take an active role in the anti-feudal as well as anti-imperialist struggles. Hence, the middle class peasantry as a whole is a reliable ally of the proletariat. The positive or negative attitude of the middle peasants is one of the factors determining victory or defeat in the revolution, and this is especially true after the agrarian revolution when they become the majority of the rural population.

They are important motive forces in the revolution. The middle peasantry can be considered as rural petty-bourgeoisie. They constitute roughly 20-25% of the rural population.

5. Rich Peasant

Rich peasants constitute 10-15% of the rural population. They possess considerable amounts of land. Some own only part of their land and lease in the remainder. Some others have no land of their own and lease in all their lands. The holding operated by them is a surplus - producing one. They generally own better instruments of production. They generally engage in labour themselves and in this sense form part of the peasantry but at the same time they always rely on exploitation for the part or even the major of their income. In general if the income of a peasant through exploitation is more than 50%, they should be classified as rich peasants. Though they adopt more or less all the existing forms of semi-feudal exploitation, their main form of exploitation is by hiring agricultural labour. They may rent out their land, may lend money or engage in trade, commerce, small business, etc. The procapitalist rich peasants use modern technology, engage in intensive cultivation, lease in land to expand scale of production and produce for the market. The growth of capitalist relations in agriculture in some pockets and the increasing reliance of the rich peasants on the market for purchasing agricultural inputs as well as for selling the produce, is bringing them into increasing conflict with imperialism and the comprador big bourgeoisie who control the market and hence they are being drawn more and more into the anti-imperialist struggles of the peasant masses. But, by virtue of their class status, they tend to compromise in face of mounting state repression. Generally they remain neutral in the agrarian revolutionary struggle. As a class, they can be considered as vacillating allies of the revolution. A section of rich peasantry comes with us, another section remains neutral and a small section joins the enemies.

6. Petty Bourgeoisie

The petty-bourgeoisie includes the handicraftsmen i.e., those engaged in small scale production, small traders, the lower levels of intellectuals such as students, primary and secondary school teachers, college lecturers, office clerks, non-gazetted officials, engineers, doctors, lawyers, and those employed in various other professions who have largely middle-class incomes that are derived mainly from their own manual or mental labour.

The petty-bourgeois class consists of three sections though they broadly belong to the same economic strata.

The first section consists of the relatively better-off i.e., those whose yearly earnings allow them to have some surplus over and above their consumption needs; the second section consists of those who in the main are economically self-supporting; and third section consists of those whose standards of living are continually declining and who find it difficult to make both ends meet.

The first section always aspires to go up the social ladder, is closer to the national bourgeoisie, has a lot of faith on liberal bourgeois propaganda and is suspicious of the revolution. This section which is a minority among the petty bourgeoisie constitutes its right wing.

The second section which is very numerous and makes up more than one-half of the Indian petty-bourgeoisie, never opposes the revolution but only hesitates to join it as it harbours doubts regarding the ultimate victory of the revolution.

The third section, equally numerous, whose living standards are fast declining, come out openly in support of the revolution and play an active role. Although these three sections differ in their attitude to the revolution in normal times, in times of war and acute crisis when the revolutionary movement is advancing towards victory, the entire petty-bourgeoisie class including even the right wing, sails with the revolutionary tide. This is because of its very class position in society i.e., its position as a class oppressed by feudalism, imperialism and comprador bureaucrat capitalism with more and more of its members facing social insecurity and becoming pauperised and being driven to the ranks of the proletariat or the unemployed with the deepening of the economic crisis. Hence as a class, this section of the petty bourgeoisie constitutes one of the motive forces of revolution and is a reliable ally of the proletariat.

Various sections of the petty-Bourgeoisie

(i) **Intellectuals and Students:** These do not constitute as a separate class or stratum in the society. Seen from the point of view of their family, living conditions and their political outlook, the majority among them may be treated as petty-bourgeoisie. Their number in India has been considerably increasing in the past few decades. The majority among them are oppressed by imperialism, feudalism and comprador bureaucrat capitalism and live in a constant fear of unemployment and social insecurity that they might be forced to abandon their studies and such other fears. Hence they tend towards revolution. Having bourgeois education and scientific knowledge and keen political outlook to some extent, they frequently stand in the forefront in the present stage of the revolution or act as a bridge between the people. It was first of all among intellectuals, students and youth that Marxism-Leninism in India had extensively spread and found acceptance.

(ii) Petty Tradesmen: Generally the small business men who engage one or two workers or self-manage their small shops without engaging anyone. They live in constant fear that they will become bankrupt due to the exploitation by imperialism, big bourgeoisie and moneylenders.

(iii) Artisans: They are very numerous, possess their own means of production and are themselves engaged in production. Their condition is similar to that of middle class peasantry.

(iv) Professionals: These are doctors, lawyers and such other engaged in various professions who derive their income more through their own labour, whether manual or mental, than by exploiting others, Those professionals who derive their income more through exploiting others than through their own labour are considered as part of the national bourgeoisie.

These sections of petty bourgeoisie are reliable motive forces in the revolution. Their weakness is that some of them are easily influenced by the bourgeoisie and hence we must carry on revolutionary propaganda and constant organisational work among them.

7. National Bourgeoisie

The national bourgeoisie in India consists in general of the middle and small bourgeoisie. This is a class with dual character which arises out of its economic position. The national bourgeoisie is a class which is politically very weak and vacillating.

On the one hand it is oppressed by imperialism and comprador bureaucrat capitalism and fettered by feudalism. Hence it has a contradiction with all these three enemies of the people's democratic revolution in India. It has neither a share in state power nor any control over the state funds. It has comparatively few ties, with imperialism. Its market is continuously being gobbled up by the imperialist-comprador bureaucrat bourgeoisie combine, its growth is being restricted and sections of it are even liquidated due to the ever-growing onslaught of imperialism. Hence it constitutes one of the revolutionary forces in the present stage of the Indian revolution.

But on the other hand, it is inconsistent and lacks the courage to oppose imperialism and feudalism thoroughly because it is economically and politically flabby, depends on the state for licenses, raw materials and finance, still has some economic ties with imperialism and feudalism, and is scared of the working class revolution. It also aspires for establishing a state under its control and to become the big bourgeoisie. It exploits labour and derives its income primarily from this exploitation.

It follows from the dual character of the national bourgeoisie that, at certain times and to a certain extent, it can take part in the revolution against imperialism and the Indian ruling classes, but that at other times, there is the danger of its tailing behind the comprador bureaucrat bourgeoisie and taking part in counter-revolution.

The right wing of this class has reactionary political tendencies, spreads illusions about imperialism and opposes the people's democratic revolution. We must unmask these sections before the people and liberate the masses from their reactionary influences. But at the same time, the majority of the national bourgeoisie either remains neutral or participates in the revolution. The targets of the New Democratic Revolution are only the imperialism, the comprador bureaucrat bourgeoisie and landlord class. Even after country-wide victory of the revolution, it will be necessary to permit the existence for a period, a capitalist sector of the economy represented by the small and middle bourgeoisie without, of course, allowing them to control the economic lifeline of the country.

In general the party adopts the policy of protection to the small and middle bourgeoisie wherever the state power of New Democracy extends.

8. The Lumpen-proletariat

This stratum of the Indian society are those who are deprived of all opportunities to participate in social production. This is due to the existence of a vast army of rural and urban unemployed which numbers over ten crores in the country and which is ever-increasing on account of the semi-colonial and semi-feudal conditions prevailing in India. The increasing in unemployment is leading to the increase in the lumpen proletariat. Petty thieves, robbers, criminals, goondas, beggar, vagrants, pimps and prostitutes and all those who are forced to make illegitimate means to make a living constitute the lumpen proletariat. They are mainly found in the slums of cities and towns. Many of them migrate to cities from the villages in search of living, but deprived of jobs due to the ever-intensifying crisis in the Indian economy, they end up as criminals and antisocial gangs. The ruling classes often utilize them as strikebreakers, disrupters or as mercenaries. Some of them are recruited by the ruling classes into counter-revolutionary militias and into the reactionary armed forces.

Due to their position in class society lumpen proletariat develops hatred towards it. Hence they respond to the slogan of smashing the existing socioeconomic structure. But these people lack constructive qualities and are given to destruction rather than construction.

Hence it has some potential to be remoulded and employed in the service of the revolution. But extreme caution is necessary recruiting them into the party as they often become the source of roving rebel and anarchist tendencies in the revolutionary movement and have an aversion for discipline.

CHAPTER-4

Two Stages of the Indian Revolution

The semi-colonial and semi-feudal character of the Indian society points out that the first task of the Indian revolution is to transform the semi-colonial, semi-feudal society into an independent, self-reliant, democratic society by solving the two fundamental contradictions of the present indian society, and then to build a socialist society so as to advance towards realising the Communist society. Hence the Indian revolution has to be carried out in two stages: the new democratic stage and the socialist stage. This is because, in India, bourgeois democratic revolution has not been completed as in the West.

The first stage of the Indian revolution can be victoriously completed only under the leadership of the proletariat. In the present era, no other class or party, except the working class and a genuine communist party as its vanguard, can lead the New Democratic Revolution to its final victory. This is due to the fact that in the present era, and particularly after the Great October Revolution, no bourgeoisie of any country is in a position to carry out a thorough-going national democratic revolution out of fear of the working class continuing the revolution to its consummation to socialism. Hence the bourgeoisie compromises with imperialism and lacks the will to wage a thoroughgoing revolution against feudalism by mobilising the peasantry. It stands opposed to the oppressed masses.

Hence, to lead the peasantry towards the New Democratic Revolution is the most important task of working class leadership. The working class of India cannot emancipate itself without uniting with the peasantry who constitute the overwhelming majority of the population in semi-colonial and semi-feudal India and who are being exploited and oppressed for ages.

It is only by organizing and leading the peasantry in the agrarian revolution and national democratic revolution that the working class can give leadership to the revolution, can open wide the path of their own liberation from wage-slavery by liberating the peasantry from the exploitation, plunder and depression of imperialism an their running dogs - the feudal lords and the comprador capitalists. And it is in this way that they can lead the revolution and it is this path of socialism which alone can emancipate the working class from the system of wage-slavery. The chief tasks of the first stage of the revolution in India are to overthrow the three main enemies of the Indian people-imperialism (and the comprador bureaucrat capitalism that is generated by imperialism) and feudalism in order to establish a new democratic India.

The national and democratic revolution, directed against the main enemies of the revolution - imperialism and their lackeys the big bourgeoisie and feudalism, though are the two different kinds of basic tasks in the entire process of Indian revolution or the People's Democratic Revolution, one cannot be separated from the other. As the imperialist and their comprador lackeys, the Indian big bourgeoisie, are the main supporters and protectors of feudalism, the struggle for the overthrow of imperialism and the struggle to uproot feudalism are interrelated to each other. Judging conversely, as the Indian society is mainly dependent on feudalism, protected under the wings of imperialism and their comprador lackeys - the comprador capitalists, so the struggle to uproot this moribund feudalism and the struggle to annihilate imperialism and the comprador bureaucrat capitalism generated by it, are inseparable from each other. So, the two fundamental tasks of the national revolution and the democratic revolution are at once distinct and interwoven. It is wrong to regard the national revolution and the democratic revolution as two entirely different stages of the revolution. The main content of the new democratic revolution is the agrarian revolution.

The task of the second stage is to establish a socialist society by carrying forward the revolution to its consummation. The first stage is the pre-condition for the second. Only by fulfilling the tasks of the People's Democratic Revolution in India we can lay the basis for the Socialist Revolution. People's democracy is an inseparable part of Socialism, an inseparable part of the world socialist revolution. It is wrong to forget the inseparable relationship between People's Democracy and Socialism. It is equally wrong and harmful to confuse the two stages and to think of reaching Socialism in a single leap.

No intervening stage of bourgeois dictatorship will come between the stages of New Democracy and Socialism.

CHAPTER-5

Basic Tasks of People's Democracy

The aim of the New Democratic Revolution is to smash the semi-colonial, semi-feudal politics, economics and culture and to establish new democratic politics, economics and culture. Only by way of accomplishing this goal, the doors for the all-embracing development of the Indian society can be opened, the poverty and misery of the people can be redressed, and the political, economic, and cultural basis for a socialist society be laid down. The struggle for people's democracy is the struggle of all the ant-imperialist and anti-feudal politics, economics and culture against the counter-revolutionary semi-colonial, semi-feudal politics, economics and culture. The struggle for people's democracy is the struggle of all the anti-imperialist and anti-feudal people on the basis of worker-peasant alliance under the leadership of the working class exerted through its vanguard, the Communist Party, against imperialism, CBB and feudalism. This is a struggle between revolution and counter-revolution.

The People's Democratic Politics

The central task of the NDR is to establish the people's democratic state by overthrowing the present semi-colonial, semi-feudal state machinery through armed struggle. The people's democratic state means the state of the democratic dictatorship of the all the anti-imperialist and anti-feudal forces, on the basis of worker-peasant alliance, under the leadership of the proletariat, and is a particular embryonic form of the dictatorship of the proletariat. The people's democratic state ensures all types of freedom, rights and democracy for the vast masses of the toiling masses, and also try to ensure the participation of the vast masses of the people in the day-to-day administrative work by adopting appropriate methods, defends the people's interests at all times, while at the same time it exercises dictatorship over the reactionary forces-imperialists, comprador big bourgeoisie, big landlords and all their hangers-on who constitute a small minority.

To build up a united front of the people i.e. a united front for armed struggle, under the leadership of the working class, exercised through the Communist Party, against imperialism, the CBB and feudalism, and to establish the people's democratic dictatorship under working class leadership is the central task of the New Democratic Revolution. This will forge close international unity.

People's Democratic Economy

The main task of people's democratic economy is to pave the way for the economic and social development of the country and to lay the basis for socialist economy by overthrowing the semi-colonial and semi-feudal economy. It is the economy of a society that is in transition from capitalism to socialism under the people's democratic dictatorship led by the proletariat.

All the industries, banks and other enterprises of the imperialists and the CBB will be expropriated and turned over to the New Democratic State; all the land of the landlords will be expropriated and distributed to the poor and landless peasants; the exploitation of the peasantry by the usurers/moneylenders and traders/merchants will be put to an end thereby releasing the initiative and the potentialities of the peasantry. Voluntary co-operatives will be set up and state trading will control the life of the country's economy. Capitalist production that has no control over public life i.e. of national capital will be allowed but will be under state restriction and regulation. However, it is the people's democratic State that will play the principal role in industry and commerce and will control the economic lifelines of the country. This will facilitate not only the building of the people's democratic economy, but also pave the way for the socialist economy. In this connection the rich experiences of socialist china under the leadership of comrade mao will be taken as the guide.

To overthrow the moribund feudalism and to accomplish the agrarian revolution, to expropriate the imperialist and comprador-bureaucrat capital and transform them into the property of the new democratic state, and thus, to open wide the path of the progress and development of the Indian economy and society by establishing the control and authority of the people's democratic state over the economy of the country-such is the essence of the New Democratic Economy. The development of the people's democratic economy will lay the basis for the socialist economy.

People's Democratic Culture

The task at the present stage of the revolution in the cultural front is the establishment of new democratic culture i.e., a scientific, democratic and mass culture, by uprooting the semi-colonial, semi-feudal culture along with the modern revisionist ideology. The people's democratic culture is an anti-imperialist, anti-feudal culture. It is an heir to all the secular, genuine democratic, and scientific aspects of the rich cultural heritage of the oppressed masses that are passed on by history.

It is impossible to arm the people ideologically, make them conscious and organise them for the people's war without the widest propaganda of people's democratic culture based on Maoism. As Mao said: "*In overthrowing a political power the first and regular task is to work in on the ideological front and to create public opinion.*" To overthrow the exploiting classes and their state machinery, the first and foremost task throughout the course of the new democratic revolution is to wage ideological struggle and create public opinion in favour of agrarian revolutionary war and the protracted people's war.

Mao says, revisionism is the main danger. Modern revisionism is one of the chief enemies of MLM and the people's democratic ideology and revolution. the anti-imperialist anti-feudal revolutionary culture of the people cannot be established without fighting against modern revisionism. in this respect MLM is the strongest weapon in the fight against modern revisionism.

Besides, in India, feudal thinking is deep-rooted and is manifested in many ways, particularly in casteist, biases against religious minorities, religious narrow mindedness, communalism, untouchability, patriarchy, and numerous other forms. The Party must educate the masses against all such anti-democratic values and cultures and replace them with those based on equality, self-respect, secularism, dignity of labour and a proletarian class view-point.

For the success of the Indian revolution the anti-imperialist and antifeudal cultural front has to be organised and constantly strengthened. The people's democratic culture will be an inseparable part of the general antiimperialist, anti-feudal revolutionary people's democratic front. One of the tasks of this cultural front is to educate the workers, peasants and the toiling masses about the anti-imperialist and anti-feudal agrarian revolutionary struggle and the protracted people's war.

The people's democratic state will take up the task of wiping out the imperialist and feudal culture from all spheres of social science like economics, politics, philosophy, military science, history, literature etc., and in their place, establish the people's democratic culture.

CHAPTER-6

The Central Task of the Revolution - Seizure of Political Power Through *Protracted People's War*

As comrade Mao said: *"The seizure of power by armed force, the settlement of the issue by war, is the central task and highest form of revolution. But while the principle remains the same (for all countries), its application by the Party of the proletariat finds expression in various ways according to the varying conditions."*

The above principle is equally applicable to the Indian Revolution too. The Central task of the Indian revolution also is the seizure of political power. To accomplish this Central task, the Indian people will have to be organized in the people's army and will have to wipe out the armed forces of the counterrevolutionary Indian state through war and will have to establish, in its place, their own state—the People's Democratic State and will have to establish their own political authority. The very act of establishment of the state machinery of the people by destroying, through war, the present autocratic state machinery - the army, the police, and the bureaucracy of the reactionary ruling classes - is the Central task of the People's Democratic Revolution of India.

It is absolutely indispensable for the Party of the proletariat in India to study the experiences of the world socialist revolution particularly the experiences of the two great proletarian revolutions of Russia and China. The application of the above principle of conducting the revolutionary war followed two different paths in the two countries depending on the special characteristics specific to their respective countries. The revolution in Russia took the form of a country-wide armed insurrection for the seizure of political power, while in China the path traversed by the revolutionary war was the path of protracted people's war. Whatever the forms assumed by the revolutionary wars in various countries, the content remains the same i.e., the seizure of power by armed force.

Protracted People's War is our Path

In order to guide the revolutionary war in India, it is necessary for us to grasp the experiences and the theoretical summing ups of these revolutionary wars made by comrade Lenin, Stalin and Mao. And particularly it is necessary for us to grasp the essence of Mao's contribution on military science.

Generalising the experiences of the proletarian revolutions in the era of imperialism, we can broadly categorise the revolutionary wars in the various countries in the world into two types according to the character of their respective socio-economic-political systems. If it is a capitalist country where bourgeois democratic rights prevail, the Party of the proletariat prepares the working class and its allies through open, legal struggles—parliamentary, trade union, general strikes, political agitation and such other activities, in order to organise a country-wide armed insurrection at an hour of revolutionary crisis, seizing power first in key cities and then extending it throughout the country, at the same time strengthens appropriate secret party apparatus and combines secret, illegal and semi-legal activities with open and legal activities in accordance with concrete conditions.

Thus the Path followed by the Russian Revolution is: Inflict decisive smashing blow, at a hurricane speed, first, on the urban center which is the well-fortified, consolidated and well-organized controlling center of the state power of the enemy, crush the heart of the enemy's state machinery. Establish the Centre of power of the revolutionary state in the urban area. Then spread the revolution rapidly to the countryside—march forward by smashing the enemy's state machinery in the countryside. Capturing the urban area first, though war of strategically quick decision, establish revolutionary authority in the urban area, and thereafter, capturing the villages and establishing the revolutionary authority in the state power of the whole country through insurrection and establishing the revolutionary political authority of the people—such is the general Path followed by the Great October Revolution in Russia.

If, on the other hand, the country is ruled directly or indirectly by some foreign imperialist power or powers and is semi-feudal where there is no independence and democratic rights for the people, the Party of the proletariat from the very beginning arouses and mobilizes the people for armed struggle, relies on the peasantry—the main force of the revolution—makes backward rural areas its main centre of work, builds a people's army and people's militia; establishes dependable, strong and self-sufficient base areas or liberated areas in the vast countryside, constantly expands them in the course of protracted people's war, (in such a situation the cities under the control of the enemy will look like small islands in the ocean of the vast rural liberated areas); encircles and finally captures cities by way of decisively smashing the state power of the reactionaries and establishing the state system and political authority of the people throughout the country-such is the Path traversed by the Chinese Revolution to win world-shaking victory in 1949. And the history of the revolutions in colonial, semi-colonial, semi-feudal countries of Asia, Africa and Latin America have shown that this Path is applicable to all such countries also. In all these countries the main form of struggle is armed struggle and the main form of organisation is the army, but other forms of mass struggles and mass organisations are also indispensable.

Before the outbreak of a war all organisation and struggle are in preparation for the war and will serve it directly or indirectly after war breaks out.

The path followed by the Chinese revolution is also applicable in semi-colonial, semi-feudal India due to basic similarities in the conditions between India and pre-revolutionary China. It is the principal characteristics of the objective conditions of India that determine the Path of the Indian Revolution as the path of protracted people's war.

The Principal Characteristics of India's Revolutionary War

1. India is a vast semi-colonial and semi-feudal country with uneven political, economic and social development, with favourable terrain for guerrilla warfare, that has witnessed a long period of armed struggle by the peasantry and also now witnessing the ongoing agrarian revolutionary guerilla struggle in which the peasantry is playing a heroic role.
2. Our enemy is big and powerful having centralized state machinery and a well-equipped modern army.
3. The Communist Party, the guerilla army and the agrarian revolutionary movement in India are still weak.
4. Our country is a prison-house of nationalities where some nationalities are engaged in bitter struggles against the Indian state to achieve their right to self-determination.

Since it is the above principal characteristics that determine the line for guiding India's revolutionary war as well as many of its strategic and tactical principles, let us analyse these characteristics more deeply.

1. Uneven economic and political development and the semi-colonial, semi-feudal character of Indian Society is the most important characteristic that basically determines our political strategy and tactics as well as our military strategy and tactics.

The unevenness in the economic and political development of India is quite glaring. On the one hand, there is a distorted capitalist economy that is being increasingly integrated into the imperialist world economy. The capitalist economy has given birth to a huge industrial proletariat and other wage earners in non-industrial establishments running to around seven crores. This ensures that the proletariat of India is strong enough both in numbers and organization to lead the Indian revolution if it is imbued with the ideology of Marxism- Leninism-Maoism.

On the one hand, the capitalist economy coexists with, and stands on, a preponderant semi-feudal base. Although capitalist relations are penetrating the feudal setup in the Indian countryside and are partially remoulding it to suit the needs of imperialism, it is impossible (given the collusion between feudalism, comprador bureaucrat capitalism and imperialism) to bring a radical structural change in the semi-feudal base and its super structure. Consequently, the vast majority of India's population still lives in the countryside and the vast majority of them languish under semi-feudal conditions of existence.

The vast majority of the peasantry is in urgent need of the agrarian revolution to change the miserable, wretched semi-feudal conditions of existence. This circumstance derives from the fact that the democratic revolution in India remains unfinished and that the land question remains unresolved. Hence the content of the new democratic revolution remains the peasant war for land and political power-a factor that can be effectively utilized by the Party to rouse and organize the vast peasant masses into the People's Army.

Hence the proletariat finds its principal ally in the peasantry and can lead them to victory in the agrarian revolutionary war if proper Strategy and Tactics are pursued. It is possible to establish strong mass base among the peasantry and mobilise them into class struggles in the form of armed struggle for the seizure of land and establishment of people's authority in place of feudal authority. Several areas in the country have seen an upsurge of the peasantry against the semi-feudal exploitation and semi-feudal production relations, particularly since the great Naxalbari struggle. In the past decades the agrarian revolutionary war has spread to several strategic regions in our country and has created the condition for an unending flow of armed peasant militants and cadres into the revolutionary movement.

The unevenness of development in India indicates that it is not possible to stage a simultaneous revolution (i.e., an armed insurrection) throughout the country and that the line of area wise seizure of power through the strategy of protracted people's war has to be adopted basing on the relatively backward and strategic areas of the countryside. This means revolutionary war has to begin in those regions that are relatively more backward and where the social contradictions are sharp. The strength of the armed forces of the reactionaries is quite inadequate in the vast countryside of India and the inadequacy of the transport and communication system and other infrastructure makes it inconvenient for the quick movement of the enemy forces. The people's armed forces - the people's army and the people's militia, on the other hand, can advance and retreat easily, according to the needs of the struggle, in the vast countryside, that is, there is enough room for their manoeuvre in face of a big military offensive by the enemy's armed forces.

Thus the vastness of the countryside, the inadequacy of the transport and communication system and the isolation of the remote countryside from the military centers, and above all, the inadequacy of the reactionary armed forces in comparison to the vastness of the country and the population, if all these are taken into consideration, the military strength of the reactionaries is relatively weak in the countryside compared to that in the cities, and hence, from the military point of view, the vast countryside is the most advantageous for the revolutionary people's army to strike at the enemy. Hence, we can transform the vast tracts of the countryside into red resistance areas, guerilla zones, guerrilla bases and liberated areas by making use of the favourable terrain which is abundant in some regions of the Indian countryside. Liberated areas can also be established in the plains when the domestic and international situation becomes more favourable and the people's army becomes powerful i.e., when the revolutionary war is at a high peak.

The semi-colonial nature of Indian society also breeds conflicts and rivalries among the various imperialist powers for their domination and control over India. This is bound to generate acute conflicts and rivalries among the Indian ruling classes. Such an unstable political situation can be utilised by the Party of the proletariat to hasten the pace of building guerrilla zones and liberated areas and thereby advance towards completing the New Democratic Revolution. Thus while the first characteristic incontrovertibly proves that protracted people's war, and not armed insurrection, is the path to be followed by the revolutionary war in India, we must analyse the other characteristics to understand how protracted people's war in India could be waged.

2. The second principal characteristic—the enemy is big and powerful with a centralized state machinery and a well-equipped, well-trained modern army, Paramilitary and other forces-makes it imperative for the Party of the proletariat to take extreme caution from the very beginning in conducting the revolutionary war. This factor underscores the need to wage our revolutionary war from the weakest links of enemy rule - the vast tracts of the backward Indian countryside. It also warns us against engaging in strategically decisive battles with the enemy's armed forces for a long time, and to use the tactics of guerrilla warfare and preservation of our forces while destroying the enemy's forces bit by bit through guerrilla methods of warfare, to accumulate strength by extending and deepening the armed struggle over ever-wider areas and to make the best use of the favourable terrain in the strategic regions in the countryside.

It should, however, be noted that the enemy is superior only from the tactical point of view. In the strategic sense, enemy's armed forces are only paper-tigers. Their interests are diametrically opposed to the interests of the broad masses and hence cannot get any cooperation from the people. Their morale and combat capacity are quite low primarily because of their mercenary nature; and the contradiction between officers and soldiers also contributes to it considerably. Moreover, since the vast majority of them are peasants in uniform, the influence of the agrarian revolutionary war will have a deep impact on them.

3. The third principal characteristic—the weakness of the Communist Party, the people's guerilla army, and the revolutionary movement in the country at the present juncture- has a profound influence on the nature of the revolutionary war in India. It shows that the people's guerrilla army that is built in the course of anti-feudal struggles and advancing the agrarian revolutionary guerilla struggles, has to accumulate strength over a period of time before being transformed into the PLA and prior to the transformation of guerrilla zones into liberated areas. It also warns us that we should not expose our forces to the enemy; should accumulate our forces considerably before entering into decisive engagements with the enemy's forces and should build a strong, stable, underground party mechanism from the very beginning. Thus from the sharp contrast of the weakness of the Party, the guerilla army and the revolutionary movement as a

whole with the strength of the enemy's armed forces, arises the strategy and tactics of our people's armed forces and the Party.

However, this weakness relates to the present situation only. The conditions for overcoming this weakness are relatively developing. Already people are getting mobilised in various parts of the country into armed agrarian revolutionary struggles under the leadership of the Communist Party, which is growing in strength day by day. People's guerrilla army is getting expanded and people's war is spreading to new areas. Since our agrarian revolution is a just one, and since it defends the interests of the majority of the people, the support of the people is increasing day by day.

The inferiority in arms and other things can be made up by relying on the mobilization of the vast masses as correctly observed by Mao:

> "*The mobilization of the common people throughout the country will create a vast sea in which to drown the enemy, create the conditions that will make up for our inferiority in arms and other things, and create the prerequisites for overcoming every difficulty in the war.... To wish for victory and yet neglect political mobilization is like wishing to "go south by driving the chariot north", and the result would inevitably be to forfeit victory.*"

Hence, by adopting appropriate and correct strategy and tactics, as the war is drawn out, the enemy's disadvantages and our advantages will both grow, and inevitably, the degree of the strength and weaknesses of ours and that of the enemy will continue to change, and changes will continue to occur in the position of relative superiority and inferiority too of both the sides, And, in this way, the military power of the people will continuously and definitely attain supremacy over the military power of the enemy and will finally decisive defeat on the military power of the enemy.

To sum up, at the initial stage, that is, up to a certain stage of development of the people's war, the military strength of ours is liable to remain weaker than that of the enemy. But this strength of the enemy and the weakness of the people are never absolute, they are relative, they are temporary. By way of relying on the vast rural areas and on the poor peasantry, by way of strictly pursuing the class line and mass line and the principles of guerrilla struggle and the protracted people's war, in words and in deeds, as shown by Com. Mao, the military strength of the people can gradually and definitely overwhelm that of the enemy as the revolutionary war draws out and can finally inflict decisive defeat on the armed forces of the enemy. However strong the forces of the enemy may be and however weak the people's forces may be at the beginning of the revolutionary war, through the realization and creative application of the total teachings of the flexible strategy and tactics of the guerrilla war and the Protracted People's War, it is possible to build up a new type of army, that is the red army, and to establish one after another-advanced base areas in the backward rural areas, and it is entirely possible to carry forward the revolution towards its final victory by gradually consolidating and expanding the people's army and the base areas through struggles. Beginning with the great Chinese Revolution, the very historical experiences of the revolutionary wars of countries like Vietnam, Laos, Cambodia, etc., bear testimony to the above truth.

4. The fourth principal characteristic—the irreconcilable contradiction between the various nationalities and the Indian ruling classes leading to incessant armed confrontation - contributes greatly to weaken the enemy and helps the advance of the revolutionary movement.

This circumstance arises from the fact that the unfinished democratic revolution in India has left the national question unresolved and it is the Party of the proletariat that should take up the historic task of solving this problem from a class perspective. A large part of the remote countryside, most advantageous for the establishment of red liberated areas form the geographical and military point of view, are being inhabited mainly by the discontented and agitated nationalities and tribes, who are engaged in a bitter armed confrontation with the Indian state. Hence, it becomes imperative for the enemy's armed forces to be deployed in large numbers in ever-wider areas to contain the armed struggles waged by the various nationalities.

Lakhs of enemy's armed troops have been deployed since long in Kashmir and the North Eastern states alone. More and more nationalities may come into armed confrontation with the reactionary Indian state that is keeping them in a state of subjugation and oppression and denying them their right to self-determination. As a considerable part of the enemy's armed forces will inevitably be engaged against the growing tide of struggles by the various nationalities, it will be difficult for the Indian ruling classes to mobilise all their armed forces against our revolutionary war. If our Party can lay down the correct basis to win over the nationalities and tribes through our policy of guaranteeing self-determination for the nationalities and political autonomy for the tribes and forge a powerful united front against the common enemy (i.e. imperialism, CBB and feudalism) with these forces we can spread the flames of armed struggle to almost all the strategic regions in the country.

Needless to say, this will be a great positive factor for the rapid advance of the people's war by developing the people's guerrilla army into the PLA, establishing several base areas and then advancing towards countrywide victory.

The above four principal characteristics determine the line for guiding India's revolutionary war as well as many of its strategic and tactical principles. It follows from the first and fourth characteristics that it is possible for our Party and People's army to grow and defeat the enemy. However, it also follows from the second and third characteristics that it is impossible for our Party and our People's army to grow very rapidly or defeat our enemy quickly. Hence the revolutionary war in India will be of protracted nature.

However, the revolutionary situation can become even more favourable for the rapid advance of the people's war due to several factors such as: further intensification of the imperialist crisis; a war with the neighbouring countries or on a world scale; intensification of the internal contradictions among the Indian ruling classes that may lead to an even more severe political crisis and instability and thereby forcing the enemy to divert his armed forces and economic resources to deal with the growing mass revolts; possibilities for the emergence of revolts among the police, Paramilitary forces as well as the army, and so on.

Some people argue that in India it is impossible to establish liberated areas, to build the red army and to carry out protracted people's war because there is relatively more industrial development, capitalist relations in agriculture and better transport and communication facilities, and because the Indian government has a strong centralised administrative system with a very big modern army when compared to pre-revolutionary China. These arguments are wrong. However strong the enemy's military power may be and however weak the people's military power, by basing ourselves on the vast backward countryside-the weakest position of the enemy-and relying on the vast masses of the peasantry, eager for agrarian revolution, and creatively following the flexible strategy and tactics of guerrilla struggle and the protracted people's war, - as a full meal is eaten up mouthful by mouthful, exactly in the same way, - by applying the best part of our army (a force few times stronger than that of the enemy) against different single parts of the enemy forces and following the policy and tactics of sudden attack and annihilation, it is absolutely possible to defeat the enemy forces and achieve victory for the people in single battles. It is thus possible to increase the people's armed forces, attain supremacy over the enemy's forces and defeat the enemy decisively.

While taking into account factors favourable to the enemy, we must, in the course of carrying out the protracted people's war, take many more precautions and we should establish liberated areas by developing guerrilla zones keeping in mind that it is not possible to build liberated areas in quick succession. We will have to mobilise people into class struggle more skillfully and cautiously based on class line and mass line. We must remember that the only positive factor that the enemy has (even that is temporary) is the superior strength of the state machinery, particularly the mercenary armed forces. On the other hand, all other factors are on the side of the revolutionary Party and the people's guerilla army-the principal among these being the just cause of our war, our historic responsibility of solving the land question and the nationality question that are the aspiration of the overwhelming proportion of the country's population, the ever-increasing crisis and contradictions within the ruling classes, and the fact that we are waging not the old type of conventional war but a people's war by mobilizing the people on a massive scale both militarily and politically. Thus the factors favourable to the enemy cannot change the protracted nature of the Indian revolutionary war which ensues from the principal characteristics of our country, as well as from the lessons drawn from the Chinese and Russian revolutions,ans mainly from the Chinese Revolution.

Not only India, but every country has, in addition to the general characteristics, its own specific characteristics and its own peculiarities. We must also remember that the revolution will suffer losses if we fail to take into account the specific characteristics and peculiarities while formulating the guiding principles of our revolutionary path. However, we have to keep in mind that these specific characteristics and peculiarities cannot alter the general characteristics of revolutionary war or the revolutionary path determined by those characteristics.

Strategic Stages

That the "protracted people's war" will pass through three strategic stages is a general principle (the experience of revolutions of China, Vietnam and other countries proved this). They are:

I. Stage of Strategic Defensive;
II. Stage of Strategic Stalemate; and
III. Stage of Strategic Offensive.

Basically our protracted people's war will also follow this general principle.

The experience of past victorious revolutions of other countries reveals the fact that in a protracted people's war, the first stage will last longer. The stage of strategic stalemate and the stage of strategic offensive, which follow it, will end in a comparatively shorter time. However, changing into the second and third stages mainly depends on domestic and international situation.

Parliamentary Elections - Our Stand

According to Marxism-Leninism, the participation or boycott of election are forms of struggle and related to tactics. But after the emergence of Khrushchov revisionism, when the parliamentary path and participation in election has become the strategy of the modern revisionists, then in the backdrop of this aspect, we cannot leave this question merely a question of tactics only. So it is wrong to say, like all other tactics this tactic too, can be utilised only if it suits the concrete conditions of the country in general and serves the revolutionary strategy, i.e., the seizure of power through protracted people's war.

In the concrete conditions of semi-colonial, semi-feudal India where bourgeois democratic revolution too has not been completed and uneven social, economic and political conditions exist, the objective conditions permit the proletarian party to initiate and sustain armed struggle in the vast countryside. In the name of preparation for armed struggle, participation in election will only sabotage the revolutionary movement. No peaceful period of preparation for revolution is required in India, unlike in the capitalist countries where the bourgeois democratic revolutions were completed and armed insurrection is the path of revolution.

Hence, generally speaking, in the conditions prevailing in our country, participation in election neither helps in developing revolutionary class struggle, nor in enhancing democratic consciousness among the people. Rather it will only foster constitutional illusions and legalist trends among the Party ranks and the masses at large.

Some say that the revolutionary party must participate in parliament and assemblies citing three reasons: 1) that there is no high tide of revolution; 2) that the subjective forces are weak at present to initiate and advance armed struggle; and 3) that people have illusions in the parliamentary system.

All these arguments are baseless and have no relation whatsoever to the concrete ground realities in India. Firstly the question of ebb and flow as explained by comrade Lenin applies to countries pursuing insurrectionary tactics where periods of ebb are used for preparation for revolution and periods of tide are used for armed insurrection or uprising. In India, a revolutionary situation is existing and the path of revolution is that of protracted people's war, participation in parliament has no relation to ebb and tide of revolution and armed struggle can be initiated and area wise seizure of power can be achieved in the countryside.

Secondly, participation in parliament does not help in developing the subjective forces. Rather it will only drive them into legalism and divert them from the arduous and painstaking task of building a secret party, intensifying revolutionary class struggle and advancing armed struggle against the state. Moreover, the experiences of participating in election for the last 50 years amply prove this fact that, most of those who participated in parliamentary election under any argument, have either turned into apologists of parliamentarism and become die-hard revisionists or only increased illusions on the parliamentary system.

The argument that the Indian people have illusions in the parliamentary institutions and hence one must participate to dispel these illusions is even more obnoxious and dangerous. The parliamentary institutions and system in India are discredited to a large extent in the eyes of the people and participation in these will only create or increase the illusions among the people. There is no objective basis in India for exposing the parliamentary system from within. It can be best done by direct propaganda and organising the people against the parliamentary and election system on the basis of the election boycott slogan.

It is only by promoting alternative institutions of people's power in the course of the intensification of ongoing agrarian revolutionary guerilla struggle that it will be possible to enhance people's consciousness and to wipe out their illusions, whatever they may have, about the present parliamentary system. Further, it is necessary for this purpose to propagate extensively and concretely to boycott the patliamentary election and, at the same time, about the alternative organs of people's power. The tactic of participation in election undermines the task of building and developing revolutionary armed struggle.

Moreover, historical experience in India until now has only proved that most of those who participated in election either became revisionist or diverted revolutionary armed struggle into legal and peaceful channels. The various Marxist-Leninist groups in our country that pursue the tactic of participation in parliamentary elections are getting bogged down more and more in the right opportunist mire, while some have already abandoned armed struggle and become revisionists.

Hence we can conclude that boycott of elections, though a question of tactics, acquires the significance of strategy in the concrete conditions obtaining in India as it is not at all compatible with the strategy of protracted people's war.

CHAPTER-7

Agrarian Revolution - People's Army-Base Areas

Agrarian Revolution is the axis of the New Democratic Revolution

Agrarian revolution is the axis of the New Democratic Revolution, and the peasantry, shattered and oppressed under the pressure of the semi-colonial and semi-feudal system, is the firmest and the most dependable ally of the working class in the national democratic revolution. The armed agrarian revolution which alone is the key to the creation of the unending flow of the armed revolutionary forces of the vast peasantry and the establishment of the invincible people's army.

It is only by leading the peasantry in the national and democratic revolution —along the path of the agrarian revolutionary guerrilla warfare and protracted people's war as shown by Mao, that a firm revolutionary alliance of the working class and the peasantry can be formed which will serve as the basis for the broader new democratic united front with all the forces opposed to imperialism and comprador bureaucrat capitalism, and feudalism—a united front for conducting armed struggle, which is one of the three magic weapons of the revolution.

Hence our Party has to propagate extensively the agrarian revolutionary programme among peasants, mainly among landless poor peasants and agricultural labourers, in the rural areas. The slogan "Land to the tiller and power to the revolutionary peasant committee" will constitute the main slogan in the period till the establishment of the guerrilla zone. Thereafter, in these Guerrilla Zones, with the development of the embryonic forms of people's political power, the central slogan will be transformed into "*Land to the Tiller - All Power to the Revolutionary People's Committee*". In the course of the development of the Guerilla Zones towards Base Areas, this latter slogan will assume the main form.

It is only by taking the agrarian revolution as the axis and by depending on the vast countryside, that we can arouse and organize the peasantry-constituting the overwhelming majority of the population and the principal ally of the revolution-for guerrilla warfare, and establish a mighty people's army through liberating them from the exploitation and oppression of the reactionaries. It is only thus we can gradually turn the vast countryside into self-sufficient, strong and dependable base areas—into great military, political, economic and cultural bastion of the revolution, and from these base areas, strike effective and strong blows against the urban areas the comparatively stronger bases of the enemy, and gradually liberate the cities from the hands of the enemy, thereby capturing power countrywide.

Base Areas, other Areas - Their Inter-Relationship

As we have seen in the foregoing, the line of area-wise seizure of power has to be adopted basing on the relatively backward areas of the countryside, i.e. the revolutionary war has to begin in those regions that are relatively more backward, where the social contradictions are sharp, where the authority of the state is relatively weak, and where terrain is more favourable for carrying on guerilla war.

Though India is a country with vast and extensive rural areas our Party at present is still weak and is confined to limited areas. Hence, the central leadership should draw up a comprehensive strategic plan consisting of area selection, cadre deployment, ideological-political-organisational-military preparations, concentration of leadership, coordination etc. As our Party cannot immediately start work in all the rural areas of the country, as part of our Strategy, the state committees should take up planned work in rural and forest areas according to their respective strength. We have to first concentrate on those areas where feudal exploitation is as its worst; where social, economic and political contradictions are intensifying; where the class struggle is sharpening, where the enemy is relatively weak and where the geographical conditions (mountains, hills, forests, and other favourable terrain) are more favourable for conducting the guerilla war. Our Party, with a perspective of building Guerilla Zones and Liberated areas in such areas, should give first priority to these in the allotment of cadres and concentration of leadership.

Strategic Areas for Establishing the Base Areas

Basing on the laws of protracted people's war in India, in order to confront an enemy, who is far more superior in strength, the revolutionary forces will have to select areas, in which the enemy is relatively weaker and which are favourable to the revolutionary forces, and develop the revolutionary war there. Our country has many such areas that are strategically important for the people's war where Liberated Areas can be established. These Bases will act as the lever or fulcrum for coordinating and advancing the people's war in the country and for seizing political power countrywide.

These strategic areas are hilly regions with dense forest cover, have sufficient economic resources, a vast population, and a vast forest area spreading over thousands of square kilometres. In such areas the enemy is weak, and these areas are very favourable for the manoeuvres of the people's army. In these strategic areas we can defeat the enemy completely by fulfilling the tasks of building and consolidating a strong proletarian party and a strong people's army; procuring the people's support and economic resources, while developing the guerrilla war aiming at the building of liberated/base areas in these areas.

We have to advance giving importance, depending on the respective concrete conditions, to the formation of several base areas or guerilla zones basing on one base area, or to the consolidation of the base areas. We should choose the objectives in this way basing on the type of the respective areas and prepare the masses mentally, imparting ideological and political consciousness to them from the beginning. We should impart consciousness to the subjective forces while training them in accordance with the above objectives, so that they will formulate proper tactics from time to time by identifying the changes occurring during the course of development of the struggles. However liberated areas too will undergo changes. Developments like a base area changing into a guerrilla zone and a guerilla zone changing into a base area will occur depending on the state of the enemy's offensive, the state of our subjective forces, and on the domestic and international situation.

Since at present, the revolutionary movements are advancing in the vast belt of people's war encompassing the extensive area of Dandakaranya, Jharkhand, Andhra, Bihar, Orissa Border, North Telangana, Koel-Kaimur - have a great strategic significance. We will be able to build these areas into a contiguous area of armed struggle, with each area influencing the other. As these areas get consolidated, we should utilize their impact on the surrounding areas and develop them into guerilla zones thus expanding the area of armed struggle. We should have the aim of developing the revolutionary movement in strategic areas of various states as the subjective forces gain strength. We should allocate our forces accordingly.

Relation Between Strategic Areas and other Areas

Basing on the concrete analysis of the concrete conditions prevailing in our country we have formulated the programme and strategy for the Indian revolution in the present stage and the future perspectives of the Indian revolution. We had drawn up the basic, principal and the immediate task of the revolution at the present stage as the establishment of the People's Army and Base Areas in the vast countryside and also decided that the principal form of struggle throughout the stage of the new democratic revolution in India is armed struggle and the principal form of organization is the people's army.

The revolutionary line, the political and military strategy of the revolution will be the same for the entire country. However, in the sphere of tactics we have to take into account the diverse economic, political, social, geographical and cultural conditions in the different regions in the country; the strength of the subjective forces and the changes in the balance of forces, the intensity of class struggle and armed struggle, etc. in different regions and formulate the appropriate forms of struggle and forms of organization, tactical slogans while keeping in mind that all these should always be subordinated to, and serve the overall strategy. How to apply the general line of new democratic revolution to the varying conditions in the different regions in the country, how to maintain the correct dialectical relationship between strategy and tactics, the principal and the non-principal forms of struggle and organization, between the principal task and the secondary tasks, between the strategic areas and other areas is a complex question in practice and we have to grapple with it by basing on the concrete conditions and creative application of MLM.

Besides the principal strategic areas as mentioned above, there are four other categories of rural areas basing on their distinct characteristics. These are:

1) Backward plain and semi-forest areas with some hilly terrain where the class contradictions, particularly between the broad masses of the peasantry and the feudal forces, are quite sharp. Terrain here may offer some additional advantage but the main factor to be taken into consideration is the predominance of semi-feudal relations that can rapidly lead to an intensification of the armed agrarian revolutionary war and transform the area into guerilla zones, and later into Base Areas depending on the overall situation in the country and the strength of our subjective forces. Guerrilla war can be waged in these areas for a long time provided we utilise the seasons and people's support to our advantage. These areas will be able to withstand the enemy's offensive by utilising the first type of strategic areas as their rear.
   We should also build up revolutionary mass movements, especially revolutionary peasant movements based on agrarian programme, in a big way in these areas that have large population and acute class contradictions. Some among the people's army recruits and leadership coming to the fore in these struggles have to be shifted to strategic areas. On the whole, these areas will be the main centres of recruitment and supplies to the people's war.
   Areas abutting lakes, small islets, some of the coastal areas with favourable terrain, islets in the estuaries etc. also can serve as seasonal Bases. Guerilla war can be waged extensively using this coastal area (heavy losses on the enemy can be inflicted by hitting at his supplies through sea routes).
   Likewise, plain areas adjacent to the strategic areas and areas with international borders should be dealt separately with a long-term perspective of transforming them into base areas.
2) Relatively advanced areas where capitalist development in agriculture has taken place to some extent, though this capitalism is very much distorted and disarticulated. Moreover, land question has not been fundamentally solved. Infrastructure like transport and communications is quite developed in these areas and the state's authority is considerably strong. Nevertheless, these areas offer ample opportunities for political mobilization on a massive scale along with preparation from the very beginning for Guerilla war.
3) The coastal areas that are adjacent to the mountain ranges and forest belts i.e. adjacent to the strategic areas. Although there is relative development of capitalist relations in the coastal areas (the areas adjacent

to the strategic areas), within the overall semi-feudal system in the country, and though there is relatively developed infrastructure, these areas are to be seen in relation to the potential Base Areas in the neighbourhood and adopt different tactics. The scope for wide political mobilization exists in these areas and here too, we must give utmost attention for the preparation for Guerilla warfare from the very beginning.

4) The numerous adjoining rural suburbs of urban centres that have daily organic links with the urban centers. These suburban areas have to be further classified into different types depending on the scale, importance and role of the particular urban centres in the economy, their proximity to the areas of armed struggle, the weightage of the various classes, particularly the working class, the traditions of working class struggles, etc. and appropriate tactics have to be formulated for the different types of the suburban areas. Mini-squads with small weapons and dressed in civil so as not to seem conspicuous, organizers working in absolute secrecy and under different covers, special action teams, may be the chief forms of organization in these areas. The main stress should be on working with a long-term perspective and also to act as a liaison between the urban and the main rural areas.

While it is necessary for the revolutionary Party to formulate different tactics for the above-mentioned types of areas, it is even more important to keep in mind the relation between the tactics and the overall strategy and the central task of revolution; between the tactics and the basic, principal and immediate task at the present time; between the strategic areas of the first type and the other areas, etc. Thus it becomes imperative for the Party to scientifically formulate the tactical principles for all these areas with a strategic understanding so as day-to-day tactics can be worked out basing on these principles.

(i) The first priority should be given to the work in the principal strategic areas in accordance with the line of protracted people's war in the concrete conditions of India, i.e. the line of building the people's army and establishing Base Areas in the vast countryside, and to advance to liberate the entire country basing on these Base Areas and the people's army. All the work in other areas should be carried out by coordinating with this most important task.

(ii) We should work with the revolutionary objective of seizure of political power in all areas from the very beginning.

(iii) The forms of struggle and forms of organization and the main slogans in the different areas should be based on the concrete analysis of the concrete conditions pertaining to the economic, political, social, cultural, and geographical spheres on the one hand, and the level of people's political consciousness and the state of our revolutionary movement. The stress should be on establishing the proletarian (Party) leadership over the oppressed masses in all these areas.

(iv) In all these areas, particularly where there is relatively more capitalist development with greater infrastructure and influence of the market, and where the influence of the bourgeois and revisionist-reformist ideology and politics hold the sway and our movement's influence is relatively weak in the present situation, we have to lay stress on taking up mass issues and politically mobilizing the masses into militant struggles against the State, making the necessary preparation for building guerilla warfare. It is only thus we can gradually bring the vast masses in these areas into our fold by placing the revolutionary alternative before them. The advance of our people's war and the growth of the people's army and the establishment of the Base Areas will bring a qualitative change in the situation in these areas too and we will be in a position to utilize the situation in our favour if proper tactics are adopted from the beginning.

(v) The Party must give special importance to make the necessary preparations from the very beginning in all these areas for building the guerilla forces along with the people's militia and strengthening them in the course of guerilla war. Utmost priority must be given to secret armed activities. We must keep in mind that all the areas other than the strategic areas will remain as guerilla zones for a relatively longer period of time and hence must be more flexible in adopting tactics. For instance, we may have to change our tactics in accordance with the changes in the seasons in matters such as the military and other campaigns, formations, shifting of the forces, etc. We may have to retreat our forces frequently depending on the intensity and magnitude of the enemy's suppression campaigns. Also we have to send forces from these areas to the strategic areas according to plan from time to time so as to accomplish the principal task of establishing the Base areas. This factor has to be taken note of in drawing up the tactics in these areas.

(vi) In states that do not have strategic areas of significance, plans must be made from the very beginning to deploy some subjective forces in the strategic areas in the neighbouring states. The central and state leaderships must create such an understanding among the cadres in these states, take concrete decisions and implement them.

(vii) The Party units in all these areas must shoulder the task of sending Party cadres, technicians, doctors and others to the strategic areas and to the people's army, to give logistical support to them, and to build solidarity movements. This will develop the correct revolutionary orientation in the entire Party, rally the entire Party around the central and basic task, establish a revolutionary relationship, cooperation and coordination between the different movements in the country.

People's Army and Base Areas as the Basic, Principal and Immediate Task

The very general line of the Protracted People's War points out that the basic, principal and the immediate task of the present stage of the revolution is to arouse and organize the people, in a planned way, for agrarian revolutionary guerrilla war in the countryside—specially in the remote countryside (which is most favourable for the building up of the guerrilla war, the people's army and the base areas), and to build up the people's army and the rural red base areas through guerilla warfare.

Therefore, while developing guerilla zones, and the guerilla war, we should concentrate our forces in the strategic areas and give importance to the establishment of liberated areas and should organise the people planfully for the agrarian revolutionary guerilla war in the countryside specially in the remote coutryside which is the most favourable for the building up of the guerrilla war, the people's army and the base areas, not only from the economic and political points of view but also from the geographical and military points of view and give importance to build up the people's army and the rural red base areas through the guerrilla war.

In the absence of liberated areas it is impossible to advance either the on-going guerilla war or the guerilla zones. The people's liberation army will have to depend on the liberated area for the preservation and expansion of its forces and for the destruction of the enemy forces. In one word, "*The guerrilla armies rely on these strategic bases to fulfill their strategic tasks*". The liberated areas constitute the rear for the guerrilla armies. Moreover, by establishing people's democratic political power in a specific area and implementing in practice the tasks of the agrarian revolution, it will become possible not only to greatly enthuse the people in other parts of the country but also to promote confidence in them and create areas of struggle everywhere. Thus by the realization of this task, it is possible to enhance and expedite the revolutionary high tide throughout the country, and through this, basis can be laid for the building up of new base areas, and the gradual consolidation and expansion of the people's army and base areas. In this way, we will be able to create serious losses to the exploitative ruling classes, quicken the tempo of the revolution, and open up the path for carrying forward the revolutionary war towards the ultimate victory.

As building up of the people's army and the red base areas is an indispensable and a very important step towards bringing about a qualitative leap in the ongoing people's war in the country, the imperative and the urgent priority before us is to firmly grasp the task of building the people's army and the base areas as the principal and the immediate task of the present time and to orient the entire work of the Party in line with this. It is our imperative duty to firmly carry on this principal and immediate task of the present time by adhering to the correct line and policy and the planning and method—to the correct line of work, simultaneously carrying out the struggle against the right and "Left" opportunism of various shades and colours on these questions.

Developing Red Resistance - Completing Preparations for Guerilla Zones

In accordance with our general line of establishing Base Areas first in the vast backward countryside and then gradually expanding to the advanced areas and finally encircling the cities, we have to first select the strategic areas to commence our rural work. The central leadership and the concerned state leaderships should play the determining role in the selection of the areas in the respective states apart from some strategic areas directly under the Central leadership. This is very much essential in order to avoid spontaneity in our work.

The area selected should be sufficiently large so as to have enough room for manoeuvre in face of severe enemy offensive. Though we may begin the work in the core area of the selected zone, we should have a concrete perspective to expand the movement to the entire zone within a time-bound plan. In selecting the area, we should also take into consideration the economic, social, political, geographical and cultural conditions. The question of economic self-reliance should also be a factor while selecting the area keeping in view the perspective of building and sustaining the Base Area. The first priority must be given to the first type of the strategic areas. In states where such areas do not exist, the second type of strategic areas can be selected or the strategic areas contiguous to the state where they exist can be selected under the guidance of the central leadership. The small towns and urban centres falling within these strategic areas must be considered as part and parcel of this work.

The concerned committees should give the first priority to these areas in allotting cadres. Sufficient leadership cadres should be allotted and cadre should be sent in accordance with the growing needs of the movement in these areas from time to time. The cadres being sent should be prepared deologically, politically, organizationally and militarily so as to grapple with the complex problems that they will encounter in course of initiating and developing the armed struggle. The entire Party too should be prepared by the leadership to orient he entire work in accordance with the work in the perspective areas.

Once an area is selected, the first important task to be fulfilled is to undertake a social investigation i.e. theconcrete form of exploitation and oppression and the concrete class analysis or the class relations in the area, decide who are our friends and who are our enemies, with whom to unite and whom to target mainly, and the issues to be taken up for the mobilization of the oppressed masses. Apart from the economic issues of the different classes, particularly the basic classes, we should also identify the major political issues for mobilizing the masses. Another major task is to undertake a concrete study of the terrain of the area to the extent possible before commencing the work. It may also become necessary for our squads or the organizers to familiarize themselves with the terrain in the very beginning depending on our assessment of the enemy.

The form of organization that has to be set up in the area should, as a matter of principle, always depend on the form of struggle that is to be taken up or is possible in the given time. Generally speaking, in all these backward areas with favourable terrain, it is possible to go for armed form of struggle from the very beginning as it is the principal form of struggle in the entire period of NDR. Hence our whole orientation, concentration, and concrete planning should accord with this principle of developing armed struggle as the principal form of struggle. This means that we have to propagate the politics of seizure of power among the peasantry, particularly the poor and landless peasantry, from the very beginning and organize them into militant struggles taking the issues of their day-to day problems and also for the basic demands of land, democracy and political power for the people. We have to organize them and arm them for these demands. We have to maintain the correct interrelationship between these four aspects, namely, propaganda, investigation, struggle and organisation. In this way we have to launch and gradually develop red resistance struggle and struggle for wiping out feudalism -lock, stock and barrel.

From the very beginning we have to mobilize the masses on the slogans: 'Land to the Tiller', "*All power to the peasant committees!*", "*without power people have nothing!*", and "*without people's army people have nothing!*".

To accord with the above slogans and forms of struggle we have to set up armed organizations of the peasantry from the very beginning in these strategic areas. Initially, when our forces are too weak, we must work secretly among the poor and landless peasantry in order to establish sufficient contacts and bring them into the mainly underground peasant organizations under the leadership of our Party. We may commence our work either in the form of underground organisers or in the form of squads directly depending on our strength and other factors. Whatever form we adopt in organizing the masses, our main thrust should be to bring the politically conscious and militant elements, particularly from the basic classes, into underground peasant organizations or Committees.

Along with the secret peasant organizations or committees, we must also form of broader and open organizations of the peasantry wherever conditions permit and initiate militant struggles on issues against the imperialist- CBB-feudal exploitation and against the state machinery. When working openly in such a situation we must take the precaution not to expose our Party cadre and to work under some cover. Depending on the situation, we may also use the open organizations, even if temporarily, to establish the necessary contacts among the masses with the aim of setting up the underground mass organizations of the peasantry. As the struggle has to be intensified and will have to take the armed form from the very beginning, we have to lay stress on building the underground organization of the peasantry from the beginning. The form of open organization of the peasantry should thus be subordinate to our general line of building underground peasant committees and raising armed guerilla units at the earliest possible time.

From the very beginning the party should concentrate on educating the peasantry with the politics of seizure of power, and from the very beginning, the people should be made aware of and tempered in secret and illegal activities. If the peasantry lacks the perspective of seizure of power and building the people's army while carrying forward the peasant struggle, however extensive and strong the movement may be, will certainly end up in economism and reformism. The principal aim should always be to arouse and organise the masses for guerrilla warfare and protracted people's war with the objective of seizure of state power and to create an unending flow of revolutionary armed forces in the countryside to develop guerrilla struggles and guerrilla organizations.

The Communist Party of China too correctly pointed this out after the outbreak of the glorious Naxalbari uprising: "*The struggles that are being fought by the poor peasantry of India against dispossession of land and for getting back the land, for reduction of rent and against various kinds of rents and taxes, are certainly necessary; but these movements are to be closely connected with the struggle for the seizure of power through armed struggle, and the armed struggle is to be developed as the principal form of struggle; because, otherwise, it is impossible for the peasantry to achieve complete liberation by way of totally uprooting the feudalism.*"

It is clear that the landlords and the reactionary state machinery will invariably launch all kinds of brutal attacks with a view to nip in the bud all the revolutionary flames of the peasant struggles. The government will deploy armed forces in a big way and will launch a campaign of suppression. Our Party organisation must get ready before hand to resist these attacks. Hence, in the phase of the red resistance struggle itself, we must not only form local guerilla squads, special guerilla squads and people's militia, but also arm and train the people of the village as far as possible in order to offer counter resistance to the attacks of local enemies and the state's campaign of suppression of the anti-feudal, anti-imperialist agrarian revolutionary guerrilla struggle.

So from the very beginning the party and the revolutionary peasant committee should educate the peasantry to face the onslaught of the landlords with arms and build the self defense squads to defend their struggles. Mobilizing the masses on a wide scale creates fear and red terror among the reactionaries. Squad actions, without having any connection with the people, only do not create such a situation; hence our effort is to involve the masses in a big way in such guerilla activities. In the process of arming the militants who are thrown up in the anti-feudal, anti-imperialist and anti- State struggles on a continuous basis, we should intensify the guerilla war. For this, a definite time-bound plan should be drawn up to build armed self-defence squads, village defence squads and the people's militia at the village level with the aim of building the PLGA. Regular forces like the LGS/LRGSs and SGSs should be formed according to plan by every Party committee. Recruitment should be mainly from the working class and the lower middle poor and landless peasantry, and also from the secondary sources like the students, youth, women and petty bourgeoisie sections.

We must take up actions for arming the people by capturing weapons from class enemies i.e. landlord class etc., and from police and para-military froces and then must take up actions against the police and other forces of the state whenever possible, and boost up the morale of the masses. We must follow the principle of dispersing the forces to rouse the masses and concentrating the forces to attack the enemy. The party should thus take the necessary steps consciously to build the people's guerilla army.

We must also build various types of revolutionary and democratic mass organizations such as the organisation of students, youth, women, etc. and must co-ordinate their activities with armed agrarian revolutionary programmes. The various Party committees should draw up proper plans to enter these sections, initiate struggles, recruit forces from these sections by selecting the advanced elements and raising their political consciousness.

The struggles in the red resistance phase will be waged in a series of waves and therefore, the party should consciously use the intermittent intervals between one struggle and the next to consolidate the results of the struggle. Here, consolidation means educating the people with the politics of seizure of state power, further strengthening of underground party organisation, revolutionary peasant organisaations and revolutionary mass organizations and village self-defense squads, peasant guerrilla squads, making them realize the necessity to forge unity with other sections of anti-imperialist, anti-feudal masses to wage still heroic battles against the common enemy improving their socialist consciousness bringing them out of all sorts of revisionist influence, and building the party with the militants emerging from the mass struggles. This process of consolidation and along with it the weakening of the grip of the landlords, on the economic social and political life of the village, and the establishment of the firm leadership of the proletariat over the broad masses in the village, will take place only through the course of intensification of revolutionary class struggle in that village and the basis will be laid for forming the Revolutionary People's Committees.

As the struggle intensifies and reaches a critical situation, any movement should either advance or decline but cannot remain marking time. At that point, it should necessarily transform itself into the guerrilla zone or otherwise it cannot preserve itself. During this course, the resistance actions in the form of guerilla actions against state's armed forces increase, the revolutionary armed forces gain strength and the struggle between them and the state's armed forces becomes principal, bringing about a qualitative change in the whole situation, which will lead to the formation of guerilla zone. In order to achieve this, the conscious role of leadership is very important. Hence the leadership should formulate appropriate tactics and chalk out time-bound plans as well as ensure their actual implementation.

It is extremely necessary to prepare the entire Party to orient its entire work in relation to the principal task of building of people's army and developing the red resistance areas into guerrilla zones and Base Areas. All other tasks should be planned so as to serve this principal, basic and immediate task and the entire Party should be ready for every type of sacrifice to fulfil this task. We must keep in mind what com. Mao has said in this regard: *"every party member should be prepared to take up arms and go to the front at any moment"* and "*the whole party should pay deep attention to war, should study military affairs and pay attention to war, should study military affairs and prepare itself for fighting.*"

The Transformation of a Guerrilla zone into a Base Area

To turn the guerrilla zone into a Base Area, we must have a strong communist party, a People's Liberation Army and a revolutionary United Front. We can achieve this objective only by developing the guerilla war with a correct political understanding and with concrete plan. The guerrilla war must aim at the establishment of Liberated Areas. The forming of a People's Liberation Army is vital for the achievement of a Base Area.

In a guerrilla zone, the guerrilla war will not go on in the same manner from the beginning to the end. The intensity of the guerilla war goes on increasing during the course of development of the people's guerilla army. We should identify different conditions existing in different areas during different times and formulate tactics, work methods and time-bound plans that correspond to the respective conditions and work with firm determination.

In the guerrilla zones, the guerrilla army, and the guerrilla war will be the main forms of organisation and struggle. As the People's Liberation Guerrilla Army goes on consolidating, the guerrilla war intensifies. In the Guerrilla Zones there will be, in the main, a contention for political power between the enemy and us. There will be the destruction of enemy's political power, and construction of people's political power. But here, it should be understood that while destruction is main construction would be secondary. When the guerrilla forces have the upper hand, the people's power can exist. The enemy rule will go on temporarily when the guerrilla forces retreat in the face of the enemy onslaught. There cannot be dual power in the same area simultaneously. It will be either the enemy's power or ours.

In the guerilla zone, the enemy will be relatively stronger than the revolutionary forces. The mobilisation of the people into the people's war is the only way to change the balance of forces between the enemy and the revolutionary forces. In order to drive out the reactionary forces, and arouse the masses in a big way into struggles the people's guerilla army must advance the guerilla war in places where the enemy is weak military. Unless the PLGA destroys the smaller units of the enemy decisively, it can neither expand nor arm the people.

The effects of the advances and retreats in a war show their impact on the mobilisation of the people and their struggles. When the revolutionary forces are advancing and gain an upper hand, the people will be ready to take on new tasks. When the enemy has an upper hand, people become demoralised to some extent temporarily. Party and army will also decrease to some extent. The Party must, as a duty, stay among the people, organise them and lead them once again during the repression when the people's forces are temporarily on the retreat. Due to this, the people will come into the struggles in a much more massive way than earlier.

We must develop the strategic areas having a good mass base and favourable terrain within the guerilla zones into guerilla bases for the establishment of people's political power, for military and political training of our own forces and for the preservation of our own forces, for advancing the revolution and for bringing about a change in the balance of forces by dealing heavy blows on the enemy. The people's militia, the party units, the organs of people's political power and various mass organisations will be relatively stronger in the guerilla bases. We will have to further intensify the guerrilla war by concentrating on wiping out the enemy in the vulnerable areas, driving him out of that area and consolidating the revolutionary forces. The relationship between the new political power, emerging and consolidating in these guerrilla bases and the political power of the enemy outside it, will have the nature of dual power. There will be contention between these two powers, with each trying to eliminate the other and to stabilise its own power. In guerilla bases like these, the people should be aroused politically, the people's guerrilla army and the people's political power should be consolidated and strengthened and the political power should be extended to the rest of the guerrilla zone areas.

Conscious effort is very much essential for establishing guerilla bases. Work should commence with a good time-bound plan and firm determination. The central leadership must pay attention. Sufficient conscious cadre must be allotted and politically motivated. Plan should be drawn up for establishing the Party and political power. PLGA and the Party cadre allotted for the RPCs should work in coordination to hasten the process of forming the guerilla base. The state and central committees should pay special concentration in order to create a guerilla base/bases and to generalize the concrete experience derived. Since these areas are politically, economically and socially very backward, the Party should pay special attention to develop the consciousness of the masses and also on the education of the masses. It should strive to politically mobilize all the people who support the revolution for the common aim i.e. to establish a new democratic society. The Party leadership should work creatively to mobilise the people by formulating concrete slogans in accordance with the general line.

When there is a serious enemy offensive in the form of 'encirclement and suppression' campaign are being conducted in such areas, we should not make futile attempt to obstinately preserve our entire strength within the area of encirclement, in the name of persistence in work, or to hold control over the area, instead we should organise speedily as mobile squads, a major portion of our strength who can be made mobile, and should spread them outside or around the area of encirclement. and at the same time, we should carry on attacks from exterior lines, simultaneously with the attacks from within the area of encirclement.

Guerrilla bases are transitory in nature. If we want to wage guerrilla war powerfully, if we want to change the Guerrilla zones into Liberated Areas, then the question of establishment of guerilla bases will have a special importance. These guerrilla bases will constitute the focal points within the guerilla zones for the development of a strong party, a strong people's liberation army and a united front while, at the same time, creating favourable conditions for the establishment of liberated areas, expanding the political power in waves and quickening the tempo of the revolution. As the new political power in the guerilla bases goes on stabilizing, changes should be brought about in the production relations while intensifying the agrarian revolution. Land should be distributed on the basis of land to the tiller and cooperative movement among the people should be promoted for the development of agriculture. The embryonic form of the new democratic state should be consolidated. Therefore it should be understood that formation of the guerilla base means a significant advance in the process of building base area. This will create a strong impact on the people in the areas around the guerilla base and will inspire them to participate in the people's war more extensively.

In order to defeat the offensive campaign of the enemy the people's guerrilla army should mobilise the people in a big way for political and military actions and should carry on enemy annihilation operations extensively which includes sabotage actions also. The people's guerrilla army transforms into the people's liberation army by acquiring the characteristics of a regular army during the course of its development. The guerrilla war develops into mobile warfare. People's power will be established in the guerrilla zones by completely annihilating the enemy in that area with the active support of the people and that area will change into a liberated area. The base areas formed in such a way may be unstable and may change hand between us and the enemy. In order to consolidate these into stable bases, we have to formulate appropriate plans.

However, there is no such precondition that liberated areas can be achieved invariably through the establishment of guerilla bases only. The people's army, when it grows to a sufficient level, and under favourable conditions, can even march directly into the guerrilla zones or strategic areas, wage decisive battles against the enemy and establish liberated areas. Under such condition, the plains too get influenced and, depending on the seasons and other such favourable factors, guerrilla bases can be formed there if we can rouse the masses on a wide scale and beat back the enemy onslaught and destroying the enemy network and enemy strength considerably in the area.

In the plains, guerilla war will go on for a long time. Utilising the seasons, temporary guerrilla bases can be developed in those areas in the plains that have some favourable terrain and a strong political mass base. Under such conditions, political power can be sustained even if it is for a short period. At the same time guerrilla war should be developed by arousing the people through the programme of agrarian revolution, and increase recruitment in a big way to strengthen the people's guerrilla army. The establishment of power in the plains will be very unstable and will be in a wave-like manner. Organs of political power will get formed in some villages where the people's consciousness is developed. But one should keep in mind that the organs of people's political power in the plains will be unstable until a stage is reached when the people's guerrilla army inflicts significant defeats on the enemy forces.

In the guerilla zones and in those areas where our work is going on with the task of forming Liberated Areas, we should organise the people into struggles by rallying them around the following concrete slogans: This takes place through the Revolutionary People's Committees, as part of the politics of capturing the state power.

1. Overthrow feudal authority; establish people's political power.
2. Take over the lands of the landlords, the lands of the government, and of other exploiting institutions and distribute them to the poor and landless peasants!
3. Build armed people's militia!
4. Stop repayment of debts and interests to landlords and moneylenders!
5. Stop paying taxes, cess, and levies to the government!
6. Right over the forest belongs to Adivasis and the toiling people, Stop the plunder of forest wealth by imperialists, CBB and big contractors!
7. Develop agriculture and cooperative movement! Increase production and achieve self-reliance in every sphere!

The implementation of the above slogans, by mobilising all the anti-feudal forces into struggles against imperialist exploitation and the exploitation of landlords and comprador bureaucrat bourgeoisie classes, will be the immediate political task. As a result of the political mobilisation that takes place on the above slogans, the peasantry will intensify the class struggle in the form of armed struggle in a big way; it will provide innumerable warriors for the expansion of the PLGA and for the development of PLGA into the PLA. It will ripen the conditions for the establishment of the liberated area.

A liberated area is a specific area where the enemy has been destroyed completely and where the rule of the revolutionary people's government is established. If such a liberated area is to be established then a well-trained people's liberation army, i.e. a regular army, well-trained under a centralised military command and having the capability of defeating the enemy should have come into existence; majority of the oppressed masses in that area should have been educated with revolutionary politics and prepared for forming organs of political power. The people's revolutionary committees, which are the organs of people's political power, will transform into Revolutionary People's Councils. A layer of these people's revolutionary councils will be built from the village level to liberated area level. The people should, in support of the People's Liberation Army, get armed in people's militia organisations. A Communist Party should provide leadership while performing all these tasks. Without these conditions, neither a liberated area can be formed nor can it be sustained after formation.

When we take into consideration one of the main specific characteristics of our country, that is, the existence of powerful centralised state machinery, then the establishment of stable liberated areas like in China will relatively be a hard task. However, while developing several backward areas in the country into guerilla zones through the intensification of class struggle, we will be able to create a condition for armed conflicts with the government armed forces. Through this, we will be able to scatter the enemy forces and will be able transform certain areas, which are advantageous geographically, into Liberated Areas. Several political developments that occur in the country and all over the world too will help this by creating favourable conditions.

For instance, as a consequence of the intensification of the internal contradictions among the imperialists, the internal contradictions among the ruling classes of India too may intensify, leading to political crisis and an unstable rule; the armed struggles of various oppressed nationalities may intensify further and this will divert the enemy's armed forces, capabilities and economic resources towards those struggles; a people's upsurge against imperialism and against the comprador ruling classes may break out in some pockets as a result of the crisis that is subjecting the oppressed masses to cruel exploitation; with the intensification and the advancement of guerilla struggle, there may be outbreaks of rebellions by some sections of the police, paramilitary, military forces; and, one cannot deny the possibility of the outbreak of wars (either local, or world wide) that can divert a part of enemy's strength and resources. All these will create an unfavourable situation for the enemy and a favourable situation for us. In short, during the course of waging the protracted people's war against the armed forces of the enemy, the revolutionary crisis is bound to erupt thereby facilitating the establishment of more and more liberated areas.

Foundations for a New Democratic Economic System

Our goal is to destroy the present semi-feudal, semi-colonial economic system, which serves the interests of the landlord, comprador bureaucratic bourgeoisie classes and of the imperialists and to build a New Democratic Economic System in its place. Hence, we must strive to promote new democratic economic system, during the course of, and in accordance with the development of the people's war. We should coordinate this effort for economic development with the people's war, so that it is subordinated to the central task of development of revolutionary war. Since the guerilla zones are unstable and face the menace of continuous enemy attacks, the economic development programmes we take up in the guerrilla zones, should not be of long term nature but should be ones that will get completed quickly. Our policies for economic development, and our efforts, should be directed towards the improvement of the people's living standards thereby encouraging them to actively participate in the revolutionary war. They should also help in facilitating the supply of food and other materials to the people's army; and for further consolidating the people's democratic state power (the RPCs). These economic policies should take into account people's welfare programmes like education, health, sanitation, public distribution system etc.

The ruling classes will impose economic blockades on our struggle areas, when the guerilla war goes on intensively, or during and after the formation of liberated areas. The enemy will resort to measures like, plundering and burning people's properties, destruction of production and implements of production, etc. In order to withstand such situations, we should make our struggle areas self-reliant from the beginning and foil the enemy blockade. The people's army should be made self-reliant, while conserving the resources through the organised might of the people.

We should intensify the agrarian revolution and mobilise the people for the cooperative movement during the course of the advance of the revolutionary war and the formation of guerrilla zones and guerrilla bases. In the beginning, primary cooperatives may come into existence to meet the needs of the people. Mobilising agricultural labourers, poorpeasants and middle peasants, can form mutual aid teams. The cooperatives should be formed on the basis of resolving the problems of labour power, bullocks, fertilisers, seeds, and irrigation. The labour and capital of the people should be the main component n this cooperative movement. However, labour is the key aspect. Consumer and credit cooperatives too should be built. This co-operativisation movement should be expanded in the guerrilla bases and thousands of people should be mobilised. The hegemony of the landless peasants, agricultural labourers and poor peasants should be established over all these cooperatives.

On the whole, the party should pay constant attention on the following attars, throughout the period of the people's war:

1. Throughout the period of People's war, i.e. From the time of commencement to the final capture of power - the revolutionary politics that state power must be seized should be in command over the work of preparing, mobilising and organising the people for the people's war.
2. Our party should wage the peoples war, constantly evaluating our and the enemies strength and adopting concrete tactics in the concrete conditions corresponding to that strength. By doing so, we will be able to keep the initiative in our hands. The intensification of the peoples war while preserving our subjective forces as far as possible and destroying the enemy gradually will be possible only in this way. We should never forget that to loose the initiative in the war means certain defeat.
3. Throughout the course of the people's war, the party must depend on the people: we must never for a moment forget about maintaining organic relations with the people. Com. Mao said: *"The revolutionary war is a*

peoples war; we can wage that war by the mobilising the people and relying on the people."

Strategic Understanding of Work in Urban Areas - Relation Between Rural Work and Urban Work

It is true that, in our revolution, which follows the line of protracted people's war, the liberation of urban areas will be possible only in the last stage of the revolution. However, this does not mean that there is no need to concentrate on the building of urban revolutionary movement from the beginning. From the beginning we will have to concentrate on the organization of the working class, which being the leadership of our revolution has to directly participate and lead the agrarian revolution and the people's war besides building a revolutionary workers' movement.

We must keep in mind the fact that the urban population has been growing rapidly due to the deepening agrarian crisis in the countryside, which is forcing the poor and landless peasantry to migrate to the urban centers in search of livelihood. The working class too is numerically many times more in India than in China during the course of the Chinese revolution. At the beginning of the decade of 1990s itself, the strength of the organised working class in both public and private industrial sectors in our country was about 260 lakhs. Their strength in the unorganised, ancillary and small-scale industries is double this figure i.e., 450 to 500 lakhs. Hence the revolutionary party cannot afford to neglect its work any more in towns and industrial areas and has far greater importance than in pre-revolutionary China. However, the majority of workers are mired in economism due to the nature of the struggles being organised for decades by the various revisionist and bourgeois trade-unions. In spite of this, the workers are increasingly participating in spontaneous struggles today and are getting rid of the illusions they had on the leadership of the respective trade-unions. The responsibility of properly guiding and organising them lies with the revolutionary party alone.

In addition, the workers in many places of our country are not only living side by side with the peasantry but also have countless ties with the rural areas. That is why the influence of the anti-feudal struggles going on in the rural areas is there to a considerable extent on the working class of the industrial centres. The working class struggles, in turn, are bound to greatly influence the peasantry.

On the basis of revolutionary workers movement we will be able to mobilise millions of urban toiling and oppressed masses and build struggles against imperialism and feudalism, struggles in support of the agrarian revolution and struggles for democratic rights. We will be able to create the subjective forces and conditions required for building a countrywide, broad, anti-imperialist, anti-feudal united front during this course only. The urban movement is one of the main sources, which provides cadres and leadership having various types of capabilities essential for the people's war and for the establishment of liberated areas. Moreover, the responsibility for the provision of supplies, technology, expertise, information and other logistical support to the people's war too, lies on the shoulders of the urban revolutionary movement itself.

Hence, we must, while giving first priority to the work, that has to be undertaken for the establishment of liberated areas, at the same time, also give appropriate importance to the task of building a strong urban revolutionary movement. If the working class struggles mainly those in the spheres of transport, communications, ordnance, power plants, mines etc. are coordinated with the armed peasant struggles, they play a key role in carrying forward the people's war. Hence Party has to pay special attention to its efforts on key industrial organisations from the beginning and allocate leadership cadres accordingly. We should not forget the dialectical relationship between the development of the urban movement and the development of the people's war in the countryside. In the absence of a strong revolutionary urban movement, the people's war in the countryside will face many difficulties.

Moreover, we should not belittle the importance of the fact that the urban areas are strong centres of the enemy. Building up of a strong urban revolutionary movement means that our Party should build a struggle network capable of waging struggle consistently, by sustaining itself until the protracted people's war reaches the stage of strategic offensive. Here we have to bear in mind, that instead of pursuing the wrong line of trying to organise 'insurrection' or 'decisive battles', we have to follow the correct line of building up struggles in the urban areas which must be coordinated with, and complementary, in serving the armed agrarian revolutionary war. We must continue to make fuller preparation from beforehand so that the cities may be liberated in proper time when urban areas are encircled from the countryside.

With this long-term perspective, we should develop a strong secret party, a revolutionary united front and urban guerilla squads and militia; intensify the class struggle in the urban areas and mobilise the support of millions of urban masses for the people's war.

We must keep in mind that, in a semi-colonial and semi-feudal country, any struggle, be it in the rural areas or in the urban areas, if isolated from the task of building up of and the development of the agrarian revolutionary armed struggle, cannot but, in the ultimate analysis, be depraved of being economist, reformist and revisionist. Before the outbreak of the agrarian revolutionary war, the aim and the task of all struggles and organizations are to develop this war. When such war has begun, the task of all struggles and organizations are to become united with this war and to further develop this agrarian revolutionary guerrilla war and protracted people's war.

The development and expansion of the agrarian revolutionary guerrilla warfare in the countryside is significant not only for the peasant struggles, it is of extraordinary significance for the development and the correct orientation of the struggles of the working class and the vast masses of the urban people too. The establishment of the Base Areas and the expansion of the people's war to the vast countryside is bound to lead to the radicalization of the urban masses and give great impetus to their struggles against imperialism, CBB and the stranglehold of feudalism in the various spheres of social and cultural life of the urban masses. It will also create massive wave of support in the urban areas for the armed agrarian revolutionary movement.

This relationship between the rural and urban work (i.e. city work is subordinate to rural work and complementary to the basic, principal and immediate task of building up of the people's army and base areas), must always be borne in mind when carrying out the work in the urban areas. In order to create a strong base of support to the ongoing people's war in the countryside and to resolve their own basic issues, and to utilize the situation for the take over of the urban centers during the high tide of revolution, the Party should undertake work among the urban toiling masses with a long-term perspective.

Henceforth, our party must have a comprehensive line of revolutionary struggle (armed struggle and other forms of struggle) for the urban areas also in conformity with the line of protracted people's war, i.e. the line of liberating the countryside and encircling the urban areas from the countryside first, and then capturing the urban areas.

CHAPTER-8
Three Magic Weapons

The three fundamental questions of the Party in the Indian revolution are the building up of the Party, the People's Army and the United Front. A correct understanding of these three questions and of its mutual relations will give the accurate direction for the entire Indian revolution.

Com. Mao explained that a correct understanding of the relationship between the Party, army and the united front is necessary for the victory of the revolution:

> *"... the UF and armed struggle are the two basic weapons for defeating the enemy. The UF is a UF for carrying on armed struggle, and party is the heroic warrior wielding the two weapons, the UF and the Armed Struggle to storm and shatter the enemy's positions. That is how they are related to each other."*

Thus it is extremely imperative for us to grasp the importance of the construction of each of these weapons from the very beginning as well as the masterful application of these to the concrete practice of the Indian revolution based on the teachings of MLM.

The Party of the Proletariat

Lenin taught us that, *"The Proletariat, in its struggle for power, has no weapon other than organization."*

And comrade Mao explained:

> *"If there is to be revolution, there must be a revolutionary party. Without a revolutionary party, without a party built on the Marxist – Leninist revolutionary*

> *theory and in the Marxist - Leninist revolutionary style, it is impossible to lead the working class and the broad masses of the people in defeating imperialism and its running dogs."*

In the construction, development and the Bolshevisation of the Party in semi-colonial, semi-feudal India we must always keep in mind the principle laid out by Mao that it is tightly linked to its political line, to its correct or erroneous resolution of the united front and armed struggle questions.

The most important question in Party building is that a correct ideological-political line should guide it. Without being guided by the most advanced theory of the proletariat-the ideology of Marxism-Leninism-Maoism-it is impossible to work out the correct programme, strategy and tactics of the revolution and hence, impossible to achieve victory in the revolution. Ideological-political line should serve as the basis for all the work of the Party both during and after the new democratic revolution and until the accomplishment of socialism and communism.

Another basic principle in Party building laid out by comrades Lenin and Mao is its underground structure or its clandestine character. Mao explained the imperative need to maintain a strictly underground Party in areas dominated by the reactionaries thus:

> *"In the beginning, our policy is to maintain the Party's organization clandestinely and make it compact, selective and efficient. To remain underground for a long period, accumulate forces and await the correct moment and not precipitate or expose ourselves."*

Comrade Mao thus established our understanding of the ideological and political basis of the construction of the Party in a semi-colonial, semi-feudal country.

The third basic principle is the unity of will and the unity of action within the Party, and the unity between the Party and the people. Building the Party on the basis of democratic centralism and pursuing the class line and mass line alone can ensure this. Conscious implementation of democratic centralism is of great importance for ensuring the unity of the Party, strengthening its centralized leadership enhancing its fighting capacity and invigorating Party life. The Party can be made strong by practicing democratic centralism to stimulate the initiative of the whole membership.

The strengthening of the collective leadership is an important precondition for the implementation of democratic centralism in the Party. In order to put into practice the combination of collective leadership and individual responsibility, the Party committee system must be strengthened. This also prevents any individual from monopolizing the conduct of affairs.

Com. Mao also developed our understanding of the struggle within the Party as a reflection of the class struggle in the society and that the struggle within the Party is the struggle between two lines which covers its entire process of development. We must adopt the "**Three Great Styles of Work**" which are one of the hallmarks distinguishing the proletarian Party from the bourgeois and revisionist Parties. These are : the style of integrating theory with practice, maintaining close ties with the masses and practicing criticism and self-criticism. Ideological-political education is the key link to be grasped in uniting the whole Party for great political struggles. Unless this is done, the Party cannot accomplish any of its political tasks.

We must build the Party based on the abovementioned Marxist-Leninist-Maoist understanding in order to make the Party invincible and lead the revolution to victory.

In order to strengthen the proletarian foundations in the Party organisation, we have to pay special attention to building the Party units in key industrial organisations in towns and cities and among the landless and poor peasants and agricultural labourers in the rural areas. Since our path is the path of protracted people's war, it is obvious that we have to mainly concentrate our work including Party building on the rural areas.

Working class leadership is the indispensable condition for New Democratic revolution in India. The working class should exercise its leadership in the revolution through its direct participation and send its advanced detachment to the rural areas. Only by organising and arousing the working class and continuously drawing its advanced section into the party that the party can be strengthened, its class basis made firm and working class leadership on the New Democratic Revolution be guaranteed.

The Party, in order to prepare the people for the people's war, has to organise the various classes into class organisations, rally them into the struggles against the state and develop the consciousness of seizure of state power.

People's Army

We cannot conceive of people's war without a people's army. The importance of the people's army in the seizure of political power is captured in the well-known statement of Mao, *"Without a people's army the people have nothing."* The people's army is the instrument in the hands of the oppressed people to capture political power without which it is impossible to smash the state machinery of the exploiting classes. Therefore the effort of the party of the working class to build and develop a people's army will be of vital significance in the revolutionary movement following the line of Protracted People's War.

In a country like ours, the revolution will go on from the beginning mainly through the form of armed struggle. Throughout the course of the new democratic revolution armed struggle or war will be the principal form of struggle and army will be the principal form of organization. Neither the work of organisation of the people nor the work of building mass struggles can go on successfully without the support of the people's armed forces. The party can consolidate the achievements of mass struggles only by expanding and developing the guerrilla war, and will thus be able to lay the foundation for the alternative people's political power.

Com. Mao also pointed out: *"the people's army is an armed body for carrying out the political tasks."* Besides fighting to destroy the enemy while preserving its own strength it should shoulder such political tasks of doing propaganda among the masses, mobilising the masses along with organizing and arming them and helping them to establish revolutionary political power; setting up and developing the party organizations; and participating in production. Com.Mao said without these objectives fighting looses its meaning and the red army looses the significance of its existence.

We will be able to steadily develop the people's war and develop the consciousness of seizure of state power among the people only by arming the people through the form of people's militia, train them and developing mass resistance against the state. The guerilla warfare waged by the people and the red army as the main force complement each other like a man's right arm and left arm. Therefore, the party should always pay attention to this effort of arming the people.

On the relation between the Party and the People's army, comrade Mao taught us that: *"The Party commands the gun, and the gun must never be allowed to command the Party."*

The people's army in an agrarian country like India will be basically an army of the peasantry, particularly the army of the poor and landless peasantry, under the leadership of the working class. It is this class composition of the people's army that is its real strength. In fact, this army is the people's army. Each and every member of this army is imbued with the great aim of serving the people and the relation between the army and the people is like that of fish and water.

The agrarian revolution is the basis that ensures the unending flow of recruits into the people's army. Armed with the theory of MLM, guided by the historic mission of the proletariat, and leading a just war of liberation, the people's army becomes invincible in the face of the most trying circumstances.

The people's army of India is an armed detachment of the world proletarian army; is guided by the principles of proletarian internationalism. While the foremost task before it is the liberation of the people of India from imperialism and all their comprador running dogs, it also considers as its imperative task to fight anywhere in the world, when the need arises, in defence of the interests of the world proletariat and the oppressed masses.

Revolutionary United Front

The United Front of the alliance of four classes is to be built for the seizure of political power and to establish the people's democratic dictatorship. The aim of the united front is to isolate, weaken and destroy the main enemies one by one and win over the maximum possible forces opposed to the main enemies. Hence, the Party has to pay particular attention to build as broad a front as possible by uniting with all those classes, groups, parties, individuals and forces that aspire to achieve the common aim of the UF, however weak and vacillating the constituents of the UF may be. In the whole process of building the united front, i.e., building particular UF on concrete problems or right from building a UF at local level to finally building a revolutionary UF for establishing people's power, the Party has to, follow without fail, the following Leninist principle:

> *"In order to properly conduct the revolution towards victory, the Communist Party in every country must, without fail, utilise every smallest opportunity to gain a friend from among the people, however vacillating that friend may be, however unable he may be, however unreliable he may be and even however temporary that opportunity may be".*

In a semi-colonial, semi-feudal country like India, the strategic united front should be built up in the course of armed struggle and for carrying forward the armed struggle for seizure of power. Com. Mao laid down the basic tactical principles of the united front to be pursued by the proletariat such as: maintaining the hegemony of the working class over the united front; maintaining the independence and initiative in the hands of the working class and relying on its own efforts in all conditions; and that the united front should serve the armed struggle.

Thus the first principle in building the UF is that the party of the proletariat should play the vanguard role in this united front. There can be no united front without the theoretical, political, organisational and military leadership of the working class and the Communist Party.

The alliance of the proletariat and the peasantry is the foundation of this United Front. This is the basic alliance in the united front and there cannot be a revolutionary united front without this basic worker-peasant alliance. There cannot be a people's army or the organs of people's democratic power at any level without the basic alliance of the working class and peasantry. This is the second principle in the construction of the revolutionary united front in semi-colonial, semi-feudal India. The rich peasants are a vacillating ally. On the one hand, they are exploited by imperialism and fettered by feudalism, and on the other they themselves exploit others. Due to this dual nature, in spite of their vacillation the rich peasants become part of UF as the immediate aim of New Democratic Front is to abolish the exploitation by imperialism, comprador bureaucrat capitalism and feudalism.

The third principle in the construction of the revolutionary united front in India is the development of the alliance with the urban petty bourgeoisie thereby forging the united front as the revolutionary alliance of all the motive forces. The ruling classes gain credibility and strength from the support of the urban petty bourgeoisie and once the Party of the proletariat wins this important social stratum to the side of the revolution the credibility of the ruling class will be at stake.

The national bourgeoisie will take part in the revolution against imperialism and feudalism at certain times and to a certain extent. This class may come with the advancement of the people's war and our overall strength if we take up a correct policy and attitude towards the national bourgeoisie.

Thus to accomplish the new democratic revolution in India, our Party has to give utmost importance to the task of forming and developing the revolutionary strategic United Front consisting of the above-mentioned four classes - the proletariat, peasantry, the urban petty-bourgeoisie, and national bourgeoisie (middle and small bourgeoisie). Of these the first three are the motive forces of the revolution, while the national bourgeoisie is a vacillating ally.

It is also important for the Party of the proletariat to take advantage of the conflicts and contradictions within the reactionary ruling classes that are bound to intensify in a semi-colonial country like ours due to the growing inter-imperialist contradictions for the control of our vast resources and markets.

This means only after establishing the four class UF under our leadership we will be in a position to utilise the contradictions within the ruling classes effectively. Whether we have to develop any issue based tactical alliances with the ruling class parties or not, that is also to be decided by the party according to the then concrete conditions.

The revolutionary united front is the real bastion that protects the revolutionary movement from fascist suppression and annihilation campaigns carried on jointly by the counter-revolutionary ruling classes. This united front can become powerful and stable only in the course of advancing the armed struggle and the armed struggle, in turn, can become powerful with the effective forging of the united front.

As the new democratic revolution cannot be organized and carried forward without the above-mentioned three weapons, precisely in the same manner, these three weapons also cannot be built up, consolidated and expanded in isolation from armed agrarian revolutionary war and the protracted people's war. The main constituents in building up these three weapons are the working class and the peasantry, particularly the poor and landless peasantry. Hence, we must pay utmost attention to build these three weapons in the process of establishing the Base Areas through agrarian revolutionary movement and protracted people's war by taking the working class and the peasantry, especially the poor and landless peasantry as the core.

Tactics

Tactics are a part of strategy, subordinated to and serving it. Tactics are not concerned with the war as a whole, unlike strategy, but with its individual episodes, with battles and engagements. The function of tactics is primarily to determine - in accordance with the requirements of strategy, and taking into account the experience of the workers' revolutionary struggle in all countries - the forms and methods of fighting most appropriate to the concrete situation of the struggle at each given moment. A most important function of tactics is to determine the ways and means, the forms and methods of fighting that are most appropriate to the concrete situation at the given moment and are most certain to prepare the way for strategic success. Consequently, the operation and results of tactics must be regarded from the point of view of the aims and possibilities of strategy.

The art of war under modern conditions consists in mastering all forms of warfare and all the achievements of science in this sphere, particularly comrade Mao's contribution in the military sphere, utilizing them intelligently combining them skilfully, or making timely use of one or another of these forms as circumstances require.

The same must be said about the forms of struggle in the political sphere. The forms of struggle in the political sphere are even more varied than the forms of warfare. They change in accordance with the development of economic life, social life and culture, with the condition of classes, the relation of the contending forces, the kind of government and, finally, with international relations, and so forth. It is the task of the Party to master all forms of struggle, which are suitable for advancing our strategy of protracted people's war, to combine them intelligently on the battlefield and skillfully to intensify the struggle in those forms which are especially suitable in the given situation.

It is a fundamental principle of Marxism that forms of organization are adapted to the forms of struggle. Hence the task of the Party is to master the forms of organization in both military and political spheres and adapt these to the changes in the forms of struggle.

Formulation of slogans, i.e. concise and clear formulation of the aims of struggle, also forms part of Tactics and the Party leadership has to master the art of placing appropriate tactical slogans subordinate to the principal aim, in accordance with the need and different aims of struggle, basing on the changes in the situation-how a propaganda slogan should be transformed into agitation slogan, the agitation slogan into action slogan, and the action slogan into a Party directive i.e., Propaganda—Agitation—Action—Party Directive. Com. Stalin's explanation of these slogans should serve as our guideline in practice.

The art of leadership consists in identifying, at any given moment, the particular link in the chain of processes by grasping which, we will be able to hold the entire chain and prepare the conditions for achieving strategic success.

> *"It is not enough to be a revolutionary and an adherent of socialism or a Communist in general,"* says Lenin. *"One must be able at each particular moment to find the particular link in the chain which one must grasp with all one's might in order to keep hold of the whole chain and to prepare firmly for the transition to the next link."*

CHAPTER-9

Party Building and Our Tasks

Three decades of practice has proved that our general line is correct. We have to develop our practice in order to properly prepare the subjective forces and to further train up the people politically based on this general line. For this, we have to follow the following principle enunciated by comrade Stalin.

> *"After a correct political line has been worked out and tested in practice, the party cadres become the decisive force in the leadership exercised by the Party ... in order to carry a correct political line into effect, we must have cadres, people who understand the political line of the Party, who accept it as their own line, who are prepared to carry it into effect, who are able to put it into effect, who are able to put into practice and are capable of answering for it, defending it and fighting for it. Failing this, a correct political line runs the risk of being purely nominal".*
>
> *(Stalin, Problems of Leninism, pages 919-920)*

Party is one of the three powerful magic weapons necessary for successfully carrying out the new democratic revolution in India to victory. This is the only weapon that can effectively utilize the other two weapons. The Communist Party has to provide the correct ideological-political-organisational- military leadership at every turning point and at every phase of revolution with great foresight. It has to apply the ideology of MLM to the concrete conditions, formulate the tactics, and implement these with unflinching determination. It should strive to resolve the concrete problems and chalk out specific policies in the light of the ideological-political line. The working class Party has to carry out its practice by placing politics in command to accord with its revolutionary objective. As a militant, organized detachment possessing iron discipline the Party of the proletariat should have the necessary revolutionary style of work so as to fulfill its historic responsibility. It should make use of the proletariat's mighty weapon of criticism, self-criticism to rectify the mistakes, shortcomings and weaknesses that cause harm to the interests of the revolution. It should conduct the rectification and education campaigns and two-line struggles in the proper method of unity-struggle-unity to rectify the non-proletarian trends that arise in the Party.

It is very essential to have an extensive, consolidated, and powerful organisational network, which has the capabilities, initiative, and creativity for formulating and implementing tactics from time to time that accord with the concrete conditions. Our Party can successfully implement our strategy for the revolution and can advance the people's war towards victory only by possessing such a foresight and organisational network. Therefore, we will have to develop leadership and an organisational network. The people's army and the united front can become powerful magic weapons only under the leadership of such a party.

The party committees at various levels have to be developed in such a way that they will be able to concretely analyse the problems of the movement and resolve them by creatively applying Marxism-Leninism-Maoism. The Party committees should be built with forces that are ideologically and politically developed, organizationally experienced, that are capable of carrying out work by applying the Party line to the concrete conditions, and adopt the revolutionary style of work. The higher-level committees in general should be built by following the method of three-in-one combination. We will be able to build strong leadership by selecting sufficient leading cadre working in various fronts who have the leadership abilities and including them in the committees. The existence of committees at all levels that acquired such an expertise, will constitute an important precondition for the victory of the revolution. Today, we are advancing in the direction of developing PLGA into a PLA and towards developing the guerrilla zones into a liberated area. This point has key significance in the present situation. The Party has to consciously make ideological, political and organisational preparations for these qualitative changes; it has to mould the movement; it has to see that it takes a leap to the subsequent higher stage. The leading committees have to play a key role during this course of development. It is essential to impart training to them so that they acquire adequate capabilities for the fulfillment of that gigantic task. Not only the Party Committees functioning in areas where work is going on aiming at the establishment of liberated areas, but also the Party Committees functioning in the plains and urban areas too, should link up all their activities with the task of advancing the agrarian revolution and building the people's army and liberated areas.

Party Building among the Revolutionary Classes

We will be able to establish working class leadership over the vast oppressed masses in all spheres of social life by absorbing into the Party the advanced elements in the mass organizations, cooperatives, organs of people's political power and its various wings, regular armed forces and the militia after the required politicization. It is only thus we will be able to greatly increase our Party membership.

Working class leadership is the indispensable condition for New Democratic revolution in India. The working class exercises its leadership in the revolution by organizing all sections of the people in anti-imperialist and anti-feudal struggles and by sending its advanced detachment to the rural areas. To achieve this, we have to free the working class from the influence of revisionist and reactionary politics. Only by organising and arousing the working class and continuously drawing its advanced section into the party that the party can be strengthened, its class basis made firm and working class leadership on the New Democratic Revolution be guaranteed. Hence we must concentrate on building Party cells among workers in key industries in cities and towns and develop full-time professional revolutionaries from the working class.

Since our path is the path of protracted people's war, it is obvious that we have to mainly concentrate our work including Party building on the rural areas. In order to strengthen the proletarian foundations in the Party organisation, we have to pay special attention to building the Party among the poor peasants and agricultural labourers in the rural areas also. In fact, the task to build up the party from among the workers and landless-poor peasants is the backbone or the basis of our party building.

We have to also give importance to the task of building our party among the students who are a revolutionary force and who are subjected to grave injustice due to the unscientific and undemocratic education policy and face a dark future. To begin with, we must make efforts to educate and consolidate them in the rural and urban areas. The advanced among them should be sent to backward rural areas to integrate with the peasantry and adivasis.

We have to give special importance to assimilate into the Party organisation the unemployed youth living in the extensive rural areas and towns and cities. Similarly, we have to give importance to Party work among teachers, intellectuals, employees in other fields etc.

We should undertake special efforts to build the party amongst the dalit masses. We should rally the dalit masses extensively by taking up struggles for their self-respect and against every kind of discrimination, oppression, degradation, physical attacks and pogroms by the upper caste feudal forces. If necessary, we may also form organisations for the eradication of the caste system with our own initiation and orientation.

The party should take special steps to ensure that dalits develop into leadership positions at all levels of the party organisation.

In the sphere of women, and particularly toiling women, the Party must make special efforts and draw them into the ongoing armed agrarian evolutionary struggle as well as into struggles against social inequalities, oppression and patriarchy. We must pay attention to giving training to develop necessary political consciousness in them in order to develop them as able party cadre and to include them in various party committees including with all other committees and promote them to leadership positions.

The party has to make similar steps in relation to the Adivasi masses. The party must give special attention in the education and training of the party members hailing from Adivasi community in ideological, political, organisational and military matters. It is only through such special attention that we will be able to help these comrades overcome the handicaps which social oppression and backwardness has forced upon them. It is only such measures that will facilitate the quick development of Adivasi comrades in the various levels of leadership in the party and the PLGA.

Just as we expand and develop the revolutionary movement to the higher stage, likewise we have to develop the Party by increasing its membership extensively and consolidating it. It is only by increasing the Party membership and consolidating the Party that we will be able to develop the revolutionary movement to the higher stage and expand it further. Conversely, only when we expand and take the revolutionary movement to the higher stage will it be possible to increase the membership of the Party and consolidate it. It is only when we understand the dialectical relationship between these two aspects, we can develop the class struggle, the revolutionary movement and develop the Party as a strong and experienced leader of the oppressed masses.

It is very much necessary to concentrate on Party building if the people's war has to advance in big leaps. There is a dialectical relationship between propaganda, agitation, struggle and organization.

If the Party organization is confined to the peasantry alone the development of the Party along with the movement will be retarded. The Party leadership should review the situation from time to time with a strategic perspective and concentrate on expanding into the working class, students, youth, women, intelligentsia and other sections. Likewise, the leadership has to strive to maintain the balance in the Party organization between strategic areas and other areas and between rural and urban areas. Special consolidation campaigns, education campaigns have to be taken up so as to increase the Party membership in a big way.

Party Fractions in Mass Organizations

Party fractions with Party members have to be set up in the executive committees of the mass organizations from the area level to central level in order to establish the working class leadership on the mass organizations and to make them work effectively in accordance with the revolutionary objective. These fractions under the Party leadership will coordinate the Party members in the executive committees in the mass organizations. Thereby the mass organizations under working class leadership will serve as the conveyor belts between the vast oppressed masses and the Communist Party. In the Base Areas they will ensure that the mass organizations serve as the foundation for establishing new democratic dictatorship. The fractions will help establish Party leadership over the mass organizations and through these over the oppressed masses.

Two Wings of Party Organization

Only when the two components of the Party organisation – the professional revolutionaries and part-time members - are strong, will the Party be really strengthened. Among them the professional revolutionaries are the core of the Party while part-timers are the base. At the same time, the parttimers should maintain lively relations with the people to the maximum extent and while continuing their professions be vigilant not to get exposed to the enemy. There should be continuity of leadership in the whole course – from the beginning, growth and development - of class struggle. As and when new members join the Party, the leading team should be formed with a good combination of old and new. The Party should be moulded in consonance with the changes in the country and international situation. The Party leadership and the rank and file experienced in carrying-out class struggle should be increased. If not, we will go on losing leadership cadres and rank and file each time the enemy starts a big campaign of suppression. We will face hurdles in building teams and cadres who have collective understanding, thereby resulting in the class struggle losing its proper direction.

Party Organization as a Secret Apparatus

As a militant organization that has to wage armed struggle against a superior enemy for the seizure of power, it becomes imperative for the working class Party to remain underground from the very beginning until the end. The Party part-timers and whole-timers in the mass organizations, cooperatives, organs of people's political power and their various wings, people's militia and the various mass fronts should remain secret, but at the same time, appear as members and leaders of these organizations. The Party members in the mass organizations should maintain the utmost secrecy. The Party members in the working class, youth, women, petty bourgeoisie and other sections in the urban areas should work strictly underground keeping the strategic perspective in mind. They should mainly work openly within the masses but under various covers. In the people's army too the Party has to work by remaining secret. It is obvious that the Party members working in the enemy's armed forces have to maintain the utmost secrecy. The Party PRs working in various fronts should build a secret mechanism that is impregnable to the enemy. Even in the Base Areas our Party organization should remain secret.

However, the enemy will hatch conspiracies and resort to various methods to smash our secret Party apparatus. The enemy on a massive scale will perpetrate brutal massacres and tortures. We have to raise the political consciousness of the entire Party, enhance its vigilance and establish proper secret mechanisms to face the brutal offensive of the enemy and safeguard our forces. It is necessary to impart military training to the Party members to confront the enemy and to escape from the enemy's clutches.

Coordination of Legal and Illegal Activities

Coordination of the legal activity with the Party itself remaining underground is one of the most important aspects in the functioning of the revolutionary Party. It is an art that has to be mastered by the Party members at every level. And it is precisely in the coordination of the legal and illegal structures and activity that the revolutionaries have the greatest confusion and commit many mistakes. This has been true in all revolutions and Lenin pointed out how the problem of the underground Party organization and legal work of Social-Democracy has been one of the principal problems in Russia. Here Russian experience should be implemented in the specific conditions of our country where there is no real independence and democracy.

In India, there is a misconception among some so-called ML forces that one cannot carry out extensive work in the masses by remaining underground or that secret nature of our organization separates us from the masses. From this wrong notions arise a legalist type of thinking or a "Left" sectarian thinking. Hence clarity on this question is very much essential for building a broadbased and extensive mass movement on the one hand and a strictly underground and unexposed Party apparatus that is impregnable to the enemy's machinations.

The question of coordinating the legal and Illegal activities should be done in the background of ongoing severe repression campaign let lose by the reactionary governments.

The principle underlying the legal-illegal coordination is to form the widest possible legal organizations inside which the Party operates secretly. Com. Lenin remarkably pointed this out:

> *"The legal organizations are the points of support which allow taking to the masses the ideas of clandestine cells. That is to say that we modify the form of influence to the objective of which the prior influences continue in the sense of clandestine orientation."*
>
> *"By the form of the organizations the clandestine 'accommodates itself' to the legal. By the content of our Party's work, legal work will 'accommodate itself' to the clandestine ideas."* (Lenin, Vol. 18, p. 392)

Thus we must know how to march together shoulder to shoulder and hand in hand with the advanced sections of the toiling masses although we are compelled to carry on exclusively illegal and clandestine activities.

Thus the Party apparatus- its structures, membership, mechanism, etc.— should be built with utmost secrecy but at the same time, the legal organizations in which the Party membership works should be as wide as possible. We should educate the entire Party about the dialectical relationship between the legal mass movement and illegal Party organization and train it to skillfully and creatively use proper methods to achieve the effective coordination between the two. While keeping in mind that it is the clandestine Party that is the principal aspect out of the two, we must know how and when to change the forms of organization depending on the changes in the situation.

Cadre Policy

All the committees must pay attention on imparting ideological and political training to the cadres freshly joining the party. We will have to concentrate on moulding them to meet all the requirements of the class struggle. The party can best play its vanguard role with the growth and development of these new cadres.

Besides training the Party Committees and the cadres ideologically, politically, organisationally and militarily, a system of proper checkup is also needed. Time-bound and planned tasks should be allotted which are to be checked up and reviewed regularly. Proper education concerning the tasks should be imparted to the cadres. In this way it will become possible to identify and resolve the problems. The higher committees can effectively guide the lower committees in this way.

Ideological-Political Education

Theoretical education is one of the most important tasks among all the Party's activities. While studying the science of Marxism and applying its principles is one aspect, participating directly in class struggle and learning from the masses is another. Based on the knowledge obtained in the above process, the Party's policies should be further enriched and the Party ranks should be developed theoretically. Therefore uniform education is essential to unify the entire Party based on study and concrete application of theory. That is why Mao explained the importance of theory in one sentence:

> *"Theoretical education is the key to unify the entire Party. Without this, the Party cannot achieve a single political task."*

To achieve this we should ensure that:

1. Plans are drawn up for conducting classes/combined study for 10-15 days every year for the education of committees at various levels. This is apart from the centralized classes conducted by the central school for the cadres at various levels. The concerned SCs/SZCs/SACs should conduct these combined study/classes keeping in view the needs and campaigns of the states/regions and special zones.
2. Comrades going to the field should make it a point to concentrate on studying the economic, social and political developments in the areas and prepare the reports based on such a concrete study. This should form an important part of their study. The class composition, class contradictions, changes in land relations, government schemes, condition of the parliamentary parties, analysis of any other special aspects, changes taking place due to the impact of the movement of the past 2 to 3 decades, problems arising in implementing the central tasks and the circulars, resolutions of the concerned committees - many such problems have to be studied by concentrating on the field. Written reports should be prepared. Developing the above mentioned methods and striving to give clarity to PMs on ideological-political issues is one of the m main tasks before us today.
3. The Party press should be in a position to educate and guide the leading cadres at various levels of the Party, the ordinary PMs, the mass organisations and the masses at large. As the average political level of our cadres is still very low, the concerned party committee should aim at a lucid and simple style of writing corresponding to their level, and for this, strive to build up the necessary writers and staff locally. We should try to prepare bulletins, pictorial stories, video films etc., for developing the understanding regarding basic marxism for new PMs and for the peasantry and the adivasi peasantry. Help should be taken from sympathiser educationists. Bringing out magazines basing on local resources and improving them during that course itself should be our policy. To achieve this we have to increase the number of experienced comrades at various levels who can carry out this responsibility. We can then train up our cadres as good communists, enhance their skills and ensure that they fulfill proper responsibilities in conducting the revolutionary movement.
4. The CC must set up a Central Publishing House for publishing ideological and political literature in English and Hindi; the local language publishing

houses of the State units will publish literature according to requirements in the local languages. The official ideological-political organ of the Party should be brought out regularly to focus on ideological-political issues. It will be published secretly and can be translated into the regional languages. The Central political organ of the Party should be brought out in English and Hindi and in other languages according to the decision of the CC. This magazine must basically take the political stand of the party on current issues and current extensive reports of the movement.

Non-Proletarian Trends and Rectification Campaigns

As the democratic revolution in our country remains unfulfilled, as it still remains a semi-colonial, semi-feudal society, feudal values, outlook, approaches and methods are still continuing strongly. Similarly, due to the relative development of capitalist relations in our country petty-bourgeois features are quite strong in the society. The wrong trends in the Party are the reflection of the above social background.

Majority of our party members and members of the guerrilla squads are young women and men hailing from agricultural labourer, landless and poor peasantry. Those from the middle peasantry and the urban middle class come in the next place. Party leadership mainly comprises of those belonging to the middle class. The number of those who came to our party from the industrial proletariat is very less in number. The imperialist cultural invasion of our society too has its influence on the various sections of the population from which our Party cadres are recruited. On the whole, when we keep in view the class composition of the party and the short-coming in the theoretical understanding of M.L.M. in the Party, one can say that ideological remoulding is on a low key, that petty-bourgeois ideas are still quite strong in the party, that the hegemony of the working class ideology is yet to be firmly established. Therefore, there is the possibility for the emergence of wrong trends in the formulation of party's policies, and in their implementation.

Since the theoretical level of the entire Party is relatively low, since there are not enough party committee members who are trained ideologically and politically in a thorough-going way, since our revolutionary movement is going on in backward rural areas and the cultural level of the party units working there is low, and due to other such reasons, there is also a greater possibility for more mistakes to occur and for the emergence of wrong trends during the course of understanding and implementing party's line and policies.

Moreover, as peasant and urban petty bourgeoisie elements are joining the party during the course of the movement, petty-bourgeois ideology, habits and work methods are penetrating into the party through them. Where proper effort is not made in time to change them through a correct method, these are emerging alien class trends in the party, causing much damage.

In order to rectify the alien class trends continuing in our party, we should undertake rectification campaigns on a regular basis throughout the Party.

Party in the People's Army

In order to successfully carry out the new democratic revolution, millions of peasants, workers and petty bourgeoisie sections have to become armed and join the revolutionary war. The Party leadership has to be established from the Party primary units to all levels in the extensive armed militia and the regular people's armed forces so as to transform them into powerful instruments for achieving the revolutionary objective. In our country people's armed forces are an important source for the Party organization. The practice of revolutionary war, the political-organisational-production effort being carried out among the masses contributes greatly for the development of the class conscious sections of the masses who participate in the revolutionary war into members of the working class Party and into leaders at various levels. By joining the revolutionary war on a massive scale the workers, poor peasantry, the agricultural labourers, and the toiling masses will have immense possibilities for releasing their initiative and creativity, enhancing their working class consciousness, and growing into Party members and leaders. Thereby they will be able to steer with their own hands the onward march of history in their role as the Vanguard representatives of working class and will develop into a significant section in the Party. Therefore, we must pay utmost attention to build and develop the Party among these sections.

Conversely, the people's army plays an important role in organizing the Party in the vast countryside. By carrying out the various tasks such as mobilizing, organizing, fighting, propagating and producing, the people's army arouses the masses into struggles on their basic and partial demands, makes them active participants in the armed struggle, and raises their political class consciousness to a great extent. It thus lays the basis for extensive building of the Party network among the basic classes.

Class Line and Mass Line

The hall-mark of a serious Party lies in:

> Whether there is serious class-analysis of the society and whether the correct class-line and the mass-line are followed in all the practical work;
>
> Whether there is genuine respect and love for the working class and its firmest ally, the poor and landless peasantry - whether there is firm reliance and faith on them;
>
> Whether there is the intention to realize the significance and the indispensability of the all-embracing leadership of the working class and of the revolutionary unity of working class and the peasantry in the revolution;
>
> Whether, in conformity with the class line, the work and activities, as well as struggles in the urban areas are being organized by completely relying on, and centering around the working class, whether the working class is being

> aroused to class consciousness and to the consciousness of the leadership, whether they are being activised in the revolutionary work, and whether in conformity with the class line itself, the works and activities in the countryside are being carried on depending on and centring around the reliable and the firmest ally of the working class, the poor and landless peasantry, and whether there is the effort to bring up more and more cadres from among them.

The advancement and the success of the National Democratic Revolution of India depend to a great extent on whether we take a correct class approach on the above fundamental questions of principle and whether all our works and activities are directed accordingly.

In fact, however revolutionary the programme drawn up by the revolutionary Party may appear, and however objective the concrete class analysis and social investigation may look, it will not be of real use to the revolution if these do not bear any connection with our day-to-day activity i.e. if the correct class line and mass line are not adopted in all our practical work.

One of the reasons for the temporary failure of the peasant struggles developed after the Naxalbari struggle is the lack of realization of the importance of correctly following the class line and mass line in practice. Lessons must be drawn from this. The importance of the role of the revolutionary intellectuals in the New Democratic Revolution cannot but be emphasized; but it must also be understood, and more clearly understood, that revolutionary struggles in the real sense, or revolutionary party or people's army in the real sense, none of these can be built up with the petty bourgeois revolutionary intellectuals alone. As a matter of fact, the revolutionary war in the real sense and the revolutionary party, the peoples army and the united front in the real sense, as the weapons of the revolution, - none of these can be built up without the active support and firm role of participation of the working class as the most advanced and the most revolutionary class of the society, and the peasantry (and specially the poor and landless peasantry), who constitute the overwhelming majority of the Indian population and who are the firmest and the most dependable ally of the working class and who are the principal force of the revolution.

Let us learn from the past experiences; firmly follow the correct class-line and the mass line; arouse the working class to class-consciousness and bring them into the leadership; build up guerrilla struggle and guerrilla army with the peasantry (specially the poor and landless peasantry). Recruit an endless stream of cadres from these basic classes who are in dire need of revolution. Such should be the line of work of Party building in semi-colonial, semi-feudal India.

Mao's understanding of democratic centralism was a significant contribution to the Marxist theory of organisational principles. He stressed on creating *'a political situation in which we have both centralism and democracy, both unity of will and personal ease of mind and liveliness'* both inside and outside the Party and said that "*Otherwise it will be impossible to arouse the enthusiasm of the masses. We cannot overcome difficulties without democracy. Of course, its even more impossible to do so without centralism. But if there's no democracy there won't be any centralism.*"

"Without democracy there can't be correct centralism because centralism can't be established when people have divergent views and don't have unity of understanding. What is meant by centralism? First, there must be concentration of correct ideas. Unity of understanding, of policy, plan, command and action is attained on the basis of concentrating correct ideas. This is unity through centralism."

Method and Style of the Leadership

Along with its highest form of organization—the Party—the working class also has its own method of leadership and work style that are indispensable for capturing power by overthrowing the bourgeoisie and building socialism and communism.

The method of leadership consists of: creatively applying the theory of MLM to the concrete conditions, combining the general call with the particular, taking the ideas of the masses, synthesizing them and taking the refined and centralized ideas to the masses; ensuring the real synthesis of centralized leadership and proletarian democracy; ensuring collective leadership and individual responsibility; pursuing a correct cadre policy; learning from past mistakes to avoid future ones and curing the disease to save the patient; correct checking and supervision of the work of the cadres; constant vigilance against the non-proletarian trends and the bourgeois line from entering the Party, and so on. Leadership should be an example of plain and simple living and hard work.

As pointed out by our Marxist teachers our approach should be to start from objective facts, not from abstract definitions, and that we should derive our guiding principles, policies and measures from an analysis of the actual conditions. It is important to keep in mind the method pointed out by Com. Mao for the leadership in order to correctly guide the revolutionary work:

> *"... if persons in leading positions confine themselves to a general call-if they do not personally, in some of the organizations, go deeply and concretely into the work called for, make a break-through at some single point, gain experience and use this experience for guiding other units-then they will have no way of testing the correctness or of enriching the content of their general call, and there is the danger that nothing may come of it."*

Thus it is not enough for the leadership to set the tasks but must also solve the problem of the methods of carrying them out.

Correct revolutionary style means combining American efficiency with Russian revolutionary sweep or becoming 'red and expert'. This means always taking class struggle as the key link and placing politics in command in solving all problems; close integration with the masses; direct participation in class struggle and not confining to giving instructions from above; fewer pompous phrases and more of plain, everyday work; overcoming inertia and routine style of work; fighting conservatism and dogmatic thinking; business-like perseverance of continuing a task once started until it is finished even if it is a minor one; putting up ideological-political struggle against unprincipled practicalism, that is pragmatism, and narrow empiricism; carrying out all our daily activities with a revolutionary perspective and vision; and such other qualities.

Only by following the proletarian method of leadership and work style the Party will be able to apply the theory of MLM creatively to the concrete conditions andin our country. Only thus we can creatively implement democratic centralism and centralized collective leadership. Without this proper method of leadership and work style we cannot achieve our objective. Training the entire Party in this correct method of leadership and work style is an important task in Party building. Only thus we can build a Party of a new type, *"one bold enough to lead the proletarians in the struggle for power, sufficiently experienced to find its bearings amidst the complex conditions of a revolutionary situation, and sufficiently flexible to steer clear of all submerged rocks in the path to its goal."*

Some Important Points for Attention

The party should keep in mind the following four important points throughout the period of its leadership of the revolution:

1. As regards the forms of organizations and struggle, the party has to take decisions basing on the level of people's political consciousness and on their organizational strength but always keeping the revolutionary objective in mind. It should, under no circumstances, take decisions basing on the subjective desires of the leadership.
2. The Party should take utmost care to ensure that it does not lose the initiative when the struggle is in transition from one stage to another. The party should evaluate beforehand the upcoming next stage and make all the necessary preparations. It shall get ready to successfully advance towards the next higher stage. It should impart proper political, ideological, organisational and military training to the cadres at all levels to ensure that the subjective forces do not face any big losses on every occasion the movement takes a turn. This is the most important the leadership has to fulfill.
3. The party should be on the constant alert against alien class tendencies like sectarianism, subjectivism, empiricism, etc. which are likely to emerge and prevail in the party. Similarly it should be careful about the right and 'left' deviations, which are likely to emerge in the party.
4. Party should ensure that the mass line is implemented in all spheres and in all matters of the movement, from the lower levels to the higher level.

CHAPTER-10

Building the People's Army

If we do not formulate a military line corresponding to the correct political line we cannot achieve our revolutionary objective. The military line should be subordinate to the political line. The correct military line takes birth in struggle, develops through struggle and takes a clear shape in the course of struggle. It is only by waging incessant ideological struggle against the Right and "Left" opportunist lines that we can successfully carry out the protracted people's war.

MLM teaches us, and is proved by the experiences of class struggles in world history and the concrete experience of the class struggles in our country's history, that the exploiting ruling classes will never relinquish or give up power voluntarily even at the time of serious crisis. Without smashing the present state machinery and the main constituent of the state power, the mercenary armed forces, the instrument of suppression of the people by the ruling classes and without the establishment of the armed power of the revolutionary people, the Indian people cannot establish their political power. Hence, in order to completely smash the state machinery of the exploiting classes or overthrowing it, the building of the people's army as the organized armed force of the masses is indispensable. That is why Mao said that "*without a people's army people have nothing,*" *and 'political power flows through the barrel of the gun'.*

The military line that was comprehensively developed by com. Mao proceeds from two fundamental points. In our people's war too, we can victoriously carry out the people's war by creatively implementing these two fundamental points: One, our army is a new type of army that is fundamentally different from the mercenary armies of the exploiting classes; it is a political army. It must be an instrument subordinate to the ideological leadership of the proletariat and serving the struggle of the people and the building of revolutionary base areas. Two, our revolutionary war is a new type of war-a people's war; it must be a war in which we recognise that the enemy is strong and we are weak, that the enemy is big and we are small, and in which therefore we fully utilise the enemy's weaknesses and our strong points and fully rely on the strength of the masses for survival, victory and expansion.

In India, people's war and people's army must be considered as the principal forms of struggle and organisation throughout the whole period of the stages of the protracted people's war. Even to build up guerrilla struggle and PLGA as the first step towards this aim. In the concrete conditions of India, we cannot build the people's army without the armed agrarian revolution and without the people's army we cannot carry out the agrarian revolution to its consummation. We cannot establish the Base Areas in the absence of the people's army. And without the Base Areas the people's army cannot carry out consistent and prolonged resistance against the enemy and it loses the meaning of its very existence.

The process of building the people's army is not the same throughout the world. The people's armies were built basing on the specific conditions of the respective countries. In countries like Nepal, Peru, the Philippines, etc. where protracted people's war is being waged under the leadership of the revolutionary Communist parties, guerilla armies and the people's militia were first formed and only later, the people's liberation armies came into existence.

Development of the People's Guerilla Army in India

In our country people's army could not be formed despite heroic armed peasant struggles right from the first war of independence of 1857 and the Santhal rebellion until our Party took the initiative to form the PLGA. The failure to form the people's army even under the leadership of the united Communist party which led the Telangana armed struggle between 1946-51, was due to the absence of a revolutionary political and military line and the dominance of a Right opportunist line for most of the period of its existence.

The upsurge of armed peasant revolutionary movements in the late 1960s and early 70s starting with Naxalbari armed revolt, through heroic sacrifices and armed struggle against the state's armed forces, could create the embryonic form of the people's army in the form of armed guerilla squads.

Thereafter, going through several ups and downs and bravely resisting the enemy's brutal suppression campaigns, guerilla war continued to develop and advance as per plan with the aim of establishing the Base Areas. Starting with irregular guerilla forces, we have formed guerilla forces in the form of people's militia locally (GRDs, self-defence squads), local guerilla squads, special guerilla squads in AP, Dandakaranya, Jharkhand and Bihar states. In this process, the acts of resistance against the state's armed forces have increased. The struggle between the guerilla forces and the state's armed forces has become the principal form leading to a qualitative change in the situation and guerilla zones came into existence.

The necessity had arisen for further intensifying the guerilla war in accordance with the changing conditions by confronting the enemy's brutal onslaught. Besides the separate guerilla squads, the need for the qualitatively higher level of platoons and companies became necessary in order to destroy the enemy forces at a specific time and in specific place. The guerilla forces working as guerilla squads, platoons and companies were brought under a centralized policy and decentralized command in order to coordinate the separate guerilla operations with further plan to destroy the enemy by relative concentration of the forces and in this way the PLGA was formed. This is the first step in the formation of the PLA and the establishment of the Base Areas.

PLGA is the armed organization to achieve the revolutionary political tasks. It preserves its strength and destroys that of the enemy. At the same time, it takes up the political tasks like propaganda among the people, organizing the masses, arming the masses, helping the masses in establishing their organs of political power, developing the Party, participating in production etc.

Three Types of Forces of the PLGA

1) Main Forces—These are the platoons, companies central/state special action teams which move anywhere to participate in the war depending on the needs of the movement under the instructions of the Commissions/ Commands.

2) Secondary Forces—Local guerilla squads, special guerilla squads, platoons and district/division level action teams.
3) Base Forces—People's militia (self-defence squads, GRDs, ARDs at the RPC level).

The people's militia is the base force in the structure of the PLGA. This will be extensive numerically. Without the people's militia it is not possible for the PLGA to develop as it is the principal recruitment source for the other two forces. Efforts should be made to arm the militia and to impart politicomilitary training so that it becomes a militant fighting force and harass the enemy forces continuously without a let up.

The secondary forces operate in a specific area. The weapons of the secondary forces are of relatively inferior quality compared to those of the Main forces.. We have to improve them further. Although these are less in number than the base forces, they are better at fighting. They lure the enemy forces into small guerilla activities, harass and tire them and destroy the enemy forces by using guerilla tactics.

Though the Main Forces are relatively less in number than other forces they are better in terms of political consciousness, quality of arms and fighting skills. Hence it is the backbone of the PLGA. Without this force it will be difficult for the other two forces to survive.

Special action teams, special platoons and companies have to be formed in order to annihilate the cruel officers belonging to the enemy forces, the anti-people notorious elements who serve the class interests of the imperialists, the CBB and the feudal forces, to conduct surprise raids on the enemy forces in key places and seize the arms, and to annihilate the enemy forces who have fortifications.

Coordination Between the Forces

In war we have to preserve our forces and destroy the enemy forces to the maximum extent.

To achieve this objective, small and big actions have to be coordinated We formed organizations that are suitable for undertaking these operations i.e. Main, Secondary and Base forces. The Main Forces like the platoons, companies etc. will concentrate the forces for the annihilation of the enemy forces and for the seizure of arms. They should be provided the opportunity to carry out the military operations and for annihilating the enemy. The Main forces, by their very nature, are better equipped and have the capacity to annihilate the enemy forces. Hence with the help of the Secondary and Base forces it becomes relatively easier to destroy the enemy. The Party committees and Commands at various levels should chalk out the operational plans so as to fulfill this aim. Coordination between these should be achieved.

The CMC provides the politico-military leadership to the PLGA on behalf of the CC. It guides the military affairs. All the Party committees from the CC to the lower levels do not form part of the PLGA. The first thing is to establish the firm leadership of the Party over the PLGA. The basic leadership system consists of the Party cells and branches in the PLGA and the collective leadership of the Party committees under which the commanders carry out individual responsibilities. PLGA carries out principally guerilla warfare. Hence there will be unified strategy and independent activities. This means that the CC and SCs/SZCs decide the general plans while the lower level commands (Regional/Sub-zonal, Zonal/district/divisional, Area commands) draw up the corresponding operational plans. In the PLGA both military commanders and political commissars are the leaders of the military units. Distinct work division exists between them. While the military commanders shoulder the responsibility of implementing the orders and instructions related to military matters the political commissars bear the responsibility of carrying out the tasks related to political matters.

The key aspect for developing and strengthening the PLGA is to establish able Commands at various levels (Area/sub-zone, district/divisional, Zonal, Regional, SC/SZC/SAC, Central level). Only thus we can oversee the proper deployment of forces, enhance the fighting capacity, ensure iron discipline, and make an orderly retreat of the forces in the course of our fight against the enemy forces and further create the condition for transforming the PLGA into PLA. Achieving political unity, military unity, coordination in political-military matters is very crucial for achieving our political objective. Therefore, various Party committees and Commands should grasp this consciously and develop the people's war unitedly, with close cooperation and coordination.

In order to enhance the fighting capacity of the PLGA, expand it and transform it into PLA, we have to set up various wings. At present the development of the guerilla war depends on the development of the departments of communications, intelligence, supplies, ordinance (arms and ammunition), artillery, medical and politico-military training.

A weak people's guerilla army is at present confronting a strong enemy force. In such a war the enemy aspires to completely wipe out the PLGA. Towards this end, he will unleash all-round offensives and encirclement-suppression campaigns in a big way. Besides using brutal force he will resort to all types of deception and cunning methods. To counter this, we should protect our leadership, our forces, people's support and arms & ammunition, keeping in view our final objective of defeating the enemy forces. Until a qualitative change occurs in the balance of forces between our forces and those of the enemy we should not go into strategically decisive battles.

The PLGA is the vanguard of the fighting people and the focal point of armed struggle. In order to fight a strong army we have to create the necessary material and subjective conditions. War continually undergoes changes. In accordance with the changing conditions we have to take appropriate decisions in appropriate time i.e. develop appropriate forms of military organizations and guerilla struggle. The enemy's armed forces should be destroyed bit by bit, as a full meal is eaten up mouthful by mouthful, through guerrilla methods of warfare, and our forces should be strengthened by extending the armed struggle to extensive areas and deepening the struggle. When sufficient arms are acquired and the guerilla forces are increasing the PLGA should be expanded by going into new formations. The PLA has to be developed by further developing the platoons and companies, improving the training, and qualitatively developing these into battalions and divisions.

To develop the regular army (PLA) we have to raise the necessary soldiers in good numbers, develop iron discipline, impart a high level of politico-military training, and acquire relatively better and larger number of arms (including modern arms) and ammunition. Leadership has to play a decisive role in achieving these. It is very essential for the leadership to make conscious planning and special effort for developing the PLGA into the PLA. Special campaigns should be continuously taken up for recruitment into the PLGA. Those who have the qualities needed for guerilla soldiers should be encouraged to join the PLGA. Thus the guerilla army should be developed in the course of the people's war into the PLA.

We have to impart ideological-political understanding among the PLGA fighters and leaders regarding our political-military line as well as enemy's changing strategic plans and tactics of deception, cunning methods, covert methods etc., from time to time thereby enhancing their overall preparedness and vigilance.

We have to make all efforts to attract to our side part of the enemy's army, Para-military and other armed police force and to create disunity among the enemy's armed forces. Mainly two aspects help our efforts in the enemy's armed forces.

We have to educate the PLGA fighters and guard against the emergence of non-proletarian trends such as purely military viewpoint in isolation from the masses, adventurism, bureaucracy, revolutionary impetuosity, ultra-democracy etc., besides several bad habits, in the light of MLM.

Discipline

In order to preserve ourselves or to destroy the enemy we have to work unitedly and with firm determination. Hence the PLGA should follow discipline as stipulated. The orders from above should be followed without fail in all military activities. This discipline is the discipline developed on the basis of the political consciousness fighters and commanders. The most important method to be followed for implementing the discipline is teaching and convincing. Following discipline voluntarily by themselves will be principal. In order to strengthen discipline the PLGA should strictly follow the **'Three Rules of Discipline'** and **'Eight Points of Attention'** formulated by com. Mao.

Five good qualities are essential for the fighters and commanders if the PLGA has to become strong: being good at learning MLM, being good in Military Training, being good in the three-eight work style, being good in accomplishing tasks, being good in Physical Training.

Offensive-Counteroffensive

The objective of the all-round offensive of the state and central governments that has further intensified with the formation of the Joint Operational Command is to completely wipe out, through military means, the entire movement and the PLGA led by our Party throughout the country, specially concentrating the attack on AP, Jharkhand, Dandakaranya, Bihar and Orissa, Chathisgarh, UP, West Bengal states. Multi-pronged offensive means to attack the revolutionary movement on all fronts-political, cultural, ideological, apart from military offensive. The objective is to brutally suppress the social and political forces that oppose the enemy.

We are presently in the phase of strategic self-defence. This means that the enemy is strong and we are weak. Hence the enemy is trying to suppress the revolutionary movement, the people's guerilla army and the masses by means of brutal onslaught. This situation will exist until a change in the balance of forces occurs. Only when our forces become stronger than those of the enemy the method of using the suppression campaign continuously will come to an end. Until that time one suppression campaign will follow another. Enemy's all-round suppression campaign-our tactical counteroffensive will be the main feature of our struggle during this period. The war will increase in its intensity and expand its theatre of operation in both the enemy's all-round offensive or the encirclement-suppression campaign and our tactical counteroffensive campaign. There will be ups and downs, defeats and victories, advance and retreats in the course of this intense struggle. Our aim is to defeat the enemy's al-round offensive and achieve the political and military objectives. The most important task in resisting the enemy's all-round offensive is the political mobilization of the masses. It is only taking up campaigns of tactical counteroffensives in accordance with the strength and capacities of our PLGA and the prevailing situation that we will be able to preserve our forces and destroy the enemy forces. We must make the arrangements necessary for resisting the enemy offensive according to plan beforehand. Losses will be less for the PLGA and the Party if the enemy suffers losses in appropriate time and place. Our PLGA should concentrate and deal heavy blows on the weak points of the enemy forces that are ready for attack against our forces with the aim of causing damage to the enemy. The tactical counteroffensive against the enemy should be carried out in the form of small and big military actions. When the concentration of the enemy forces in a given place becomes dangerous to our existence, we should temporarily retreat our guerilla forces to a strategically favourable place with the aim of carrying on the war for a long time. When the chances for enemy attack are more the guerilla squads and platoons should take the necessary precautions to remain secret and concentrate on smashing the enemy attack at the opportune moment. In this way by protecting the PLGA, the Party and the movement from enemy attacks. we should acquire the skill in conducting tactical counteroffensives.

Moreover, we have to apply comrade Mao's military line creatively according to our concrete conditions.

Army Role in Extension

Initially in the places where guerilla war is going on, the PLGA should concentrate its forces to conduct attacks on the enemy forces with the objective of annihilating the enemy forces and stalling the enemy attacks. Later the newly formed guerilla formations should launch attacks on the outposts, communication network, operational bases, central bases in the enemy territories and thus constantly harass the enemy. In the forests and isolated hilly areas these attacks should be conducted both during night-time and daytime. But in the plains where the enemy patrols are frequent these attacks can be undertaken during the night. To undertake these the cooperation of the masses and a grip on the terrain are essential. The life of the PLGA is determined by these two factors every moment. Besides studying the present areas of operation the PLGA should also undertake the study and survey of future areas of expansion.

By involving the working class, peasantry, and other oppressed masses in small guerilla actions the area of guerilla operations and armed resistance in the forests, plains and the urban centers will expand. The expansion of the area becomes necessary in order to defend the main guerilla area or the guerilla base. The guerilla areas have to be strengthened and transformed into Liberated areas in the course of conducting the guerilla war.

While consolidating a guerilla area we have to make the necessary preparations and send our forces in a planned manner to future areas of expansion with the aim of opening new battlefronts. It is very much essential to have enough room for manoeuvring when the enemy intensifies his suppression campaigns. Besides, the guerilla bases and base areas cannot be sustained in the absence of an extensive area of guerilla war in the surroundings.

Hence recruitment and arms should be increased according to a well-laid out plan and the guerilla forces should extend to new areas continuously. The correct balance between consolidation and expansion should be maintained by concretely assessing the needs of the movement from time to time. One-sided stress on either consolidation or expansion is harmful to the interests of the movement. The enemy will try to obstruct our extension. To counter the moves of the enemy the /PLGA should confront the enemy during extension and go to higher formations such as platoons and companies in accordance with the situation.

Forms of Revolutionary Warfare

Commencing the war with guerilla warfare and then going through the forms of mobile and positional warfares will resolve the question of state power. Protracted people's war is in constant development. In accordance with the changing conditions and keeping the ultimate aim in mind decisions have to be made with swiftness, initiative, and mobility. By destroying the enemy forces by means of guerilla warfare and mobile warfare, we have to bring a change in the balance of forces between the enemy and ourselves and ultimately destroy, or render impotent, the enemy forces through positional warfare. In order to achieve this we have to first build the guerilla army from small guerilla units and then transform it into the PLA and solve the question of state power. The general principles of these three types of warfare will be as follows:

Guerrilla Warfare

Guerrilla warfare is a method of warfare by means of which the working class and the oppressed masses of the peasantry liberate themselves. As guerrilla warfare is a phase in the protracted people's war, it will be waged in accordance with some specific scientific principles due to the special features it has. Whoever neglects the implementation of these principles will be defeated. In every country these general principles have to be creatively implemented depending on the political, economic, social and geographical conditions.

Guerrilla warfare is a war waged by the vast masses. It is a people's war. PLGA will be the focus of the fighting masses. It is a method of warfare that is waged when one is short of resources by basing on heroic revolutionary spirit. Not resorting to fighting when the enemy is strong but conducting attacks when the enemy is weak; dispersing the guerrilla forces at one time and concentrating the forces at another time; retreating at times and destroying the enemy at other times; being ever prepared to confront the enemy anywhere—such are the methods of guerrilla warfare.

Guerrilla warfare is a method of war through which the weaker side in terms of weapons, training of troops and army formations than its enemy, defends itself by delivering blows on its enemy through hit and run methods and wipes out smaller enemy troops. Alertness, swiftness, mobility and sudden attack in the shortest time i.e., short, swift and sudden—these are the strategic points of guerrilla war.

Having a grip on enemy's condition and terrain conditions, it will adopt the methods of delivering a lightning blow on the enemy and withdrawing in a moment. It adopts tactics like seeming to come from the east and attacking from the west, choosing and attacking vulnerable positions of the enemy, etc.

Divide our forces to arouse the masses, concentrate our forces to deal with the enemy.

Since in a guerilla war, the lower level units have to operate independently, on their own, they will have relatively more independence in military operations. Especially in the fluid situation in enemy controlled areas, the lower units will be given initiative to some extent. As a result flexibility in changing tactics and operations, which is vital to a guerilla war will be obtained.

In a guerilla war, the supply system will be totally decentalised and all the units should be self-reliant. For this, they will have to mainly depend on the people and on the enemy. In all matters, people's support is the lifeline of a guerilla war.

In the all-round offensives and the encirclement-suppression campaigns unleashed by the enemy we have to enhance the capacity of the masses to face difficulties and their heroic fighting spirit.

In a guerilla war, do not go in for protracted battles. Operations of quick decisions should be taken up. The essence of guerilla war is -when the enemy advances, we retreat; when the enemy camps, we harass, when the enemy tires, we attack; when the enemy retreats, we pursue.

Seen from a strategic perspective guerilla war creates many losses and difficulties for the enemy. His morale will be broken and will become tired. The sum total of victories in several small battles render impotent the manpower of the enemy. The dispersed battles will develop into a more centralized war. For destroying the enemy troops on a large scale and to establish the Base Areas the guerilla warfare has to transform itself into mobile warfare.

Guerilla war by itself cannot win a revolutionary war as an all-independent form. The guerilla war will continue to develop until the guerilla army grows gradually and acquires the features of a regular army (PLA). After the development of the PLA, victory will only be possible when the enemy is destroyed by developing the guerilla warfare into mobile and positional warfare and is waged in co-ordination with them.

Mobile Warfare

The mobile warfare is a war, a regular army wages by concentrating its forces in a vast area with fluid battle-fronts and deployments and often changing from one place to another. It will have the mobility of attacking the enemy at his relatively vulnerable spots and withdrawing quickly and the potential for changing tactics when the conditions change.

> *"Fight when you can win, move away when you can't"* - this is the real essence of mobile warfare.

Mobile warfare will not aim at retaining or capturing territories, instead it aims at wiping out enemy troops.

In a mobile war, the moment advantage slips out of the hands of our troops, that territory will be vacated immediately.

While the safety of troops in positional warfare is secured through defence positions and fortifications, in mobile warfare it is secured through quick fluidity, through rapid counter attacks and through the extensive utilization of concentration - dispersal.

In the mobile warfare too, primarily, battles of quick decisions should be waged.

The important difference between a guerilla war and a mobile war is that, in mobile warfare, the troops will be concentrated in large numbers. The troops engaged in mobile warfare, will comprise of regular soldiers who have relatively higher political consciousness, greater discipline and military training. The guerilla forces engaged in guerilla war will be of a relatively lower level in the above matters.

This mobile warfare which possesses the elementary features of regular warfare, will have the ability to annihilate the enemy forces in a big way. By thus wiping out the enemy forces on a big scale, this will serve as a key strategy to gain the upper-hand over the enemy and for transforming the war from the stage of strategic defensive to the stage of strategic stalemate or equilibrium and from the stage of strategic equilibrium to the stage of strategic counteroffensive.

Positional Warfare

Positional warfare is a war waged face to face with the enemy, from fixed positions either to capture or to retain a territory. The positional warfare primarily depends on the theory that retaining of a territory will ultimately lead to victory.

Though the above three types of war have their separate distinct characteristics, there is no Chinese Wall demarcating the three in the period of transition. The guerilla operations undertaken by small guerilla squads, will have guerilla nature to a greater degree. However, as the people's guerilla army grows and as guerilla operations conducted by concentrating them increase, they will acquire some elementary features of a mobile warfare. Similarly, in the preliminary phase of mobile war, guerilla nature will be somewhat more, and the mobile war, which goes on with increased concentration of troops, the primary features of positional warfare appear.

When taken as a whole, in our revolutionary war, mobile warfare comes first and guerilla warfare will be secondary, and in the last stage of strategic offensive, we will capture state power through full-scale positional warfare.

Strategic-Tactical Principles of the PLGA

The following basic principle of the military line developed by Mao should be followed under all circumstances by our people's guerilla army: *"You fight your way and we'll fight ours: We fight when we can win and we retreat when we cannot."*

"The guiding principle of our strategy must be to prolong the war". The above general principle stated by Mao will be the strategy of our people's guerilla army. This is because time is required for preparing the masses for the war by mobilizing

and consolidating them, for annihilating the enemy forces and render them impotent, to gradually bring a fundamental change in the balance of forces, to turn the domestic and international situation in favour of the people's war and to achieve an upper-hand over the enemy.

Our people's guerilla army should creatively apply the following tactical principle pointed out by Mao:

> *"In every individual campaign and from a tactical view point we must achieve rapid settlements."* The enemy must be annihilated in a methodical, sector-by-sector process, in which superior forces suddenly strike him when he is unprepared, weary, eating or sleeping. The guerrillas strike at the less mobile enemy's communication lines, harass him constantly, render his forces lame, lost, hungry, thirsty. As the enemy's strength and morale are sapped, guerrilla strength increases and morale improves. And as the war drags on, the guerrilla army will gain experience, will acquire recruits and arms.

The PLGA should strive to implement the under-mentioned important tactical principles:

Protracted people's war is arduous and torturous. The spirit of prolonged self-endurance should be upheld. In campaigns and battles it must oppose the use of the few to defeat the many and must adhere firmly to the use of the many to defeat the few. To confront a strong enemy it should rely on the masses and its own forces. PLGA should integrate with the masses.

> *"We must mobilise the people to support our armed forces enthusiastically and to fight the enemy together with them. The people are the eyes and ears of the army; they feed and keep our soldiers. It is they who help the army in sabotage and in battle. The people are the water and our army the fish."*

PLGA should rely on the battle front in order to enhance its fighting capacity; rely chiefly on the enemy for arms; be frugal in supplies; increase its patience; overcome difficulties; participate in production and increase production; establish arms factories for the production of weapons; and strive to carry on the people's war in the most trying circumstances.

CHAPTER-11

United Front and Work in the Basic Masses

What should be our concrete tactics to realize the revolutionary or strategic united front of the four classes-the working class, the peasantry, the urban petty bourgeoisie and the national bourgeoisie-and make it an effective instrument for advancing the armed struggle?

Firstly, we should concentrate on organizing the masses of these various classes into revolutionary mass organizations, the people's army, the militia, the revolutionary organizations of the nationalities, anti-imperialist fronts, and so on led by our Party. It is in the process of organising these various sections of the population and giving leadership to their struggles, and transforming them into armed struggle for the seizure of state power that the revolutionary United Front begins to take concrete shapes. The nucleus of this United Front is the four-class alliance based on worker-peasant unity which assumes the form of the RPCs at various levels led by the Party.

The Party, the People's Army, the revolutionary mass organisations, the nationality organisations having the new democratic programme and various other revolutionary and petty bourgeois organisations supporting the new democratic progamme will be part of this New Democratic Front. Although the formation of the NDF at the All India level requires a relatively strong People's Army, a strong Party with country-wide political influence, and a considerably wider area of armed struggle with organs of people's political power at various levels, we should strive to form the revolutionary UFs at the village, area, regional and state/special zonal/special area levels depending on the strength of our Party, army, revolutionary mass organisations, and the extent and depth of our armed struggle. We should allot some subjective forces according to plan for work in the towns falling within and around the areas of armed struggle with the aim of the building the UF. Though formation of the NDF at the all India level will take time, still we may try to form this UF in embryonic form on ant-imperialist, anti-feudal basis and based on the support of the revolutionary struggle.

What do we mean when we say that the UF is an instrument for advancing the armed struggle and the vice versa? Firstly, the revolutionary united front mobilizes the masses politically for the capture of state power. Wherever the organs of new democratic people's power are set up as the concrete form of this revolutionary united front, these organs act not only as organs of power, but also as organs of armed uprisings of the masses. They are the *"most powerful organs of the revolutionary struggle of the masses, of the political action of the masses of the uprising of the masses."* They politically arouse the masses, arm the masses and lead the masses to defend the political power and the political gains made. A huge army of the toiling masses is raised and people's militia is established wherever the revolutionary united front takes its concrete expression as an organ of new democratic people's political power. In this way, armed struggle of the masses led by the Party reaches a qualitatively new phase. And, conversely, this armed struggle further consolidates the revolutionary united front.

Even where the organs of the people's political power are not set up in the real sense but the revolutionary united front projects itself as the alternative provisional revolutionary government, it facilitates the political arousal of the masses and the advance of the armed struggle.

Since they are the most democratic organs, they are also the most authoritative organizations of the masses which facilitate to the utmost their participation in the struggle for building the new social order and brings into full play the revolutionary energy, initiative, and creative abilities of the masses in the struggle for the destruction of the old order.

Our united front tactics at the present juncture should be based on the fact that a significant chunk of the people belonging to the four classes that form part of the revolutionary UF are presently under the influence of the comprador-feudal political parties, revisionist parties, and various shades of reformist and petit-bourgeois organizations. The majority of the organized workers are in the various trade unions belonging to the ruling class parties and other revisionist parties; the peasantry, youth, students, employees, women etc. are also organised into different associations and federations affiliated to, or under the influence of, the above-mentioned parties. These sections should be brought under the leadership of the revolutionary party by taking up their sectional demands, raising their political consciousness and dispelling whatever illusions they may have on these parties through incessant political exposure of these parties and ideological-political education of the masses. In order to achieve this, we must concentrate primarily on building the UF from below.

In order to rally all these people, all these sections into the protracted people's war, into the revolutionary united front, the party of the working class, has to build several types of tactical united fronts at various levels, with diverse class forces and with different aims. But we have to try to develop those struggles subordinate to our main aim and objective.

Moreover, provided the revolutionary movement acquires enough strength, if opportunities to utilise the contradictions among the ruling classes in favour of advancing the people's war arise, efforts should be made to utilize them too. However, we must be cautious against the infiltration of notorious anti-people elements belonging to ruling class parties into such united front activity. The principles mentioned for building the United Front in the strategy part of this document should be taken as the guidelines in building the tactical fronts on issues with the various political parties.

All our tactical alliances or UFs in the form of joint activity with various oganisations belonging to the, anti-imperialist anti-feudal classes at whatever level should be subordinate to the aim of building the strategic UF i.e. the NDF. Our orientation in UF activity should be to accelerate this process by rallying these classes on the basis of our New Democratic programme. And all this activity should serve to intensify and extend our armed struggle further. Any joint activity or tactical alliances that do not serve the cause of the PW will be a futile exercise. All our work in the various revolutionary mass fronts, nationality organizations, and other revolutionary and petty bourgeoisie organisations and so on should be evaluated from this perspective only.

We must always keep in mind that the united front activity in whatever form is a method of drawing the masses into the struggle and to isolate and weaken the enemy classes. The Communist International defined the tactics of the united front as the Leninist method of drawing the masses into the revolutionary struggle, as a method of establishing closer ties with the masses. We must find and advance those slogans and forms of struggle that arise from the vital needs of the masses, from the level of their fighting capacity at the given stage of development. At the same time, Communists must not for a moment abandon their own *independent initiative* and work of education, organization and mobilization of the masses. However, to ensure that the toiling masses find the road of unity of action, it is necessary to strive at the same time both for short-term and for long-term agreements that provide for joint action with trade unions of various colours and other organizations of the working people against the class enemies of the proletariat. The chief stress in all this must be laid on developing *mass action*, locally, *to be carried out by the local organizations* through local agreements. At the same time, we must not lose any opportunity of making use of united front tactics also from above wherever and whenever it helps in bringing the broad masses into mass action and in the politicization of the masses.

Oppressed masses and various sections should be rallied through various forms of forums like united action or people's action forums, strike committees, struggle committees etc., on their respective demands from the primary level onwards i.e., from village, factory, basti, college etc., level onwards. Effort should be made to mobilise all the people - including those from various political parties and organisations- who can be rallied on various issues into the united front being built from the lowest level. The Party can rally the people on their partial and sectional demands, and can wage struggles and agitations even amidst conditions of severe repression only by building various such above-mentioned forums. We can take up coordinated actions with the various organizations on issues as diverse as: economic demands of the workers in individual enterprises or whole industries; wage demands of the agricultural labourers; remunerative prices for the agricultural produce of the peasantry and against the exploitation by the moneylender-trader nexus; in the defense of the interests of the dalits, adivasis, women; rendering aid to political prisoners and their families; in the struggle against social reaction and fascist attacks; coordinated actions on a local, regional, national or international scale, for carrying out mass political actions, and innumerable such issues.

We can bring these various sections of people under the influence of revolutionary politics and into the revolutionary organisations and can expand the Party organisation during the course of waging struggles through such forums.

We will be able to build such joint action forums from higher level downwards too, depending on the development of the revolutionary movement, depending on the strength of the subjective forces and on the position of the classes, parties groups and institutions which can be united on their respective issues. Such a united front can come into existence through agreements between various political parties, groups and institutions, which represent various classes. However, if a country-wide or state-wide broad joint action forums are formed, which are relatively stable and which can function for a somewhat longer period, on a minimum revolutionary basis and orientation. We may also try to build the corresponding joint forums at the lower levels.

We may also form a platform at higher level to take up general democratic issues and launch militant mass movement against imperialist exploitation, domination and anti-people policies of the state and its repressive measures. It is also necessary to build solidarity movement in support of anti-imperialist anti-feudal and anti-state struggles of the peasantry.

In multi-national India, where the nationalities are waging armed struggle since long for their self-determination, the party has to pay special attention on building a united front with them. The party of the proletariat should support their just demands in their fight for self-determination against the Indian ruling classes and their state. It is one of the most important tasks of the proletarian Party to mobilise people in support of these struggles and forge unity with these nationalities while at the same time organsing the masses on the Party's programme to draw these masses as part of the New Democratic Revolution. Strong UF between the proletariat and the struggling nationalities against the common enemies (i.e. imperialism, CBB and feudalism) will enable them to formulate tactics jointly to defeat the tactics of the enemy.

Whatever the tactics used (depending on the situation and our strength vis-a-vis the movement), a proletarian stand must be adopted towards every nationality movement, seeking to influence it with a consistent anti-imperialist, anti-feudal viewpoint. While forging united front with the struggling nationalities, the party of the proletariat must strive to establish its leadership over the united front. Some allies from this front may accept the new democratic revolutionary programme and turn into our strategic allies during the course of building such a UF and the united struggle against the common enemy. However it need not be taken as a precondition for forming united fronts with those struggles. One should not cause the disruption of the united front, adopting sectarian methods in the name of establishing proletarian leadership over the united front. At the same time, we should be careful to see that we do not tail behind the petty bourgeois, or ruling class elements who are participating (or leading) various nationality movements and must participate in the united front with our own independent programme.

Whatever be the nature of these tactical united fronts built at various levels, they must serve in isolating the targets of our revolution, in advancing the people's war, and in building and strengthening the strategic revolutionary united front necessary for the establishment of a new democratic system.

Mass Organization and Mass Movement

Mass Organisations are absolutely indispensable for the victory of any revolution. The principal aim of building mass organisations is to organize the masses for revolution. Without mobilising the masses into innumerable struggles and raising their political consciousness in the course of those struggles, they cannot realise the need to overthrow the state power of the exploiting classes, they cannot acquire the necessary consciousness and collective will to overthrow the oppressive state machine, and, needless to say, the Party cannot lead the masses to victory in the revolution. For this, it is absolutely necessary to draw a clear line of demarcation with the revisionistled mass movement and mass organisation. In the background of the specific condition in India, the orientation of our mass movement and mass organization will be according to the strategy of protracted people's war.

For the masses to realise the need for overthrowing the state machine and understand the Party's calls and slogans, they must be convinced through their own daily life experiences - through the experiences gained by organizing themselves and participating in militant mass struggles. Mass organisation is thus a powerful weapon to convince the masses and instill confidence in them that they can liberate themselves from all oppression and exploitation through collective organisation and struggle.

This, of course, does not imply that the masses will automatically get the political consciousness necessary for overthrowing the State machinery and to build a New Democratic society and Socialism. As Com. Lenin had repeatedly warned, this consciousness should be instilled in the toiling masses from outside; they cannot acquire it through struggles on their economic or partial demands. Hence it is the most important task of the Party within the mass organizations to arouse the masses politically and to imbue the masses with the revolutionary politics of seizure of power through armed means. The masses can grasp the Pary's policies and make them their own in course of implementing them in their day-to-day struggles.

Forms of organisation and forms of struggle differ according to differing conditions in different regions in the country. Moreover, the conditions in the same region, state or the country as a whole, do not remain static but keep on changing continuously thereby bringing to the fore the need for effecting corresponding changes in the forms of organisation and forms of struggle. This is the most important feature that should be taken into account in evolving appropriate tactics in each region or state and at each given time. Unless we adopt a dialectical approach to the forms of struggle and forms of organisation, we are bound to fail in building effective mass organisations and powerful mass movements.

Relation Between Mass Struggle and Armed Struggle

While recognising the importance of mass organisations and mass struggles, we have to also keep in mind that in the revolution as a whole, it is war or armed struggle against state that will be the main form of struggle and the army the main form of organisation.

As Com. Mao had pointed out:

> *"... War is the main form of struggle and army is the main form of organisation. Other forms such as the mass organisation and mass struggle are also extremely important and indeed indispensable and in no circumstances to be overlooked,*

> *but their purpose is to serve the war. Before the outbreak of war, all organisation and struggle are in preparation for war....After the war breaks out, all the organisations and struggles are coordinated with the war directly or indirectly."*

This is an extremely important formulation, which our Party had taken as a guideline for the Indian revolution too. Whatever may be the differences in the objective conditions between India and pre-revolutionary China, the underlying principle concerning the relationship between mass struggle and armed struggle remains the same : the mass organisations and mass struggle should serve the war between people's armed forces and enemy's forces once it has broken out, or, should be oriented towards the preparation for war.

This means from the very beginning, our orientation, perspective and the method of building mass organisations and mass struggles should be to serve the war directly or indirectly. The mass organisations which are built without such a perspective would be unfit to advance the revolution. Here the idea of transforming mass struggles and mass organisations gradually into armed struggle is to be recognised as wrong thinking.

If this direction is lost, our mass organisations and mass struggles will get bogged down in legalism and economism, and we will be unable to prepare the masses for the seizure of political power. Herein lies the source for Right opportunism and Revisionism.

While mass organisations and mass struggles serve the armed struggle and war, the latter, in their turn, help to further advance the mass movement. Such is the dialectical inter-relation between mass struggle and armed struggle. As Mao pointed out; *"giving stress on armed struggle does not mean abandoning other forms of struggle; on the contrary, armed struggle cannot achieve success unless co-ordinated with other forms of struggles."*

There is also a tendency to forget the above truth that armed struggle cannot achieve success unless it is coordinated with other forms of struggle, and herein lies one source for "Left" adventurism and sectarianism. This will amount to leaving behind the masses and going ahead with only the advanced sections. Hence, the main point to keep in mind is that we cannot achieve victory in the revolution without anyone of these; both armed struggle and other forms of struggles are indispensable, but the principal and decisive form is armed struggle.

The forms of mass organisation and mass struggle change continuously with the advance of the armed struggle. Every advance made in armed struggle helps the mass organisations to expand and deepen their base and to advance the mass movement further. And, conversely, every advance in the mass movement, particularly the political mobilization or arousal of the masses boldly against the principal enemies of our revolution, will contribute to the deepening and expansion of the armed struggle. Our Party's experience has proved this beyond any doubt.

When we organised the first mass struggles, we could only mobilise a few hundred, and later a few thousand at most. But with the spread of the politics of people's war and the growth of our armed strength, notwithstanding severe enemy repression, people gained more confidence in the Party and revolution and began to participate in numerous struggles and pour out in lakhs for meetings and demonstrations when calls were given by the Party and mass organisations even when the latter went underground. Such a massive show of support to revolution and the spurt in the militant struggles by the masses is due to the advance of the people's war and the growth of the armed strength of the people. The ability of our armed forces to face the reactionary onslaught of the state and feudal forces is an important factor to boost up the morale of the masses and instilling confidence in them on the politics of people's war.

And the masses who are politically aroused through the efforts of our mass organizations, in turn, became a main source of recruitment into the Party and the revolutionary movement. It became possible to involve more and more people into the armed struggle. Hence we have to educate the Party rank and file that the intensification of armed struggle against the state has direct bearing on the further increase in mass mobilization and mass struggles, and this mass mobilization should, in turn, raise the cadre and soldiers for the Party, People's army and involve a larger number of people in the armed struggle.

Broadly speaking, mass organisations can be categorised into three types depending upon their nature and functions:

1) Underground Revolutionary Mass Organizations: The first type of mass organisations are those which remain strictly underground and propagate the Party's revolutionary line among the masses rousing them for armed struggle. They openly call upon the masses to participate in the people's war, propagate the central task drawn up by the Party at any given time, secretly organise the masses into struggles, and directly serve as the base for recruitment for the Party and the people's war. These mass organisations are built clandestinely and conduct secret propaganda. Examples of such mass organizations are Communist Student-Youth Leagues, armed cultural organizations, Red Guard organizations, etc.

2) Open or semi-open Revolutionary Mass Organizations: The second type of mass organizations are the open and semi-open mass organizations which openly propagate the politics of New Democratic Revolution and prepare the people for armed struggle. These organisations make use of the available legal opportunities to carry on revolutionary propaganda and agitation openly and try to mobilize anti-imperialist - anti-feudal forces as widely as possible. Thus, these mass organisations too directly serve the people's war as long as scope for open revolutionary work exists. Revolutionary Women Organisation, Revolutionary Student and Youth organizations, Revolutionary Art and Cultural Associations, Revolutionary writers' Associations, New Democratic Associations of various sections, etc. can be formed for carrying out open revolutionary propaganda and agitation.

3) Mass organizations not directly linked to Party: These mass organizations, which are not directly linked to the Party and work under some cover with a limited programme, belong to the third type. These are broad-based organisations that try to unite non-Party forces on a common programme. They may take up anti-imperialist, anti-feudal programmes openly or may work with a more limited programme. These organisations become indispensable under conditions of extreme state repression where opportunities for open revolutionary mass organizations are very much restricted. They may also be formed in normal conditions as complementary to the revolutionary mass organisations that directly serve armed struggle. Although we have been carrying on our work based on the above understanding in general, there are still some shortcomings due to lack of a deeper grasp of the above, especially in concrete application. The third type of organisations can further be subdivided into three broad categories: a) fractional work, b) party-formed cover organisations, and c) legal democratic organisations:

(i) *Fractional Work:* Here the Party works through the numerous traditional mass organisations that operate in the rural and urban areas. These traditional mass organisations are the organizations normally set up by the masses to fight for their sectional interests or otherwise fulfill their needs. The Party, through its members or other activists, penetrates such organisations without exposing any links with the Party. Through the activities of the organisation, the masses, while being mobilised for their sectional interests, are attempted to be drawn towards the revolution. This method of organising, if properly conducted, offers the best opportunity for cover work for a long period of time. It is therefore indispensable in areas of severe repression. The best organisations are those which are more oriented to struggle, like trade unions, slum and other locality based organisations, youth organisations, unemployed organisations, students associations and unions, women's organisations, commuter associations, etc. Besides there are also other organisations which are welfare oriented, community based or are self-help organisations - like workers' cooperatives, cultural organisations, sports clubs and gymnasiums, libraries, bhajan mandals, non-governmental welfare organisations, women's welfare organisations, welfare organisations for oppressed castes, nationalities and minorities, etc.

(ii) *Cover organizations:* Cover organisations are indispensable in areas where our mass organisations are not allowed to function openly. We may also form cover organisations in other areas according to necessity. The purpose behind forming cover organisations is to keep our forces unexposed to the enemy while carrying on open mass work. We must keep in mind that cover organisations are not a substitute for the legal or underground mass organisations. We must form the Party units within the cover organisations and direct them.

(iii) ***Legal democratic organizations***: These are the organisations formed on an explicit political basis with some or all aspects of an antiimperialist, anti-feudal programme, and with a programme of action and forms of struggle that broadly fall within a legal framework. These serve as the Party's attempts at the political mobilization of the vast masses. The scope of the legal democratic organisation is very wide, extending to the broad coalitions and alliances formed against repression, globalisation, Hindutva forces and right up to the all-encompassing bodies formed with the banners of anticapitalism or people's struggles. Such organisations can be formed at various levels - town/city level, district level, state level, regional level, all-India level, or even at the international level.

Several wrong trends are likely to show up in our work in the mass front such as: legalist trend of organizing and building only legal type of organizations and neglecting the semi-legal and underground organizations thereby exposing our forces to the enemy; the trend of economism of taking up only, or mainly, the partial or economic demands of the masses and losing sight of the most important aspect of political mobilization of the masses against the State and the various policies of the ruling classes; the trend of spontaneity in giving one-sided stress on the aspect of mass struggles and neglecting the aspect of consolidation; subjectivism in mechanically copying the forms of struggle and forms of organization of one region in other regions without taking into consideration the concrete conditions; and, most important of all, not orienting the mass work so as to serve the armed struggle.

Hence, utmost importance must be given to educate the Party rank and file about the danger of the above non-proletarian trends that emerge in the course of building mass organizations and mass movements and must guide the entire work with the proper orientation of serving the armed struggle at all times. The leadership of the mass organizations must always keep the politics of seizure of power in command, bring the vast masses to these politics by evolving the appropriate political slogans and rallying the masses around these. Attention must be paid on conducting wide political propaganda of the revolutionary politics through various means-open, semi-open and secret, and concentrating on political exposures of the policies of the ruling classes, the anti-people nature of the Parliament and the government, the attacks and atrocities on women, Dalits and Adivasis; the persecution of the religious minorities; the oppression and suppression of the rights of the nationalities; and the viciousness of the exploiting social system. It is possible to rally the vast masses if the correct tactical slogans are advanced in the appropriate time and forms of struggle and forms of organizations are evolved to take up such issues with the correct orientation.

We must keep in mind the Leninist tactical principle: "*To put in the forefront precisely those forms of struggle and organization which are best suited to the conditions prevailing during the flow or ebb of the movement at a given moment, and which therefore can facilitate and ensure the bringing of the masses to the revolutionary positions, the bringing of the millions to the revolutionary front, and their disposition at the revolutionary front.*"

Of course, while applying this principle into practice we have to keep in mind the specific condition and specific strategy of our revolution and also we have to realise the differences among the various forms of struggle and organisation from the point of view of our specific strategy i.e protracted people's war.

In the background of the above discussion,we must allot some able and experienced PRs and organisers to work in the legal democratic organizations, cover organizations and for fractional work. Without such able organisers it is not possible to work in these organisations without getting exposed and with a long time perspective. Our organisers may also belong to a Party Committee at some level. But, while working openly in these organisations they should not be identified in any manner with our Party. Once they are exposed to the enemy, they should immediately go underground or be shifted elsewhere.

CHAPTER-12

Special Social Sections and Nationalities - Our Tactics

Women, dalits, adivasis and religious minorities are the most important of the social sections to be taken cognisance of by the party of the proletariat leading the revolution in the concrete conditions evailing in India. All these sections have special problems of their own and specific types of traeconomic oppression apart from the class oppression. We have to pay due attention to solve their special problems and to chalk out special tasks to mobilise them effectively into the revolutionary movement. Towards this end, we have to not only bring these sections into class organizations along with other oppressed masses, but also evolve the necessary forms of organizations and forms of struggle for the widest mobilization of these sections on their special problems both on a short-term and long-term basis. Broader joint fronts too should be formed wherever and whenever necessary to address the specific grievances.

However, while taking up specific tactics on the special problems related to these sections, we should keep in mind that the tactics should always be subordinate to our strategic line. We should place the specific programme for the solution of their specific problems in relation to, and in the overall context of, the on-going people's war in the country. We must educate these sections how their problems are essentially class questions; how the material basis for the final solution of their problems can be laid only by liberating themselves from class oppression; and hence, the imperative need for waging war against the common enemies-feudalism, imperialism, and comprador bureaucrat capitalism, that are oppressing the vast toiling masses in the country-unitedly with other oppressed masses under the leadership of the proletariat.

We must demonstrate in practice how the people's war and the ongoing class struggle is bringing these sections increasingly into the center stage; how the latent potential and creative energies, the revolutionary initiative and capacities of these oppressed sections are being released in the course of the people's war and the deepening class struggle. It is only by paying special attention and making conscious effort based on concrete planning by the leadership of the Party to develop the oppressed among these sections, that we can bring a qualitative change in their overall status in the Party and position in the revolutionary movement. Hence, in all our guerilla zones and areas of class struggle, firstly we have to follow the class line and mass line seriously, i.e to work mainly among the landless and poor peasantry and agricultural labourers generally who belong to dalit section. basing firmly on this aspect, we have to take up a special programme for bringing these sections to the forefront in all fronts, apart from drawing up specific forms of struggle and organization to mobilize broader masses of these sections on their specific demands with a clear-cut plan to involve the advanced elements from these sections into the Party and the class organizations.

By pursuing the above-mentioned general line and approach, we will be able to draw the clear line of demarcation with the parliamentary and revisionist parties, with the reformist NGOs and other petty bourgeois organizations, as well as with the so-called Communist Revolutionary organizations in our country with regard to the solution of the problems of these special social sections. We must also take up consistent political exposure of the various bourgeois-reformist-revisionist trends within the movements of these sections.

Let us now analyse the nature of oppression and the problems of each of these sections separately.

Special Social Sections

(i) Women: Women constitute almost one-half of the country's population and an overwhelming majority of them belong to the oppressed and exploited classes. But in addition to feudal and capitalist oppression, they suffer from male-chauvinist domination, oppression and patriarchy. The women of our country have to face extreme insecurity of life due to our patriarchal system, which denies any rights and independence and denies them access to property despite formal legal rights. They are denied equal educational and employment opportunities. All domestic labour, which is unpaid labour, is performed by women. This labour is looked down upon by the society as menial, as of no value, and there is neither any recognition nor respect for women's labour in the existing patriarchal society. It is only a double burden on women that thwarts their initiative, creativity and role in public life. The orthodox Hindu and Muslim traditions look down upon women treating them as inferior beings and weaklings fit only to serve the men-folk and to breed and rear children at home. This outdated and reactionary outlook is being reinforced by the growth of the Hindu religious chauvinist forces on the one hand, and the Muslim fundamentalists on the other.

Recently, with the proliferation of consumerism and increased penetration of imperialist culture and decadent values into our society, women are being rapidly converted into commodities and their condition is further degrading. Women are subjected to varied forms of sexual harrasment and domestic violence. Rape is used as a weapon to counter rightful assertion by women. It is also used as a very specific repressive measure by the state against women in struggle. Thus the Indian women have become victims of social, economic, political, and cultural discrimination and deprivation of all sorts. Thus the Indian women should be organised not only against class oppression but also against all types of patriarchy, male domination, and discrimination. Special effort should be made to bring more and more women into the revolutionary movement by bringing them out of feudal and obscurantist ideas which restricts them to the home.

So in order to emancipate women, besides the class-struggle, we have to carry on struggle in political, economic, ideological and cultural sphere for equal rights for women. We should support the struggles of women that are breaking out either spontaneously or under the leadership of petty bourgeois, feminist organizations against social degradation, discrimination, oppression and exploitation while at the same time we should expose the limitations of those leadership. The party should help organise them in the correct revolutionary direction and strive to transform their protest into mighty struggles. We must expose the politics and influence of the bourgeois, petty-bourgeois, revisionist and reformist parties and organizations, including feminist organisations, that have been trying to depoliticise and demobilize the women and to divert the women's movement from the real path of liberation. We should also try to bring more and more women into the revolutionary movements by imbuing them with the politics of new democratic revolution and making them realize that there cannot be women's liberation without the liberation of the oppressed masses from feudalism, imperialism and comprador bureaucrat capitalism.

(ii) Dalits: The dalits or Scheduled Castes should be treated as a special social section that is peculiar to the obnoxious caste-ridden Indian society. Though the vast majority among them (over 90%) belongs to the poor and landless peasantry and to the proletariat and other wage-earning sections, they are also victims of social oppression and upper caste atrocities and discrimination in all spheres of life. The most heinous and inhuman manifestation of this social oppression is the practice of untouchability still practised in most parts of India. The real solution to the problems of dalits lies in smashing the existing semi-feudal, semi-colonial setup by successfully completing the agrarian revolution on the basis of distributing land to the tiller.

While mobilising the vast masses of the dalits who constitute around 17.5% of the Indian population into the agrarian revolution, we must also lay special emphasis upon the task of fighting all forms of social oppression and caste discrimination practised by the upper castes against them. Appropriate organisational forms should be evolved at various levels to fight the evils of untouchability, upper caste atrocities against the dalits and other forms of discrimination based on caste. At the same time, we must desist from forming exclusively caste-based organisations for the dalits, which will only lead to their further segregation.

The Party must fight for equal rights, reservations and other special privileges for dalits and other backward castes. Simultaneously we must expose the hollowness of the policies of the ruling class parties and the state on these issues. We must also expose the opportunist dalit leaders who build their own electoral fortunes in the name of taking up dalit issues. We must take up struggles on these issues with our own independent programme, through our mass and class organisations, without forming separate caste-based organisations.

The petty bourgeoisie Dalit sections in certain states have formed some exclusive organizations of Dalits and are organising movements on some issues related to their problems. Depending on the concrete situation, if it is helpful for the ongoing revolutionary movement, we may sometimes work ointly with these petty bourgeoisie Dalit organisations on these issues while exposing the reformism and opportunism of the leadership. It is only due to lack of a revolutionary alternative that exclusive Dalit organizations are proliferating in various parts of the country. Such organizations will become irrelevant if the revolutionary Party and mass organizations take up the issues of Dalits and build a broad-based movement by including all sections of people.

(iii) Adivasis: The Adivasis, or the tribes residing in the hilly regions, forests or less-developed plains in India, constitute about 7% of the Indian population. Representing relatively more backward forces of production, their economy, society and culture differ significantly from those in the rest of India. The imperialists, comprador bureaucratic bourgeoisie, unscrupulous contractors, moneylenders, traders and government officials have deprived the Adivasis of their land and other traditional means of livelihood. The process of breaking up of their traditional economies, society and culture and their forcible assimilation into the semi-colonial, semi-feudal setup by the Indian ruling classes serving imperialism is proceeding at an unprecedented pace particularly after the transfer of power. The attempts to convert Adivasis into various religions with the backing of the state have been going on since a long time. Whereas during British rule, Christianity spread on a considerable scale into the vast tracts inhabited by the Adivasis, after the transfer of power it is the Hindu chauvinist organisations that are aggressively spreading Hindu religion in these areas. As the regions inhabited by the Adivasis are rich in mineral deposits and forest wealth, imperialists and comprador bureaucratic bourgeoisie are evincing special interest in exploiting these regions through mining, quarrying and such other activities. Some infrastructure too has been developed towards this end. The state and central governments have been carrying on construction works, luring a section from the Adivasis under the name of welfare schemes. In the main, tribal chiefs, are benefiting from government schemes and are trying to turn the people in favour of the government and, in some areas, a tiny section of adivasis have become rich and have developed themselves as local oppressors. Both of them constitute the social basis for the ruling class parties or parties in the name of welfare of various tribes and nationalities.

Proper tactics have to be adopted to ensure the eradication of the influence on the Adivasi masses of this intermediary section which is divorced from labour, while at the same time proper tactics have to be adopted so that a strong unity within the toiling adivasi people could be achieved and also a strong unity between toiling people of tribals and non-tribals can be developed maintained.

These regions have strategic importance for the Indian revolution from the military viewpoint due to their favourable terrain that facilitates the establishment of base areas. Hence the Party should organise Adivasis with the slogans, "*Right over the forest belongs to people and Adivasis*", *"Politica Autonomy to the Adivasi territories"* and transform the territory as exploitationfree territory i.e 'red land', 'don't be divided, be united' 'unite the real friends against the real enemies'.'right over all the resources including water, forest etc.' 'right for protecting their own culture and development', and draw up a specific plan for work among them to mobilise them against economic, political, social and cultural oppression by imperialism, CBB and feudalism.

(iv) Religious Minorities: The religious minorities like the Muslims, Sikhs, Christians and others comprise around 15% of the Indian population. They are often the targets of attacks by Hindu chauvinist political parties and Hindu fascist gangs and suffer from discrimination by the Indian state that is biased towards the Hindu majority. Among the religious minorities the Muslims are being specially targeted in recent times.

The party should oppose, expose and fight against the growing threat of these Hindu fundamentalist forces ideologically, politically and also fight against them at the local level by adopting all the appropriate means. At the same time we must also continue to expose the fundamentalism of other religions. But we must be clear that the real purpose of the chieftains of the Hindu fundamental forces is to divide and divert the people's attention from their growing upsurges and thus blunt their class consciousness. Hence, the party must continue to focus its attention in advancing the actual class struggle, that is, the protracted people's war, which will finally put an end to this threat.

We must widely propagate the politics of new democratic revolution among the people of the religious minorities and make them realize that they too are oppressed by the three big mountains weighing down the backs of the entire Indian people and it is only by fighting unitedly with their class brethren among the Hindu majority that they can put an end to the religious persecution. We must take class struggle as the key link in solving the problem of communalism permanently.

Our Work among the Nationalities

Leading the revolution in a big multi-national country inhabited by scores of nationalities and national minorities oppressed by the Indian State in league with imperialism, our Party faces the special task of correctly addressing and resolving the national question.

We must beware of two wrong trends prevalent on the nationality question among the various revolutionary organizations in India: one, the view that the struggles of the various nationalities, especially those that are being waged with the demand of secession from the Indian Union, as imperialist-inspired and as disrupting the unity achieved by the Indian people in the course of the ong-drawn-out struggle against British imperialism, and that it is not the usiness of revolutionaries to get involved in these struggles since these are neither class struggles nor are led by the proletariat; two, the bourgeoisnationalist view of supporting all nationality struggles without analysing their aim and objective, replacing class struggle with national struggle through their line of organising every nationality in India separately and fighting for secession irrespective of the stage of historical development of the particular nationality, the level of development of class struggle and political consciousness among the people of a particular nationality.

Hence the question before us is: How to unite these struggles of the various oppressed nationalities into a common fighting united front against the common enemy - the Indian State? And what should be the programme of the Indian proletariat to solve the national question in India? In laying down the policy of the proletariat towards the national question we must take as guideline the teachings of our teachers. In resolving the question in Russia, com. Stalin observed:

> *"The essence of this policy can be expressed in a few words: the renunciation of all 'claims' and 'rights' to regions inhabited by non-Russian nationalities; the recognition (not in word but in deed) of the right of these nationalities to exist as independent states; the formation of a voluntary, military and economic union of these nationalities with Central Russia; the granting of aid to the backward nationalities in their cultural and economic development, without which what is known as 'national equality' becomes an 'empty sound' and the basing of all this on the complete emancipation of the peasants and the concentration of the entire political power in the hands of the toiling elements of the border nationalities - such is the national policy of the Russian Communists".* [***'The October Revolution and the National Policy of the Russian Communists' (1921)***].

When explaining this problem, comrade Mao said: *'in the final analysis the national question is a class question and hence, is a part and parcel of class struggle.'* Under the background of this basic principle we have to realize that today without the leadership of the working class and its party, the Communist Party, the people belonging to different nationalities cannot achieve their liberation in the truest sense.

A distinguishing feature of the national oppression in India is that it is being carried out not by any one particular dominant nation as was the case in Russia, but by feudalism, imperialism and comprador big bourgeoisie –the three main enemies of the Indian people- and by their agent, the Indian state. As long as these three big mountains weigh down the nationalities, there cannot be any genuine development of their economies, culture, language and so on. Complete democracy, which is the basis for the elimination of national oppression, cannot be achieved without overthrowing these three monsters. Once these oppressors are overthrown, a voluntary Indian Federation can be formed consisting of the various national People's Republics which will have the right to unhampered secession.

Thus the task of the Indian proletariat is to lead the struggles of these various nationalities against the above enemies with the specific programme of equality of all nations and languages in the country and recognising the right of all nationalities for self-determination including secession. Each and every struggle of the nationalities should be supported if it is directed against the Indian state. While supporting the rights of the various nationalities we must expose the conspiracies of the imperialists along with the ruling classes to divide the people on the basis of nationality and strive for the unity of all oppressed. As Com. Stalin had pointed out:

> "*When we put forward the principle of the right of peoples to selfdetermination we thereby raise the struggle against national oppression to the level of a struggle against imperialism, our common foe. Unless we do so, we may find ourselves in the position of people who bring grist to the mill of the imperialists*" ***(Report on the National Question, 7th All Russian Conference of the RSDLP, 1917).***

In taking up the national question, we must make a distinction between the nationalities of the North East and Kashmir on the one hand and those in the other states of India on the other. The former have never considered themselves as part of India since they were actually annexed by the British and added to India. The ruling classes of India have continued their occupation of the territories of these nationalities after the transfer of power despite promises made prior to 1947 that in the present concrete conditions, we must extend complete and unflinching support to the demand for secession of these nationalities as long as their struggle is directed against our common enemies. But at the same time, we have to try to make them understand very patiently that without having a comprehensive plan and programme and without being a part and parcel of the NDR, their complete political and economic emancipation cannot be fully achieved. We must try to give a revolutionary orientation to the nationality movements keeping in mind that the leaderships of these movements often tend to strike a compromise with the ruling classes or even surrender their cause in the midst of the struggle.

We ourselves should lead the struggle for a voluntary union of the Indian nationalities. Even if some regional comprador-feudal parties rake up the national issue to the point of secession in those states, the proletariat should expose them and try to convince the people that secession is against their basic interests and that coming together into a voluntary federation is advantageous to their interests from both political and military points of view. If, however, the entire people of that nationality insist on seceding, we must not oppose it. By following such a policy alone it will become easier for us to unite with them again after a lapse of time after gaining their confidence through our consistently democratic policy towards them.

Communists must, of course, be in the forefront of every democratic demand of the nationalities whether it is for autonomy; for equal status for their languages; for separate statehood; against economic, social cultural and other forms of oppression by a certain dominant nation (oppression by Bengalis over Assamese and over other nationalities of the North East; the oppression by the Assamese over the small nationalities in the state of Assam such as the Bodos, Karbis, Mishings etc); against the policy of discrimination exhibited in any field towards particular nationality, and so on. Appropriate forms of struggle and organisation should be evolved to fight every manifestation of national oppression taking all care, at the same time, to bring the people of the particular nationality out of national aloofness and to promote a spirit of international solidarity among them. Such should be the essence of the Marxist- Leninist approach to the nationality question in India.

The Basis for the Unity of the Nationalities

To sum up, the policy of the communists, the people's democratic front and the people's democratic states on the problem of nationalities of India is:

a) To mobilise the peoples of all nationalities in an united front against the common enemies and lead them towards agrarian revolution and the national and democratic revolution or people's democratic revolution; to fight against nation l chauvinism encouraged by the reactionaries - fight against big and advanced nation-boast-fullness and arrogance on the one hand, and narrow sectarian nationalism on the other; to fight against every conspiracy of the imperialists and their agents to create division and disunity amongst different nationalities.

b) To uproot the national exploitation of the people's of the 'backward' nationalities and sub-nationalities and to guarantee an equal and all-embracing economic, political and cultural development (development of national languages also) of all nationalities and sub-nationalities.

c) To fight for the principle, both in words and deeds, that all nationalities are independent, equal and sovereign and to build up a relation of unity and love among the peoples of all nationalities on the basis of equal rights and the right of self-determination for all nationalities (that is, to be united within a voluntary Federation of People's Democratic Republics of India on the basis of equal rights and the right to establish separate state, if so desired).

This policy is fully compatible with the final goal of the international great union, on a voluntary basis, not only of the Indian nationalities but also of the nationalities of the whole world.

It goes without saying that without consistent struggle against diehard bourgeoisies nationalism - against big and advanced nation chauvinism on the one hand, and the petty bourgeoisie national sectarianism on the other - encouraged by imperialism, and their 'Indian' henchmen, without fighting against national inequality, exploitation and oppression, the nationality movements will remain to a great extent under the influence of petty bourgeois politics and sectarian nationalism. As a result, these struggles cannot be elevated to the stage of class struggle and the revolutionary democratic instincts inherent in them cannot be led to the path of revolution.

It is only by remaining loyal to the politics of the proletariat and the ideology of Marxism-Leninism-Maoism and maintaining its own political and organisational independence that the working class can give leadership and liberate the peoples from the sectarian nationalism and arouse them and bring them into the path of revolutionary national struggle in its true sense (as part and parcel of the new democratic revolution). No other class except the working class and its vanguard party can take the leadership of this work. To neglect this task or not to give proper attention to this task in a multinational country like India is harmful to the revolution.

CHAPTER-13

Work in Urban Areas

Work in the urban areas has a special importance in our revolutionary war. Our urban areas today mirror the distorted development-taking place in the semi-feudal, semi-colonial production relations, in tune with the interest of imperialism. In fact, vast masses of the urban population remain under the clutches of unbridled exploitation and oppression of imperialism and CBB.

The fact that the working class is heavily concentrated in these areas is a matter of great significance. Lakhs of workers in these metropolises, and other industrial cities and towns, are working in modern industrial enterprises, in which the socialization of labour has taken place at a high level. Moreover, the urban petty-bourgeoisie section, who are reliable allies of our revolution are also concentrated here in big numbers. On the other hand, it is here itself, the state power and the ad inistrative machinery of the ruling classes are concentrated; and it is from here itself they have been regulating the economic life-lines of the country. Thus, along with the positive factor that the leading force of the revolution-the working class, and another basic motive force, the petty bourgeoisie, are concentrated here in big numbers, the urban revolutionary movement also faces a negative factor, that these are very strong-centres for the enemy. Hence we will have to build the revolutionary movement keeping both these factors in mind.

The urban movement is one of the main sources, which provides cadres and leadership having various types of capabilities essential for the people's war and for the establishment of liberated areas. Moreover, the responsibility for the provision of supplies, technology - expertise, information and other such things, to the people's war, too lies on the shoulders of the urban revolutionary movement itself. Hence Party has to pay special attention to allocate leadership cadres accordingly to work in urban movement. We should not forget the dialectical relationship between the development of the urban movement and the development of the armed agrarian revolutionary war. In the absence of a strong revolutionary urban movement, the growth of the people's war will face limitations and difficulties in its advancement.

Objectives of Our Urban Work

Work in the cities and towns involve a number of tasks. All these tasks can however be combined under three broad objectives. They are as follows:

1) **Mobilizing and organizing the basic masses:** This is the main activity of the Party. It is the Party's most important task to organize the basic class in the urban areas, i.e., the working class, as well as other classes and sections like the semi-proletariat, students, middle class employees, intellectuals, etc. It also has the task of dealing with the problems of special social groups like women, dalits, and religious minorities and mobilizing them for the revolutionary movement. It is on this basis that the masses are politicized and the advanced sections consolidated into the Party.
2) **Building the United Front:** This involves the task of unifying the working class first, and then building worker-peasant solidarity and alliance, uniting with other classes in the cities, building the fronts against exploitation and oppression of imperialism and the CBB, imperialist war designs and globalization, against Hindu fascism, against repression, etc. This is a very important aspect of the work of the Party in the city.
3) **Military Tasks:** While the PLGA and PLA in the countryside perform the main military tasks, the urban movement too performs tasks complementary to the rural armed struggle. These involve the sending of cadre to the countryside, infiltration of enemy ranks, organizing in key industries, sabotage actions in coordination with the rural armed struggle, logistical support, etc.

Of the above three, the first task of organizing the basic masses is fundamental and primary. Without widely mobilizing the masses it is not possible to perform any of the other tasks such as building of UF and performing the military tasks.

Factors Governing All-India Perspective-Plan

Drawing up the All-India perspective-plan means basically selecting the cities, industries or regions where we should concentrate and give priority. It can further mean the evaluation of the available subjective forces and deciding on suitable allocation.

Suburbs and nearby villages also depend on urban centres for employment. So we should incorporate the work in these areas as part of the urban work. Many industries and other infrastructure also exist. Hence, depending on the concrete conditions plans for organizational work should be drawn. The urban working masses, particularly the youth, and all the pettybourgeois sections are leading an insecure life lacking employment opportunities and even the daily necessities. This objective condition is favourable for building a strong revolutionary urban movement. However, due to the weakness of the revolutionary forces, the ruling classes are able to utilise this atmosphere in their favour, even though temporary, to some extent or the other. CPI and CPI(M) revisionists are still powerful in the sphere of trade unions and have considerable grip over other sections of the urban population in major cities. We have to raise the vigilance of the people against he danger of economism and capitulationism being spread by these revisionists.

To achieve this a revolutionary class-consciousness should be ensured through our political activity in the urban poor. We have to build up a vast network of secret party units with the advanced section of the working class that comes to the fore, particularly through political mobilization. We have to build up secret armed defence squads and open defence teams, from the very beginning itself with the working class youth to organize resistance against the attacks from goondas engaged by managements and other exploiting sections and also from the state's armed forces.

The working class is the most advanced revolutionary force of our society. We have to impart revolutionary consciousness in the course of their struggle/movement to unleash the revolutionary potentialities latent within the class. We endeavour to ensure their leading role as a class in the ongoing NDR. For this purpose first, we have to expose and free them from the reformist and revisionist thinking and practice, and consolidate politically the advanced sections of the working class and guide them to rouse the entire class for NDR.

Work in Key Industries

Our presence today in the key industries is extremely low. With the advance of the people's war, it is a pressing need that we enter into key industries and establish a strong base there. Some industries like transport, communications, rail, dock, power, oil and natural gas, defence production, etc. can play a crucial role in our revolution. In the course of war development disruption of production in these industries has an immediate impact on the enemy's ability to fight the war. It is thus the responsibility of the urban organization to establish a presence and influence in such key industries.

The key industries have normally been in the public sector. Now however with the policy of privatization, many of the old units are being privatized and new units are being set up directly in the private sector. Thus some of these industries, like the electricity boards and telecommunications department, are experiencing many militant struggles in opposition to the privatization policies and there has been a significant revival of the trade unions. In the context of the general upswing of the workers' movement, the workers of other key industries too are resorting to struggle. We can therefore make use of this situation to try and influence the workers in these industries.

Our Plan for the Key Industries should Operate at Two Levels

One. We can influence the workers in these industries from outside through various forms of propaganda, particularly during the struggles of these industries. This can be done through legal TU organizations, workers' magazines, secret pamphleteering and even through Party statements.

Two. We should send comrades to secretly develop fractional work from within the industry's existing TU, according to the opportunity. This work should be done with a long-term approach taking care to avoid exposure.

Due to the critical character of these industries, the enemy too is very conscious of the need to prevent any revolutionary or other genuine struggling forces from entering such industries. We therefore have to be very guarded and careful while entering and working within such enterprises. All work in such places should be under cover of some sort. Fractional work is the normal method. The work in such industries should normally be separated from the other work in the area

Work in other Fronts

The main focus of mass political mobilisation and organising in the cities should be the working class. We should pay particular attention to the trade unions and other working class organisations. We should also organise in the bastis and slums where the working class resides along with other sections of the urban poor. In some urban centers a section of the basic masses, who hail from the areas of armed agrarian struggles, are influenced by revolutionary politics.

Apart from the working class and the urban poor, we have also to pay special attention to our work among women, students, youth, teachers and middle class intellectuals in other professions who have grown considerably in recent decades. Youth and cultural organizations also play a good role in the activities of the city movement.

A section of the student community has imprinted their death-defying advanced role in the history of the country's revolutionary struggles. They again and again played a role of fore-runner of revolutionary struggles/ movements.

They have shouldered the responsibility of spreading revolutionary politics. They have also been playing an important role in the ongoing PPW. It is our task to further deepen our activities within the student community. Considering the present situation we should develop suitable organizational forms to imbue them with revolutionary politics, and organise and mobilize the vast majority of them politically. They can be mobilised politically on both domestic and international issues.

The objective situation is favourable for the political mobilisation of all these sections apart from organising them on their sectional or partial demands. We must give great importance to mobilizing them around the tactical political slogans given in the Political Resolution. From the beginning, we have to build secret party units among them. The advancement and victory of the movement is based on the political experience gained by all these classes.

In fact,the role of women in various fields in the urban areas is increasing. In addition to students, women employees, labourers and those working in other handicrafts, there are thousands of women working in big and small industries at low wages. They live in abject poverty and pathetic living conditions. Besides, they are subjected to constant sexual harassment at the workplace. Therefore, in order to organise women more attention should be paid by the Party at all levels, particularly in towns.

In the past few years, the strength of the communal forces in towns has increased considerably. The people of religious minorities are becoming prey to the attacks of the Hindu communal forces whose social base in the towns is relatively developing. To rein in such forces and bring out the oppressed people from the influence of communalism, the Party units, cadres and committees should exhibit initiative and stand by the side of the religious minorities and formulate necessary slogans and timely tactics as and when required.

Urban areas also offer scope for uniting with sections of the national bourgeoisie that oppose imperialism and the CBB. In our tactics towards this class, we must take into account their vacillating and exploitative nature and adopt a policy of unity-struggle with them. Though they will come into the strategic united front at the later stages of the revolution, we must strive to bring them in tactical united fronts. However, on no account unity with sections of the national bourgeoisie be achieved at the cost of the basic classes within the united front. Thus while uniting with the national bourgeoisie we should never lose sight of the struggle aspect of our relationship with them. We should not have any misconception that unity with the national bourgeoisie implies concessions in trade union struggles with these sections. It is the strength of the working class and not its weakness that will be the force attracting the national bourgeoisie to the front.

The ceaseless attacks of the imperialists and their Indian agents are daily pushing the national bourgeoisie into more conflict with the ruling classes. Thus today the practical possibilities of unity from below are growing. These possibilities are greater in cities with a stronger national bourgeois presence. Local party organisations should try to achieve issue-based unity like preventing relocation or closure of industries, opposing anti small industry laws and tax increases, etc. while keeping in mind the above principles.

By mobilizing the urban masses and classes in the above-mentioned manner, we should work with the aim of creating an upsurge of people's movements against the stranglehold of imperialism and the repressive policies of the Indian State. To achieve this, we should concentrate our work mainly on the vast section of the working class and other democratic sections.

Military Tasks of the Urban Movement

While the and PLA in the countryside perform the main military tasks, the urban organization too performs tasks complementary to the rural armed struggle. There are numerous ways through which the urban movement can assist the rural armed struggle and particularly, the base areas and the guerilla zones. Some involve direct and immediate help in terms of materials and personnel; others involve the long-term preparation for the decisive battles in the later stages of the peoples' war.

It is very important to penetrate into the military, para-military forces, police, and higher levels of the administrative machinery of the state. It is necessary to obtain information regarding the enemy, to build support for the revolution within these organs, and even to incite revolt when the time is ripe.

The nature of urban work being primarily defensive, the military tasks directly related to the urban movement are basically defensive in nature and will remain that way till the final period of the revolution. However even a defensive urban movement requires the military type organization of the armed defence of the urban masses against the peoples' enemies. These enemies are of various types - mafia, criminals, goonda gangs acting in the service of the ruling classes, social fascist gangs led by revisionists, Hindu fascist organizations and their militias, vigilante gangs specifically organised by the state to attack activists and sympathisers of our movement, state forces themselves, etc. Without standing up to such forces it would not be possible for an organisation to survive and develop. While we cannot and should not, at this stage, organise for armed offensive confrontation with the state, we should definitely build such defence organisations as are suited to the concrete situation. However we have to form open and secret defence teams to resist the repression of all kinds unleashed by the ruling classes.

Logistics Support

The enemy gets all its logistics support from the urban areas. The People's Army however relies as far as possible on the rural areas and the rural masses.

However for certain crucial things there is need for upport from the urban areas. Depending on its strength, the urban organisation should make all efforts to provide such support.

Supplies or contacts for supplies of certain types of materials such as arms and ammunition, spare parts, medical supplies, etc. are only available in the urban areas. Technical help in the form of repairs and maintenance of fighting, communication and other equipment of the PLGA, development of new technologies for the people's war, and sending comrades with technical, electrical, electronic and other skills to settle in the countryside is another task of the urban organization. Propaganda and publications to fulfill the needs of the rural movement is also one of the important tasks in the urban centres.

Urban Area in the Vicinity of Liberated Areas and Guerrilla Zones

There is a special significance to the work in the small towns, (district towns, kasbas and small mining centres) inside, and in the vicinity of the base areas and the guerrilla zones. Such towns act as business centres. Some towns are the supply centres for forest produce and raw materials. In such towns, the enterprises of the comprador bureaucratic bourgeoisie, of the TNCs, and of the national bourgeoisie have interests in areas such as mining enterprises for extracting raw materials like coal, iron etc, and some medium and heavy industries based on these raw materials. As a consequence, working class too is concentrated to a notable extent in these towns. Such towns will have importance.

On the whole all the towns in and around these areas are the centres of government machinery. As the government machinery in the rural areas around these towns is either too weak or paralysed, these towns turn into main centres for counter-revolutionary rule in that area. It is basing on these towns that, the enemy forces launch attacks of suppression campaigns on the guerrilla zones and the liberated areas: On the other hand, when compared with other towns, the impact of revolutionary politics and of the people's war will be very high. The oppressed masses will show much greater inclination towards the revolution.

In such towns, opportunity for open and legal work will in general not be available, either to our Party or to the mass organisations. Therefore, our Party has to work, in the main, through cover organisations only. We will have to conduct open activities through broad united front formed on the basis of a limited programme.

The Party has to function through secret methods, very cautiously, with an organisational structure impregnable, to the enemy. As the revolutionary movement in these towns, has to play a key supporting role in many ways to the guerrilla zones and liberated areas, it is very essential in such towns that the underground network of Party organisation should spread extensively and people's support should be mobilised in a big way.

On the occasions the enemy launches encirclement and suppression campaigns and onslaughts on the base areas, the urban people's armed squads need to serve the people's war by destroying enemy supplies, transport communication facilities etc.

Even amidst brutal fascist conditions of repression of whatever scale this urban revolutionary movement must ensure that its organic links with the guerrilla zones and liberated areas do not get snapped. We should concentrate on building such a party, which is impregnable to the enemy, in these urban centres. Then that urban movement can fulfil its role in the protracted people's war. The people's war can advance breaking the military and economic blockades of the enemy only if such an extensive organisation is in existence.

It will also be possible for us to capture some small towns during the course of intensification of people's war and establishment of liberated areas.

Party Structure

The question of the Party structure in the urban areas presents quite different problems from that in the rural areas where our Party is based. These relate to the problem of building and running stable structures, the continuity of party leadership, the coordination between open and secret work, between lower and higher bodies, and between the city organisation and the leadership based in the rural areas. We cannot resolve these problems without the close attention and study by the higher-level bodies and the development of concrete and practical solutions. We also require however a broad common approach on the objectives, tasks and methods to be adopted for building and advancing the urban Party structure.

The essential principle forming the basis of our Party structure is political centralisation combined with organisational decentralisation. This means that all PMs and all bodies, particularly at the lower level, should have solid ideological-political foundations, so that they are able to independently find their bearings and take the correct organisational decisions according to the political line of the Party.

This is particularly important in the urban areas because of the technical difficulties of maintaining close and constant links between the secret higher bodies and those at the lower levels engaged in direct open work. This is also important because urban work often demands immediate and quick responses to the events of the day. With rapid advances in electronic communication and media, delays of days and sometimes even hours in politically reacting to major events can hinder the impact that our Party can have on the urban movement. This thus depends on the strength of the bodies that form the foundation of our urban Party structure - the cells and the lower level committees - as well as on the Party fractions that link the Party with the mass organisations.

Comrades in leadership positions should not directly guide or maintain contacts with the individuals, organisations and shelters that become exposed to the enemy. Work should be decentralized at all levels. We should prevent loss of leadership or unnecessary sacrifices due to lack of seriousness in technical matters and becoming prey to spontaneity. In spite of all the precautions we take, as we are fighting with a powerful enemy, there is a danger of our Party members (part-timers and professional revolutionaries) getting exposed to the enemy due to mistakes committed by our subjective forces, lack of understanding and experience. Under such circumstances all such comrades should be sent underground and ensure that the party organisation is not put to loss. At the same time, the Party should educate the rank and file regarding the danger of left-adventurism and right opportunism rearing their head while observing all technical precautions

Another problem related to the urban Party structure is the links with the rural party organisation as well as the functional departments of the higher Party bodies. There is often a need of urban help of various types, for which the urban organisations involved in day to day mass work are regularly used. Therefore it is important to put a stop to such short cut methods and separate structures should be set up in the cities for this purpose.

From the beginning of the revolutionary movement to its end, the urban areas will remain as strong recruiting centres for the revolutionary party. Cadres have to be continuously sent as organisers and as leaders at various levels to the areas of armed struggle by imparting the necessary ideological and political knowledge.

The entire urban work should be reoriented based on the above policy and guidelines and the committees at various levels should draw up plans accordingly.

Intensify and Expand our People's War based on our Strategy and Tactics

Dear comrades,

The strategy and tactical principles for the Indian revolution have been evolved based on the concrete economic, political, social, cultural, historical and geographical conditions of India and taking into account the rich experiences of the world revolution, particularly the great Chinese revolution. They took final shape in the course of the protracted ideological-political struggle against revisionism of various hues and in the course of the long practice of armed struggle in India. The protracted people's war, with armed agrarian revolutionary struggle as its principal content, being waged in our country ever since the great Naxalbari revolt, had incontrovertibly proved the correctness of the political-military Strategy and the various Tactical principles adopted by the Maoist revolutionaries 36 years ago. These have been further enriched in the course of advancing the armed struggle.

Implementation of our strategy of overthrowing the three big mountains weighing down the Indian people-imperialism, CBB and feudalism-by first concentrating on the backward rural areas that have strategic importance for developing the guerrilla zones and the establishment of Base Areas, and orienting our work in all other areas and fronts to conform with the above basic, principal and immediate task, has led to great advances in the revolutionary movement in the country. Several guerrilla zones could be formed in the past three decades of struggle; the people's guerrilla army came into existence in the form of the PLGA; political power of the revolutionary masses could be established in some pockets in the countryside; and, several tactical successes could be achieved in the guerrilla war against a vastly superior enemy. The line of protracted people's war has thus become firmly established as the only path for the liberation of our country.

By unequivocally rejecting the parliamentary path and the participation in the elections in any form, we had drawn a clear line of demarcation between the revolutionaries on the one hand and the revisionists and the Right opportunists on the other. Our practice has vindicated the correctness of our understanding that parliamntary elections and protracted people's war are incompatible with each other in the concrete conditions of India.

All the party members must advance with unflinching determination basing on the synthesis of our experiences of work in all fronts-from the strategic areas to the urban areas-which has been incorporated into the present document, and basing firmly on the ideological guidance of MLM in solving the problems that arise in the course of our practice. The party's leading committees must play a conscious role in implementing the principles worked out in the present document.

The entire party ranks must base their entire work on the correct class line and mass line, integrate themselves and maintain ties with the masses like fish in water, and by recruiting an unending stream of the basic classes into the revolutionary movement, transform the /PLGA into the PLA, defeat the growing enemy offensive thereby accomplishing greater advances. They must have strategic firmness and tactical flexibility, grasp the correct interrelationship between strategy and tactics, and creatively apply these principles by concretely analysing the specific conditions and make conscious effort to transform the unfavourable conditions into favourable ones. Let us base our tactics by seeing the enemy as a paper tiger strategically but a real tiger tactically.

We must concentrate on mobilising the broadest masses opposed to imperialism, CBB and feudalism in accordance with the political strategy of building the four-class alliance through armed struggle. By establishing Base Areas and guerrilla zones in the vast rural tracts of the country and intensifying revolutionary guerrilla war we must create a revolutionary upsurge of the masses, and utilise the excellent international and domestic situation to accomplish the new democratic revolution in India. We must concentrate on building and strengthening the three magic weapons – a strong proletarian Party, a mighty People's Army and a Revolutionary United Front – throughout the country in order to accomplish the above tasks.

Today, imperialism worldwide is facing an unprecedented crisis unheard of ever since the end of the Second World War. All the fundamental contradictions are further sharpening. A new tide of revolutionary struggles, national liberation struggles and various people's movements against imperialist aggression, oppression, exploitation and the reactionary ruling classes is unfolding everywhere. Let us utilise this favourable situation to make great leaps in the ongoing people's war in our country and advance towards the establishment of a new democratic/ socialist India.

Dare to Fight ! Dare to Win !
Final Victory belongs to the People in this Just People's War !!

***

URBAN MOVEMENT

In their earlier avatar *as the People's War Group (PWG), the rebels had successfully organized themselves in some towns and cities of the North Telengana region in Andhra Pradesh. Effectively, they determined the prices of grocery in the markets, the fee that would be charged by hairdressers in saloons and the price of a ticket in a cinema. As late as in 2002, on Christmas day, a PWG squad blasted the Hanamkonda police station, which is located a few hundred meters away from the office of the district police chief (Superintendent of Police) of Warangal.*

Owing to the challenging task of building the movement in various parts of the country and consolidating the organization after the formation of the CPI (Maoist), the rebels did not find adequate time to spreading the urban movement. However, in December 2006, the Central Committee decided to launch the urban movement on a wider scale across the country. With this in view, an Urban Sub Committee was formed and was tasked with preparing an 'Urban Perspective Plan', and was asked to prepare it by September 2007. According to security force officials, Kobad Ghandy alias Rajan, ideologue and Polit Bureau member, who is presently lodged in the Tihar Central Jail in New Delhi, played a significant role in the preparation of this plan.

In the Maoist scheme of things, the objectives of the urban movement can be classified under three broad heads: (a) mobilize and organize the basic masses and build the party on that basis, (b) build the United Front and (c) military tasks. They hope to gain control over the working class movement and use it appropriately at a later stage when their so-called New Democratic Revolution advances and furthers. In the immediate to short-term their objective is to gain control over key strategic industries with a view to inflicting damage on the state's capacity to fight the Maoists, either through organizing sabotage activities or bringing production to a halt. The industries they plan to penetrate include communication, oil and natural gas, coal, transport, power, defence production, etc. This could, indeed, have disastrous consequences.

The following is the Maoist blue-print on how to organize and conduct the urban movement.

OUR WORK IN URBAN AREAS

CONTENTS

1. Introduction

The Strategy and Tactics document adopted at the Ninth Congress of 2001 explains the importance of urban work within the strategy of Indian Revolution in the following manner:

> "Work in the urban areas has a special importance in our revolutionary work...in our revolution, which follows the line of protracted people's war, the liberation of urban areas, will be possible only in the last stage of the revolution. However, this does not mean that there is no need to concentrate on the building of urban revolutionary movement from the beginning. From the beginning we will have to concentrate on the organization of the working class, which being the leadership of our revolution has to directly participate and lead the agrarian revolution and the people's war and on building a revolutionary workers movement. Moreover, on the basis of revolutionary workers movement we will be able to mobilize millions of urban oppressed masses and build struggles against imperialism and feudalism, struggles in support of the agrarian revolution and struggles for democratic rights. We will be able to create the subjective forces and conditions required for building a countrywide, broad, anti-imperialist, anti-feudal united front during this course only. The urban movement is one of the main sources, which provides cadres and leadership having various types of capabilities essential for the people's war and for the establishment of liberated areas... We should not forget the dialectical relationship between the development of the urban movement and the development of the people's war. In the absence of a strong revolutionary urban movement, the people's war will face difficulties.
>
> "However, we should not belittle the importance of the fact that the urban areas are the strong centers of the enemy. Building up of a strong urban revolutionary movement means that our Party should build a struggle network capable of waging struggle consistently, by sustaining itself until the protracted people's war reaches the stage of strategic offensive. With this long term

> perspective, we should develop a secret party, an united front and people's armed elements; intensify the class struggle in the urban areas and mobilize the support of millions of urban masses for the people's war." [Pages 69-70, S&T].

However, there have been serious shortcomings and mistakes in our understanding and practice over the last thirty years. The Political and Organizational Review of the Ninth Congress thus reviewed as follows, "The importance of urban work in the ongoing people's war in the country is well-recognized by our Party and is elaborated in our Strategy-Tactics document. However we have been extremely deficient in perspective, policy and methods of work. We have only made piecemeal changes from time to time, to the policy, contained in the document "Our Work in Urban Areas" brought out by APSC in 1973. We have yet to develop a comprehensive and long-term approach, which takes into account the changing developing trends in urbanization, as well as the policies of the enemy to isolate and crush us in the urban areas. This has led to frequent ups and downs in our urban work in most areas and serious loss of cadres in the areas of repression." [Page 141, POR]

Thus the Congress decided on "A time-bound programme for preparing policy and guidelines for urban work, particularly working class work. This should include a review of our understanding and practice with regard to revolutionary trade unions, mini-guerilla squads, selfdefence squads, and workers' magazine among other things. This should be followed by a campaign to reorganize our work according to the guidelines." [Page 149, POR]

The present document is part of the attempt to implement the above Congress decision. Part 2 gives a brief picture of urban India, presenting the trends in urbanization and the changes in class composition, particularly since the policies of liberalization. Part 3 is the main section which lays out the policy and guidelines for work - our strategic approach and objectives, forms of organization and forms of struggle, the party, united front and military tasks, propaganda, tech mechanism, and planning. Part 4 reviews the main shortcomings in our understanding and practice of the past 30 years. Part 5 identifies some immediate tasks.

Besides this a separate document, 'Guidelines for Our Work in the Working Class', explains details with regard to working class work.

2. Urban India

According to the census of 2001, 27.8% of India's population now lives in the towns and cities. The total urban population is 28.5 crores, which is larger than the total population of the world's third most populated country - USA. Most of this urban population is situated in large cities. Almost two thirds stay in cities with a population of over one lakh, and 10.8 crores (i.e. 38%) are in 35 metropolitan centres with a population of over 10 lakhs. Three of the world's twenty mega-cities, with a population of over one crore each, are from India.

The centre of the economy has also moved away from the rural areas. In 1950-51 56% of production came from agriculture, but today less than 25% comes from agriculture. Today most of the country's production is from the industries and services sectors, which are mainly based in the towns and cities. The urban share in the Gross Domestic Product (GDP) is thus now over 60%.

India's urban population size, proportion, and economic weight today are much higher than what was there in China at the time of the revolution. China, then had only about 10% of its production coming from industry and only 11% of the people staying in the urban areas. This would mean that India's urban areas would have to play a relatively more important role in the revolution, than the cities played during the Chinese revolution.

This however does not mean any change in our basic strategy, which is based on the uneven economic and political development and the semi feudal, semi-colonial character of Indian society. Current international experience too shows various semi-colonial countries with large proportions in urban areas successfully advancing the people's war basing on rural armed struggle. Though our urban population is large and constantly growing, its proportion is still much lower than the percentage of most other semi-colonial countries with movements seriously engaged in armed agrarian revolution. Thus Philippines have 59%, Peru has 73%, and Turkey has 75% urban population. Only Nepal has a lower 12% urban population, though the rate of growth of its urban population is almost double that of India.

2.1 Urbanization Pattern

Since 1947, four major metropolitan cities, which served as regional capitals under the British, have dominated the process of urbanization in the country. These were Kolkata, Mumbai, Delhi and Chennai, who respectively served as the central hubs of the east, west, and north and south of the country. Since the sixties they have continued to experience growth, though at different paces. Further newer metropolitan centres like Bangalore, Hydrabad and Pune, are emerging as new hubs of urban growth. The policies of liberalization are bringing further changes and new patterns of urbanization have been emerging, which are changing the positions and importance of even the old metropolitan centres.

Delhi continues to maintain its all-India importance, mainly as administrative capital and also due the rapid industrialization in its surrounding areas. Mumbai as financial capital, has been continuing to grow rapidly and is now among the five largest cities in the world. Kolkata and Chennai continue to maintain their regional importance, but Kolkata has lost its all-India importance as a centre of industry and commerce.

The ups and downs of these main centres is however only a reflection of the country's sharply unequal pattern of urbanization. Kolkata is falling back because of its placement in the poorest and least urbanized eastern part of the country, whereas all the new stars are emerging in the most urbanized south and the west.

The old hierarchy of four mega cities located in different regions of the country is thus giving way to urban corridors and clusters of new investment located mostly in the southern and western parts of the country.

With the exception of the Delhi region and adjacent areas in Haryana, Punjab, Rajasthan and Uttar Pradesh much of the north, the east and the centre of the country have been bypassed. This vast area covering the eastern half of UP and stretching across Bihar, West Bengal, the North-Eastern states, Orissa, Madhya Pradesh and the eastern part of Maharashtra is remaining as an area of urban backwardness, with old industrial bases and high unemployment. These areas are thus the main sources of cheap migrant labour for the large metropolitan cities.

The above inequalities are being encouraged by the policies of the government. In the earlier period under industrial licensing there were some small attempts at bringing about balanced industrial development and this led to some projects being set up in relatively backward areas like the central India minerals belt. Now under the liberalization policies investment is not regulated and goes to the areas promising the greatest profits. Thus the main investment is centred in and around a few areas of growing urban concentration. The main such areas are:

a) **Ahmedabad-Pune Corridor:** This stretch of Western India is the main concentration of high industrialization and urbanization in the country. It includes four of the top ten cities in the country - Mumbai, Ahmedabad, Pune and Surat - besides two other cities over ten lakh - Vadodara and Nashik. The industries cover almost all the main industrial groups—engineering, chemicals, textiles, automobiles, telecommunications, electronics, etc. These cities and the adjoining districts attract the largest amount of new investment in the whole country. The working class is the most diverse, having migrated from all parts of the country.

b) **Delhi Region:** The capital region together with the adjoining areas of Gurgaon and Faridabad in Haryana, and Ghaziabad and NOIDA in UP is a massive urban and industrial zone. It is continuing to advance at a rapid pace in engineering, automobile, electronics, etc. The working class here too is diverse, but mainly from north India.

c) **Bangalore:** This has for some time been a centre of many major public sector establishments, besides textiles and silk weaving. Electronics and computer software and hardware are the main growth industries, with Bangalore being the software capital of India. It is a fast growing centre.

d) **Chennai:** The Greater Chennai region has become the industrial hub for the entire south. It has a very diverse range of industries - automobiles, textiles, chemicals, petroleum products, electronics, etc.

e) **Coimbatore-Erode Belt:** This is the area of fastest growing urbanization in the country. The principal industries are centred around textiles - mills, power looms, knitwear, etc. There are also small and medium engineering units.

f) **Hyderabad:** Though the actual growth is not as much as the media propaganda of the AP Chief minister, Hydrabad is also a fast growing urban centre. Besides the earlier public sector undertaking and other industries, the new investments are mainly in electronics and information technology. In AP, Vishakhapatnam has also been a centre of growth, attracting big investments.

Most urban centres in other areas are not receiving much investment and are therefore experiencing some level of stagnation. They are however major centres of industry with a large working class. They also play a very important role in their regions. Some of these centres are:

a) **Kolkata:** Though it has lost its all-India importance, it remains the centre for the whole of eastern India. It has a large and diverse industrial base, but no major new area of industrial growth. The city too is growing at a slow pace. It has got new investment but a large part is for the expansion of existing plants. The working class is diverse, but basically from eastern India. Due to slow industrial growth unemployment rate is relatively higher.

b) **Industrial Cities of Central India:** The investments coming into these areas are mainly for power and fuel, and metallurgical industries. However new projects are relatively few and overall unemployment there is growing.

c) **Cities of the Gangetic Plain:** These cities including old major industrial centres like Kanpur, are not receiving much new investment and are thus stagnating. The cities however continue to grow due to influx from the rural areas.

The above trend and pattern of urban growth has to be taken into account while drawing up a perspective and plan for urban work.

2.2 Changes in Class Composition and Structure of Cities

Besides the changes at the all-India level there are also significant changes taking place within the cities, particularly the largest cities. This is resulting in changes in the nature and composition of the work force, as well as the geographical placement of various classes and communities.

2.2.1 De-industrialization of major cities

Over the years most major cities have seen a decline in manufacturing activity as compared to business activity in banking, finance, and other service sectors. This process started first with the largest cities, with the close down of many of Kolkata's jute mills and other industries from the late sixties. This process however became very generalized from the early eighties with the decline of the textile mills in Mumbai, Ahmedabad, Chennai, and other centres. Lakhs of blue-collar jobs were destroyed without the setting up of any new industries within the city. Since the last twenty years now, hardly any new industry has been located within the major old cities. New industrialization is normally taking place on the outskirts of the main city, or in the nearby towns and cities. This is combined by an increase of white-collar jobs in the field of services, with investment normally going into these areas.

This process has led to a change in the class composition of most cities, particularly the metropolitan cities. Aggregate data on urban areas as a whole show a gradual decline in the percentage of male workers engaged in manufacturing from 27 per cent in 1983 to 23.6 percent in 1993-94. For female workers, the decline was from 26 per cent in 1983 to 23.6 percent in 1993-94. Over the same period, the percentage of male workers engaged in the services sector has increased from 24.8 per cent to 26.4 per cent, the increase for women workers being from 31.4 per cent to 38.8 per cent. Here services have been defined to include finance, insurance and business services and all other services, including community and social services. This indicates that the overall proportion of the industrial proletariat in urban areas throughout India is falling as compared to the employees engaged in offices, marketing establishments, hotels, etc.

While the above figures give the overall picture, the actual situation with regard to particular cities will be different. Since this factor is very important for our organizational perspective, plans, and tasks at the city level, all the respective committees should conduct city level class analysis regarding the situation and trend in their areas.

2.2.2 Changes in the Workforce

With closures of industries and the accompanying loss of jobs, many workers are forced to take up casual work or earn on their own through hawking, plying rickshaws, running roadside tea stalls and food joints, etc. At the same time new youth entering the work force do not get regular jobs immediately (unemployment rate is the highest in the 15 to 24 age group) and are forced to take casual employment or also run some small trade. This trend is increasing in recent years in the urban areas. At the same time more and more women are being employed in jobs but at much lower wage rates. This trend, which had started since the early eighties in most cities, has further accelerated since the liberalization policies.

The percentage of urban males in regular work has dropped and the percentage of self-employed and casual labourers has gone up. At the same time the percentage of women in regular work has gone up, though this does not affect the total size of the working class so much because women compose only 17% of the total urban workforce.

This then means a change in the composition of the working people. **Firstly** there has been an increase in the proportion of the semi-proletariat (i.e. self-employed); **secondly** there has been an increase in the proportion of women workers being paid very low wages; and **thirdly** there has been an increase in the casual labour force.

Besides the above given changes, another change has been the shift of jobs from the larger factories of the organized sector to the small workshops and industries. In recent years the percentage of workers in the organized sector as compared to the total workforce has fallen from 8.5% in 1991 to 7.1% in 1997 to 6.9% in 1999-2000. As the workers are divided into smaller units their potential for unionization also reduces.

All the above changes in the workforce have been presented here at the all-India level. These changes have significant consequences for our planning at the city and area levels. We should conduct local class analysis and plan accordingly.

2.2.3 Division or Segmentation of Cities

Cities and towns in India, basing on the colonial pattern, have always had a rich British section and a poorer Indian section. This separation however reduced to some extent in the process of growth of the metropolitan cities. Thus it became quite common to have slums adjoining posh high-rise buildings, and hawkers and vendors occupying space right next to the offices of multinationals in the heart of the central business district. Periodically drives would be taken up to demolish slums or evict hawkers, but they would most often manage to struggle and maintain their space within the centre of the city.

In the liberalization-globalization period however the ruling classes in most major cities, aspiring to make them 'global' cities, have in a coordinated and planned manner launched numerous measures to push the poor out of the core of the city and preserve it for the economic and social use of imperialist and comprador capital. This process has and is taking place in an intensive manner in Mumbai, Delhi, Bangalore, Hydrabad, Kolkata, Chennai, and in some other metropolitan cities. Similar patterns are however to be seen even in relatively smaller cities.

This process of dividing or segmenting the city is done through various measures. These measures extend from the old measures of slum demolition and hawker eviction to new forms like closure of 'polluting' factories, banning of protests in central areas, law changes encouraging privatization and localization of urban finance and urban facilities, regulations encouraging concentration of development in the richer zones, etc.

The role of the state is most prominent. Bureaucrats and urban planners operating under direct instructions from the World Bank, Asian Development Bank, and other imperialist institutions have formulated laws, regulations, policies and master plans, which have given up even the earlier pretence of the slogans of equity and alleviating of urban poverty. Now the basic thrust of the plans are on 'efficiency' and 'clean and green' cities, which means basically providing sanitized five star enclaves with the best infrastructure and communication facilities for the offices, houses, and entertainment facilities of the corporate managers and elites, while pushing the urban poor along with their 'unclean' slums and 'polluting' industries to the borders of the city. The basic thrust of the National

Capital Plan for Delhi and the 1993 Mega-City programme for the other 5 top cities mentioned above basically have this objective. The High Courts and Supreme Court, aided by anti-people so-called environmentalists, have also played a very active role in this process giving numerous court rulings to speed up this process in the name of 'public interest' litigation.

Numerous struggles of the working class and the urban poor have erupted against these measures. The November 2000 revolt of the Delhi working class and national bourgeoisie, and the struggles of Mumbai slum dwellers and Kolkata hawkers are some examples. However despite these struggles the remapping of the mega-cities and other metropolitan cities is proceeding ahead, and the socio-geographic pattern of cities like Mumbai has already changed considerably.

This process has to be dealt with by us at two levels. At one level we must participate in the mass struggles against the process of eviction and fight for the right of the working class and urban poor to live and work in their old areas. At another level we must take account of the changed pattern of the city in our analysis and planning. As part of our class analysis we should also map out the geographical locations of the various classes, both residential and work place. We should take it into account in our plans for organization, protest, self-defence, etc.

2.2.4 Ghettoisation

A ghetto is a slum or locality inhabited mostly or completely by one community. When a particular community is attacked repeatedly and forced, for their safety, to concentrate in particular areas this process is called ghettoisation. Localities formed on the basis of nationality, caste and religion are very common in almost all Indian towns and cities. However not all have been formed by a process of ghettoisation.

Urban mass violence on the basis of nationality has comparatively infrequent examples like Cauvery riots in Bangalore where the Tamil national minority was attacked, or the 1967 Mumbai attacks on south Indians by Shiv Sena national chauvinists. This is to a great extent because of relative lack of support for such acts from the integrationist all-India ruling classes and the Central state machinery.

Caste violence and caste riots are more numerous, with some towns and cities repeatedly witnessing attacks on dalits. Anti-reservation riots in many parts of the country are a constant form of caste attacks. Such upper caste violence has led to further sharpening the division of many towns and forcing all dalits to live in separate areas to better organize their self-defence.

The main form of violence has however been the attacks and organized pogroms by the Hindu communalists and fascists, primarily against the Muslims, but also against the Sikhs and Christians. This has led to the sharp segregation of the Muslim community and the creation of Muslim mohallas in almost all towns and cities where they have any existence. However with the metropolitanisation of some cities there has been some small shift out of Muslims into other areas. This too is being sought to be drastically reversed by the Hindu fascists during the eighties and the nineties.

The eighties and the nineties have seen the largest number of anti- Muslim pogroms associated with the political ascent of the Hindu fascists of the Sangh parivar. The major centre for this has been the western corridor with massacres of Muslims in almost all the major cities in this belt - Ahmedabad, Vadodara, Mumbai and Surat, as well as other smaller cities like Bhiwandi, Malegaon and Bharuch. The major urban centres of the south too have been centres for communal riots—Coimbatore, Hydrabad, and Bangalore, besides other smaller cities like Mangalore, Bhadravati, etc. Some have also taken place in the cities of Central India and the Gangetic plain. Most of these attacks have been done with the full connivance and even participation of the state forces. Of all these, Gujarat is being taken up by the fascists as a laboratory for an experiment in ethnic cleansing, with systematic physical and economic annihilation of Muslims.

As the Hindu fascists' campaign spreads in other parts of the country, ghettoisation is bound to sharply intensify in most cities. Purely Muslim areas, suspicious of all others, and organized for self-defence will become essential for the survival of the community. Sharpening of divisions on communal basis can become a serious barrier to building class unity. Our Party in the urban areas has to seriously take the ghettoisation process into account in all plans. Sharp ghettoisation leads to lack of jobs for Muslims and pushes larger sections of them into the semi-proletariat. Thus merely organizing within industry will not enable us to enter this oppressed community. Unless we base ourselves in the middle of the ghetto, we will not be able to gain entry into organizing the community, we will not also be able to build the united front against the Hindu fascists. Thus, in our planning, we have to clearly identify the ghettos of a city and draw up our plan for gaining entry into them. While doing this, we need to organize them on their basic needs and day-to-day problems too.

3. Policy and Guidelines

3.1 Strategic Approach in Urban Work

3.1.1 Role of Urban Work within the Political Strategy

As the Ninth Congress says, "Working class leadership is the indispensable condition for the New Democratic Revolution in India. The working class exercises its leadership in the revolution through its direct participation. Apart from rising under the leadership of the Communist Party in the overall struggle for democracy and liberation and thereby uniting all other sections of the people in anti-imperialist and anti-feudal struggles, the working class organizes the agrarian revolution by sending its advanced detachment to the rural areas." [Page 36, S&T]

Thus, being the centres of concentration of the industrial proletariat, urban areas play an important part within the political strategy of the New Democratic Revolution. It is the task of the party in the urban areas to mobilize and organize the proletariat in performing its crucial leadership role. Urban work thus means, firstly, forming the closest possible links with the working class, and, through the class struggle, establishing the party as a proletarian vanguard; further, it means the mobilization and unification of all other sections under proletarian leadership in the struggle to achieve the tasks of the revolution.

3.1.2 Role of Urban Work within the Military Strategy

The specific characteristics of revolutionary war in India "determine the military strategy to be one of protracted people's war - of establishing revolutionary base areas first in the countryside where the enemy is militarily weak and then to gradually surround and capture the cities which are the bastions of the enemy forces." [Page 8, S&T]

Thus it is clear that the armed struggle and the movement in the rural areas will play the primary role, and the work in the cities will play a secondary role, complementary to the rural work. However, while giving first priority to the rural work, we must also give due importance to the urban struggle. Without a strong urban revolutionary movement, the ongoing people's war faces difficulties; further, without the participation of the urban masses it is impossible to achieve countrywide victory. As Com. Mao says, "the final objective of the revolution is the capture of the cities, the enemy's main bases, and this objective cannot be achieved without adequate work in the cities." (Mao, Selected Works, Vol. II, Pg. 317).

Thus the correct dialectical relationship has to be maintained between the development of the urban movement and the development of the people's war. We should, by building up a strong urban movement, ensure that the urban masses contribute to creating the conditions that will obtain success for the armed struggle in the countryside. As we have seen in the earlier section, India has a larger proportion of the population in urban areas and a much larger working class than at the time of the Chinese revolution. This too increases the relative importance of urban work in the particular conditions of Indian revolution.

3.1.3 Long-term Approach

The cities and big industrial centres are the strongholds of reaction where the enemy is the most powerful. In these places the police, army, other state organs, and other forces of counter-revolution are concentrated and are in a dominant position from which they can suppress the people's forces. At the same time our Party's work and organization is extremely weak and generally cannot achieve a dominant position till the final stages of the people's war. It is this objective reality, which determines our policy towards work in the urban areas.

In such a situation, where the enemy is much stronger, we cannot have a short-term approach of direct confrontation in order to achieve 'quick results'.

Rather, we should have a long-term approach. The task of the Party is to win over the masses, including the vast majority of the workers, and to build up the enormous strength of the working class in preparation for the decisive struggle in the future. Now is not the time for this final struggle between the revolution and counter-revolution, and we should therefore avoid engaging the enemy in such a fight while the conditions are not in our favour. This means that we should act chiefly on the defensive (and not on the offensive); our policy should be one of protecting, preserving, consolidating and expanding the Party forces, while mobilizing and preparing the broad urban masses for revolutionary struggle.

As Com. Mao, while outlining the tasks of the Party in the urban and other white areas dominated by the reactionaries, explained, "the Communist Party must not be impetuous and adventurist in its propaganda and organizational work...it must have well-selected cadres working underground, must accumulate strength and bide its time there. In leading the people in struggle against the enemy, the Party must adopt the tactics of advancing step by step slowly and surely, keeping to the principle of waging struggles on just grounds, to our advantage, and with restraint, and making use of such open forms of activity as are permitted by law, decree and social custom; empty clamor and reckless action can never lead to success." (Mao, Selected Works, Vol. II, Pg. 318)

In order to mobilize the broadest possible sections in struggle it is absolutely essential that we should utilize all possible open and legal opportunities for work (and not reject the use of legality). Broad mass organizations help the Party to have wide contact with masses, so that it can work under cover for a long time and accumulate strength. While exploring the open opportunities, it is essential that we organize people into secret organizations too.

Broad, open and legal forms of organizing the masses have, however, to be combined with the strictest methods of secrecy, especially with regard to the link between the open and underground organization. All precautions should be taken to protect the identity of our comrades in the open organizations and contacts with the underground organization should be maintained at the minimum. At the same time particular care should be taken to ensure that the underground structures do not get exposed and smashed. For this a long-term approach and patience are absolutely essential. We should be even ready to sacrifice the short-term requirements of doing a particular job well in order to avoid endangering the long-term existence and functioning of the underground structure.

3.2 Main Objectives of Our Urban Work

Work in the cities and towns involve a number of tasks. All these tasks can however be combined under three broad heads or objectives.

They are as follows:

1) **Mobilize and organize the basic masses and build the Party on that basis:** This is the main activity of the Party. It is the Party's task to organize the working class, as well as other classes and sections like the semi-

proletariat, students, middle class employees, intellectuals, etc. It also has the task of dealing with the problems of special social groups like women, dalits, and religious minorities and mobilizing them for the revolutionary movement. It is on this basis that the masses are politicized and the advanced sections consolidated into the Party.

2) **Build the United Front:** This involves the task of unifying the working class, building worker-peasant solidarity and alliance, uniting with other classes in the cities, building the fronts against globalization, against Hindu fascism, against repression, etc. This is a very important aspect of the work of the Party in the city.
3) **Military Tasks:** While the PGA and PLA in the countryside perform the main military tasks, the urban movement too performs tasks complementary to the rural armed struggle. These involve the sending of cadre to the countryside, infiltration of enemy ranks, organizing in key industries, sabotage actions in coordination with the rural armed struggle, logistical support, etc.

Of the above three, the first task of organizing the basic masses is fundamental and primary. Without widely mobilizing the masses it is not possible to perform any of the other tasks such as building of UF and performing the military tasks.

3.3 Mass Mobilization and Party Building

We need to build the broadest mass base by building various types of mass organizations, such as, open revolutionary mass organizations, legal democratic organizations, secret mass organizations, cover organizations, etc. Depending upon the situation one or other type of organization becomes primary for that period. But keeping in mind long-term approach, we need to build several types of mass organizations simultaneously.

Thus the general principle with regard to urban forms of organization is that the mass organizations should be as wide as possible. As the Indian political situation is uneven, we need to explore right combination of various types of mass organizations. While there is no possibility to form open revolutionary mass organizations in AP, there are several states in which still such possibility still exists.

Thus we may organize the people in several forms, depending on the situation. But Party building should always be done with utmost secrecy. As the experience of work in Shanghai city, where the white terror was utmost, during the Chinese Revolution shows, "the party organization should be secret, the more secret, the better. Whereas, a mass organization should be open, the wider, the better." This principle could be creatively applied to our conditions. Those organizations, which openly propagate Party politics, should generally function secretly. Those organizations functioning openly and legally, generally cannot openly identify with the Party, and should work under some cover with a limited programme.

Correctly coordinating between illegal and legal structures, we should have an approach of step-by-step raising the forms of struggle and preparing the masses to stand up against the might of the state.

3.3.1 Types of Mass Organizations

Our POR identifies three types of mass organizations:- 1)secret revolutionary mass organizations, 2)open and semi-open revolutionary mass organizations, and 3)open legal mass organizations, which are not directly linked to the Party. Urban work within the third type of organizations can further be subdivided into three broad categories:- a)fractional work, b)party-formed cover organizations, and c)legal democratic organizations.

3.3.1.1 Secret Revolutionary Mass Organizations

These organizations remain strictly underground and propagate the Party's revolutionary line among the masses rousing them for armed struggle. They openly call upon the masses to participate in the people's war, propagate the central task drawn up by the Party at any given time, secretly organize the masses into struggles and directly serve as the base for recruitment for the Party and the people's war. These mass organizations are built clandestinely and conduct secret propaganda. They are built around a clear-cut and explicit revolutionary programme. Acceptance of the aims of the revolution and willingness to work secretly are thus minimum criteria for membership.

In our party such mass organizations were not formed as a plan. They emerged in and around the struggle areas when the open revolutionary mass organizations were forced to go underground under severe repression. Later they were consciously formed even in areas with relatively less repression. Today with the imposition of an All-India ban under POTA, mass organizations in many more areas will be built underground. Many of these organizations are principally functioning in urban areas. Though such secret organizations may be formed in any section of the masses, we have so far, in the urban areas, mainly set them up among the youth, students, and workers.

In urban areas these secret organizations perform the important task of propagating the Party line among various sections of the masses. They are the main vehicles of revolutionary propaganda. Due to the dominant position of the enemy in the cities, the important task of rousing the masses through revolutionary propaganda must be performed through a secret structure. The secret structure of the Party however cannot be the only medium to propagate revolutionary politics. This would limit the extent and depth of the impact of our propaganda. It is therefore necessary to develop separate secret organizational structures among various sections of the people, which will carry the message of the Party's calls to those sections in particular, as well to other sections of the broad masses. This therefore is the principal task of the secret revolutionary mass organizations in the urban areas.

It is the task of the secret units and committees to plan the forms and methods of propagating the Party line, the dissemination of Party propaganda, and the formulation and propagation of the revolutionary standpoint on various issues of the day - particularly the issues affecting the section which they are organizing. These can be done through secret posters, voices, pamphlets, cassettes, booklets, and other forms of propaganda; it can be done through personal contact by the organization members; it can be done through planned dramatic actions like attacks on imperialist, comprador, and other ruling class targets, etc. Through sustained and effective propaganda, and planned actions, the secret revolutionary mass organization must aim to reach a position where it influences, guides and even determines the actions and decisions of the non-Party organizations and the masses in its field of operation.

There could be some limitations for the secret mass organizations in organizing and mobilizing the masses in struggle in a big way. But there are occasions wherein secret mass organizations—though their actual organization is limited and their influence is significant—could lead important struggles in which lakhs of workers par Secret forms of struggle can and must be used. SiKaSa is an example for that.

Secret revolutionary mass organizations may not rally masses in a wide and broad way as that of open revolutionary mass organizations. When an open revolutionary mass organization is forced to go underground, while changing the work methods from open methods to secret methods by sending exposed cadre to UG, etc., wherever possible, unexposed portion of the organization's forces should be shifted so as to work in other types of organizations such as cover organizations, fractional work, legal democratic organizations, and so on.

Secret organizations are the not organs for leading and directing the legal organizations, which are not directly linked to the Party. This will create an unnecessary semi-party form of layer between the Party and such organizations. We should thus also generally avoid forming units of the secret organization within the open organization so as to lead the open bodies. The Party fractions and cells functioning in the area should do this leadership. The secret organization performs its revolutionary role by giving calls and conducting propaganda to guide and push the open organizations in the correct direction. However this too should be avoided in areas where the field of fractional or cover work is too small or where the open revolutionary propaganda may lead to exposure that we are doing such work in that area. If it is necessary for the secret organization members to actively work within the open organization, they will work as ordinary open members of the organization, while taking special care to safeguard their political identity. It is better to avoid combining of the tasks of the secret organization activist and open organization leader; wherever possible different comrades should be assigned these separate tasks.

Thus the secret mass organization should serve as vehicle of revolutionary Party propaganda in the urban areas. It is the form of organization that is suited for implementing this important task.

3.3.1.2 Open Revolutionary Mass Organizations

These are the open and semi-open mass organizations, which openly propagate the politics of New Democratic Revolution and prepare the people for armed struggle. These organizations make use of the available legal opportunities to carry on revolutionary propaganda and agitation openly and try to mobilize anti-imperialist, anti-feudal forces as widely as possible.

Our Party has formed and run such open revolutionary mass organizations since the seventies, particularly in the period following the lifting of the Emergency in 1977. These open organizations were then the main organs of mass mobilization both in the rural and urban areas. They were the banners under which thousands and lakhs were mobilized, particularly in the struggle areas of AP and Bihar. These mobilizations reached their peak in the 'open' periods up to 1986 and during 1991 in AP. They played the role of attracting the broad masses towards the revolution. However with the onset of repression most of these organizations were denied any legal opportunities and were forced to go underground. Direct bans were imposed in AP and Bihar, whereas serious restrictions and surveillance were placed on the organizations in other states. Thus the scope of such organizations has drastically reduced with the rise in repression on our Party throughout the country. Today only very small open bodies exist in some cities.

As is clear from experience, this form of organization can only be used when the ruling classes, due to various reasons cannot or do not bring repression. This being the case there is limited scope for this type of organization in the urban areas. Since the enemy generally has the strong upper hand in the urban areas, there are few situations where repression cannot be brought about. Thus as the people's war sharpens, the scope for legal opportunities is either because of the weakness of the ruling classes due to internal contradictions, or due to a plan of the state to keep watch on our forces or due to some other temporary reason.

Whatever be the reason, we should however evaluate the situation and try to make the best use of the legal opportunities available, while keeping in mind the long-term perspective. This means that if we are to get the opportunity to mobilize the masses in large numbers under our direct banner, we should make use of the chance. At the same time we should expose only a small section of our forces and make sure that the majority of our cadre remain hidden from enemy surveillance. We should on no account indulge in small demonstrations where all our activists are easily identified and even video filmed for easy targeting in future. We should understand that the period of legal opportunities for open revolutionary organizations will generally be short and we should make the best use of the period for long-term gains. While attempting to mobilize the largest numbers of the masses in struggle on the openly revolutionary platform of the open mass organization, the Party should concentrate on strengthening and consolidating the elements from these struggles who will serve the long term interests of the protracted people's war.

Thus we must be clear that the open revolutionary mass organization cannot be a permanent form of mass organization in the urban areas. It can and must be utilized in the periods and situations of legal opportunities, and we must be ever alert to make use of such opportunities whenever they arise. However while doing so we must be ever conscious of the long-term interests of the Party and the class struggle and make sure that they do not suffer in order to obtain some short-term gains.

3.3.1.3 Fractional Work

Here the Party works through the numerous traditional mass organizations that operate in the urban areas. These traditional mass organizations are the organizations normally set up by the masses to fight for their sectional interests or otherwise fulfill their needs. The Party, through its members or other activists, penetrates such organizations without exposing any links with the Party. Through the activities of the organization, the masses, while being mobilized for their sectional interests, are attempted to be drawn towards the revolution. This method of organizing, if properly conducted, offers the best opportunity for cover work for a long period of time. It is therefore indispensable in areas of severe repression. However it can and should be used in all urban areas because it also provides excellent mass forums for approaching large sections of the people; and if we do not disclose links with the Party we can function for long periods without suffering enemy repression.

Work of this nature can be carried out in various types of organizations. The best organizations are those which are more oriented to struggle, like trade unions, slum and other locality based organizations, youth organizations, unemployed organizations, students associations and unions, women's organizations, commuter associations, etc. Besides there are also other organizations which are welfare oriented, community based or are self-help organizations - like workers' cooperatives, cultural organizations, sports clubs and gymnasiums, libraries, bhajan mandals, non-governmental welfare organizations, women's welfare organizations, caste based and nationality based welfare organizations, minorities' bodies, etc. There are also many organizations, which emerge on a particular issue, for a particular period, or for a particular festival, etc.

Most of these organizations emerge naturally due to needs of the masses. However many of them will have either direct affiliations or indirect links with ruling class parties and organizations. This however does not need to affect our plan to work among them at the lower levels. Our main considerations while deciding to work in a particular organization are, firstly, whether the masses are or can be mobilized through that organization, and secondly, whether the situation of the organization is such that there is scope to politically influence the masses and draw some elements towards the Party.

Sometimes there are various mass organizations of different affiliations operating in the same area, e.g. multiple trade unions within a single factory. At such time we may have to decide which organization to work within. This decision again should be broadly according to the conditions given above. We may even decide to work in more than one organization if it suits our plan for the area. However our general approach would be to oppose the splitting of the unity of the masses and to stand for the unity of all representative mass organizations working in a particular area.

Once we have decided to do fractional work within an organization we should strive to achieve a leading position in it. This means we should be in a position to influence and guide the decisions of the organization. If it is necessary to takeover office bearers' posts in order to achieve this influence, then we should make attempts to do so. This however does not mean that we should always push for PMs to be in office bearers' posts. If our plans can be fulfilled through non-PMs or even through leaders belonging to other parties it is the best. This will not only better maintain our cover, but also will leave our PMs free to perform other tasks. However if there is no other alternative, and it is the will of the majority, we should not have any ban on even PMs taking up such posts.

Whether we take up office bearers' posts or not, the important point in fractional work is the skillful exposure of the reactionaries and reformists leading or participating within these organizations. This exposure is essential to draw the masses away from their influence. This must however be done without exposing ourselves to the enemy. The forms of exposure will thus differ depending upon the concrete situation. In vast areas where risk of direct exposure of our fractional work activists is low, we can use propaganda by the secret revolutionary mass organization or even direct calls by the Party. In smaller areas like a single factory or slum we may have to mainly or only use word-of-mouth propaganda. Sometimes we can create artificial banners like 'angry workers', 'concerned slum dwellers', etc. for doing our propaganda. Very often we may have to use a combination of various methods. Whatever is the method it should be applied carefully, skillfully, and consistently? It should ensure that the masses are drawn away from the influence of reactionaries and reformists; it should also at the same time ensure that we do not get prematurely exposed and face losses.

There are two types of deviations in fractional work. One is to sink to the level of the reactionaries and reformists leading the organization and refuse to do any political work in the name of having a long-term approach and preventing exposure. The other is to get rapidly exposed due to our desire to achieve 'quick results'. Both deviations should be avoided. The main problem in our fractional work so far however has been our lack of a long-term approach. Our mistakes range from excessive revolutionary rhetoric, to simple errors like singing Party songs or distributing Party literature without ascertaining the reliability of those whom we are giving the literature to. Though much experience exists in the international communist movement and though we ourselves have gained many lessons in practice, we have not yet successfully been able to internalize and implement these lessons in our day-to-day activity. Though we have recognized this error in our documents, we have to yet educate all levels to concretely bring this into practice. The in-depth participation of the leadership is necessary for this.

The crucial point is to achieve the correct balance of making the fullest use of the legal opportunities without crossing the boundaries set by social customs, habits, existing forms of struggle, etc. Our speech and actions should suit the normal functioning of the activists and masses in the particular area. This will of course vary from situation to situation. While it may not be abnormal to resort to gherao among many sections of industrial workers, we may have to restrict to black badges and dharnas for bank employees; while militant anti-dowry and anti-caste struggles may be normal in some areas and states, social norms in other states or areas may be such that they would draw immediate suspicion if we tried to engage in such struggles through cover organizations. We would probably have to restrict ourselves to propaganda in such situations. Thus we should plan our activities, and our issues and forms of struggle according to the concrete situation of the class struggle, so that our Party identity is not quickly suspected and exposed. We should of course not reduce ourselves to mere tails of the masses. We should be skillful enough to remain one step ahead of the masses, without getting exposed. We should use opportunities to push the struggle to the maximum socially acceptable limits, while raising the political consciousness of the masses above their earlier level. We should thus through a long-term approach continuously advance the movement.

Once we have implemented the correct approach and methods in our fractional work it can become a powerful tool in our urban work. This was widely used form of organizing in urban work in the Chinese Revolution.

3.3.1.4 Party-formed Cover Mass Organizations

It sometimes becomes necessary for us to directly form mass organizations under cover without disclosing their link with the Party. Mostly, such a need arises due to the absence of any other suitable mass organization within which we can do fractional work. An example is the case of unorganized workers, where the established trade unions have a limited presence and we often have no option but to set up our own trade union organization to take up the unorganized workers' demands. This however is not the only area where we may form cover organizations. In fact, cover organizations can be of as many varied types as the organizations for fractional work we have mentioned in the earlier section. They can range from trade union type struggle organizations to welfare type organizations to issue-based organizations, etc. The methods of mass work too are not very different from the areas of fractional work. The main difference is of course that we do not have the task of exposure, as when working within the reactionary and reformist organizations.

Wherever we form such cover organizations our programme will be of a limited nature, similar to other such organizations working in the area. While utilizing these cover organizations to mobilize the masses on their specific demands, we will try to draw the best elements into the Party.

We should be careful (especially in repression areas) not to attract the attention of the state by far exceeding the socially acceptable limits of militancy for that area. For example if the normal weapons used in the area are knives and swords we should not resort to firearms, or we should not normally resort to annihilations in a new area where there has not been any history of such actions.

We have had some experience of building cover organizations now since the last few years. We have committed various mistakes (mentioned in our POR) leading to the quick exposure of our forces in many areas. While learning from these mistakes we should inculcate the correct long-term approach to preserve such organizations for a long period of time while making them strong bastions of mass struggle.

3.3.1.5 Legal Democratic Organizations

These are the organizations formed on an explicit political basis with some or all aspects of an anti-imperialist, anti-feudal programme, and with a programme of action and forms of struggle that broadly fall within a legal framework. Some such organizations may be those catering to a particular section like trade unions, student bodies, women's fronts, caste abolition organizations, nationality organizations, writers' associations, lawyers' organizations, teachers' associations, cultural bodies, etc. Others may be formed with issue-oriented programmes focusing on particular core questions like contract labour system, unemployment and job losses, caste atrocities, communalism, imperialist culture, violence on women, saffronisation of education, corruption, regional backwardness and statehood, etc. The scope of the legal democratic organization is very wide, extending to the broad coalitions and alliances formed against repression, globalization, Hindutva, and right up to the all-encompassing bodies formed with the banners of anti-capitalism or people's struggles. Such organizations can be formed at various levels - town/city level, district level, state level, regional level, all-India level, or even at the international level.

Our Party has been initiating or participating in the formation of such organizations only since the last few years. Our experience thus has been limited. But rather than experience, the problem has more been the lack of a clear understanding regarding the concept, role and importance to the legal democratic organization. This has led to spontaneity, a trial and error approach, and mistakes in practice. This has resulted in our organizations remaining within a narrow base of support. It has prevented us from actually implementing in practice the full scope of the legal democratic organizations. It has prevented us from making the fullest use of legal opportunities for the widest mobilization of the masses.

Actually the legal democratic organizations serve as important means to the Party's attempts at the political mobilization of the urban masses. This is because repression normally prevents the open revolutionary mass organizations from functioning. The legal democratic movement is thus the arena where the masses can participate in thousands and lakhs and gain political experience. It thus has a very important role in the revolution, complementary to the armed struggle in the countryside. Revolutionaries in other countries, particularly the Philippines, have participated within and utilized the legal democratic movement very effectively. In India too there is excellent scope to participate within, build, promote and develop legal democratic organizations and movement to advance the interests of revolution. The masses suffering under the yoke of imperialism and feudalism, regularly participate in countless small or big, militant, day to- day struggles. Innumerable grassroots level organisations and leaders with a restricted perspective and functioning within a legal framework lead these. It is these struggles and organizations that provide the concrete material basis for the setting up of broad democratic organizations. And it is through the legal democratic movement that these struggles are brought out of their narrow confines, are unified, and gain political direction.

Thus it is necessary that our Party in the urban areas should give considerable importance to the task of participating in and building up a strong and broad legal democratic movement. We should join, form, or join in the formation of legal democratic organizations of various types - sectional, issue-oriented or broad-based; depending on necessity and feasibility, this can be at any level ranging from the town/area level to the all-India/international level. While taking up this task and allocating forces for it however, we must also guard against a tendency to overemphasize one-sidedly the sweeping mass mobilizations and struggles at the cost of the central tasks of consolidation and party building. The legal democratic movement itself too can grow from strength to strength and remain on the correct political course only if we concentrate sufficiently and simultaneously on developing the secret Party core within it. Thus while giving due importance to the legal movement, we should take care to maintain the correct dialectical balance between the needs and importance of the legal and illegal work, the open and the secret organization.

Maintaining relations between the open and secret also means strict adherence to tech precautions. This means protecting the Party leadership from exposure and danger, as well as protecting the legal leadership from being exposed as belonging to our Party. Meetings between open and secret leadership should as far as possible be avoided and guidance should normally be through written communication and other means which should be done by protecting the Party link. When a meeting has to take place, proper care should be taken that the legal comrades are not allowed. Similarly errors like meeting public figures in front of entire squads thus directly exposing their links, should be avoided.

Generally we should avoid exposing our Party's influence within a particular organization, as well as the identity of our PMs and other comrades close to us. However as its activities expand and intensify, we cannot prevent the enemy from growing suspicious, launching surveillance and indulging in harassment.

However, this does not mean that they will be able to easily launch full-scale repression and bring a ban. As long as the organization adheres to the principles of legal democratic functioning, and as long as it has a broad enough base of support, it will be difficult for the state to close it down.

The crucial central point in this however is the broadness of the organization. If we set up a narrow organization limited only to our Party forces, we cannot expect it to continue for long even if we use all tech precautions to conceal our identity. On the other hand, if broad sections of the masses are rallied and if a wide range of non-Party forces is united, the enemy will not be in such an easy position to suppress fully. Even if they launch attacks they risk the possibility of still wider protests and support.

However in order to achieve broad unity, it is necessary for us to have such an approach in whatever legal democratic effort we participate in. We should broaden our efforts far beyond the revolutionary camp and attempt to involve and unite with a wide spectrum of struggling forces on various fronts. A minimum political understanding for any organization should be the basis for our unification efforts. Our basic condition should be serious adherence to a minimum political programme. We should in fact target such organizations and individuals that are seriously committed to struggle and try to involve them in any effort at broad unity. If we have such an approach and are able to allocated suitable forces we will definitely be able to soon achieve much success. It is through such efforts that we will be able to see the legal democratic movement emerge as a powerful urban force, complementing the rural armed struggle and helping to advance the revolution throughout the country.

3.3.2 Organizing at the Place of Residence

Though the workplace organization is the primary organization of the workers, we should also pay attention to organize the workers within the slums and localities. Through this we can get contact with new workers from various industries, we can draw the families of the workers into the movement, and we can organize the semi-proletariat and other sections of the urban poor living in the slums and poor localities.

In slums and other poor localities there are already numerous traditional organizations in existence. Constantly living in precarious conditions, the urban poor naturally come together to help each other and unite within organizations to fight for their rights, to secure better living conditions, to solve problems among themselves and to better organize their social and cultural activities. The common types of traditional organizations are slum-dwellers organizations, basti or chawl committees, mahila mandals, youth clubs, sports clubs, cultural bodies, committees for various festivals like Ganesh festival, Durga puja, Ambedkar Jayanti, etc. There are also some organizations that are peculiar to certain regions, cities, and areas. Since such organizations offer the best cover we should try to make the best use of these traditional organizations and mainly work from within them. Even if there is a need to form new legal organizations, we should normally give them the forms already existing among the masses.

Struggle issues are a regular feature of locality work, particularly slum work. Fights for basic amenities like water, electricity, toilets and sewerage, against corruption and exploitation of ration shop owners, adulterators and black marketers, against slumlords, goonda gangs and other lumpens, and against demolitions are some of the regular issues. We should organize the struggles on these issues through the local committees and the slum-dweller organizations. As women and unemployed youth play a leading role in most of these struggles, the mahila mandals and youth clubs should also be involved and struggles can even be led under their banners.

Besides the above struggle issues and organizations, we should also pay attention to the welfare and cultural needs of the masses. We should make use of cultural bodies to promote democratic culture. We can also initiate the setting up of libraries and reading rooms that can provide progressive education. We should also pay attention to solving the contradictions among the people. Traditional forms like panchayats should be transformed and rid of feudal and exploitative practices.

We should always propagate and educate against the activities of the Hindu fascists. In areas prone to communal tensions we should set up permanent all community peace committees and open self-defence teams. Similar suitable steps may also be taken up in areas of caste or nationality based tensions. Self-defence should also be organized against the goondas and lumpens. If such teams are well organized, they can even play a role in leading the mass resistance at times of demolition.

A problem peculiar to slum work is the problem of imperialist funded NGOs. They are today in existence in almost all the slums of the main cities of the country. We should educate the slum masses and particularly the activists about the sinister role of such organizations and the agencies financing them. We should particularly expose them when they stand in the path of the people's struggles. However if such organizations come forward for struggles we can have issue-based unity with them. In situations of repression we can also work within them.

Through the traditional mass organizations, we can and should organize political propaganda, but it will be of a limited nature. For higher level of propaganda and mobilization we should use the legal democratic organization banners or can even affiliate some of the traditional organizations to these legal democratic organizations. Thus the issues of the slum can be broadened and linked to the broader fight against globalization and imperialism.

For propaganda on direct Party positions however we should use secret organizations like the secret revolutionary workers' organization and the secret revolutionary youth organization. They should however only be used while keeping in mind the precautions to prevent exposure of our locality work. Thus if the slum and locality work is very small and narrow, we should avoid propaganda by the secret organizations in such an area.

We should consolidate the activists emerging from the struggle first into basti activist groups and then into Party candidate cells and full cells. The basti activist groups, the Party cells and the basti Party committees are the cores for planning and leading all the activities and struggles in the bastis, for political propaganda and education, and for recruiting new members into the Party.

The situation of the urban poor in the slums and poor localities is worsening continuously. The slum population of India today stands at 4.1 cores, spread in 607 towns. The largest mega city, Mumbai, has 49% of its population in the slums. Our Party has so far paid limited attention to the organizing of this section. Other revolutionary parties, particularly the Peru Communist Party (PCP) have been particularly successful in this respect. In fact the shantytowns of Lima have been the strongholds of the revolutionaries for a long period. We too should work at creating such strongholds in India's major cities.

3.3.3 Party-Building

Mass struggles and mass organizations are absolutely necessary for preparing the masses for revolution. They however are not sufficient by themselves without the conscious consolidation and development of the vanguard - the Party. Thus the best elements that emerge through the struggles should go through a process of politicization in struggle, ideological and political education in activist groups, study circles and political schools, and consolidation into candidate and party cells. This process is relatively a slow painstaking process as compared to the spontaneous sweeping element of the mass movement. Consolidation cannot emerge by itself spontaneously without a conscious programme for it and consistent monitoring and implementation at all levels. In urban areas the Party cell is the crucial body for systematic and serious Party building. However all higher bodies must constantly follow-up and pay attention to this task

In the urban areas the main concentration has to be on the consolidation of the vanguard elements from the industrial proletariat class. This is doubly important considering the present weak working class composition of our Party. We have to thus concentrate on the struggles and organizations of the working class, both at the work place and in the bastis, and have a target of drawing the largest numbers of the best members of the working class into the party. Besides the working class, we should give importance to the consolidation from the semi proletariat, the students, the intellectuals and other sections of the petty bourgeoisie.

3.3.3.2 Activist Groups

The secret activist group is a crucial unit in the Party-building and recruitment process. It is the preliminary organizational form for consolidation of the most active and sincere elements emerging from the class struggle. It is the unit through which the activities of its members are given political direction, through which they receive ideological and political education, through which their life decisions are politicized, and through which they are chosen to become members of the Party.

The activist group may be formed at the workplace - factory, mine, industrial estate, shift, department, section, office, branch, or any other level which is a unit for organizing; it may be formed at the place of residence - the slum, chawl, street, society, or any other level which is a unit for organizing; it may be formed in schools, colleges, or other institutions; and where the organizing is based on a particular section, the activist group can be formed at the level suitable for that section.

The main basis for selection into the activist group is activity. All activist group members should be regular, or prepared to be regular, in activity. Other criteria are broad sympathy to revolutionary politics and steadfastness to the cause and interests of the section of the masses who are being organized.

The activist group will be built from the advanced elements within the masses. It should be formed as soon as possible after a certain level of activity. Depending on the concrete situation the group can consist of 3 to 7 members. Normally at least one capable PM should be given the responsibility for leading a particular activist group. This however should normally be without disclosing his/her identity as a PM.

The tasks and responsibilities of an activist group will differ concretely according to the field of work. However for all organizing among the basic masses these responsibilities can be broadly divided into 3 categories. **Firstly** there is the task of guiding and transforming the organizations of the masses into bodies genuinely representing the masses interests. If no mass organizations exist it should try to form such organizations. **Secondly** the group should be given the task of politicizing the broad masses. **Thirdly** it should organize their self-defence. These responsibilities should be discussed in the activist group and concretely allocated among the members.

While leading the group in the above responsibilities, it is the task of the PM in charge to conduct the ideological and political education of the group. While classes and joint study should be conducted, great importance should also be given to other more flexible methods like informal discussion, films, individual reading, etc. As the group develops, where feasible, there should be collective discussion on personal and family problems and this should be used to help the members to take political decisions in their personal life.

Through the above process some or all or even none of the activist group members may develop to become candidate members and members of the Party. This will lead to the formation of a cell in the same area where the activist group had been operating. Once such a cell has been formed, the activist group should be dissolved or reconstituted without exposing the cell-formation to the non-PMs. As far as possible an activist group and party cell should not simultaneously exist having parallel responsibility for the same unit at the same level - e.g. there should not be an activist group and a cell simultaneously for the same department within a factory, though there may be a cell for the whole factory and an activist group for the department at the same time.

Thus the activist group is a transitory form of organization. Its purpose is to facilitate the consolidation of the advanced sections of the masses and build them into the vanguard. If it is conducted in a systematic and planned manner it can play a crucial role in the Party-building process.

3.3.3.3 Political Education

Urban work activists and cadre function within the areas dominated by the enemy and are thus faced much more by alien class trends and the ideological influence of the bourgeoisie. Being normally distant from the zones of armed struggle there is a tendency to swing to extremes, deviating from our basic line. In situations when the urban movement is low there is the tendency towards despondency and lack of confidence in the revolutionary line. When the urban movement is on the upswing, there is the scope to overplay the importance of urban work and give less importance to the rural armed struggle. Such deviations can be prevented and rectified through continuous ideological and political education. There is thus always the need for solid and systematic education in Marxism-Leninism-Maoism and the line of protracted people's war? This is necessary not only for advancing the movement but also for fighting off the degenerative influence of the reactionaries.

Despite this need, political education in the urban Party is a much-neglected area. Independent organisers who remain for long periods out of the contact of the higher committees mostly conduct urban work. In the absence of systematic planning and follow up, the task of political education is thus left to the capabilities and initiative at the lower level. There is also thus a greater possibility of being caught up in the urgencies of the immediate practical work and neglecting the long-term ideological requirements. Another problem is the tech problem of conducting classes and schools in the city. While risks from the state can be reduced by better secrecy methods, there still remains the problem of conducting numerous small batches to prevent exposure of comrades working in different areas. Mixing comrades can sometimes reduce this problem of exposure from distant towns or even from different states, but this cannot always be the solution.

All this however implies that political education tasks in the city cannot be fulfilled without the active intervention of the higher committees. Courses, methods of conducting schools and taking classes, tech methods, training of teachers, plans for education at different levels - all require the personal attention of the higher committee members.

At the higher levels of AC and above it would be necessary, for the present, to systematically implement the programmes and courses decided by SCOPE. However in the future it will be necessary to develop special courses and training to particularly cater to the needs of urban work. One constant need, peculiar to urban work, would be that of developing the numerous teachers to take the number of small batches that urban work requires.

While thorough and continuous political education at the higher levels is the key to proper Party leadership, political education within the mass organizations and at the cell level is necessary to provide a sound foundation. The task of political education at these levels is all the more important in the urban areas because the normal area of activity for such comrades are the fractional and cover mass organizations where they cannot disclose their identity and where they have to constantly function among non-party forces and even ruling class elements.

Mass organizational education should use open forms of mass education for all topics permissible without attracting the attention of the state. We should try to adopt and adapt all locally prevalent forms used by the ruling classes and other classes. These can be like libraries, street corner reading posts and other such means which can be used to disseminate progressive literature among other general books; lecture series during festivals, debate competitions, elocution competitions, etc. where our comrades express progressive views; public speaking courses, personality development courses, etc. with political topics included in the syllabus; mass organization training camps, and the like. The level of political education possible through such methods will of course be very low, but it is very essential to be conducted on a regular basis to keep up a political atmosphere among even the more backward sections within the mass organization. For the more advanced sections we have of course to use different forums and methods - e.g. the activist group.

Political education for the activist group, candidate cells and party cells, will have to be planned at the level of the responsible committees. While education materials provided by SCOPE should be the basis, the committees should also select materials, which will suit the local urban conditions and also the particular sections being educated. While planning it must be kept in mind that the urban education system needs to be as decentralized as possible. This means that the courses and materials should be such that they can be easily implemented and used by the responsible organizers and PMs who will finally be performing the task of teachers. Where necessary they have to be given the attention and help to enable them to put the plan into implementation.

A well planned decentralized political education system, with sufficient teachers and regular follow-up from the committee is thus what every urban area requires.

3.3.4 Party Structure

The question of the Party structure in the urban areas presents quite different problems from that in the rural areas where our Party is based. These relate to the problem of building and running stable structures, the continuity of party leadership, the coordination between open and secret work, between lower and higher bodies, and between the city organization and the leadership based in the rural areas. We cannot resolve these problems without the close attention and study by the higher-level bodies and the development of concrete and practical solutions. We also require however a broad common approach on the objectives, tasks and methods to be adopted for building and advancing the urban Party structure.

The essential principle forming the basis of our Party structure, particularly in the urban area, is political centralization combined with organizational decentralization. This means that all PMs and all bodies, particularly at the lower level, should have solid ideological-political foundations, so that they are able to independently find their bearings and take the correct organizational decisions according to the political line of the Party. This is particularly important in the urban areas because of the technical difficulties of maintaining close and constant links between the secret higher bodies and those at the lower levels engaged in direct open work. This is also important because urban work often demands immediate and quick responses to the events of the day. With rapid advances in electronic communication and media, delays of days and sometimes even hours in politically reacting to major events can hinder the impact that our Party can have on the urban movement. This thus depends on the strength of the bodies that form the foundation of our urban Party structure - the cells and the lower level committees - as well as on the Party fractions that link the Party with the mass organizations.

3.3.4.1 Party Cell

The urban Party cell can be formed on the basis of unit of production—for workers this could be factory, shop, department, section, shift, production line, industrial estate, etc. for students and middle class employees it could be the college, school, institution, office, etc.; the cell can also be formed on geographical basis (i.e. the place of residence) - this would be the slum, chawl, street, society, etc. Wherever the number of PMs in a particular unit (e.g. factory) is less that three they can be combined with adjoining units to form a cell. However this should not be done indiscriminately in the urban areas as this would lead to unnecessary exposure. Where the work is integrated a common cell may be formed. In other cases it is better to wait for further recruitment before formation of a cell.

The cell is the body leading all other organizational units within its sphere of responsibility. It performs its basic tasks under the leadership of the next higher committee. **The basic tasks of the urban cell include organizing the masses, politicizing them, educating the advanced elements and recruiting them into the party, and preparing its members and other activists to go to the countryside to work for the success of the agrarian revolution.**

The cell should develop its own secret network of shelters and meeting places. As far as possible meetings should not be held in the areas where the members do their political work among the masses. Generally cell members should not be transferred from cell to cell as this would lead to unnecessary exposure.

Where there are at least three PRs functioning in an area and are known to each other, a Professional Revolutionary Cell (PRC) may be formed. The PRC however should not play the role of a Party committee and become a centre for planning the activity of the areas of all the PRs. This would result in unnecessary exposure of various structures and areas of work and could lead to losses. For the purpose of work planning, each PR can be a member of the cell responsible for his/her area of work. Where this is not possible, the planning should be done with the concerned organizer or committee member. The main function of the PRC is to provide the political training and development to the PR, which would not be possible within the time constraints and other limitations of a part timer cell. Longer political education programmes, collective study and debate, and other similar activities can be conducted through the PRC. Thus it can play a positive role in rapidly developing the future Party leadership. This advantage however should be balanced against the risks of exposure and losses in urban work. Thus if a PR is functioning in an unexposed area, or if he/she shows signs of vacillation, he/she should not be included in a PRC.

3.3.4.2 Part-Timer Party Committees

Wherever there are two or more cells functioning in a particular locality or unit of production we should take up the task of forming the Factory/Industrial Area Party Committee or Basti Party Committee or College Party Committee as the case may be. These may be composed completely of part timers, or may include PRs or may in come cases include organizer level comrades. This is the level of Party Committee between the Area Committee/Organizer and the cells. It is the body that leads and guides all the cells, candidate cells, party fractions and other bodies within its field of responsibility. It is the body that ratifies the recruitment of candidate members and decides their full membership.

The Factory/Basti Committee is a very important layer in the urban Party structure. It improves Party functioning by providing more day-to-day attention to the functioning of the party cells and other lower level bodies. It also reduces the risk to higher-level committees by providing another layer and eliminating the need for the higher committee member to always meet all the cells. Despite its importance we have not paid sufficient attention within our Party to developing this layer in the urban areas. We have as yet very few areas where such committees have been created and our experience is thus very limited. The main aspects we should concentrate upon while setting up these committees is proper selection of reliable committee members, stress on setting up a proper secret network for shelters, communication and meetings, and extreme care not to expose the identity of the committee members to all the PMs. Where necessary, precautions may also be taken while reporting, so that the actual identities of PMs and activists are protected. Generally we should adopt a long-term approach towards building such committees and sustaining for a long period of time. A proper network of such committees can considerably improve the functioning of our urban Party structure.

3.3.4.3 Party Fractions

Besides the cells and the Party committees, the Party sets up fractions in various non-Party organizations in order to ensure that members functioning within these organizations express a single will, pursue uniform tactics and act in harmony. They are the agencies through which the Party exercises influence over these organizations and carries through its policies. Since most of the work in the urban areas is done through non-Party organizations, properly functioning fractions are a very important part of the urban Party organization. They are necessary for uniting and coordinating the Party forces within the non-Party organizations and ensuring that they play a leading role.

The relevant Party committee may form fractions in any organization or executive body where there are at least three PMs. Where all the PMs are from a single cell there is no need to form a separate fraction as all the functions of the fraction can be performed by the cell. Similarly, if the main forces within a particular organization or executive are in one cell or Party committee, or due to some other practical considerations, the Party committee may decide not to form a fraction. However wherever the members are from various forums, or where the work of the organization is substantial, it is advantageous to form a fraction.

The fraction functions under the guidance and supervision of the relevant Party committee. Thus the fraction within a factory trade union committee will function under the Factory Party committee, whereas the city level trade union fraction will function under the Party City committee. The relevant Party committee decides to form the fraction with all or some of the PMs in that area. It also has the right to send PMs to the fraction and to recall any members of the fraction. Urban work may sometimes require that PMs who are very exposed and under surveillance be not included in the fraction forum, though they are playing a prominent role in the organization. This may also be necessary sometimes to protect the Party identity of a comrade. In such cases the Party committee should devise special means and methods of coordinating with such comrades and seeing that they function in unison with the fraction and according to the direction decided upon.

The Party fraction guides the work of the organization in which it operates. All questions coming up in the organization in which it is perating are discussed in the fraction. All PMs must speak and vote within the organization in accordance with the decisions taken by the fraction. Similarly it is the responsibility of the Party committees to work through the fractions to see that the whole organization is guided according to a single policy and plan.

3.3.4.4 *Layers*

Layers refers to the various levels in the urban Party organization like city committee, area committees, factory/basti/college committees, cells, candidate cells, as well as the links to the mass organizations like activist groups and fractions. Due to greater enemy threat in the urban areas it is always necessary to maintain a number of layers from the lowest to the highest levels, and it is important to work through these layers without bypassing them.

We have since some years now been stressing in our documents the need and the importance of functioning basically through layers. We have however not achieved much progress in this regard. Most city organizations have not concentrated on building sufficient layers, and even where some layers exist there is a tendency to deal directly with the lowest levels in order to obtain quick results. We must quickly get rid of such wrong notions and practices and develop a system of layers in every city.

The core question for functioning through layers is to see that each layer is trained and developed to independently perform the functions at the particular level. This requires the close guidance and follow-up of the next higher level. The guidance should be directed to developing the independent capabilities of the comrades at that level as well as the team functioning of the committee. This is the key to decentralized organizational functioning according to a centralized political line and policies. It is the only long-term approach to building a party structure that will preserve our cadre and leadership and develop the forces for the future.

3.3.4.5 *Coordination and Links with Other Party Structures*

Most of our city work, particularly in the guerilla zone areas, is coordinated and led from the rural areas. Even the DCM leading the city work is often based in the rural areas and periodically has to call the city comrades to the squad areas for discussing and planning the urban work. This results on the one hand in serious exposure problems, and on the other hand to insufficient guidance, without a deep understanding of the actual problems of the urban work.

Coordination therefore is best done through a Party structure of at least DC level that is based in the urban areas itself. In cities which are large enough and where the extent of work and the Party structure warrants it, the DC can be built in that city itself. In some states where the coordination problem is particularly acute due to repression, it can be done through a special sub-committee for urban work formed under the SC. Where the suitable leading comrades are very exposed, they could be allocated far away from their earlier areas, or even to other states. Another problem related to the urban Party structure is the links with the rural party organization as well as the functional departments of the higher Party bodies. There is often a need of urban help of various types, for which the urban organization involved in day to day mass work are regularly used. Such links on a regular basis is dangerous for all involved, as well as affects the regular functioning of the urban organization. Therefore it is important to put a stop to such short cut methods immediately. Separate structures not linked to the running urban organization should be set up in the cities for this purpose. Comrades can be transferred out of the urban organization and allocated these tasks.

Here too what is basically required is a long-term approach. We must realize that it is only through the implementation of systematic and long-term plans that we can build the different structures required, to mobilize the urban masses, to provide logistical and other help to the rural work, as well as for other requirements.

3.4 United Front

The urban areas are the centres for struggle by various classes, under the leadership of several organizations representing them. It is essential that we unite with such struggling organizations and build up broad struggles against the ruling classes Thus a significant part of the party's work in the urban areas concerns joint front activity. This includes the formation of various tactical united fronts, as well as building the worker peasant alliance, which is the basis of the strategic united front. This extends from the task of building basic working class unity, to solidarity with the peasantry, to unity with the other revolutionary classes like the semi-proletariat and petty bourgeoisie, right up to maintaining relations and even joint activity with national bourgeois and even ruling class organizations. Let us look at the main forms of such united front activity.

3.4.1 Working Class Unity

The working class is the main focus of concentration of our work in the urban areas. Since the working class is in an extremely divided state today, a crucial Party task is to build the broadest possible unity of the class. This task of unity is at two levels - one is to organize and unite the maximum possible numbers from the workers under genuine organizations that follow the democratic line and programme, the other to build a broad workers' united front against the present assault of the imperialist backed bourgeoisie on the rights and economic conditions of the working class. This means taking the initiative, or joining in other initiatives, to build united struggles on various issues like contract system, change in labour laws, privatization, exit policy, etc. It also means working towards building united organizations with all genuine forces within the working class movement who are ready to work for a broad anti-imperialist, anti-feudal programme.

Joint trade union fronts are important for increasing the fighting strength of the working class. These joint fronts may be issue-based or based on a minimum political understanding and programme. They may be organized at various levels - industry, area, city, region, all-India, and international.

Our policy is to be ready for issue-based unity with even the reactionary and revisionist unions, if they have a mass following and are ready to participate in the struggle. However a decision for temporary unity should not only be to serve the needs of the moment, but also to advance the long-term aim of drawing the mass of workers towards the revolution. The legal democratic working class joint front organizations can play a very useful role in achieving this long-term objective. It is such organizations that form the democratic nucleus within the broader unity with the reactionaries. If these organizations function effectively they can rally around larger sections of the working class on a democratic programme. They can play the leading role within the broad issue-based united fronts. They can utilize the temporary alliances with the reactionary unions to serve the interests of the democratic programme. They can inspire, mobilize and unite the other revolutionary classes in the urban areas on an anti-feudal, anti-imperialist programme.

3.4.1.1 Industry-Based Unity

Due to the multiplicity of unions in India, in most industries there is very low possibility of achieving the 'one industry, one union' principle. In such a situation we should work for or support the next best option of forming co-ordination committees of the unions within a particular industry. We should try to draw all the unions with significant membership into such bodies. Such unity can start on issue basis and can later advance to a more permanent minimum understanding.

Similarly it is necessary to unite the various factory level unions within a particular company. Such unity can start at the co-ordination committee level or be formed as a federation.

In the present globalization scenario where the production in one country is easily transferred across international borders, international workers' unity is also very important and necessary. Such unity is today very weak. We should however support initiatives for building the international unity of workers within a single multinational or within a particular industry. Even where it is not possible to give the unity an organizational form we should push for solidarity struggles and strikes and do propaganda in this regard.

3.4.1.2 Issue-Based Unity

These are joint fronts of various unions and political organizations formed to oppose particular policies or actions of the government or to take up particular trade union, social or political issues. Our approach in such joint fronts is to build the broadest possible struggling unity of all organizations that have a minimum common stand on the issue. At the same time there should be no compromise on basic principles. Very often joint front bodies tend to become ineffective top-heavy bodies, or forums for endless debate. Our approach should be to see that the joint front builds the broadest possible unity of the masses and is not merely the joint front of a few leaders. The attempt should be to take the masses forward in militant struggle and politicize them in the process.

We should within these fronts pay due attention to both unity and struggle. While the requirements of unity require some level of adjustmen with the reformists, revisionists, and reactionaries, in the formulation of demands, we should constantly prepare the masses and struggle against any attempt by them to betray the struggle.

When there is a wide range of different political forces within a joint front, we should establish co-ordination with those who have a closer common understanding so as to act in unison with a common approach and line of action. Such co-ordination can be on the basis of relations with other parties of the communist revolutionary camp or through existing legal democratic organizations having a common programmatic basis or on any other basis.

3.4.1.3 Area-Based Unity

This unity can be for an industrial area, town/city, region, state, all-India etc. Unity in a particular industrial area or locality may be restricted to only putting up a common front against problems faced by the workers of the area like goondas, transport, sanitation, water, etc. However area unity at higher levels is normally based on some minimum political understanding. It is the unity of like-minded unions and other bodies, who agree to struggle together to achieve a common set of demands or issues or stand by common political goals. This is thus the most common type of legal democratic workers' organization.

We should give considerable importance to such type of unity. In the present struggles against globalization the scope and need for such unity is constantly growing. We should direct our efforts to make this unity as broad-based as possible by pushing for the regular and wide mobilization of the masses. At the same time we should pay simultaneous attention to consolidating the activists emerging from these mobilizations. We should thus while planning at the local level allocate forces both for leading such fronts and organizations, as well as for the tasks of consolidation and party building within the movement.

3.4.1.4 Workers' Platforms

Another form of uniting the working class on a political basis is to directly form legal democratic workers' organizations as forums or platforms with a minimum workers' programme. Such platforms do not principally attempt to unite the unions, but target the worker activists of various unions and attempt to rally them politically. Such bodies use meetings, demonstrations, talks, seminars, cultural programmes and various means of propaganda to draw the advanced sections from among the workers on a political basis. They should also mobilize for agitations and struggles on political and other issues. The aim should be to draw the widest possible non-Party forces who can be united around the programme.

Another variation of this form is to use the banner of a workers' cultural organization or workers' magazine as a platform for unity. Here the programme of the platform is widely propagated and worker activists encouraged to perform cultural programmes, or to write articles and reports for the magazine, to distribute it, etc. and to participate in preparing and mobilizing the masses in struggles.

There are thus several various forms of uniting the worker masses. We cannot of course attempt to implement all forms in a particular area. The relevant committees should therefore decide on the suitable methods depending on the objective situation in their area and the subjective forces available. What is important however is to recognize the importance of this ask, particularly during the present upsurge of workers struggles and therefore to allocate necessary forces for it.

3.4.2 Worker-Peasant Alliance

This is the basis of the four class strategic united front and we should therefore work towards building and strengthening this alliance right from the very beginning. The aim is to generate workers' support to the peasant struggles and build up the closest possible links between the two most important classes of the democratic revolution.

The work of building and strengthening the worker-peasant alliance should be taken up from all areas of our working class work. The stress on particular aspects may however differ according to the area of work. Thus in metropolitan cities somewhat delinked from the rural areas and from the agrarian struggle, a major concentration will be on continuous education and propaganda to raise the consciousness of the workers. In the towns in and near the guerrilla zones where the worker and peasant masses are closely linked, the focus can be on concrete issues and practical help to the movement. Various organizations too perform different roles.

The revolutionary workers' organization has a particularly important role to play. It has to take on the main responsibility of propaganda and agitation regarding the agrarian war. Constant and continues propaganda regarding the progress of the rural movement, the victories achieved, and the repression it faces, and the need for solidarity of the workers with this movement should be an essential part of the work of this organization. Since the organization has to normally function secretly it will not be possible to organize open solidarity demonstrations by the workers. However the revolutionary organization activists can use the method of secret shock actions for propaganda purposes to highlight issues concerning the agrarian struggle.

The legal democratic worker organizations can be the forums through which open mobilizations of the workers are organized. Forms of such mobilizations can extend from signature campaigns to solidarity demonstrations and protest actions. These should be organized in support of the revolutionary movement as well as the peasant struggles led by non-revolutionary organizations. We should however not organize open demonstrations in support of our movement if we expect the mobilization to be low, as it will only result in the exposure of our forces. We should in fact plan such actions in order to mobilize non-Party forces in large numbers. Another type of programme, which can be taken up through the legal democratic organizations, is large joint mobilizations of workers and peasants on common issues like WTO, state repression, etc.

Worker-peasant alliance work can also be taken up through the trade unions. Where possible they can mobilize and participate in the programmes of the legal democratic organization with or without its own banner. Depending on the cover other programmes can also be taken up - like education regarding the exploitation and repression in the backward rural areas, aid teams during disasters, support statements to peasant struggles of various organizations, etc.

The industrial Party committees should regularly pay attention and follow up the implementation of such tasks. Depending on changes in the situation, new and more creative methods should be worked out. Party statements and calls to the workers should be issued when the situation demands. However, whatever be the level of worker-peasant alliance activity possible, it holds central importance in our united front tasks. It should not be neglected, given secondary importance or subordinated to the other united front tasks in the city.

3.4.3 Unity of the Urban Exploited Classes

Besides the working class, the other exploited classes and sections of the urban areas include the semi-proletariat, the urban poor concentrated in the slums, the students, teachers, employees, and other sections of the middle classes, etc. The Party sends its cadre to organize and lead the mass organizations of all these classes. This however is not the only way by which the working class and its Party unites and provides leadership to all these classes. Solidarity struggles and united front activity are the important means by which the working class inspires and leads all other classes in struggle.

Propaganda and agitation on issues and incidents of repression on various other urban classes are the main means by which the working class and the Party expresses its solidarity with the affected sections. Issues can be of several types - the eviction of hawkers, demolition of slums, suppression of student rights, funds for teachers' salaries, etc. While it may not be possible to hold a solidarity action on every such issue, the Party should be ever alive and respond in whatever manner possible - propaganda pamphlet, poster, press statement, or dharna, demonstration, or some more militant action. Our main effort however should always be to draw the masses of workers out in solidarity.

The other medium through which the urban united front is built is through joint fronts on various issues concerning the general mass of the urban population, like price rise, corruption, closure of a key industry or many industries, or various urban problems like water shortage, commuter problems, sanitation issues, etc. Such issues unite all classes but mainly involve the exploited sections. The joint fronts on such issues may be issue-based or may built as legal democratic organizations on a political basis linking the issue to the democratic programme.

Such tactical united fronts draw larger sections of the urban masses closer to the revolution and pave the way for bringing them into the purview of the strategic united front.

3.4.3.1 Unity with the Semi-Proletariat

The semi-proletariat, living in extremely poor conditions, is the urban class with the greatest potential for unity with the proletariat. In recent years the new economic policies have led to a steep rise in their numbers. Many workers are being thrown into the ranks of the semi-proletariat and many rural migrants who come in search of jobs end up in petty trades or in doing sundry odd jobs. Because of their dispersed nature they are not as well organized as the proletariat. It is therefore the task of Party to organize this class and build about its close unity with the industrial workers.

a) **Trade Unions of the Semi-Proletariat:** In many towns and cities these sections remain completely unorganized. According to our subjective forces and town plan we can take up the task of building their organizations. Hawkers' unions, head-loaders and hamal unions and panchayats, rickshaw pullers unions, auto-rickshaw and taxi drivers/ owners unions, rag-pickers unions, are some of the organizations that can be formed. Since the capitalist class does not directly employ the semi-proletariat, the enemy is normally the state through the various government authorities, municipal bodies, etc. Issues concern harassment and corruption of officials, imposition of unjust taxes, fights for increase in rates, fight against eviction, etc. Some sections like market hamals and rag pickers have demands directed against particular groups like traders, scrap dealers, etc.

Due to the dispersed nature of the workforce and the lack of a proletarian sense of organization, building the unity of these sections is a painstaking and full-time task. However once organized they prove to be militant fighters.

In most towns and cities where these sections remain unorganized, work in these sections will involve the setting up of cover unions. In the large cities where they are already organized we can take up fractional work.

b) **Solidarity with the Semi-Proletariat:** In many large cities, particularly those aspiring to become 'global' cities, some major sections of the semi-proletariat are under heavy attack. Hawkers particularly face intensive eviction drives and harassment of officials. Auto-rickshaws and taxis are accused of pollution. The courts, anti-people environmentalists and the reactionary media are also targeting them. They are accused of obstructing the drives of these elements for 'clean and green' cities. Though they fight militantly they are often isolated in their battles. It is therefore of utmost importance that the workers' unions should express solidarity with hawkers and such other sections. The legal democratic workers' organizations too should organize campaigns in their support and expose the anti-poor urban plans of the development authorities and imperialist agencies.

Another area of unity of the workers and the semi-proletariat is in slum work. These two classes are the main sections of the urban poor who live in the slums and poor localities. Besides the basti struggles where both classes fight side by side, the trade unions and other workers organizations too should organize solidarity actions.

Where possible, alliances to oppose the current reactionary trend of urban development should also be set up, involving slum dweller associations, hawkers organizations, trade unions, and even groups of progressive professionals and intellectuals. While uniting all directly affected sections they should also aim to educate the middle class sections who are inclined to get misled by the 'clean and green' propaganda of the ruling classes. The aim should be to build broad unity of all exploited sections against the anti-people programmes of globalizes.

3.4.3.2 White-Collar Employees

The rapid spread of computerization and automation in modern industry and increasing share of the services sector in the economy has resulted in a significant increase in the number and proportion of white-collar employees. A large number of them are in the public sector and they are mostly unionized. Examples are the unions of the banks, insurance companies, teachers, government employees, etc. There has also been a more recent growth of unions and associations of higher level employee professionals like electricity, telecommunications and other department engineers, resident doctors, pilots, etc. Many of the above unions are powerful and have shown their ability to hit and paralyze the economy.

While all the white-collar employees are reliable allies of the working class and the revolution, certain sections sometimes tail the bourgeoisie and become victims of reactionary propaganda. It is therefore necessary for the industrial proletariat to always maintain close links with the employees' section and lead it away from vacillations in the class struggle. In all industries and enterprises we should therefore always struggle for unity of both white collar and blue-collar sections into one union. We should generally oppose the backward practice of having separate 'workers' and 'employees' unions. Where separate unions exist however, we should, where possible, allocate forces for fractional work within them.

In the globalization period the ruling classes have launched a concentrated propaganda attack against this section as an overpaid, under worked section whose salaries and numbers should be reduced. Thus some sections are being forced to agree to very meager rises in salary and cuts in earlier allowances. They have also been the target of various privatization and VRS schemes. Though they have been struggling continuously they often do not receive the sympathy and support of other sections. Our workers' unions, legal democratic and secret workers organizations, and sometimes even the Party should make it a point to express solidarity in various ways with the struggles of the bank employees, teachers, journalists, etc. When joint trade union bodies are formed at the town/city level we should try to draw in all the local branches of the employees unions. This can help in organizing joint programmes and mutual solidarity during times of repression and struggle.

3.4.3.3 Other Sections of the Petty Bourgeoisie

Some section or the other of the petty bourgeoisie is often in struggle. The students come out in agitations, the lawyers resort to strikes; the shopkeepers also have their protests and bandhs. When these struggles take a militant turn they face the attacks of the state. The working class should be alive to the struggles of these sections. We should, through the trade unions, legal democratic organizations and even the Party, express solidarity. Where possible we should not restrict ourselves merely to statements of support. During major struggles and repression we should make all attempts to mobilize the workers in large numbers to come out on the streets in support. Where there is sufficient support we should attempt to widen the scope of the issue and involve as many sections as possible in support.

Among the urban petty bourgeoisie students and youth constitute important category. They react to the events and historically from the anti-British movement they played a significant role. In the wake of Naxalbari their role is exemplary. Our party has good experience in organizing them. While working in urban areas, we must pay necessary attention to organize them.

There is need to emphasize the necessity of uniting with intellectuals. We need to allot sufficient cadre to work among them and some special effort be put in to unite and organize them.

3.4.4 Relations with the National Bourgeoisie

Due to the vacillating and exploitative nature of the national bourgeoisie, its wide participation in the strategic united front generally takes place only at later stages in the revolution. However there is scope in the urban areas, for supporting or uniting with various sections of the national bourgeoisie in tactical united fronts.

A large part of our working class work is in the small industries of the national bourgeoisie in the unorganized sector. They are often the immediate enemies of the workers that we organize. It is thus often difficult for the mass of workers to accept the concept of support or unity with these exploiters and 'enemies'. It is however a reality that the national bourgeoisie is coming out in struggle against the government, imperialism and the CBB. We should render all support to them in this struggle and wherever possible even unite to wage common battle against the ruling classes.

A normal method of uniting with the national bourgeoisie is for the Party to directly or indirectly through some mass organisation declares support to the demands and struggles of the national bourgeoisie against the government, imperialism or/and the comprador bourgeoisie. These can be on various issues like reduction of taxes, cut in electricity rates, anti small industry policies and court decisions, protest against entry of multinationals and foreign goods, exploitation of ancillary producers by big industry, etc. Our support can take the form of propaganda or even extend to militant mobilizing of workers on the issue.

Another mode of unity could be through joint front bodies with national bourgeois organizations. Mostly such unity will be issue-based like preventing relocation or closure of industries, opposing anti small industry laws and tax increases, etc. However as the anti-globalization and anti-WTO movement picks up we will have to try our best to draw the more progressive sections and organizations of the national bourgeoisie into the movement

While making efforts in bringing the national bourgeoisie in opposing and imperialism, such unity can on no account be achieved at the cost of the basic classes within the united front. Thus while uniting with the national bourgeoisie we should never lose sight of the struggle aspect of our relationship with them. We should not have any misconception that unity with the national bourgeoisie implies concessions in trade union struggles with these sections. All such issues will be decided according to the normal principles of trade union struggle and will basically depend on the relative strength of the contending forces and the overall conditions of the industry where the struggle is taking place. It is the strength of the working class and not its weakness that will be the force attracting the national bourgeoisie to the front.

The ceaseless attacks of the imperialists and their Indian agents are daily pushing the national bourgeoisie into more conflict with the ruling classes. Thus today the practical possibilities of unity from below are growing. These possibilities are greater in cities with a stronger national bourgeois presence like the Delhi belt, the Coimbatore-Erode belt in Tamil Nadu, Surat in Gujarat, etc. Local party organizations should where possible utilize such opportunities, while keeping in mind the above principles.

3.4.5 Front Against Repression

The PR and POR adopted by the Ninth Congress have given the call to mobilize the masses against the fascist repression of the ruling classes and against the black laws. All sections of the masses in the urban areas face the brunt of this repression and stand opposed to it. It is therefore the task of the Party in the urban areas to unite all forces that are ready to wage militant struggles to oppose these policies and build a broad democratic movement against repression.

The organizations that most consistently oppose state repression and black laws are the various civil liberties organizations active in different parts of the country. We can work to some extent through them. They however have a poor mass base and limited political programme. Thus, while we should work to broaden and strengthen such organizations they cannot be the only forums for building the front against repression.

Fronts against particular black laws like POTA have the potential of uniting the widest sections. We should initiate or may join such fronts with our own programme. Since such fronts are formed at various levels we can intervene in different fronts through separate cover organizations suited for such work. Some of these fronts however have various ruling class forces and parties with a long record of suppressing people's movements. We should therefore decide on our participation only if we are able to conduct vigorous exposure of such opportunist forces. Since such exposure is normally only possible at the lower levels we should not participate at the higher levels where we would only become a pawn of such forces.

Another excellent form of building broad fighting unity against repression is to take up particular cases of brutal state repression and immediately mobilize all sections of the masses in militant struggle. Police firings, lock up deaths, rape by security forces, are some of the examples that can be used to rouse the masses into open battle. There have been many instances like the Rameeza Bee case and others, where such incidents proved to be the turning points for building not only militant struggle but also much broader democratic movements. In some cases where the above methods lead to broad movements we can work with others for the formation of organizations of a more long-term nature with a broad anti-fascist repression programme.

3.4.6 United Front Against Hindu Fascist Forces

An important call of the Ninth Congress is to build a broad UF of all secular forces and persecuted religious minorities such as Muslims, Christians, and Sikhs against the Hindu fascist forces. Since a large proportion of the minorities are urbanized and since the attacks of the Hindu fascists are as yet mostly concentrated in the cities, this UF has basically been the responsibility of the urban organization. This task has appeared in our documents now from many years, but very little has as yet been done. One of the explanations for this failure is the weakness of our urban organizations, but the other more important reason is our neglect of work among the minorities.

The above UF cannot be built merely by uniting some secular individuals on the basis of a political programme. In order to be effective it has to involve the masses, particularly the masses from the minorities. This therefore means that we must have substantial grassroots work among the minorities, particularly the Muslim masses who are the most numerous and the worst victims of the Hindu fascists' atrocities. However due to extreme ghettoisation in almost all Indian cities, this is only possible if we take a conscious decision to shift out at least some forces from Hindu dominated areas and base them in the slums and localities inhabited by the Muslim poor. This would be the first step to building any united front..

The actual UF organizations would generally be in the form of legal democratic bodies uniting various genuine secular forces as well as organizations of the persecuted minorities. Such organizations should have a programme basically targeting the Hindu fascist organizations and aiming to unite the masses of all communities. We should on this basis conduct propaganda and agitation among both minority and majority sections and attempt to unite the many to isolate and defeat the few Hindu fascist diehards. Booklets and other propaganda aids explaining the organizations' stands and exposing the fascist organizations' positions should be used. In areas with a history of communal conflicts, genuine peace committees, mohalla committees, and all-community protection teams should be set up.

Issue based joint front organizations can also be built. These could be to fight for the punishment of the perpetrators of pogroms on the minorities, to oppose Hindu communal legislation, to fight against the saffronisation of education, etc. These fronts too should have a mass approach and attempt to widely mobilize secular sections, as well as those most affected.

As the Hindu fascists push ahead with their agenda, the task of building this UF becomes all the more urgent. All urban organizations should plan concretely to bring this into practice.

3.4.7 Front Against Globalization, Liberalization and Privatization

This too is a call of the Ninth Congress whose implementation requires considerable efforts by the Party organization in the urban areas. As the globalization policies are impacting all sections of the urban masses, discontent is growing and there is great potential for the urban areas to become powerful centres of anti-imperialist struggles. Though the struggles have not yet reached the heights of the anti-capitalism and anti-globalization protests in many cities around the world, the movement in India too is growing. The industrial working class is the leading force in these struggles, with numerous demonstrations, rallies, bandhs and long drawn out strikes, against privatization, changes in labour laws, contract system, exit policy, and other aspects of the globalization policies. These struggles, which took an upturn from the year 2000, have not only been increasing in size and intensity, but also been taking clearer political positions against the WTO, against globalization, and even against imperialism.

The line of action for building anti-globalization fronts should thus rely primarily on the working class, while rallying around all other sections in the struggles against the imperialist policies. Thus we should aim at drawing the different working class fronts against the various anti-worker policies into the front against globalization. Similarly the anti globalization fronts should consciously give importance to workers' issues in their programmes.

Other classes and sections of importance we should try to draw into the anti-globalization front are the peasants' organizations and the farmers' bodies, slum bodies, students organizations, intellectuals, writers and cultural activists, pro-people environmental groups, teachers and other middle class employees associations etc. The scope of the anti-globalization movement is so large that it includes practically all classes who are part of the strategic UF. While the separate organizations formed by these sections against various aspects of globalization objectively form part of the movement, we should nevertheless try to draw all such organizations into common united struggle on a common anti-imperialist programme.

Reactionaries like Swadeshi Jagran Manch, revisionists like CPI, CPI (M) and foreign funded NGOs- are some of the forces involved in anti-globalization movement. These forces are linked to the ruling classes or part of them. We must keep away from the reactionaries in any joint front. With regard to the revisionists who are part of ruling classes, we our selves should not invite them into any joint front, but if they are part of a front called by others, we need keep away because of their presence. The revisionists and foreign funded NGOs may participate to some extent but there is always danger of them attempting to sabotage the movement at higher levels of struggles. We must alert to this danger.

The front against the globalization has the potential to encompass a wide range of forces. The urban Party organization should thus plan concretely to participate most effectively in this movement.

3.5 Military Tasks

As explained earlier, the urban movement plays a secondary and complementary role in the military strategy of the revolution. While the PGA and PLA in the countryside perform the main military tasks, the urban organization too performs tasks complementary to the rural armed struggle. Due to the spread of urbanization, the growth of a number of mega cities, and the sharper division of the cities into rich and poor sections, the possibility and importance of urban military operations increases. These however yet remain second to the rural military tasks. The varied military tasks performed in the urban areas relate to, 1) the defence of the urban movement, 2) help by the urban organization to the rural armed struggle, and 3) direct military operations conducted under central direction. These thus form the main categories of military tasks and forms of organization in the urban areas.

3.5.1 Defence of the Urban Movement

The nature of urban work being primarily legal and defensive, the military tasks directly related to the urban movement are basically defensive in nature and will remain that way till the final period of the evolution. However even a defensive urban movement requires the military type organization of the armed defence of the urban masses against the peoples' enemies. These enemies are of various types - goonda gangs acting in the service of the ruling classes, Hindu fascist organizations and their militias, vigilante gangs specifically organized by the state to attack activists and sympathizers of our movement, state forces themselves, etc. Without standing up to such forces it would not be possible for an organization to survive and develop. While we cannot and should not, at this stage, organize for armed offensive confrontation with the state, we should definitely build such defence organizations as are suited to the concrete situation.

3.5.1.1 Open Self Defence Teams

Wherever necessary the legal organizations should organize defense against the local enemies. Examples of such self-defence teams are union self defence against lumpen strike breakers, basti self defence teams against goonda gangs, mahila organization self defence teams against eve-teasers and molesters, mohalla all-community self defence during communal riot situations, mass self defence against slum demolition, etc. Open self-defence teams should be organized in such a way as to mobilize sizeable sections of the masses in this task, particularly motivating the youth to participate in large numbers. When such defence is organized systematically involving the broad masses, it greatly strengthens the legal organization, gives confidence to the rank and file and the local leadership, and releases the creative energies of the masses. If such activity grows in an area it gives rise to new creative forms of militant mass fighting. Conversely, it demoralizes and paralyses the enemy, and prevents him from using his old forms of repression.

Often such open self-defence is organized on a temporary basis for a particular situation or period. However wherever possible we should plan and attempt to give this mass self defence a permanent form and structure, allocating specific responsibilities, and linking with the mass organizational committees. Such bodies can run vyayamshalas, martial arts centres, sports clubs, etc.

3.5.1.2 Secret Self Defence Squads

Secret squads are necessary to supplement the open defence teams, or where, due to repression, it is not possible to form such teams. They too are formed with the broad objective of defending the urban mass movement. However they take up different tasks, without exposing themselves. One significant form of activity is to participate along with the masses and give them the confidence to undertake militant mass action. Other tasks are to secretly hit particular targets who are obstacles in the advance of the mass movement.

The secret squads require proper military training, and military and political education. The extent and depth of the training will depend on the facilities available, but we must make the best efforts to ensure that the squads are properly trained and armed. The arms used will depend on the situation in the area. As far as possible arms which are not normally used in the area should not be employed.

Due attention should be paid to the discipline of such squads. Selection of members should not be merely on the basis of military abilities, but should consider the political level and discipline of the comrades. All squad members maintain their jobs or other responsibilities and only combine for the purpose of training or actions. They disperse again immediately after that.

The squads should function under direct and strict party control, with each squad functioning under a responsible Party comrade. As far as possible no two squads should be combined for performing an action. The knowledge of existence of such squads too should be as restricted as possible. Each squad is a separate entity and there should not be any separate line of command within the self-defence squads. All State committees should periodically review the activities of such formations and give guidelines to the committees immediately responsible for them.

3.5.1.3 Urban Militia

At this stage of the revolution all the open and secret organs of people's defence will maintain a separate identity and the Party will be the only body coordinating their activities. Today there is no scope for bringing together all or many of the self defence teams and squads under a single organizational mechanism to form a militia. This may be possible during certain periods of upsurge when significant sections of the urban population are ready to take up arms either against the fascist militias or against the state. At such times the Party should take immediate initiative to launch urban militia without exposing all its forces. The concrete organizational form of such an urban militia would however depend on the particular situation and the specific forces operating at that time.

3.5.1.4 Local Intelligence

Intelligence is a much-neglected function in our Party. Very often we suffer severe losses, or lose good opportunities due to the absence of proper intelligence. In the urban areas intelligence is also very necessary to protect and preserve the urban Party as well as the mass movement. Thus the task of information collection and analysis should be taken up from the beginning itself and responsibility should be allocated accordingly. As the organization grows this task and responsibility should exist at all levels and should be integrated into the functioning of the organization.

The objectives of our intelligence work should be to learn about and study the tactics and plans of the enemy forces in the area, to study the activities of informers, to prevent infiltration into the organization, etc. The methods and structure, particularly at the lower levels, should be as simple as possible and should utilize to the maximum the forces available to us from among the masses.

3.5.2 Help to the Rural Armed Struggle

There are numerous ways through which the urban movement can assist the rural armed struggle and particularly, the base areas and the guerilla zones. Some involve direct and immediate help in terms of materials and personnel; others involve the long-term preparation for the decisive battles in the later stages of the peoples' war.

3.5.2.1 Work in Key Industries

Some industries like transport, communications, power, oil and natural gas, defence production, etc. can play a crucial role in the peoples' war. Disruption of production in these industries has an immediate impact on the enemy's ability to fight the war. If struggles in such industries are coordinated with developments in the peoples' war they can provide direct assistance to the PGA/PLA. Party led units within such industries can also perform industrial sabotage actions, which would provide effective assistance during certain points in the war. It is thus the responsibility of the urban organization to establish a presence and influence in such key industries.

Such operations will normally be necessary at later stages in the war. However we have to make long term preparations from today itself so that the workers in such industries can be sufficiently politicized to play such a role. This means that we have to give importance to allocation of cadre for such industries right from the beginning.

The key industries have normally been in the public sector. Now however with the policy of privatization, many of the old units are being privatized and new units are being set up directly in the private sector. Thus some of these industries, like the electricity boards and telecommunications department, are experiencing many militant struggles

in opposition to the privatization policies and there has been a significant revival of the trade unions. In the context of the general upswing of the workers' movement, the workers of other key industries too are resorting to struggle. We can therefore make use of this situation to try and influence the workers in these industries.

Our plan for the key industries should operate at two levels. At one level we can influence the workers in these industries from outside through various forms of propaganda, particularly during the struggles of these industries. This can be done through legal democratic workers' organizations, workers' magazines, and secret pamphleteering and even through Party statements. We can also mobilize in solidarity with them. This method can create some broad influence among the workers and a level of unity from above with the trade unions already operating within these enterprises.

At another level we should send comrades to secretly develop fractional work from within the industry. This work should be done with a long-term approach taking care to avoid exposure. The comrades doing propaganda and extending solidarity from outside need not know about the existence of the work being conducted from within. It is also not necessary to do work at both levels at the same unit.

Due to the critical character of these industries, the enemy too is very conscious of the need to prevent any revolutionary or other genuine struggling forces from entering such industries. We therefore have to be very guarded and careful while entering and working within such enterprises. All work in such places should be under cover of some sort. Fractional work is the normal method. The work in such industries should normally be separated from the other work in the area. Even reporting in committees should be restricted, particularly at the initial stages, before any base is established. Cadre allocated to such work should not be such as would quickly retreat. Once allocated they should not normally be transferred for a long period of time. PRs generated from such industries should as far as possible be maintained within the same industry, without asking them to leave their jobs.

Considering the present opportunities available and considering our neglect so far, we should plan to use our limited subjective forces immediately in the best way possible. Depending on our contacts and the quality of our forces we should decide on certain areas and industries on which we should concentrate. Since such work is not easy to start and maintain it requires the attention and guidance of the higher levels. Considering the importance of this task for the future of the people's war, the State Committees should pay attention to it.

3.5.2.2 Infiltration into the Enemy Camp

It is very important to penetrate into the military, para-military forces, police, and higher levels of the administrative machinery of the state. It is necessary to obtain information regarding the enemy, to build support for the revolution within these organs, and even to incite revolt when the time is ripe. Other types of technical help are also possible.

The cities are the strongholds of the enemy and have a large concentration of enemy forces. It is therefore from the cities that attention must be given to this task. Such work can be done by following up contacts obtained from the civilian sphere, or by directly allocating comrades to penetrate the enemy ranks. Whatever be the method, the work is of a very special type, which requires a high degree of political reliability, skill and patience. Such work should be without the knowledge of the lower level committees and the details of the work should only remain with the comrades directly responsible.

Associated with this task is the need for a plan to work in the cantonment towns spread out throughout the country. Such work even among the civilian population of these towns can give us valuable information and openings for penetration in the enemy ranks.

3.5.2.3 Sending Cadre to the Rural Areas and the PGA/PLA

A steady supply of urban cadre is necessary to fulfill the needs of the rural movement and the people's war. This is necessary for providing working class leadership, as well as technical skills to the people's war.

This then is the responsibility of the whole urban Party organization, from the cell upwards, which should inspire comrades to be prepared to take up rural responsibilities. The task of generating new cadre for the rural movement should always be before the various Party forums, which should send up such proposals for transfer of suitable cadre. It is the higher-level bodies, particularly the State Committees, which will however take the decision in this regard. Decisions of transfer of cadre should take a balanced account of the needs of the movement and organization in both rural as well as the urban areas.

To fulfill the need of recruitment from workers in large numbers and sending them to rural areas, we need to work in the unorganized sector where overwhelming percentage of working class is there. While we need to work in key industries, which are organized sector for the strategic reasons, we must mobilize and organize millions of workers who are in the unorganized segment. The working conditions are horrendous in this sector and militant struggles are bound to come up here. Most of the working class has live connections with backward rural pockets, in some of which already armed struggles are going on. If we work patiently we can get good recruitment that we can send to the areas of armed struggle zones.

3.5.2.4 Logistical Support to the Armed Struggle

The enemy gets all its logistics support from the urban areas. The People's Army however relies as far as possible on the rural areas and the rural masses. However for certain crucial things there is need for support from the urban areas. Depending on its strength, the urban organization should make all efforts to provide such support.

Supplies or contacts for supplies of certain types are only available in the urban areas. Examples of such supplies are arms and ammunitions, spare parts, certain types of medical supplies, etc. Helping the People's Army to establish the supply lines in this regard is a task that the urban organization can perform. However once such a supply line is established it is best maintained by the rural organization. As the needs of the base areas and guerilla zones grow there will be even a need to establish a separate supply and transport wing in this regard.

Medical networks of sympathetic doctors and use of hospital facilities to treat PGA/PLA fighters are also necessary in the urban areas. This is necessary for certain cases, which cannot be treated with the facilities available in the guerilla zone areas. Here too the urban Party should always be on the lookout for sources and contacts to set up such a network in various cities. Once a network has been established however it should be separated from the Party bodies leading the urban mass work

Technical help in the form of repairs and maintenance of fighting, communication and other equipment of the PGA/PLA is another area where the urban organization has to provide assistance. Preparing comrades with technical, electrical, electronic and other skills to go and take up such responsibilities in the countryside best do this. It can also be done be sending city comrades to conduct training courses for the PGA/PLA. In some cases where necessary the repair of some equipment can be done in the urban areas. Providing the contacts to help set up a network for production of certain items in the urban areas is also another area of necessary help.

Development of new technologies for the People's War is another crucial area. With the daily advance of technology, there are numerous new devices that could be adapted in the service of the people's war. Since the large metropolitan centres are the points where such technologies or the information regarding such technologies are obtained, it would be the responsibility of all comrades in such areas to be ever alert to any opportunity in this regard. Proposals and devices obtained or developed should be sent to the higher committees for consideration and implementation. Since it would in the future be necessary to set up separate research and development wings in this regard, it would be the task of the urban organization to developed suitable comrades for such work.

All the above logistical tasks can be implemented successfully only when all urban comrades are alive and alert to these needs and constantly present suggestions, proposals and contacts in this regard. And the wider and deeper the urban mass base, the better is the possibility of actually providing assistance to the rural work. However we must realize that this task cannot be performed spontaneously in response to emergency needs. Logistical networks should be established in absolute secrecy over a period of time. Separate comrades should be allocated for such work and once they are so allocated they should be released from other work and delinked completely from the mass work. It is only in such a manner that we can create networks that can serve the long-term needs of the people's war.

3.5.3 Urban Military Operations under Central Direction

Though the countryside is the main area of operations of the People's Army, there are certain military objectives that need to be performed through operations in the urban areas. This even requires the setting up of permanent structures of the PGA/PLA in the cities and towns.

3.5.3.1 City Action Teams

These action teams are small secret teams of disciplined and trained soldiers of the PGA/PLA who are permanently based in the cities or towns to hit at important, selected, enemy targets. Such targets may be annihilation of individuals of military importance or sabotage actions like the blowing up of ammunition depots, destroying communications networks, damaging oil installations, etc. These action teams, which form part of the main force of the PGA/PLA, perform these actions under the guidance and orders of their respective command. Thus these teams should have no connection whatsoever with the local urban Party structure. The selection of targets and timing of operations too would be based on the overall political and military needs of the people's war. However the secret team should have some broad understanding of the schedules and plans of the programmes of the open mass organizations. This could where possible help prevent problems due to clashing between the open and secret plans.

Details regarding the role, the Central Military Commission (CMC) should undertake tasks, training and education of the city action teams.

3.5.3.2 Central Intelligence

Since the enemy is centred in the big cities, it is very important that our Party develops a network to obtain and analyze political and military intelligence at higher levels. Besides human intelligence, we can make use of the Internet and other modern electronic means for gathering information by entering the enemy's networks. For this it is necessary to allocate separate responsibility. Urban Party organization may provide contacts and individuals for this work. However once they are assigned to this work they do not maintain any links with the local organization. Such networks are led and directed by the highest bodies of the Party.

3.5.3.3 Cyber Warfare

We should, to the extent possible, make use of computers and the Internet network to further the military objectives of the revolution. Though we are today quite distant from this possibility, we should have the perspective of setting up units with the task of damaging the military and other important networks of the enemy. The possibility of setting up such a structure however depends primarily on the development of the urban mass movement and the ability of the urban Party organization to draw in and consolidate comrades with the required skills for such work.

3.6 All-India and State-Level Plans

The above given policy and guidelines give the political and organizational orientation for our urban work. This is the basis on which our work in the various towns and cities should be reorganized. However it is not sufficient to only reorient our work at the level of particular towns and cities. Equally important is the task of giving a plan and direction to the overall urban work in a particular state, and in the whole country, based on the concrete objective conditions and situation of subjective forces. It is also necessary to relate and coordinate the tasks of the urban movement to the overall needs of the revolution in the country or in a particular state. There is also to some extent the need to coordinate the urban movement with our international responsibilities both at the South Asia as well as the global level.

The job of drawing up such plans and the committees at their respective levels should take up implementing them. We present here the broad basis for drawing up such plans.

3.6.1 Factors Governing All-India Perspective Plan

Drawing up the All-India perspective-plan means basically selecting the cities, industries or regions where we should concentrate and give priority. It can further mean the evaluation of the available subjective forces and deciding on suitable allocation.

The main factors for deciding on areas of concentration are:

1) All-India perspective and plan for guerilla zones and base areas: Since the urban movement basically plays a role complementary to the rural armed struggle, the All-India plan for developing the armed struggle is a crucial factor for deciding on our pattern of concentration for urban work. We should give importance to cities and towns that can play a direct role in helping and strengthening our base areas and guerilla zones.
2) Concentration of the Working Class: The working class is the main focus of our efforts in the urban areas. We should therefore target such cities and regions, which have a high concentration of the industrial working class. We should judge the importance of a region's working class, not only on the basis of numbers, but also take into account its role in terms of struggle. The working class in some centres has a tradition of struggle thus influencing and providing leadership to the surrounding areas. Some cities have strong working class organizations that play a decisive role in All-India level struggles. Such factors too must be taken into account for giving importance to a particular centre. Another important short-term consideration is the sharpening of class contradictions. A centre or industry experiencing sharp and growing struggles is more suited for starting work.
3) Importance for the Ruling Classes: Some cities like Delhi and Mumbai have great political and economic significance for the ruling class. Strong movements in such cities cripple and paralyze the ruling class and have greater impact.
4) Key Industries: The centres of key industries should be given importance as they have the potential of playing an important role in the people's war.
5) Towns of Military Importance: These too should be given importance because they present the opportunity to infiltrate into the enemy ranks.

3.6.2 State Plans

State Committees should analyze and identify the main types of urban and industrial areas in their states. On the basis of such analysis the priority areas should be selected keeping in mind the following criteria: i) All-India and state gz/rural perspective, as well as the All-India urban perspective ii) concentration of working class and sharpening of class contradictions iii) concentration of students and other petty bourgeois sections and their struggles iv) political importance within state v) key industries. Class analysis of the major towns selected for work should also be done.

Deciding on the priority areas gives the broad direction for the allocation of subjective forces, which are or may become available. The concrete plan depends on the nature of forces that are actually available.

4. Review of Our Understanding and Practice

Following the Naxalbari upsurge and at the time of the Eighth (First) Congress of our Party in 1970, we had considerable impact and influence in a number of cities. We were a powerful force in Kolkata, at that time the largest city in the country. The revolutionary wave inspired workers in various industrial centres, in particular Kolkata, Durgapur, Coimbatore, Jamshedpur and Dhanbad.

However due to the wrong understanding regarding mass organizations and mass struggles prevailing in our Party at that time we could not preserve and develop our influence. Our policy was that "it is not our task to organize trade unions or to bring them under our control, or to bother ourselves about the trade union elections. Our task is to build secret party organizations among the workers." (Our Party's Tasks among the Workers, Deshabrati, March 12, 1970). We thus in fact boycotted the trade unions and as a consequence were alienated from the working class.

Similarly wrong understanding of laying stress on urban guerilla warfare, when there were no conditions for it, led to setback of our city work.

At that time though there were no circulars or policy documents regarding urban or working class work there were some articles and notes by Com. CM, which appeared in the Party magazines, which served as the guidelines for our work.

4.1 Earlier Circulars and Policies

Subsequently our Party made certain attempts to draw up guidelines for our urban and working class work. These have been very few but significant. Besides the sections on urban work in our various strategy and tactics documents and conference reviews, the main documents regarding policy have been the circular on 'Towns and Cities: Our Programme and Organization' brought out by the Andhra Pradesh State Committee in 1973, the 'Guidelines for Working Class Front' brought out by the Central Organizing Committee of the erstwhile PU in 1987, and the 'Review of Our Document "Method of Working in Towns"' brought out by the APSC of the erstwhile PW in 1995, where the earlier 1973 document was reviewed.

4.1.1 1973 Circular

Though this document was only intended to be circular giving methods to resolve contradictions between the needs of open and secret work, it also gave an explicit understanding regarding the programme, tasks and forms of organization for the working class, students and other fronts. It therefore served as the principal document guiding urban work in the erstwhile PW for many years.

The 1973 document played an important role in giving a correct direction to urban work. The crucial points on which it presented a correct understanding were:

1) It corrected most of the earlier wrong notions regarding mass organizations and mass struggle.
2) It broadly gave the correct strategic approach to urban work, that the Party in the cities and towns should use secret methods to preserve itself from the enemy, till the last stage of the liberation of the cities from the countryside.
3) It correctly stated that in the cities and towns we should concentrate mainly among workers.

Coming to its limitations, it was not a comprehensive document on urban work and it dealt more about the immediate problems that we then faced in the urban areas. It had some wrong understandings such as: we should not take up office bearers' posts in the unions, we should not organize independent trade unions by ourselves, and so on. This was a continuation of the earlier wrong understanding regarding mass organizations.

The 1973 circular played a significant role in the initial period. But in later years with the rapid spread of mass organizations in the urban areas there was no attempt to correct the understanding and further develop the circular in a comprehensive manner. Thus many of the important formulations of the document were not implemented in practice. Though the document had stated that the main concentration should be on the working class, the emphasis in the urban areas was more on the students and youth. The ban on taking union office-bearers' posts and the opposition to forming separate trade unions too were not implemented in practice. These were done without formally developing a new policy understanding.

4.1.2 1987 Guidelines

These guidelines were formulated in accordance with the call of the 1987 Central Conference of the erstwhile PU to "grasp the work in the working class front seriously." This document presented in a concise and clear manner the objective and subjective situation in relation to the working class, our tasks and policies, and a plan for work. The document was significant in presenting a correct understanding regarding the leadership role of the working class in the revolution. It stressed the leadership role of working class struggles and sending advanced detachments to the countryside, and the Party's responsibility in preparing the working class for this role.

The major defect of the document was its neglect of the strategic approach to urban work. Thus there was no understanding regarding the relation and coordination between open and secret work and the need to preserve and develop our urban forces for a long time till the later stages of the people's war.

The plan of the document was not seriously implemented nor was it reviewed. It thus could not have major impact.

4.1.3 1995 Review

The erstwhile PW's APSC's Review did not restrict itself to just a review of the earlier document. It also laid down the goals and tasks of the urban movement in AP. It was a development on the 1973 circular.

A significant point that the document correctly reviewed was the lack of necessary concentration on the urban work. It concluded that though we correctly gave importance to agrarian revolution and guerilla zones, we did not concentrate to the extent required on the cities. It analyzed the spontaneous shifts from urban to rural areas and pointed out the lack of a long-term perspective for urban work. It also corrected the 1973 document's wrong understanding regarding not taking up office bearers' posts in the unions.

The document however did not try to present a comprehensive policy for urban work. It also did not bring about the necessary reorganization of the work.

4.2 Our Main Shortcomings

The above documents and the reviews done at conferences and plenums at various levels have pointed out to various faults and weaknesses in our urban work at various points of time. It is necessary to develop a comprehensive picture of our main shortcomings as a whole.

4.2.1 Lack of Concentration on Urban Work

Throughout the past thirty years, and in most of the main areas of the Party's work there has been a disregard towards the tasks of the urban movement and Party. As the Ninth Congress POR concluded, "We have failed to grasp the dialectical relationship between the rural and urban movements. Having understood the formulation that rural work is primary and urban work is secondary in a mechanical way, we concentrated most of our leadership forces only in rural work."

Therefore, a culture was created in the organization where only the rural work was seen as fieldwork or struggle area work, whereas the urban areas were seen to be out of the field, and non-struggle area work. All the best and most committed cadres would therefore opt for, and be transferred out of the urban field. Therefore, as many examples in the 1995 review point out, cadre were spontaneously transferred out to rural areas without considering the future of the urban areas which were being emptied out.

The more serious manifestation of this understanding was however in the serious lack of concentration and specialization by the higher committees. Very few were allocated to the tasks of the urban movement and even those who were given the responsibility were normally burdened with numerous other tasks. This led to severe problems at various levels. Without higher-level cadre in the field directing the work, there was low possibility of correcting the wrong understanding at the lower levels regarding the long-term strategic approach, though this mistake was referred to time and again in our reviews and documents. Without specialization also there was no hope of the higher committees themselves deepening their poor understanding of the problems of implementing the strategic approach. Without specialization and allocation of higher-level comrades the old mistakes only continued.

All this took place despite our understanding repeated in documents that the importance of the urban areas in India is growing, that the percentage of the working class and the urban population in India is much higher than it was at the time of the Chinese revolution, and that therefore the urban areas and the working class in India will have a relatively more important role to play in the revolution.

Today the urban areas with 28.7 %of the population and over 60% of the Gross Domestic Product, with many major mega cities and a working class of ____ crores, have a growing role to play in the country and the economy, and also in the revolution. It is therefore absolutely necessary to quickly correct the imbalance in our concentration on the tasks of the urban movement. It is necessary most of all to increase our allocation of higher-level comrades to urban fieldwork. It is necessary to increase the specialization and knowledge levels of the higher-level committees regarding the urban work. And it is also necessary, where possible, to allocate suitable comrades at other levels too, or at least give greater consideration to the needs of the urban movement also when deciding regarding transfers out of the cities.

4.2.2 Lack of Concentration on the Working Class within Urban Work

The 1973 document had correctly stated that in the urban areas we should mainly concentrate among workers. Since our movement had faced a severe setback by 1972 and plans were afoot to put our movement on the track, we needed to strengthen our subjective forces at a faster pace. To achieve this, we concentrated on the students and youth from a practical angle, but this practice was not based on any theoretical premise. When our forces grew and we were in a better position, we made plans to penetrate into the working class. In the process of enemy's onslaught, and our continued weaknesses in our work in the urban areas, we became much weakened as losses mounted steeply. Lack of a comprehensive approach towards urban work and lack of concentration from the leadership are the main reasons for our weak roots in the working class.

4.2.3 Neglect of Developing Party Leadership from the Proletariat

Despite being the Party of the working class, recruitment from the workers has been low, and leadership from the proletariat still lower. Part of the reason for this was due to our deficiency in concentrating on the workers, and particularly on the organized workers who have a greater potential for leadership. Building leadership from among the workers requires conscious attention and effort. Unless we realize the importance of building working class leadership we will not put in the necessary efforts to achieve it. It is only in the Ninth Congress that we have specifically resolved to give importance to this task. We should now bring it into practice.

4.2.4 Lack of Deep Understanding of the Strategic Approach in Urban Work

We have regularly given prime importance to the long term strategic approach in our documents and for some years have been reviewing that the lack of this approach has been the cause of most of our losses in the urban areas. However we have merely understood or explained it at the level of stricter implementation of tech precautions and secret methods of functioning. We have not understood that correct strategic approach is essentially a task of basically reorienting and reorganizing the whole urban work basing on the effective combination of illegal and legal forms of organizations. Without accepting, deeply understanding and educating all levels regarding this strategic approach towards the urban movement, we cannot bring about a qualitative change in our urban work.

The widest possible mobilization and organization of the masses is essential to challenge the overwhelming domination of the enemy in the urban areas. Secret functioning and the long-term preservation of our forces are only possible within the context of a wide and deep mass movement.

Since we are working in the back drop of the semi-feudal and semi colonial conditions, we need to go in for militant struggles and actions against the management as the majority of the industrial working class is employed in the unorganized sector and is forced to work under unbearable conditions without any access to minimum protective labour laws. However, we cannot repeatedly replicate in the city the offensive tactics suited to the rural movement and expect to survive merely on the basis of stricter tech functioning. Strategically understanding the strength of the enemy in the city means accepting that we cannot openly challenge him on a military basis. Thus we cannot expect to regularly use armed strength to threaten factory owners, conduct negotiations through secret organizers, or annihilate managers, as would be possible in rural areas of a guerilla zone. And we cannot hope that we can do all such things and still survive merely by using better tech methods.

This does not of course deny the absolute importance in urban work of the strict maintenance of tech precautions, natural covers, functioning through layers, and all other means of proper secret functioning. We must thoroughly re-evaluate our tech methods in all cities and a total revamping of our secret mechanism should be an essential part of reorganizing our urban work. We must however understand that secret functioning is only one important aspect of the strategic approach of preserving our forces for a long time. Secret functioning itself is based on the mobilization and support of the broad masses.

4.2.5 Lack of Clarity on Combining the various Types of Mass Organizations

We did not have the clarity regarding the various forms of mobilizing the masses in the urban areas and how to skillfully use these in combination depending upon the concrete situation, ebb and flow of the movement.

We first placed main stress on the open revolutionary mass organizations, which maintained clear links with the Party. With the onset of repression we tried to operate these organizations secretly and still tried to mobilize the masses principally through them. It was only much later that we realized that secret mass organizations could not be the only form of mass mobilizing in the urban areas in the repressive conditions. It was only then that we introduced the concept of the cover organization.

Even at this time we laid excessive stress on the formation of new cover organizations by us and did not give sufficient importance to fractional work within the existing mass organizations already working among the people. We did not understand that such type of fractional work is an important form of mass organizing in the urban areas, which are all controlled and repressed by the enemy. We thought that only those organizations explicitly under the control of the Party are revolutionary organizations. We did not see that through proper fractional work we could remain under cover and yet guide an organization to play a revolutionary role.

Our education regarding cover organizations too gave a one-sided emphasis on the aspect of maintaining the cover of the organization and preventing its exposure. We did not stress the aspect that the broadest mobilization of the masses and the unification of large sections of the non-party masses under the mass organizations provide the best cover possible.

Further we did not understand the concept, role and importance of the legal democratic organizations and movement. Here too we only understood that we should restrict the programme and tasks so as to maintain legality. We did not see the importance of uniting the broadest sections ready to work resolutely on a minimum programme. After years of experience we have corrected some sectarian misconceptions. But we yet need to further develop our understanding and education at all levels regarding the role, importance and use of the legal democratic organization within the urban movement.

We formed several secret mass organizations at various times. Many of these secret mass organizations were formed after severe repression on the open revolutionary mass organizations, which prevented them from functioning. Our response to the repression then was to run these same organizations from the underground.

Our only change while running the secret organizations was regarding the methods of secret functioning. We expected that the secret organizations would perform the same functions and tasks that were earlier performed by the open organizations. We did not see the need to substantially change the role, tasks and structure of the new secret organization.

We should understand the limitations of the secret organizations in carrying out broad mass mobilization like the earlier open revolutionary mass organizations. We should therefore assign such tasks to the secret organization, which it is best able to perform - like secret revolutionary propaganda, organizing the masses secretly and carrying out militant actions when necessary. Further we should reallocate those unexposed forces of the old open revolutionary organization, to fractional, or other type of cover work. This would ensure the continuation of the task of mass mobilization through other means.

4.2.6 Negligence in Secret Functioning

Our POR has listed in detail the various lapses in secret functioning like not building covers, not building and functioning through layers, and other technical errors. At the root of these errors is our superficial understanding of our long-term strategic approach, and our lack of a proper grasp of the balance and relationship between open and secret work. A quick results, short cut, approach and liberalism are further reasons for the mistakes.

4.2.7 Lack of an All-India Perspective

This is also a shortcoming. In the earlier period when urban work was restricted to a few pockets the seriousness of this deficiency was relatively less. However with the intensification of the people's war and the spread of the Party to most of the major urban centres in the country, the need to have an All-India urban and working class perspective has become urgent. We should draw up such a perspective and plan the deployment and utilization of our subjective forces on that basis.

4.3 Principal Defect in Our Understanding

The above shortcomings are basically rooted in our defective understanding regarding the role of urban work and particularly the role of the working class in the Indian revolution.

As mentioned earlier in this document (point 3.1.1), the Ninth Congress has given a precise and unambiguous understanding regarding the role of the working class in the revolution. Though we had the correct understanding about the role of working class leading the revolution, we could not provide sufficient cadre to concentrate on the working class. There was not much concentration on the part of the leadership as we concentrated on building the agrarian revolution. Though we allotted cadre for the development of working class movement, because of the lakh of long-term approach and due to repression, we lost many valuable cadre who were working in the urban areas, and we faced severe losses. Though not existing at a theoretical level, there was to some extent a wrong notion in the minds of the party committees at various levels, that we need to depend upon the petty bourgeois sections, like students, for developing leading cadre. This was reflected in our practice in various states, to a considerable extent. An important factor that had contributed to this practice is the relative ease with which we can recruit cadre from the students and youth when compared with the workers and the pressure of immediate needs of revolution to be fulfilled.

The Ninth Congress has given the task of building proletarian base and to develop leadership cadre from the working class. If we rectify our mistakes, taking lessons from the past, we can certainly overcome the present shortcoming.

5. Immediate Tasks

After formulating the policy and guidelines for urban work, and after reviewing our past, the Ninth Congress POR calls upon the Party to launch a campaign to reorganize the work according to the new guidelines. Implementing this campaign call of the POR systematically and thoroughly should thus be the main focus of our immediate tasks. Depending upon the objective reality and subjective situation in our respective areas, and basing on our Policy and Guidelines, we should draw up a step-by-step area wise programme to educate the Party, evaluate our work, identify the areas for change, and draw up concrete plans and perspectives, and follow-up their implementation in a thorough manner.

5.1 Introduce Urban and Working Class Specialization in the Higher Committees

The highest committees must be the starting point. In the CC, PB, and RBs, and in those SCs where there is possibility of substantial urban work, there must be allocation of members to specialize in the urban work. Where the volume and nature of work demands it, sub-committees should be formed.

Their tasks will be to thoroughly implement the urban policy and guidelines; to closely study and solve problems in the field; to study the enemy, anticipate its moves and preplan accordingly; to theorize based on the field experiences, and to thus centralize the wealth of new ideas constantly emerging from the field so that they may be quickly implemented at all places. At this stage the same comrades will also have to concentrate on the tasks of the working class field. This means coordinating the working class work in various centres, guiding the working class organizations and fronts, preparing syllabus and materials for political education and training of cadre in the working class work, studying the developing trends in the working class movement and planning accordingly, and responding with quick decisions at the political and tactical level to the numerous spontaneous events occurring amidst the ongoing upsurge of working class struggles.

5.2 Draw up All-India and State-level Perspective-plans

The higher committees (and particularly the comrades allocated to specialize) should formulate and decide upon the perspective urban areas and industries at their respective levels. Deciding on the perspective gives the priority and direction in which to concretely plan. It ensures that the allocation of subjective forces does not move spontaneously but according to a plan.

By studying the urban process in the light of our policy and strategy, and on the basis of a town analysis and industrial analysis, the cities/ towns and industries to be focused upon should be decided. Simple class analysis of existing work areas and potential towns should also be conducted. This will help in deciding the priority and taking concrete decisions.

The actual allocation will naturally be on the basis of the subjective forces available and the overall plans of the responsible committee. However we must while allocating forces for the urban work be cautious and only allot comrades who will have a good chance of adjusting to the urban work and continuing for some time. Unlike the rural areas where retreat by a comrade need not lead to much exposure, the retreat of an urban comrade can lead to considerable problems for an urban organization.

5.3 Reorient and Reorganize the Urban Organizations with a Long-term Strategic Approach

Many of our urban work areas are not working according to a long-term strategic approach. Many areas have had to close down because of exposure and losses. Many areas have tried to introduce a strategic approach through a trial and error method derived from the day-to-day field experiences of facing the enemy. They have made considerable progress but deficiencies remain. Thus today different areas follow different practices based not only on the different levels of repression they are facing, but also on subjective factors like the approach of the area and state leadership or the differing work patterns and styles inherited from the past. This has continued due to the neglect of urban work in general, and in particular due to the absence of a common set of policies and guidelines throughout the Party. Having now adopted common policies and guidelines we should work to reorient and reorganize the urban work throughout the Party with a long-term strategic approach.

This task should be taken up as a campaign closely guided and monitored by the state committees. It should be a step by step process involving the education of all urban cadre according to the urban policy, particularly stressing on various aspects of the long term strategic approach; evaluating the functioning and structure of the urban organization at all levels - both Party and mass organizational - and taking decisions to correct or improve existing practices; setting targets for implementing the changes decided upon and following up so that they are implemented according to plan; and if necessary reallocating of forces according to the above evaluation and also according to the perspective plans drawn up by the higher committees.

The essential element in the effective implementation of such a campaign is the closest participation by the higher committees. Questions, doubts, and practical problems are bound to emerge in the course of implementation. To solve this requires the involvement of higher committee members who can provide answers and devise ways to resolve any problems that may come up. What we should aim to do is to see that every PM and activist operating in the city deeply understands the long term strategic approach, has full faith and confidence in this understanding, implements it in day-to-day practice, and tries to develop it to new levels.

5.4 Widely Mobilize the Urban masses, particularly the Working Class

Regarding mass mobilization, we must firstly correct the misconception that the long-term strategic approach of preserving our forces means restricting our mass organizing only to narrow secret mass organizations. All comrades must understand that the preservation and protection of our forces is only possible in the lap of the broad masses. We must therefore resort to the widest possible legal mass organizing while maintaining a correct balance between legal and illegal forms of organization and struggle. This direction towards broad mass organizing should therefore be one of the crucial components of the campaign to reorient and reorganize the Party.

We should mobilize through fractional work in various types of existing organizations and through different cover organizations and constantly devise new creative means to go among the masses without being exposed. We should not worry excessively that our struggles and slogans are not red and revolutionary enough. As long as we are among the masses and drawing them into struggle, we will be able to politicize them and draw them to the revolutionary line and Party.

Where necessary, and where it is possible to mobilize on a large scale, we should also form, or participate in, legal democratic organizations. We can thus bring out the masses in large numbers on a democratic programme. We should however not do such mobilizations where the numbers are likely to be small and our forces are likely to be exposed.

The main focus of mass mobilizing and organizing in the cities should be the working class. We should pay particular attention to the trade unions and other working class organizations. We should also organize in the bastis where the working class resides along with other sections of the urban poor. After the working class and urban poor we should pay attention to the organizations of the students and other sections of the petty bourgeoisie.

5.5 Recruit and Develop Party Leadership from the Working Class

We should have a strong proletarian orientation in our Party-building process. In this regard we should pay particular attention to the Ninth Congress resolution in this respect. We should therefore concentrate on building the Party in the factories and other centres of working class work. Even within the organizations of women, youth and students, we should pay particular attention to recruiting from proletarian backgrounds. We should pay particular attention to the education of proletarians in order to quickly bring them into the Party in larger numbers. After recruitment we should have measures and programmes for training and developing Party leadership from among them.

5.6 Reorganise the Tech Mechanism in the Cities

Except for the cities and towns within and adjacent to the guerilla zones, facing severe repression, the tech mechanism in most cities is very loose and primitive. We are mostly developing our tech methods as a process of reacting to the immediate enemy threat, rather than as a plan based on a long-term strategic approach. This spontaneous approach is very dangerous and must be drastically changed.

We must therefore thoroughly overhaul the tech mechanism and methods of coordinating our open and secret work. For this a gradual piecemeal process will not work. Such a process remains at the most partial and does not bring about the change required. Besides the enemy is moving fast to set up its network in cities throughout the country. We should therefore drastically revise our basic assumptions regarding tech requirements. We must realize that we cannot plan on the basis of the immediate actions and appearances of the enemy. The state is planning on a long term and all-India basis. Our planning too has to be on a long-term basis and cannot make much distinction between repression and 'non-repression' cities.

The basic norms regarding operating under natural covers, functioning strictly through layers, cover organization methods, and techniques of communication should be brought into implementation in all our urban work. This however should only be the first step. We should remember that our enemy is constantly studying and developing new methods against us. Our approach and method too therefore has to be dynamic and creative. Thus in the course of implementation of our guidelines, each one of us should further make additions, adaptations and developments to these guidelines. Our tech mechanism, while standing on certain basic concepts and principles, should always advance and improve, thus always proving to be one step ahead of the political police.

5.7 Prepare the Self-Defence Organs of the Urban Movement

In this respect we are relatively backward. Though all city organizations form teams for performing specific actions, there has been hardly any progress and very little experience in building more stable self-defence formations. This is true of both open teams as well as the secret self-defence squads.

We should fix targets and not now delay this task any longer. Where preparations are necessary we should make the necessary preparations and form the teams. For open teams, a simple political-organizational basis and a code of conduct should be drawn up. For secret squads, preparations for the necessary political and military education are important. There should also be full clarity among concerned comrades about the squad's line of command. Senior comrades should take responsibility to see to the successful completion of this task.

5.8 Take up Work in Key Industries

Our presence today in the key industries is extremely low. With the advance of the people's war, it is a pressing need that we enter into key industries and establish a strong base there. All higher committees should therefore keep this in mind while drawing up plans. We should make plans for key industries basing on the importance of the industry, the openings available for entry and the subjective forces we have available for such type of work.

5.9 Infiltrate into Enemy Organizations

This too is another area where we are practically non-existent, and where we must make a beginning. We should thus plan for this at various levels.

We should make use of opportunities for entry into the police, para military and military forces. We should very secretly follow up contacts of those already within these forces. Where possible we should enter into them from outside. Such work should be guided directly by the higher committees without informing the local bodies.

We should regularly conduct propaganda regarding the problems of the ordinary constables and soldiers. We should pick up the burning issues concerning them and arouse them to agitation.

We should also make a study of cantonment towns, ordnance factory areas, etc. with the purpose of formulating a plan for work in such zones. We should also try to collect and generate the type of forces who would be able to do such sort of work.

5.10 Build the United Front in the Urban Areas

Our urban united front work involves on the one hand, the building and strengthening of the worker-peasant alliance, and on the other hand, the building of unity between the working class and other urban sections and classes.

As mentioned earlier, the worker-peasant alliance is not only the task of those towns adjacent to the guerilla zones and other areas of rural struggle. The metropolitan and industrial cities relatively delinked from the countryside should particularly concentrate in various ways to advance the worker-peasant alliance. Propaganda, solidarity struggles, participation of workers in peasant agitations, direct help to the rural struggles, is some of the programmes to be undertaken. At the same time, basing on the concrete situation, other new and more creative ways of strengthening the unity of the two basic revolutionary classes should be developed.

The united front with other classes will mainly be through issue based or programme-based joint front organizations. Though these may be legal for quite sometime depending on the broadness of the front, we should be prepared to run the UF organizations from underground too, like the NDF in the Philippines, when confronted with brutal, fascist rule. While participating widely in these we should correct our sectarian errors in building such joint fronts and our bureaucratic dealings within them. The higher committees should constantly guide and plan for advancing and broadening our united front work.

As pointed out throughout this chapter, the policies of liberalization, globalization and privatization have had great impact on the urban areas. Almost all the toiling sections in the cities have been hit badly by these policies. This has time and again led to spontaneous outbursts of various sections on various partial issues without a clear direction. Now however the struggles have got more organized and focused against the very policies themselves, with the working class coming out in the leading role. Since the beginning of 2000, numerous major working class struggles have broken out, and continue to spread and grow unabated. Not only are these struggles spreading to all corners of the country, they are also marching in time with the anti-capitalist struggles going on in various parts of the globe. Even the reactionary wind after the military advances of imperialism in Afghanistan, has not been able to beat back the growing struggles.

These working class struggles have been joined by the struggles of the employees, teachers, etc. They are also inspiring the urban poor in the slums and the struggles of the semi proletariat with anti-demolition and anti-eviction struggles again taking on a militant character. Even the national bourgeois small capitalists are militantly taking to the streets against industry shifting, new taxes, high electricity rates, etc. The roots of most of these struggles emerge from the imperialist policies of globalization, liberalization, and privatization, and are therefore being focused more and more directly against these policies. Thus, a favourable condition exists in the urban areas for the building of broad fronts against imperialism and this situation is likely to continue for quite some time more.

****

PEOPLE'S GOVERNMENT

This document was originally prepared by the PWG and was released by the Dandakaranya Special Zone Committee (DKSZC), the most volatile of all the guerrilla zones of the Maoists, presently. Largely, the geographical area that comprises the DKSZC is co-terminus with the area that is known as Bastar, in the central Indian State of Chhattisgarh. Also, what the rebels term as their version of the people's government, which they named as Janatana Sarkar, *is best manifest in all its forms in the DKSZC area.*

According to the Maoists themselves, the Janatana Sarkar *is as yet in an "embryonic stage". In Maoist jargon the* Janatana Sarkar *is known as "New Democratic Revolutionary Power". In the Maoist scheme of things, this is 'new state power' and shall, over time, metamorphose/ grow as the 'new state', i.e. the governing authority (government) at the pan-India level, as the people's war intensifies and more areas fall under total rebel control, to eventually seize/capture state/political power at the country-level.*

This document describes in considerable detail the structures, polices and tasks of the people's government. The original spelling as mentioned in the document— 'Janathana', *instead of* 'Janatana', *is retained through the text of this document reproduced below.*

The document makes no mention of the structure of the Constitution of the new democratic people's government; nor does it provide any indication on how it would be drafted. However, it mentions under the sub-section of Amendment to the

Constitution: "Necessary amendments may be made to the fundamental policies and tasks in the people's assemblies/representative assemblies with ¾ majority and send them to the high[er] level government." Thus, one would be persuaded to suggest that this document is a precursor to a Constitution which the Maoists wish to draft at a later stage.

At the same time, this document lists out the following:

Rights and duties of the people;

Activities of the new democratic government;

Structure, election to and method of functioning of the government, and the relation between various levels of government;

Method of amendment to the Constitution; and

Composition and functions of the members of the government committee

Further, this document also lists out the various departments/organs of the government and mentions that members of the government committee shall be in-charge of the various departments. The various departments listed in the document are as follows:

Finance Department;

Agriculture Department;

People's Defense Department;

People's Judicial Department;

People's Education and Cultural Committee;

Public Health – Social Welfare Department;

Forest Protection Committee and

Public Relations Department

In the Maoist scheme of things, depending upon the need departments could be annulled or new ones created.

JANATHANA SARKAR

INTRODUCTION

We are now forming janathana sarkars successfully as a result of the great struggles the Dandakaranya revolutionary masses are taking up to successfully go forward with the ultimate aim of establishing Socialism-Communism by destroying the semi colonial, semi feudal system in India through People's War and establishing People's Democratic system. We are declaring the necessary policy [and] program.

This policy [and] program shall be implemented across Dandakaranya wherever the janathana sarkars are formed. Where they are not yet formed and serious efforts are going on for their formation, that is, in the guerilla zones, this shall be the basis of struggle. In the areas where revolutionary movement is expanding newly, that is, in the perspective areas this shall be the issue of propaganda.

FIRST PART
Fundamental policies-tasks of the People's Democratic Government

1. The central task of Indian Revolution is to seize political power, to destroy the semi colonial, semi feudal state, its politics, its economic system and culture and establish a New Democratic State. The aim of New Democratic Revolution is to establish the political and economic system and culture of this New Democratic state. By achieving this aim the doors will be opened for the development of the whole Indian society. The poverty and misery of the masses will be eliminated. A political economic and cultural base will be formed for the Socialist state. Struggle for People's Democracy means struggle to establish anti imperialist, anti feudal, anti big bourgeois politics, economics and culture. People's Democracy means the struggle of the masses against imperialist, feudal, big bourgeois classes under the leadership of proletarian class under the direction of Communist Party on the basis of peasant alliance.
2. In order to fulfill the above central task Indian masses must join the People's Army. They have to eliminate the armed forces of the Indian state and its total mechanism through War. They must establish people's democratic state in its place.
3. The line of People's Democratic Revolution is a protracted People's War. People's Democratic Revolution will be successful countrywide with the formation of self-sufficient base areas in the broad rural area, the consolidation of people's governments and expansion. Ultimately the towns are liberated. Thus people's democratic government will be established throughout the country. The existence of janathana sarkars, their consolidation, their expansion are linked with one another. So the janathana sarkars will strive at their best to strengthen themselves, to expand the people's War and develop it.
4. People's Democratic Government will establish the collective dictatorship of the proletariat, peasantry, petty bourgeois and national bourgeois classes under the leadership of proletariat class. The four class United Front is a definite necessity for the success of People's Democratic Revolution. This four class UF will mobilize all the oppressed nationalities; the religious minorities that are facing harassments and other oppressed social sections and fight. The janathana sarkar will strengthen the four classes UF in the respective levels and strive for countrywide success.
5. The People's Democratic Government shall guarantee all kinds of freedom and rights of the broad toiling masses. It shall protect the interests of people in all times. It guarantees the following fundamental rights to the people.
    1. Right to express (speech, write, publication)
    2. Right to meet
    3. To form organization

4. To conduct strikes and demonstrations
5. To live according to one's wish
6. To have primary education
7. To have primary medical treatment
8. To gain minimum employment

In addition to these rights the people will have to fulfill the following duties

1. To protect the country
2. To respect the constitution and law
3. To protect the government properties
4. To provide military services
5. To pay taxes
    1. People will have the right to elect the government representatives and to be elected in all the levels according to the constitution of People's Democracy. They will have the right to summon and if necessary, call back the elected representatives if they are not committed to the manifesto.
    2. The state shall not discriminate towards anyone in terms of tribe, caste, religion, nationality, gender, language, region, education, post and status. It shall deal all as equals. It shall give equal opportunities to all.
    3. State shall be separated from the religion and will have a secular character. Religion shall be the personal affair of individuals. It shall avoid indulging in luring and threatening people with partiality towards one particular religion. Citizens will have the right to believe or disbelieve religion. State shall oppose all kinds of religious fundamentalism. It shall put an end to religious chauvinism.
    4. The People's Democratic economic system shall have the main task of destroying the semi colonial, semi feudal economic system, lay a path for the economic and social development of the country and establish Socialist economic system. This is the social economic order in the process of the transition of capitalist system to Socialism under the dictatorship of People's Democracy under the leadership of proletariat.

It will confiscate the lands of landlords and the religious organizations and distribute them to the poor, landless peasants and agricultural laborers on the basis of 'land to the tiller'. It will not seize the properties of the rich peasants. It will put a stop to the moneylenders' exploitation of the peasants. It will bring out the initiative and potential of the peasants. It will establish voluntary cooperative organizations in all the sectors. It shall strive for the development of agriculture. It shall take up industrialization in a big way on the basis of agriculture.

It will confiscate all the industries, banks and other organizations of the imperialists and comprador bureaucratic bourgeois classes. It will confiscate all the industries, banks and business institutions of the government, imperialists, and comprador bureaucratic class. It will dissolve all the imperialist loans. It will dissolve the unequal financial agreements that the exploiting government made with the imperialists.

It will seize the capital, mobile and immobile properties of the government and the CBB. It will take up the governance of all the monopoly industries and commerce depending on 'control of capital'.

The New Democratic Government shall not come in the way of capitalist production that is not in a position of controlling the people's life. It will control and dictate the small industries, middle level industries that are the industries of the national capitalist class. It will help for the development of cottage industries and handicrafts through cooperative organizations.

It will adopt the above agricultural, business and industrial policies and facilitate the way for people's democratic economic system.

It will implement an eight-hour working day for all the workers in the New Democratic system. It will dissolve the contract worker system and the child labor system. It will provide equal wages for women and men according to the principle of equal wage for equal work. It will provide social security and protective working conditions to all the workers.

It will arm the people in order to protect the country. It will enthuse and encourage the masses to join the People's Army. People's government will pay special attention for the necessary sources of the People's army. It will put People's Army under the command of revolutionary politics. It will unite it with the masses.

It will give special importance for the task of looking after the families of soldiers, martyrs, those dependent on them, those injured in the war and the handicapped.

It will hand over the recollections (personal belongings) of the people's soldiers who laid their lives in their heroic fight with the enemy forces to their families. It will appreciate their sacrifices and stores their details. Whenever possible it will build memorial columns.

1. It will implement a progressive judicial system on the basis of mass line. It will form people's courts in various levels for this purpose.
2. It shall be the task of the government to establish a new culture, scientific and democratic, by destroying the semi feudal, semi colonial culture in the present revolutionary phase. It shall continue the secular, genuinely democratic and scientific factors of the cultural heredity that the history handed over to the oppressed masses.
3. It will strive to dissolve all kinds of discrimination on women and to end patriarchy and male domination. It will liberate women from household

drudgery and make them part of social production, political, military, government administration and other such activities. It will guarantee equal share in property. It will take up special policies to remove unequal laws in a fast pace that the women are experiencing. It will ban prostitution, provide rehabilitation to the women and recognize them as ordinary citizens.

Marriages shall be on the basis of mutual love and agreement. The age limit for marriage would be 20 years. It will ban child marriages. It will encourage widow remarriages. Women shall have a right to abortion. It will make special arrangements for the welfare of children.

It will grant divorce if both the husband and wife wish so. If only one of them asks for it, it will make the necessary investigation and announce the decision. It will distribute the common property equally. In case of children, men must take up two third parts and women one-third part of the responsibility. It shall be the responsibility of the men to repay the common loans after divorce.

1. The New Democratic Government will recognize the right to self-determination of the oppressed nationalities and national minorities. It will integrate the country by recognizing the right to separate and the right to self-determination to these nationalities. The nationality minorities in various levels from the village to the state or in places where they are a majority, they will have the right to ask for autonomy. These autonomous areas will be according to the People's Democratic system and will reflect the aspirations of these minority people. The national minorities shall have appropriate representation according to their population in the people's assemblies, and the representatives' assemblies in the areas they reside.

   There are regional disparities in the country as a result of the unequal policies followed by the exploiting ruling classes. So some areas are backward and some areas are linked with the development of the nationalities. The People's Democratic Government will eliminate all kinds of regional disparities and strive for the development of the backward areas. If necessary it will also provide regional autonomy.

1. It shall guarantee comprehensive development of the adivasi societies. It shall provide absolute power on the forest to the people. It will bring to stop the exploitation of the natural sources by the comprador big bourgeois, imperialist and multi national companies. It will work for the development of the language and culture of adivasis. It will adopt corresponding policies.
2. It will eliminate discrimination and disparities of caste. It will eliminate the caste system totally. Until then it will take up special programs to uplift them in all sectors and implement the same.
3. It will eliminate the present system of education. It will introduce a

scientific, democratic and socialist system of education in its place. It will link it with production according to the necessities of Democratic India.

4. Government shall give equal status to the languages of all the nationalities. It will help to develop the languages that do not have a script. It will not impose a language on other nationalities in the name of national language, link language or in any other form. It will try to bring forward the generally accepted language depending on unanimity.
5. It will provide proper financial and social security and good social and cultural atmosphere to all those who are physically handicapped, mentally handicapped, old persons, orphans and the helpless. It will introduce a people helping medical system that provides free treatment and good health, mainly to workers, peasants and other toiling masses.
6. It will follow five principles regarding the relations with the countries having various social systems. They are – geographical integrity, mutual respect towards sovereignty, no mutual occupation, and non-intervention in each other's matters, equality, mutual interest and peaceful coexistence. It will provide help to all the anti capitalist system and anti imperialist struggles across the world, mainly to the revolutionary struggles and revolutionary wars under the various Maoist revolutionary forces. It will work as a base for New Democratic and later Socialist India, to facilitate the success of World Socialist Revolution. Keeping in view the historical relations of India with the masses in the subcontinent, it will closely integrate with the revolutionary Maoist forces and struggles in South Asia. It will dissolve all the unequal treaties the old government made.

SECOND PART

Structure of the government

Name

Janathana sarkar

Flag

Hammer and sickle with red flag with the length and breadth of the ratio 2:3.

Song

Must sing communist international in front of the flag.

Formation of government

Village Janathana sarkars may be formed in areas of 500-3000 population.

Structure of the government

People will elect the people's assemblies/representatives assemblies on the basis of general adult vote in the village/town, area, district/division, special zone/ state levels in revolutionary bases formed in the process of the ongoing People's

War. The committees elected through these assemblies shall work as the revolutionary governments. The revolutionary government shall be absolutely in the hands of the masses. The supreme people's Congress of the Federation of the People's Democratic Republic in the all India level or the Central level after achieving countrywide success in considerable areas in the country shall be the highest organ of the government.

After the People's War achieves success in Dandakaranya or in a considerable area dandakaranya, autonomous government will be formed. The present Dandakaranya consists of South Bastar, West Bastar, North Bastar, Maad and Gadchiroli divisions. The majority masses in this area are suffering with exploitation and misery for generations together. The natural development process took a distorted turn. The adivasis are still in the pre feudal production relationships. So the Dandakaranya people's government shall work as their autonomous government and provide special opportunities for their development.

Election of government

All adults those who have the age of 18 years will participate in elections. One needs to complete 20 years to be elected. Landlords, anti people hierarchs, stooges of exploiting government and anti revolutionary forces are disqualified to participate in elections. The elections are held through secret ballot. Election commission will conduct the elections. The elected representatives shall be answerable to the people's assemblies or the representative's assemblies that they represent. If the elected representatives do not conduct their duties properly the people's assemblies/representative assemblies can call them back. The people's assemblies/representative assemblies can call the representatives back only with a 2/3rds majority. The president and the vice-president of the autonomous governments shall be from the masses, reflecting the aspirations of the majority masses. Minority nationalities and tribes from other areas shall have proper representation according to their population in the autonomous areas. The rest of the adivasis must be considered as local adivasis.

The people's democratic government will be formed with the democratic classes, sections, parties, organizations, the representatives of teams, the representatives of people's army and democratic individuals. People from workers, peasants, petty bourgeois class and national bourgeois class constitute the government. This will be formed as the revolutionary United Front government. This will exercise the power as a genuine democratic government.

Now we are forming organs of revolutionary government in a secret manner. So it is not possible to elect revolutionary people's governments with direct elections in the place of exploiting class governments from the village to upper level. We can conduct elections through the people's representative assemblies in a limited number in such conditions.

In all levels, the people's assemblies in the people's assemblies/people's representatives in the representative assemblies will elect the revolutionary people's governments. These governments will establish various government departments, their responsible persons and mechanism to conduct the administrative responsibilities. They will make the necessary laws.

Method of functioning of the government

Democratic centralism shall be the fundamental policy of the structure and method of functioning of the government. As per the principles of democracy individuals shall be committed to the government, minority to the majority, lower level government to the higher level government, lower level to the gram sabha and higher level to the representatives assembly.

Coming to the higher level autonomous governments, they shall make acceptable decisions reflecting the aspirations of the masses regarding the language, culture and development. Normally these decisions will not be mandatory orders to be implemented. The autonomous governments can ratify them with certain exceptions and amendments. On the other hand the autonomous governments shall view the development of their areas and future as a part of the development and future of the whole country and implement the decisions of the high level government.

People shall have total control on the People's Democratic government. It will make the broad masses participate in the daily work of the government by adopting proper methods. People's opinion will have much importance in the decisions and in solving problems. It will make the people have an active role in the implementation of decisions and in the review. It will facilitate the supervision of the work of the government representatives.

Relations between the village level and area level janathana sarkars

1. Janathana sarkars shall send their budget reports and the details of the necessary funds to the area janathana sarkars.
2. The village janathana sarkars shall send the annual report of their activities and the annual accounts to the area janathana sarkar.
3. The AJS will release the necessary funds to the village janathana sarkars in its jurisdiction. It will also provide help and guidelines. It will go through their annual reports and accounts. It will inspect the activities of the village janathana sarkars. It will give the necessary orders and review the decisions. It will introduce its annual reports and accounts for a discussion.

All the departments of the janathana sarkars and the members bearing various responsibilities in these departments should work with dedication, sincerity, and simplicity, sacrificing nature, hard work, collectivity and other such revolutionary characters. They must not let bribes, gifts, partial nature, bad habits, misbehavior towards women, male domination, harshness towards people and other such immoral, anti people policies. They must not deny the laws. They must fulfill their duties in a proper manner. They must always remember that they are serving the people.

Amendment of constitution

Necessary amendments may be made to the fundamental policies and tasks in the people's assemblies /representative assemblies with ¾ majority and send them to the high level government.

Government committee

It shall be elected with 7-11 members along with the president and the vice-president of the janathana sarkar.

Duties of the president

1. Presiding over the meetings of the government
2. Informing the dates of the meeting and the agenda to the members one week earlier
3. Maintaining and protecting the government records
4. Maintaining the responsibilities of office and personnel
5. Coordinating all the activities of the government in the status of the president.

Duties of the vice-president

1. Fulfilling the works assigned through the president
2. Presiding over the meetings in the absence of the president. Conducting the responsibilities of the president.

The other members of the people's government committee shall bear the responsibility of the various departments as per their work division

Government departments—departmental committees

In view of the present necessities it shall form 8 departmental committees – (1) Financial, (2) Defense, (3) Agriculture, (4) Judicial, (5) Education – Culture, (6) Health, (7) Forest protection, (8) Public relations.

The departments might be reduced or increased basing on the needs. All the departments shall consist 3-7 members. People's assemblies/representatives assemblies shall elect them (except the defense department).

Meetings

Elections will be held once in three years to the people's governments. The elected village janathana sarkars shall meet once in a month and area janathana sarkars once in 2 months. It will hold meetings once in 4 months with all the members of the departmental committees. It will review the method of functioning of the government in the meetings of the people's assemblies/representatives assemblies once in 6 months in the initial stage of the formation of the government. Later it must hold such meetings once in a year. Normal meetings will be held in the stipulated time. Meetings will be held only if there is a quorum of 2/3rd it will make general decisions according to the opinion of majority. If 1/3rd members ask so, meeting can be held.

Standing committee

The standing committees are formed with the responsible persons of the president, vice-president, finance, defense departments for taking up daily works and supervision of the governments in the respective level. The standing committees will provide the daily guideline to implement the decisions the committees took in between the meetings of the governmental committee.

1. Finance department

1. It shall adopt the annual budget as per the decision of the government according to the proposals of the various departments. Budget shall be set from 1st January to 31st December.
2. Income is in the form of taxes and donations from the people and fines from the anti people elements. This shall be in the form of cash or paddy. Government shall decide the taxes. Finance department shall bear the responsibility of collecting them.
3. It will strive for the development of business, handicrafts, domestic industries and small industries based on agriculture and forest products, in the individual level on the basis of cooperation. It will encourage private business in the specific fields. But it will control the exploitation of the traders in transaction.
4. It will collect royalty from the traders and contractors that take the local resources, with the permission of the janathana sarkar.
5. It will mobilize the masses widely with the aim of developing the economic system to fulfill the necessities of the masses and that of the People's War and takes up all the necessary actions.
6. The finance department will release the annual accounts of the government only after all the departments submit their accounts.
7. They shall be closely linked with the cooperative organizations and shall give loans and grants if necessary.
8. It will release bonds whenever necessary, for the government as capital.
9. The finance department shall maintain the details of the properties of the government.

2. Agriculture department

1. It shall distribute the lands people's government seized to the agricultural laborer, landless peasants, poor peasants and lower middle class peasants on the basis of 'land to the tiller'. It shall give priority to the families of soldiers in the People's Army, to the families of martyrs and those

dependent on them, injured in the war as per the class line. It will give importance to till the lands of the families of full timers in revolution that cannot work in their lands to the sufficient extent, the lands of those families that do not have the necessary number to work, that of old people, that of women not allowed to till, that of those who lost husbands and that of helpless persons. It will give land equal to a middle peasant to the landlords that surrender and shall confiscate the rest of the land. It will implement the rest of the land reforms phase wise as per the preparation and the strength of the movement. It will take charge of the immobile properties. It will utilize them for the people's needs.

2. It will prepare the record of land ownership. It shall strive to develop the cooperative movement and agriculture.
3. It will release joint patta in the name of families and in the name of wife and husband.
4. It will record the details of transfer of land and transaction of lands. One must take the permission of this department if they want to buy or transfer lands to the non-adivasis. Those who want to leave their house and lands must inform the local janathana sarkar.
5. It shall strive to solve land disputes between the local and non-local persons, among the local people and among the non-locals as per the class line and with the view to mobilize and integrate the masses of all the democratic classes.
6. It will decide the minimum wages and working day not above than 8 hours according to the situation in the area. It will decide equal wages for equal work.
7. It will dissolve and ban illegal interest.
8. It will see that land is taken up for agriculture family wise or collectively. It will help those that do not have cows, seeds and agricultural tools to arrange the same through the government. It shall distribute cattle, seeds and agricultural tools seized from the landlords and hierarchs to the necessary peasants. Though there is private ownership over land, it will encourage collective work through mutual labor cooperation of the peasants in leveling the land, tilling, transplantations, weed removing, harvesting, growing vegetables, raising fruits, fish, cattle raising and other such agricultural and agriculture related works. It will thus develop the cooperative movement. It will strive to increase productivity and production so as to fulfill the necessities of food grains to the people and give importance to the development of agriculture. The collective lands, collective plantations, collective ponds, fish rising and other such things shall be in the control of this department.
9. It will encourage the peasantry to store the seeds, raise two crops, grams and oil seeds. It will oppose utilizing the seeds of imperialist multinational corporations.

10. It will encourage and develop the usage of local fertilizers. It will test the fertility of land and takes up measures for its protection.
11. It will take up the building of canals to facilitate water to the fields instead of growing paddy in the ponds like it is done now. It will build check dams and small irrigations projects as a part of irrigation.
12. It will see that production will not suffer in the time of enemy repression. It will try to re grow the lost crop as soon as possible. It will help the peasants to store their properties, mainly crops from the enemy attack.
13. This department will look after the cattle house of the village.

3. People's defense department

1. This will conduct the defense duties of the janathana sarkar. It will provide protection to the people's department. It will follow class line and mass line in all affairs of defense.
2. It will suppress the local enemies. It will expose the enemy informers and CIDs and expose them among the masses. It will arrest them and summon them before the people's court. It will actively move the militia and the masses in identifying and controlling them. It will pass information about such persons to the janathana sarkar, Party, People's Guerilla forces and the various departments.
3. It will take up all the necessary actions the janathana sarkar decides to defeat the enemy conspiracies and control the conspiratorial actions of the enemy.
4. It will encourage all those qualified to join the people's militia. It will strive to arm them and train them. It will encourage and mobilize the youth to join PGA forces.
5. It will establish government intelligence and make it work. It will establish a 'protective department' (security force) to protect the law and order in the masses. This department will see that the bad elements, hierarchs do not provoke anti revolutionary ideas and create riots in the village. It shall help the people to intensify the People's War by protecting law and order in the village.
6. Jails shall be in the control of this department. This department will implement the punishments the people's court gives them.
7. It will mobilize the people to fight back and defeat the encirclement and suppression attacks and campaigns of the enemy forces. It will cooperate with the main, secondary forces and command in this area in retaliation.
8. This department too shall have in its control the people's government armed forces.

4. People's judicial department

1. The people's courts will work as per the new principles of justice, class line and mass line. The judicial department will solve the problems

between the people so as to enhance their integrity. Normally it does not punish to solve them. When it tries landlords, hierarchs, heads of the ruling class parties, exploiting government officers, police, paramilitary, military forces, goondas, anarchists, thieves, deceivers, conspirators, police agents and others it isolates them from the people and punishes them in the necessary way including confiscation of their properties. It follows methods to increase the role of people in avoiding crimes. It gives death sentence to those who indulge in counter revolutionary crimes. Before it implements death sentence the local janathana sarkars have to obtain permission from the higher courts. Except for counter revolutionary crimes, it will send those indulged in murder, attempt to murder, atrocities on women, informing the exploiting police and other such things to the labor camps. In these camps, they are made to do labor. They are taught revolutionary politics and are reformed. It will help to develop the people's judicial system by passing verdict on disputes, crimes and conspiracies. It will also keep in view the customary traditions while giving verdict. The number of judges must be according to the character and intensity of the cases. The judicial committee solves the normal cases. In critical cases the number of judges may be enhanced to nine.

2. There are yet certain forums to solve the disputes among the people in the adivasi society. According to the intensity of the problem and the character they are brought forth. The people's court must bear this in mind. The people's courts will strive to develop these forums to be people oriented and work for the integrity among the people.
3. Whatever the case or dispute may be, it will collect the related information about the case beforehand, listen to the arguments of both the parties during the trial, listen to the evidences totally and then pass a verdict. Normally the trial is open and the people can tell their opinion freely. Thus their role in the judicial system will increase.
4. In each and every case there must be voting among the judges and verdict must be given according to the opinion of the majority. It may be given with slight majority also. But in critical cases the verdicts must have 2/3 rd majorities. The president of the judicial departmental committee or the judge that presided the trial shall announce the verdicts. They must give the necessary explanation.
5. Those who are not satisfied with the verdict of the local judicial committee can appeal to the area court and even above it.
6. All the citizens shall have fundamental and ordinary rights. No citizen should be arrested without proper legal basis. The citizens must consider the arrest as a proper action done in a democratic legal method. Otherwise they can challenge the arrest warrant.
7. The people's judicial committee shall take the help of the other departments, mainly the defense committee in trying the cases.

8. If the members of the Party Committee or the PGA forces commit mistakes in dealing with the people they will be summoned in the people's court with the permission of the concerned Party Committee.
9. The people's courts will make a comprehensive and deep study regarding the families of the soldiers, martyrs and injured in the people's army and regarding the 'pado' (spouses) of those that are recruited into the Party and pass verdict.

5. *People's education and cultural committee*

1. This departmental committee shall look after the educational and cultural responsibilities for the development of scientific, democratic culture among the masses. In addition to the political consciousness and scientific knowledge it will strive to create primary knowledge about administration, organization and state affairs.
2. It will run primary, middle and adult schools and libraries for general education. It will strive to prepare new textbooks. It will make efforts to teach primary education in mother tongue.
3. It will raise the consciousness of the masses against the feudal, imperialist culture and develop democratic culture among the people. It will raise the consciousness of the masses so that they will come out of the feudal and bad traditions.
4. It will enlighten the people so that they oppose the media that propagates drinking liquor, gambling, prostitution and obscene literature (songs and films). It bans the same. It will enlighten the people so that they consider untouchability, discrimination of caste and tribe, violence on women, attacks on minorities as crimes and mobilizes them against the same.
5. It will conduct revolutionary festivals. It will conduct sports competition. It will strive to develop the youth physically and mentally. It will utilize the educated youth, intellectuals and teachers for the development of education and culture.
6. The committee shall conduct meetings and conferences for the development of education and culture whenever necessary. In addition to the development of education it will seriously try to develop New Democratic Culture and values in the personal, family and social life. It will highlight the people's art. It will pay attention to protect them. It will make a study on the local customs and traditions, festivals, marriages, death, deliveries and other such things and try to reduce the expenditure on them. It will try to bring the necessary reforms in this regard.
7. It will encourage inter caste, inter tribe and inter religious marriages with the aim of developing New Democratic Culture. It will support those who marry so.
8. It will totally oppose the attempts to Hinduise the adivasis. It will

condemn and oppose marriages of adivasi goddesses with the name of Hindu goddesses, building temples, make the adivasi children sing divine songs and conducting Hindu festivals. It will oppose the attitude of those who transformed into Hindu religion considering adivasis as untouchables and discriminating them branding as 'katwa' (sudra). It will condemn and oppose the propagation of ramayana, mahabharatha and other epics. It will stop the process of proselytizing the adivasis to Hindu religion and the construction of churches in the adivasi areas.

9. It will not allow Saraswathi sisumandir, Sevabharathi, Vanavasi Kalyan Ashram and other such things that are distorting history and other subjects through the texts with Hindu religious ideology in the name of education.
10. It will oppose and shall not allow the activities of NGA and INGO (international non government organizations) that is misleading the masses from class struggle in the name of education, medicine and other such services with the help of imperialist and multinational corporations and their funds.
11. It will take care that the 'aarogato', 'pothum kabad', 'paaro' and other such methods do not be useful for the hierarchs for economic exploitation. It will try to develop the cooperative nature and integrity in the adivasi traditions.
12. It will discourage long duration collective hunting. It disturbs the agricultural development works. It will encourage the people to utilise this time for productive activities.

6. *Public health - Social Welfare department*

1. This department will strive for the protection of people's health to better their living conditions. It will develop their understanding towards physical fitness, the importance of exercises in order to continue People's War and strives to take the necessary actions.
2. It will pay special attention for the health of women and children.
3. It will strive to utilize the local methods of medicine. It will try to remove the unscientific ideas in the traditional medicine like manthra and encourage the herbal medicine they practice. It will send volunteers for primary training to fulfill the primary medical necessities of the people and use them as doctors. It will run medical centers locally. The doctors will go to the patients and the patients need not necessarily go to the doctor or those who have medicine. It will encourage the people to take medicines from the medical center. It will buy the necessary medicine for the medical center. It will collect funds for the medical center through collective labor or in the form of donations. It will collect medicines from all sources including the voluntary organizations. It will also utilize the services of doctors with democratic ideas. It will conduct medical camps.

4. It will try to eliminate the blind superstitions in the people regarding health.
5. It will caution the people about the seasonal diseases. It will propagate the precautions to be taken. It will enlighten the people about nutritional diet, personal and social hygiene and against the bad habits. If anyone needs to go the hospital the committee shall help him or her in all ways.
6. It will record births and death.
7. It will mobilize the people and protect hygiene. It will conduct meetings and propaganda campaigns to develop the knowledge of people about health and hygiene. It propagates in various forms.
8. It will pay special attention towards the handicapped, old persons, orphans, children and welfare of victims of repression.
9. It will try to arrange houses and house sites for those who do not have, with the help of the people.
10. It will try to create clean drinking water and will mobilize the people for the same.

*7. **Forest protection committee***

1. It will protect the forests maintaining the traditional boundaries. It will protect the environment.
2. It will allow the people to use the trees that fell in the forest as fuel.
3. One has to obtain timber for domestic purposes and agricultural tools with the permission of this department.
4. It will regulate the trading of forest products for profit. It will oppose procuring of herbs, fruit trees and other valuable trees that are helpful for medical services in methods that would destroy them.
5. It will strive for developing forests. It will stop illicit timber business. It will arrest those who do illegal timber business and those who help for the same and hand over them to the people's court.
6. It will oppose the plantations of the exploiting government that destroys environment.
7. It will work against the exploiting government policies that are trying to send away the adivasis from the forests in the name of construction of Vanyaprani abhayaranyas, National Parks and other such things.
8. Those who need lands for agriculture must cut the forest only with the permission of this department.
9. It will allow the traditional hunting of adivasis. But hunting for the sake of business is banned. It will also ban business of flesh, horns, skin and other such organs of the animals.
10. It will ban the use of chemical pesticide to catch fish, animals and birds.
11. It will oppose all kinds of heavy projects that lead to the destroyal of forests in a big way and displace the adivasis and destroy the environment.

8. Public relations department

1. It will take the government policies to the people through the various mass organizations. It will have a close relation with the mass organizations for this purpose. It will not intervene in their internal matters.
2. It will strive to make the mass organizations play a main role in implementing the government policies in a regular manner.

It will widely propagate the activities and policies of the government. It will release the necessary propaganda material.

SECTION II
INTERVIEWS WITH TOP-LEADERSHIP

Interview with Ganapathy, General Secretary, CPI (Maoist) - I

Ganapathy is a native of Bheerpur village in Karimnagar district of Andhra Pradesh. He is a teacher by training and profession and joined the Maoist underground at the inception of the origanisation in its earlier avatar *as the CPI-ML (People's War) along with its founder Kodnapalli Seetharamaiah. In 1992, he ousted Seetharamaiah and replaced him as the general secretary of the outfit. Ganapathy over-saw the merger of the outfit with Party Unity in 1998, and later with Maoist Communist Centre of India in 2004 and now heads the CPI (Maoist).*

He rarely gives interviews to the media. Lately, on the few occasions he did, they were through the e-mail after collating questions sent by various journalists. On one of those extremely rare occasions, he met with an Indian journalist and a foreign national at an undisclosed location and gave the following interview.

The Maoists consider that the uncertainty and chaos witnessed in Largarh in 2009 and thereafter is 'Second Naxalbari'. Explaining the events of the Lalgarh movement he says that it was "a new model of mass movement in the country" and goes on to that the participation of several adivasi women gives it the unique character of being a 'truly democratic movement'. He also vows to replicate the Lalgarh experiment in other parts of the country and adds that the Maoists have learnt important lessons from it. He says that by building the broadest fighting front, and by adopting appropriate tactics of combining the militant mass political movement with armed resistance of the people and our PLGA (People's Liberation Guerilla Army), we will defeat the massive offensive by the Central-State forces.

In line with the Maoist rhetoric Ganapathy contends that the Union government proscribed the Maoist outfit at the behest of "comprador bureaucratic bourgeoisie and the imperialists, particularly US imperialists, in order that they could exploit the mineral wealth and natural resources of the country and exploit the Adivasis, unhindered." He puts up a brave face and claims that the Union government is also 'scared' of the rising popularity of the Maoists and the success of their model of development through Janatana Sarkars *and Revolutionary People's Committees and has, therefore, proscribed the outfit. He also boasts that with wider mass mobilization, increased military offensives and preparing all organs of the outfit, they shall be able to defeat the 'offensives' of the security forces.*

He attributes to several mistakes the "serious set-back" encountered by the Maoists in Andhra Pradesh, and as if to console his comrades he holds that in any revolutionary movement there shall be advances and defeats, but the final victory shall be achieved.

He also discusses the global situation and his organization's linkages with various other terrorist groups. Importantly, he refutes all allegations of any links with the Laskar-e-Toiba and any other terrorist organization operating from Pakistan. Ganapathy supports the Tamil aspiration for a separate homeland in Sri Lanka. He does pin-point the reasons for the defeat of the Liberation Tigers of Tamil Eelam (LTTE), but lambasts the Sinhala people as chauvinist and claims: "By adopting a proletarian outlook and ideology, adopting new tactics and building the broadest united front of all nationalist and democratic forces, it is possible to achieve the liberation of the oppressed Tamil nation [in Sri Lanka]." However, he is of the opinion that this can be achieved by Maoist forces alone.

He admits that, at the pan-India level the Maoist movement is in a stage of "strategic defensive". He declines to predict how long this stage would last. He concludes with the ususal Maoist jargon and rhetoric and finally says, "... we are confident that the vast masses of the country will join the ranks of revolutionaries and take the Indian revolution to the next stage."

"WE SHALL CERTAINLY DEFEAT THE GOVERNMENT"

The supreme commander of CPI (Maoist) talks to *Open* magazine on October 17, 2009 in his first-ever interview

At first sight, Mupalla Laxman Rao, who is about to turn 60, looks like a school teacher. In fact, he was one in the early 1970s in Andhra Pradesh's Karimnagar district. In 2009, however, the bespectacled, soft-spoken figure is India's Most Wanted Man. He runs one of the world's largest Left insurgencies—a man known in Home Ministry dossiers as Ganapathi; a man whose writ runs large through 15 states. The supreme commander of CPI (Maoist) is a science graduate and holds a B Ed degree as well. He still conducts classes, but now they are on guerilla warfare for other senior Maoists. He replaced the founder of the People's War Group, Kondapalli Seetharaamiah, as the party's general-secretary in 1991. Ganapathi is known to change his location frequently, and intelligence reports say he has been spotted in cities like Hyderabad, Kolkata and Kochi.

After months of attempts, Ganapathi agreed to give his first-ever interview. Somewhere in the impregnable jungles of Dandakaranya, he spoke to RAHUL PANDITA on issues ranging from the Government's proposed anti-Naxal offensive to Islamist Jihadist movements.

Q: *Lalgarh has been described as the New Naxalbari by the CPI (Maoist). How has it become so significant for you?*

A: The Lalgarh mass uprising has, no doubt, raised new hopes among the oppressed people and the entire revolutionary camp in West Bengal. It has great positive impact not only on the people of West Bengal but also on the people all over the country. It has emerged as a new model of mass movement in the country. We had seen similar types of movements earlier in Manipur, directed against Army atrocities and Armed Forces Special Powers Act (AFSPA), in Kashmir, in Dandakaranya and to some extent in Orissa, after the Kalinganagar massacre perpetrated by the Naveen Patnaik government.

Then there have been mass movements in Singur and Nandigram but there the role of a section of the ruling classes is also significant. These movements were utilised by the ruling class parties for their own electoral interests. But Lalgarh is a more widespread and more sustained mass political movement that has spurned the leadership of all the parliamentary political parties, thereby rendering them completely irrelevant. The people of Lalgarh had even boycotted the recent Lok Sabha polls, thereby unequivocally demonstrating their anger and frustration with all the reactionary ruling class parties. Lalgarh also has some distinctive features such as a high degree of participation of women, a genuinely democratic character and a wider mobilisation of Adivasis. No wonder, it has become a rallying point for the revolutionary-democratic forces in West Bengal.

Q: *If it is a people's movement, how did Maoists get involved in Lalgarh?*

A: As far as our party's role is concerned, we have been working in Paschim Midnapur, Bankura and Purulia, in what is popularly known as Jangalmahal since the 1980s. We fought against the local feudal forces, against the exploitation and oppression by the forest officials, contractors, unscrupulous usurers and the *goondaism* of both the CPM and Trinamool Congress. The ruling CPM, in particular, has become the chief exploiter and oppressor of the Adivasis of the region, and it has unleashed its notorious vigilanté gangs called Harmad Vahini on whoever questions its authority. With the State authority in its hands, and with the aid of the police, it is playing a role worse than that of the cruel landlords in other regions of the country.

Given this background, anyone who dares to fight against oppression and exploitation by the CPM can win the respect and confidence of the people. Since our party has been fighting uncompromisingly against the atrocities of the CPM goons, it naturally gained the confidence and respect of the people of the region.

The police atrocities in the wake of the landmine blast on 2 November [in 2008, from which West Bengal Chief Minister Buddhadeb Bhattacharjee had a narrow escape] acted as the trigger that brought the pent-up anger of the masses into the open. This assumed the form of a long-drawn mass movement, and our party played the role of a catalyst.

Q: *But not so long ago, the CPM was your friend. You even took arms and ammunition from it to fight the Trinamool Congress. This has been confirmed by a Politburo member of CPI (Maoist) in certain interviews. And now you are fighting the CPM* *with the help of the Trinamool. How did a friend turn into a foe and vice-versa?*

A: This is only partially true. We came to know earlier that some ammunition was taken by our local cadre from the CPM unit in the area. There was, however, no understanding with the leadership of the CPM in this regard. Our approach was to unite all sections of the oppressed masses at the lower levels against the *goondaism* and oppression of Trinamool goons in the area at that time. And since a section of the oppressed masses were in the fold of the CPM at that time, we fought together with them against Trinamool. Still, taking into consideration the overall situation in West Bengal, it was not a wise step to take arms and ammunition from the CPM even at the local level when the contradiction was basically between two sections of the reactionary ruling classes.

Our central committee discussed this, criticised the comrade responsible for taking such a decision, and directed the concerned comrades to stop this immediately. As regards taking ammunition from the Trinamool Congress, I remember that we had actually purchased it not directly from the Trinamool but from someone who had links with the Trinamool. There will never be any conditions or agreements with those selling us arms. That has been our understanding all along. As regards the said interview by our Politburo member, we will verify what he had actually said.

Q: *What are your tactics now in Lalgarh after the massive offensive by the Central and state forces?*

A: First of all, I wish to make it crystal clear that our party will spearhead and stand firmly by the side of the people of Lalgarh and entire Jangalmahal, and draw up tactics in accordance with the people's interests and mandate. We shall spread the struggle against the State everywhere and strive to win over the broad masses to the side of the people's cause. We shall fight the State offensive by mobilising the masses more militantly against the police, Harmad Vahini and CPM goons. The course of the development of the movement, of course, will depend on the level of consciousness and preparedness of the people of the region. The party will take this into consideration while formulating its tactics. The initiative of the masses will be released fully.

Q: *The Government has termed Lalgarh a 'laboratory' for anti-Naxal operations. Has your party also learnt any lessons from Lalgarh?*

A: Yes, our party too has a lot to learn from the masses of Lalgarh. Their upsurge was beyond our expectations. In fact, it was the common people, with the assistance of advanced elements influenced by revolutionary politics, who played a crucial role in the formulation of tactics. They formed their own organisation, put forth their charter of demands, worked out various novel forms of struggle, and stood steadfast in the struggle despite the brutal attacks by the police and the social-fascist Harmad gangs. The Lalgarh movement has the support of revolutionary and democratic forces not only in West Bengal but in the entire country. We are appealing to all revolutionary and democratic forces in the country to unite to fight back the fascist offensive by the Buddhadeb government in West Bengal and the UPA Government at the Centre. By building the broadest fighting front, and by adopting appropriate tactics of combining the militant mass political movement with armed resistance of the people and our PLGA (People's Liberation Guerilla Army), we will defeat the massive offensive by the Central-state forces. I cannot say more than this at the present juncture.

Q: *The Centre has declared an all-out war against Maoists by branding the CPI (Maoist) a terrorist organisation and imposing an all-India ban on the party. How has it affected your party?*

A: Our party has already been banned in several states of India. By imposing the ban throughout the country, the Government now wants to curb all our open activities in West Bengal and a few other states where legal opportunities exist to some extent. The Government wants to use this draconian UAPA [Unlawful Activities (Prevention) Act] to harass whoever dares to raise a voice against fake encounters, rapes and other police atrocities on the people residing in Maoist-dominated regions. Anyone questioning the State's brutalities will now be branded a terrorist.

The real terrorists and biggest threats to the country's security are none other than Manmohan Singh, Chidambaram, Buddhadeb, other ruling class leaders and feudal forces who terrorise the people on a daily basis.

The UPA Government had declared, as soon as it assumed power for the second time, that it would crush the Maoist 'menace' and began pouring in huge funds to the states for this purpose. The immediate reason behind this move is the pressure exerted by the comprador bureaucratic bourgeoisie and the imperialists, particularly US imperialists, who want to plunder the resources of our country without any hindrance. These sharks aspire to swallow the rich abundant mineral and forest wealth in the vast contiguous region stretching from Jangalmahal to north Andhra. This region is the wealthiest as well as the most underdeveloped part of our country. These sharks want to loot the wealth and drive the Adivasi people of the region to further impoverishment.

Another major reason for the current offensive by the ruling classes is the fear of the rapid growth of the Maoist movement and its increasing influence over a significant proportion of the Indian population. The Janatana Sarkars in Dandakaranya and the revolutionary people's committees in Jharkhand, Orissa and parts of some other states have become new models of genuine people's democracy and development. The rulers want to crush these new models of development and genuine democracy, as these are emerging as the real alternative before the people of the country at large.

Q: *The Home Ministry has made preparations for launching a long-term battle against Maoists. A huge force will be soon trying to wrest away areas from your control. How do you plan to confront this offensive?*

A: Successive governments in various states and the Centre have been hatching schemes over the years. But they could not achieve any significant success through their cruel offensive in spite of murdering hundreds of our leaders and cadres. Our party and our movement continued to consolidate and expand to new regions. From two or three states, the movement has now spread to over 15 states, giving jitters to the ruling classes. Particularly after the merger of the erstwhile MCCI and People's War in September 2004 [the merger between these groups led to the formation of the CPI (Maoist)], the UPA Government has unleashed the most cruel all-round offensive against the Maoist movement. Yet our party continued to grow despite suffering some severe losses. In the past three years, in particular, our PLGA has achieved several significant victories.

We have been confronting the continuous offensive of the enemy with the support and active involvement of the masses. We shall confront the new offensive of the enemy by stepping up such heroic resistance and preparing the entire party, PLGA, the various revolutionary parties and organisations and the entire people. Although the enemy may achieve a few successes in the initial phase, we shall certainly overcome and defeat the Government offensive with the active mobilisation of the vast masses and the support of all the revolutionary and democratic forces in the country. No fascist regime or military dictator in history could succeed in suppressing forever the just and democratic struggles of the people through brute force, but were, on the contrary, swept away by the high tide of people's resistance. People, who are the makers of history, will rise up like a tornado under our party's leadership to wipe out the reactionary blood-sucking vampires ruling our country.

Q: *Why do you think the CPI (Maoist) suffered a serious setback in Andhra Pradesh?*

A: It was due to several mistakes on our part that we suffered a serious setback in most of Andhra Pradesh by 2006. At the same time, we should also look at the setback from another angle. In any protracted people's war, there will be advances and retreats. If we look at the situation in Andhra Pradesh from this perspective, you will understand that what we did there is a kind of retreat. Confronted with a superior force, we chose to temporarily retreat our forces from some regions of Andhra Pradesh, extend and develop our bases in the surrounding regions and then hit back at the enemy.

Now even though we received a setback, it should be borne in mind that this setback is a temporary one. The objective conditions in which our revolution began in Andhra Pradesh have not undergone any basic change. This very fact continues to serve as the basis for the growth and intensification of our movement. Moreover, we now have a more consolidated mass base, a relatively better-trained people's guerilla army and an all-India party with deep roots among the basic classes who comprise the backbone of our revolution. This is the reason why the reactionary rulers are unable to suppress our revolutionary war, which is now raging in several states in the country.

We had taken appropriate lessons from the setback suffered by our party in Andhra Pradesh and, based on these lessons, drew up tactics in other states. Hence we are able to fight back the cruel all-round offensive of the enemy effectively, inflict significant losses on the enemy, preserve our subjective forces, consolidate our party, develop a people's liberation guerilla army, establish embryonic forms of new democratic people's governments in some pockets, and take the people's war to a higher stage. Hence we have an advantageous situation, overall, for reviving the movement in Andhra Pradesh. Our revolution advances wave-like and periods of ebb yield place to periods of high tide.

Q: *What are the reasons for the setback suffered by the LTTE in Sri Lanka?*

A: There is no doubt that the movement for a separate sovereign Tamil Eelam has suffered a severe setback with the defeat and considerable decimation of the LTTE. The Tamil people and the national liberation forces are now leaderless. However, the Tamil people at large continue to cherish nationalist aspirations for a separate Tamil homeland. The conditions that gave rise to the movement for Tamil Eelam, in the first place, prevail to this day. The Sinhala-chauvinist Sri Lankan ruling classes can never change their policy of discrimination against the Tamil nation, its culture, language, etcetera. The jingoistic rallies and celebrations organised by the government and Sinhala chauvinist parties all over Sri Lanka in the wake of Prabhakaran's death and the defeat of the LTTE show the national hatred for Tamils nurtured by Sinhala organisations and the extent to which the minds of ordinary Sinhalese are poisoned with such chauvinist frenzy.

The conspiracy of the Sinhala ruling classes in occupying Tamil territories is similar to that of the Zionist rulers of Israel. The land-starved Sinhala people will now be settled in Tamil areas. The entire demography of the region is going to change. The ground remains fertile for the resurgence of the Tamil liberation struggle.

Even if it takes time, the war for a separate Tamil Eelam is certain to revive, taking lessons from the defeat of the LTTE. By adopting a proletarian outlook and ideology, adopting new tactics and building the broadest united front of all nationalist and democratic forces, it is possible to achieve the liberation of the oppressed Tamil nation [in Sri Lanka]. Maoist forces have to grow strong enough to provide leadership and give a correct direction and anti-imperialist orientation to this struggle to achieve a sovereign People's Democratic Republic of Tamil Eelam. This alone can achieve the genuine liberation of the Tamil nation in Sri Lanka.

Q: *Is it true that you received military training from the LTTE initially?*

A: No. It is not a fact. We had clarified this several times in the past.

Q: *But, one of your senior commanders has told me that some senior cadre of the erstwhile PWG did receive arms training and other support from the LTTE.*

A: Let me reiterate, there is no relation at all between our party and the LTTE. We tried several times to establish relations with the LTTE but its leadership was reluctant to have a relationship with Maoists in India. Hence, there is no question of the LTTE giving training to us. In spite of it, we continued our support to the struggle for Tamil Eelam. However, a few persons who had separated from the LTTE came into our contact and we took their help in receiving initial training in the last quarter of the 1980s.

Q: *Does your party have links with Lashkar-e-Toiba or other Islamic militant groups having links with Pakistan?*

A: No. Not at all. This is only mischievous, calculated propaganda by the police officials, bureaucrats and leaders of the reactionary political parties to defame us and thereby justify their cruel offensive against the Maoist movement. By propagating the lie that our party has links with groups linked to Pakistan's ISI, the reactionary rulers of our country want to prove that we too are terrorists and gain legitimacy for their brutal terror campaign against Maoists and the people in the areas of armed agrarian struggle. Trying to prove the involvement of a foreign hand in every just and democratic struggle, branding those fighting for the liberation of the oppressed as traitors to the country, is part of the psychological-war of the reactionary rulers.

Q: *What is your party's stand regarding Islamist jihadist movements?*

A: Islamic jihadist movements of today are a product of imperialist—particularly US imperialist—aggression, intervention, bullying, exploitation and suppression of the oil-rich Islamic and Arab countries of West Asia, Afghanistan, Pakistan, Somalia, etcetera, and the persecution of the entire Muslim religious community. As part of their designs for global hegemony, the imperialists, particularly US imperialists, have encouraged and endorsed every war of brazen aggression and brutal attacks by their surrogate state of Israel.

Our party unequivocally opposes every attack on Arab and Muslim countries and the Muslim community at large in the name of 'war on global terror'. In fact, Muslim religious fundamentalism is encouraged and fostered by imperialists as long as it serves their interests—such as in Saudi Arabia and other Gulf countries, and Kuwait, Afghanistan, Iraq, Pakistan.

Q: *But what about attacks perpetrated by the so-called 'Jihadis' on innocent people like it happened on 26/11?*

A: See, Islamic jihadist movements have two aspects: one is their anti-imperialist aspect, and the other their reactionary aspect in social and cultural matters. Our party supports the struggle of Muslim countries and people against imperialism, while criticising and struggling against the reactionary ideology and social outlook of Muslim fundamentalism. It is only Maoist leadership that can provide correct anti-imperialist orientation and achieve class unity among Muslims as well as people of other religious persuasions. The influence of Muslim fundamentalist ideology and leadership will diminish as communist revolutionaries and other democratic-secular forces increase their ideological influence over the Muslim masses. As communist revolutionaries, we always strive to reduce the influence of the obscurantist reactionary ideology and outlook of the mullahs and maulvis on the Muslim masses, while uniting with all those fighting against the common enemy of the world people—that is, imperialism, particularly American imperialism.

Q: *How do you look at the changes in US policy after Barack Obama took over from George Bush?*

A: Firstly, one would be living in a fool's paradise if one imagines that there is going to be any qualitative change in American policy—whether internal or external—after Barack Obama took over from George Bush. In fact, the policies on national security and foreign affairs pursued by Obama over the past eight months have shown the essential continuity with those of his predecessor. The ideological and political justification for these regressive policies at home and aggressive policies abroad is the same trash put forth by the Bush administration—the so-called 'global war on terror', based on outright lies and slander. Worse still, the policies have become even more aggressive under Obama with his planned expansion of the US-led war of aggression in Afghanistan into the territory of Pakistan. The hands of this new killer-in-chief of the pack of imperialist wolves are already stained with the blood of hundreds of women and children who are cruelly murdered in relentless missile attacks from Predator drones in Afghanistan and Pakistan. And, within the US itself, bail-outs for the tiny corporate elite and attacks on democratic and human rights of US citizens continue without any change.

The oppressed people and nations of the world are now confronting an even more formidable and dangerous enemy in the form of an African-American president of the most powerful military machine and world gendarme. The world people should unite to wage a more relentless, more militant and more consistent struggle against the American marauders led by Barack Obama and pledge to defeat them to usher in a world of peace, stability and genuine democracy.

Q: *How do you look at the current developments in Nepal?*

A: As soon as the Communist Party of Nepal (Maoist) [CPN(M)] came to power in alliance with the comprador-feudal parties through the parliamentary route in Nepal, we had pointed out the grave danger of imperialist and Indian expansionist intervention in Nepal and how they would leave no stone unturned to overthrow the government led by CPN(M). As long as Prachanda did not defy the directives of the Indian Government, it was allowed to continue, but when it began to go against Indian hegemony, it was immediately pulled down. CPN-UML withdrew support to the Prachanda-led government upon the advice of American imperialists and Indian expansionists. We disagreed with the line of peaceful transition pursued by the UCPN(M) in the name of tactics. We decided to send an open letter to the UCPN(M). It was released in July 2009.

We made our party's stand clear in the letter. We pointed out that the UCPN(M) chose to reform the existing State through an elected constituent assembly and a bourgeois democratic republic instead of adhering to the Marxist-Leninist understanding on the imperative to smash the old State and establish a proletarian State. This would have been the first step towards the goal of achieving socialism through the radical transformation of society and all oppressive class relations. It is indeed a great tragedy that the UCPN(M) has chosen to abandon the path of protracted people's war and pursue a parliamentary path in spite of having *de facto* power in most of the countryside.

It is heartening to hear that a section of the leadership of the UCPN(M) has begun to struggle against the revisionist positions taken by Comrade Prachanda and others. Given the great revolutionary traditions of the UCPN(M), we hope that the inner-party struggle will repudiate the right opportunist line pursued by its leadership, give up revisionist stands and practices, and apply minds creatively to the concrete conditions of Nepal.

Q: *Of late, the party has suffered serious losses of party leadership at the central and state level. Besides, it is widely believed that some of the senior-most Maoist leaders, including you, have become quite old and suffer from serious illnesses, which is also cited as one of the reasons for the surrenders. What is the effect of the losses and surrenders on the movement? How are you dealing with problems arising out of old age and illnesses?*

A: (Smiles...) This type of propaganda is being carried out continuously, particularly by the Special Intelligence Branch (SIB) of Andhra Pradesh. It is a part of the psychological war waged by intelligence officials and top police brass aimed at confusing and demoralising supporters of the Maoist movement. It is a fact that some of the party leaders at the central and state level could be described as senior citizens according to criteria used by the government, that is, those who have crossed the threshold of 60 years. You can start calling me too a senior citizen in a few months (smiles). But old age and ill-health have never been a serious problem in our party until now. You can see the 'senior citizens' in our party working for 16-18 hours a day and covering long distances on foot.As for surrenders, it is a big lie to say that old age and ill-health have been a reason for some of the surrenders.

When Lanka Papi Reddy, a former member of our central committee, surrendered in the beginning of last year, the media propagated that more surrenders of our party leaders will follow due to ill-health. The fact is that Papi Reddy surrendered due to his loss of political conviction and his petty-bourgeois false prestige and ego. Hence he was not prepared to face the party after he was demoted by the central committee for his anarchic behaviour with a woman comrade.

Some senior leaders of our party, like comrades Sushil Roy and Narayan Sanyal, had become a nightmare for the ruling classes even when they were in their mid 60s. Hence they were arrested, tortured and imprisoned despite their old age and ill-health. The Government is doing everything possible to prevent them from getting bail. Even if someone in our party is old, he/she continues to serve the revolution by doing whatever work possible. For instance, Comrade Niranjan Bose, who died recently at the age of 92, had been carrying out revolutionary propaganda until his martyrdom. The social fascist rulers were so scared of this nonagenarian Maoist revolutionary that they had even arrested him four years back. Such is the spirit of Maoist revolutionaries—and power of the ideology of Marxism-Leninism-Maoism which they hold high. When there are serious illnesses, or physical and mental limitations to perform normal work, such comrades are given suitable work.

Q: *But what about the arrests and elimination of some of your senior leadership? How do you intend to fill up such losses?*

A: Well, it is a fact that we lost some senior leaders at the state and central level in the past four or five years. Some leaders were secretly arrested and murdered in the most cowardly manner. Many other and state leaders were arrested and placed behind bars in the recent past in Jharkhand, Bihar, Chhattisgarh, Orissa, West Bengal, Maharashtra, Haryana and other states. The loss of leadership will have a grave impact on the party and Indian revolution as a whole. We are reviewing the reasons for the losses regularly and devising ways and means to prevent further losses. By adopting strictly secret methods of functioning and foolproof underground mechanisms, by enhancing our mass base, vigilance and local intelligence, smashing enemy intelligence networks and studying their plans and tactics, we hope to check further losses. At the same time, we are training and developing new revolutionary leadership at all levels to fill up the losses.

Q: *How do you sum up the present stage of war between your forces and those of the Indian State?*

A: Our war is in the stage of strategic defence. In some regions, we have an upper hand, while in others the enemy has the upper hand. Overall, our forces have been quite successful in carrying out a series of tactical counter-offensive operations against the enemy in our guerilla zones in the past few years.

It is true that our party has suffered some serious leadership losses, but we are able to inflict serious losses on the enemy too. In fact, in the past three years, the enemy forces suffered more casualties than we did. The enemy has been trying all means at their disposal to weaken, disrupt and crush our party and movement. They have tried covert agents and informers, poured in huge amounts of money to buy off weak elements in the revolutionary camp, and announced a series of rehabilitation packages and other material incentives to lure away people from the revolutionary camp. Thousands of crores of rupees have been sanctioned for police modernisation, training and for raising additional commando forces; for increasing Central forces; for training Central and state forces in counter-insurgency warfare; and for building roads, communication networks and other infrastructure for the rapid movement of their troops in our guerilla zones. The Indian State has set up armed vigilante groups and provided total support to the indescribable atrocities committed by these armed gangs on the people. Psychological warfare against Maoists was taken to unheard of levels.

Nevertheless, we continued to make greater advances, consolidated the party and the revolutionary people's committees at various levels, strengthened the PLGA qualitatively and quantitatively, smashed the enemy's intelligence network in several areas, effectively countered the dirty psychological-war waged by the enemy, and foiled the enemy's all-out attempts to disrupt and smash our movement. The successes we had achieved in several tactical counter-offensive operations carried out across the country in recent days, the militant mass movements in several states, particularly against displacement and other burning issues of the people, initiatives taken by our revolutionary people's governments in various spheres—all these have had a great impact on the people, while demoralising enemy forces. There are reports of desertions and disobedience of orders by the jawans posted in Maoist-dominated areas. Quite a few have refused to undertake training in jungle warfare or take postings in our areas, and had to face suspension. This trend will grow with the further advance of our people's war. Overall, our party's influence has grown stronger and it has now come to be recognised as the only genuine alternative before the people.

Q: *How long will this stage of strategic defence last, with the Centre ready to go for the jugular?*

A The present stage of strategic defence will last for some more time. It is difficult to predict how long it will take to pass this stage and go to the stage of strategic equilibrium or strategic stalemate. It depends on the transformation of our guerilla zones into base areas, creation of more guerilla zones and red resistance areas across the country, the development of our PLGA. With the ever-intensifying crisis in all spheres due to the anti-people policies of pro-imperialist, pro-feudal governments, the growing frustration and anger of the masses resulting from the most rapacious policies of loot and plunder pursued by the reactionary ruling classes, we are confident that the vast masses of the country will join the ranks of revolutionaries and take the Indian revolution to the next stage.

***

INTERVIEW WITH GANAPATHY, GENERAL SECRETARY, CPI (MAOIST) - II

In deference to requests from various journalists from different parts of the country, after a very long gap Ganapathy agreed to share his thoughts on a wide range of issues. Fearing for his safety, the elusive Maoist supremo got the questions sent to him by e-mail, put them together and sent his answers through e-mail. This interview was reported in parts in various newspapers in India and was widely circulated on the Internet. The Nepalese Maoists reproduced the interview in their official organ, The Worker. *The interview assumes significance for a couple of reasons. The Nepalese*

Maoists decided to come over-ground by then. Also, this was the first interview from him after the joint interview with Kishanji, the erstwhile general secretary of the Maoist Communist Centre of India, on the occasion of the formation of the CPI (Maoist).

In this interview, he explains the decisions taken at the Unity/9th Congress of the CPI (Maoist) held in January 2007, which has been discussed in great detail in a separate section in this volume. Notably, he mentions that the Congress has decided to expand the people's war to all parts of the country and heighten military activities, i.e. take the movement to the next higher level in all areas of its operation.

His assessment of the ground situation Andhra Pradesh is the same as in the interview he gave two years later, in 2009 (reproduced above). He goes on to add: "No force on earth can stop this high tide of revolution whatever losses and setbacks we might be facing today in AP". Thereafter, his vitriol against the Andhra Pradesh government and his lambasting of its security and development measures is the best compliment which that State government could have hoped to secure from any one for its successful handling of the rebels and virtually bolting them up in very limited and isolated pockets of the State.

Importantly, he says that their plan is to expand the guerrilla activities to as many areas as possible in order that the security forces shall be distributed thinly across a wider swath of area. He has correctly understood that there are only limited number of forces available for deployment against the rebels at any given point in time.

On Salwa Judum *he says that the counter-revolutionary force was committing various heinous crimes and adds that it was created "to establish peace of the graveyard and clear the way for the unhindered loot" of mineral wealth by MNCs and Indian big industry. He warns of chilling massacres of the security forces if* Salwa Judum *was not disbanded.*

Identifying factors such as "soaring prices, unemployment, growing insecurity of life, steep increases in family expenditure due to high cost of education, health, transport, etc he concludes that there is increasing "frustration" among the middle class in India. The rebels hope to mobilize the middle class on issues of its concern and, thus, co-opt them into their fold/win their sympathy and support. Thus, he goes on to convey his opinion on parliamentary democracy, democratic elections, universal adult suffrage, etc and lampoons them, thus, reiterating the well-known Maoist stand that parliamentary democracy is a sham.

Ganapathy asserts that violence is a pre-condition to effect systemic changes and argues that their violence is merely counter-violence. In other words, his contention is that the present day ruling classes resort to the use of force to suppress dissent, provide no room for peaceful accommodation of the aspirations/interests of the toiling masses, and, therefore, violence is the only recourse they are left with.

Even as he admits that there have been peaceful, mass protests that brought about changes he quickly adds that they were mere regime changes, but not systemic changes. In the ultimate analysis, he contends that, unless there is a violent upsurge, power does not get transferred from one ruling class to another. Ganapathy clearly states that the Maoist military actions are meant to 'grab state power'.

INTERVIEW WITH COM. GANAPATHY

[Comrade Ganapathy is the General Secretary of the newly formed Communist Party of India (Maoist) after the unity between the erstwhile CPI (ML) (PW) and MCCI and he was also General Secretary during the period of CPI (ML) (PWG) and thereafter CPI (ML) (PW) which was formed after the merger of erstwhile CPI (ML) (PWG) and CPI (ML) (Party Unity). This interview was prepared by CPI (Maoist) by collecting the questions sent by various news papers and media including the BBC and the reply given by Com. Ganaathy. Hoping that it will help many readers of various parts of the world who strive very hard to get information of the revolutionary activities of the world in general and that of South Asia in particular which is considered as the storm centre of the world revolution, this interview has been published here by selecting some of them. —Editor]

Q: What are the major decisions of the Unity Congress will there be any change in your overall plans and tactics now?

The general direction of the Congress is to intensify the people's war and to take the war to all fronts. Concretely it decided to take the guerrilla war to a higher level of mobile war in the areas where guerrilla war is in an advanced stage and to expand the areas of armed struggle to as many states as possible. The destruction of the enemy forces has come into the immediate agenda in these areas without which it is very difficult to consolidate our gains or to advance further. Likewise, there is an immediate need to transform a vast area into the war zone so that there is enough room for maneuverability for our guerrilla forces, and in expansion the element so secrecy is very important; keeping in view the massive deployment of the central forces and special police forces of the states the Congress had drawn up plans to adopt various creative forms to cause serious damage to the enemy forces. The police and central forces will be taught how dangerous it is to enter our areas. We decided to strengthen the Party and the PLGA, mobilize the masses actively to resist the enemy forces, and to transform these areas into our strong bases by destroying the enemy's power in all forms. And all this will be achieved by wide mobilization of the masses into the war. As it is, hundreds of people, and at times even more than a thousand, are involved in the attacks against the enemy as you can see from the recent counter offensive operations as in Rani Bodili, Riga, CISF camp in Bokaro district, and so on in the past one month itself.

With the experience we gained in AP in the midst of ever-increasing and continuous state repression and state-sponsored repression, it is all the more important that our forces are not exposed wherever they are working. But at the same time we shall be in the forefront of every people's movement. The Congress has decided to take up struggles against the SEZs [Special Economic Zones] which are nothing but neo-colonial enclaves on Indian territory. They are not just snatching fertile farmlands of the peasants but are transforming the entire country into special zones for the unhindered ruthless exploitation and control by imperialists and the comprador big business houses. The congress gave the call to go deep into these struggles. We have no illusions on the cruel, fascist nature of the Indian state, and hence there is utmost need for maintaining secret methods of work as well as to be prepared for every kind of sacrifice.

Q: Finally, how do you sum up the achievements of your Unity Congress and its significance?

Ans: Our Unity Congress is an event of great historic significance in the history of the revolutionary movement of India. It not only marks the near-completion of the process of unification of the Maoist forces in the country but also the consolidation of the Party and the political line for the Indian revolution. The reaffirmation and enrichment of the revolutionary political line established by our founder leaders—comrades CM and KC—is the biggest achievement of significance is the establishment of a unified centralized leadership for the Indian revolution.

After a long time in the history of the revolutionary communist movement in India since the 1970s, a single directing centre has come into existence, with the merger of the MCCI and CPI (ML) [PW] in September 2004 and this center has become further consolidated and firmly established in the unity congress with the approval of the entire Party.

Q: There have been serious losses in Andhra Pradesh in recent times. What are the reasons? Has your movement become weakened overall? How do you plan to overcome these losses and regain the initiative?

Ans: I agree that the losses in the state of Andhra Pradesh are quite serious. They certainly have a considerable impact on the revolutionary movement in the country as a whole. AP, particularly the region on North Telangana, has been an important centre of revolutionary movement for a long period and a great inspiration to the revolutionary masses of our country. But we have to keep in mind that so far as the question of establishing base areas goes, it has been the more backward areas falling in central and eastern India that were selected by the Party, with the immediate task of liberating these vast areas. Hence the focus of our movement had gradually shifted to Dandakaranya and Bihar-Jharkhand.

You must have known that AP was made into a model state, an experimental state where the imperialists, particularly the World Bank, and the Indian ruling classes had concentrated to implement their multi-pronged LIC strategy against the revolutionary movement, with its focus on brutal suppression and reform. No other state affected by the Naxalite movement has such a massive police commando force as in AP, nowhere do you find such extensive intelligence network, infrastructure, funds training in counter insurgency warfare, and unlimited powers to the police. No other state had witnessed such a bloodbath as AP had for the past four decades and particularly from the mid-1980s. There are hardly any political prisoners in AP jails since the policy had always been to bump off the revolutionaries—where they are members of the central committee or sympathizers—after they are arrested. Fake encounter killings had been the tradition right from the time of Vengal Rao during the struggle of Srikakulam almost 40 years ago. Thousands of crores have been spent on so-called reforms with the aim of weaning away a section of the people from the revolutionary movement. It is a fact that a small but articulate and influential section in the countryside has been won over through these reforms. In a word, we can say that the Party and the revolutionary movement in AP bore the brunt of all the counter-insurgency measures initiated by the reactionary ruling classes in the initial stages. Today these are being implemented in several other states. We are making an in-depth study of enemy's counter-revolutionary tactics, plans and methods and taking lessons from these. The movement in AP, at the cost of huge sacrifices of thousands of comrades has given us invaluable experiences on how to counter and defeat enemy's tactics and plans. With these, the party is now more equipped to defeat the enemy's tactics in other states.

Setbacks and losses are not unnatural in protracted people's war. Revolution proceeds along a zig zag course and not along a straight line. The movement in AP has seen many ups and downs. But always it rose up like the proverbial Phoenix. No doubt, at the present juncture, we are facing a tough situation in AP and the enemy has the upper-hand from the tactical point of view. We had lost a good part of the state leadership and cadre but the most promising aspect is that the people are still with our party. The support base of the Party has not eroded much although they meet us secretly, ask to solve their problems, and they work without getting exposed to the brutal state. For them our Party is the only hope. People are pained at every loss suffered by the revolutionaries. You can gauge the mass support from the turn out at the funeral meetings of out martyrs. In spite of the threats and restrictions imposed by the police goons, more than 20,000 people had turned up at the funeral of comrade Chandramouli (BK) and Karuna in the former's native village of Vadkapur in Karimnagar district. The pent-up anger and hatred of the people for the reactionary rulers and their police—Grey Hounds—SIB goons will grow into a movement of such great proportions that it will wash away the exploiters and oppressors and all the muck accumulated in society for long. No force on earth can stop this high tide of revolution whatever losses and setbacks we might be facing today in AP; that is why while boasting that Maoists in the state had become completely weakened and that AP will serve as a model on how to deal with the Maoist movement, the fascist YSR government has initiated several measures with a long term plan such as a hundred percent increase in the strength of the Grey Hounds commando force, acquitting helicopters for anti-Naxal operations, sanctioning of Rs. 2000 crores of central aid to deal with the Naxal movement, and so on.

The present historical epoch is an epoch of great turmoil with tumultuous changes taking place worldwide. Even the mist powerful militarized imperialist power like the US is finding it impossible to suppress the national liberation struggle in a small country such as Iraq or Afghanistan. In India the ruthless exploitation and oppression of the people by the ruling classes in collaboration with imperialism has created an explosive situation. Utilizing the excellent international and domestic situation prevailing today we are confident we will be able to come out of the temporary setback in AP.

And what is more important, we made advances in many other states in spite of the losses we had suffered in AP. The situation is now qualitatively different from that of the earlier periods in that we are now able to advance the movement in a number of states even if we suffer losses and setbacks in one or two states. Way back they could suppress a Naxalbari, a Srikakulam, a Birbhum, a Mushahari, a Kansksa or Sonapur but today the revolutionary movement has become further strengthened, has spread to large tracts of the backward countryside, has well-knit party structures, Army and vast mass base. It is advancing through centralized planning and direction. Hence it is not an easy thing for the state to suppress the movement as in the past although it might achieve an upper hand in one place. The congress had chalked out a concrete plan to overcome the setback in AP by transforming the unfavorable factors into favorable ones. Overall there is great future for the Party and revolution.

Q: Recently your PLGA had inflicted one of the biggest blows to the police force and the salwa judum by killing a huge number of police and SPOs in Bodili in Chhattisgarh. Do you foresee more such attacks in near future? And do you believe the salwa judum can be stopped through such actions?

Ans: The daring tactical counteroffensive operation carried out by the PLGA led by our Party, the CPI (Maoist), on March 16 on a police base camp in Ranibodli in Bijapur police district in Chhattisgarh in which 68 policemen including Special Police Officers (SPOs) were wiped out is an inevitable consequence of the brutal reign of terror unleashed by the state and central governments in the name of salwa judum. You must know the actual ground situation in Dandakaranya to understand why such a massive operation had to be planned.

For almost two years since June 2005, the BJP government in Chhattisgarh and the Congress-led UPA government in the Centre had sponsored a counterrevolutionary terrorist campaign of mass murder, torture, and arrests of thousands of the adivasi peasantry, gang rapes and murder of hundreds of women, destruction of thousands of houses, food grains, and all property of the adivasis, killing or taking away thousands of cattle, forceful evacuation of tens of thousands of people from almost eight hundred villages and issuing threats and intimidation to anyone suspected of being a member of revolutionary mass organization or sympathetic to the Maoists in Dandakaranya, particularly in Dantewara, Bastar, Kaner, Bijapur and Narayanpur districts. Over 5000 youth were inducted into a state mercenary armed force, paid monthly salaries, and pitted against the native adivasis who are fighting for land, livelihood and liberation under the leadership of the CPI (Maoist). The Naga and Mizo Battalions were specially brought in along with a huge CRPF and other special police forces to Chhattisgarh who had been committing the most barbaric and inhuman acts against the adivasi population.

All these cruel at acts against an entire population are meant to establish peace of the graveyard and clear the way for the unhindered loot [by] rapacious hawks like Tatas, Ruias, Essars, Mittals, Jindals and imperialist MNCs. Over one lakh rupees worth of MOUs were signed by the Chhattisgarh government with these corporate comprador big business houses to drain the rich mineral and forest wealth of the state. At the behest of these day-light robbers, adhivashi dalals like opposition leader of the Congress, Mahendra Karma, Home Minister Ramvichar Betham of the BJP and others have been leading this counter-revolutionary war against the adivasi population.

A huge central force is deployed which is now more than 13 battalions, recruited 10 additional battalions of state forces and inducted even minors of 14 years of age into their mercenary police force. KPS Gill, notorious for the mass murders of youth in Punjab, was specially appointed as advisor to the Chief Minister. A carpet security system is initiated with police camps in close proximity in order to strike among the people.

We, on behalf of the CC, CPI (Maoist), once again warn the state and central governments that our Bhurmkal Sena and PLGA and people will carry out attacks on a much bigger scale if the murder campaign in the name of salwa judum is not disbanded immediately. We declare that the sole responsibility for such needless loss of lives of hundreds of policemen and SPOs lies squarely on the shoulders of the state and central governments. Large-scale armed retaliation by the adivasis led by our Party is inevitable if the atrocities on the adivasi people continue in the name of salwa judum. Like George Bush who can only think in terms of using more brute force to control the fire of national liberation in Iraq, the Indian ruling classes too can only think of sucking in more and more repressive forces in order to suppress the people's war and grab the mineral wealth of Dandakaranya. However, they will only end up in further escalating the civil war in Dandakaranya.

We do share the grief of the families of the dead policemen and SPOs but we are being compelled to wipe out the police and mercenary gangs who are obeying the orders of the ruling classes and their imperialist mentors to suppress the revolutionary movement for looting the wealth in the state. We appeal to the jawans of the central forces, particularly the Naga and Mizo battalions, to disobey the orders of the rulers and to withdraw from Chhattisgarh. We appeal to the SPOs who are being pitted against the adivasi people to quit the mercenary force as they are fighting an unjust war against their own brothers and sisters in the interests of the reactionary rulers. We call upon the democratic organizations and individuals and the vast masses of the country to condemn state terrorism on the adivasi people of Dandakaranya, to demand immediate disbandment of salwa judum and the mercenary SPO force, to fight for the withdrawal of the notorious central forces from the region, set up a judicial enquiry into the killing of over 500 adivasis by the police-salwa judum mercenary combine.

Q: History shows, the middle class wants status quo. Indian middle class is growing more powerful. How do you plan to co-opt them?

Ans: It is true that the Indian middle class has grown in number. At the same time, a sizable chunk of the middle class is facing acute crisis due to soaring prices, unemployment, growing insecurity of life, steep increases in family expenditure due to high cost of education, health, transport etc., which have become privatized to a great extent and had gone beyond the reach of a significant section of the middle class. In short, despite the numerical growth of the middle class it is at a receiving end. Hence we see that the growing frustration in large sections of the middle class is forcing them into streets for their demands as witnessed in strikes and other forms of struggles by teachers, government employees, students, and even shopkeepers who are affected by the shopping malls and FDI in retail sector. Another important factor has to be noted—most of yesterday's luxury consumer goods have become today's daily necessities. And the list of necessities is growing by the day with the large-scale proliferation of consumer goods and the promotion of consumerism by the market-place. Hence frustration is growing among members of this class as they are unable to procure these goods since much of their incomes have to be spent on the basic necessities such as food, clothing and shelter.

Middle class is terribly affected by such issues as price-rise, insecurity, corruption, unemployment for their children, high cost of education and health-care, threats from real estate mafia etc. Keeping these in mind our party has drawn up plans to mobilize the middle class into struggles on such issues.

Q: Why armed struggle is a must? (Isn't it a fact that violence pushes a large chunk of people away from the Party?)

Ans: The question of armed struggle or non-violence struggle is not based on the subjective whims and wishes of any individual or Party. It is independent of one's will. It is a law borne out by all historical experience. It is a fact of history that nowhere in the world, nowhere in the historical development of the class society, had the reactionary ruling classes given up power without resorting to violent suppression of the mass protests, without violent resistance aimed at clinging on to power until they are thrown out by force. Of course, one can cite instances of regime changes occurring through peaceful movements, through massive protests, but all of these were mere regime changes—not systemic changes. A section of the ruling classes might give up power to another section of the same class without the need for a violent upheaval but the same is not the case when one ruling class is replaced by another with diametrically opposing class interests.

However, we find that even these regime changes are not infrequently marked by violent clashes as witnessed in several parts of Africa, Asia and Latin America.

We will indeed be the happiest people to bring about systematic change without the need for armed struggle.

When we began the struggle it was basically a peaceful movement on the various issues of the people such as land, livelihood and liberation from feudal and imperialist exploitation and oppression. It needs hardly any genius to grasp the fact that no feudal lord would give up his land or power just because the masses demand it as their democratic right. The landlord would use all means at his disposal to suppress the mass resistance by brute force. He would get the local police and special forces, the central Para-military forces and, if needed, the army. We had seen this whenever we had initiated the anti-feudal struggle. In Jagtyal during the late 1970s, social boycott of the landlords imposed by the peasantry had forced them to flee the villages our revolutionary movement had spread to over a hundred villages which shook the powers that be. What happened next to this non-violent struggle should be an eye-opener to all those who harbor illusions or biased against armed struggle. After few weeks landlords came back with the mercenary forces and unleashed large-scale violence and cruel repressive measures such as arrests, torture of peasants, destruction of their property, declaration of the area as disturbed, clamping down on the civil rights of the people, and so on. It was at that juncture that the Party was compelled to take up arms and not out of any romantic notion. The same is the case with anti-imperialist struggles and nationality movements, who would want to give up their precious lives and undergo harsh, rigorous lives tortures and hardships when the demands of the masses such as land, national self-determination and liberation from imperialist exploitation and oppression are achieved through peaceful means? All movements began as peaceful movements but had to take the form of armed struggle due to the moves of the reactionary ruling classes. The case of Iraq is a classic illustration of how an entire population has been compelled to take up arms due to the unbridled violence unleashed by the imperialists for satisfying their insatiate greed for oil. The same is the case with Palestine, Kashmir or elsewhere.

The second part of your question is a big myth. Nowhere had the masses been repelled from the Party on account of armed struggle. Rather it is the lack of effective resistance that is acting as a discouragement wherever the state had bared its fangs. Without destroying and defeating the armed forces of repression it is impossible to rally the people or give them confidence. In fact, it is not our guerrilla squads alone that are putting up resistance. The people are playing a great role in heroically resisting and actively supporting the PLGA in its armed resistance to the police forces. Well, that's the ground reality notwithstanding what the intellectuals analyzing events from their ivory towers might think and theorize.

Q: Why there can not be protest in a non-violent way?

Ans: You must rather put the question the other way round. You must ask the reactionary ruling classes—the big landlords, the big business houses, the imperialist MNCs, the powerful Indian state and its armed forces, the state police and the bureaucracy—if at all they would listen, as to why they do not allow protest in a peaceful way. Why do they beat up, arrest, torture, and kill people who dare to go on strike? Why do they terminate the services of workers and employees for going on strike? Why do they send their mercenary police forces, the CRPF and the army to open fire upon people staging peaceful marches, dharnas and meetings without any provocation, why do they allow the khaki gangs to rape women, destroy property, enact fake encounters in violation of all provisions of the Indian Constitution, and for all these crimes against humanity, are let scot-free? Why do they create a Kalinagar, a Nandigram, an Arwal, an Indravellim and scores of such barbaric acts? Why peaceful protests of people in Kashmir against disappearances are not just ignored but even attacked with such ferocity? Why do they continue to enforce the savage Armed Forces Special Powers Act in Maniput when it is actually the Indian army and the police forces that are committing atrocities upon the people as the case of the rape of Manorame classically illustrates? Can you ever forget the savage beatings of the protestors by these khaki clad or olive green goods breaking their skulls, and not sparing them even after they fall down seriously injured?

No ruling classes anywhere in the world had allowed the people to achieve their basic demands of land and liberation from oppression in a peaceful way; even the so-called democratic states allow it only to the extent they do not pose a threat to the status quo, to their exploitation and amassing of super profits. Ahimsa (non-Violence) and Karma (fate) are the ideological bases and the dubious catch words of the exploiting classes to perpetuate their violence and hegemony over the vast masses.

To begin with, none would or could go directly to violent ways to solve their problems. It is only after their peaceful marches, rallies, dharnas, hunger-strikes, general strikes etc., go unheeded or sought to be crushed that they are forced to resort to violent methods. This is an incontrovertible fact whether it is the anti-feudal armed agrarian struggle led by the revolutionaries, nationality movements of the North East, Kashmir or the anti-imperialist struggles. You only have to take a glance at the origin of the armed movements anywhere in the world, not just India, to appreciate this universal truth. To put it shortly, forms of struggle adopted by the people always depend upon the moves of the ruling classes and not vice versa. And you should also bear in mind that even today we use both violent and non-violent forms of struggle and not just violent forms.

Q: Is your violence for self-defence or to grab state power?

Ans: Strictly speaking you cannot separate the two. In the long-term perspective, or ultimately our goal is to seize state power without which it is impossible to liberate the people of our country from the clutches of imperialism, feudalism and the big comprador bourgeoisie i.e. change the existing unjust socio-economic system. But in the process of preparing the people for the ultimate goal of establishing their own power, the ruling classes are resorting to savage repression on the party, the masses and the revolutionary movement as a whole. Hence in the course of mobilizing the masses into movements we are compelled to take up arms for self-defence even at an early stage. And for a relatively long time our war will have this nature and all our tactical counter offensive operations and campaigns should be seen as part of the war of self-defence at this stage.

Q: Why can't you fight [in] elections and go [to] the Parliament and raise issues in a democratic way?

Ans: It is indeed a logical question which anyone who sees only the outer shell of so-called parliamentary democracy would ask. What is important is the kernel, the essence, the content and not just the form. When you strip off the outer garment of democracy you find the rotten, stinking corpse inside. That is why Lenin described Parliament as a pig-sty and a mere talking shop. Why are we calling it a talking shop?

Firstly, the real problems of the people can never be addressed by the Parliament and Assemblies, not to speak of solving them. The Parliamentary institutions are not meant for that. They have no real power. They may pass some resolutions that seem to do good for the people but these have to be implemented through the Executive which has the real power. We know the fate of the Lank Ceiling Acts, legislation on untouchability, dowry, etc which are only showpieces. It is the executive which carries out everything. In periods such as Emergency during Indira Gandhi's regime, when the Parliament itself was subverted, the real power of the Executive had come openly to the fore. But, the man on the street knows how it is the revenue official, policeman, and the local magistrate who decide his life. However good a legislation act might seem to be, it is money power, muscle power and nepotism that decide every aspect of his life.

Secondly, Parliamentary institutions are meant to defend the status quo, not to change the system. They do, of course make some cosmetic changes now and then to maintain their credibility among the masses. Most important of all it is the imperialists comprador big business houses, big landlords, contractors and the mafia which control the Parliament. Those who enter the Parliament are the representatives or mere puppets in the hands of these powerful lobbies. Even a good intentioned parliamentarian cannot go beyond the rules drawn up by these bigwigs. If you see the business transacted in the parliament, you would find that more than 90% of it is just trash, with no bearing on the real problems of the country.

That the system of elections is a big farce needs no elaboration as it is known even to a school child. Do you call it democracy to purchase votes with liquor and money, whip up caste, religious, and ethnic sentiments? And even after the election, purchasing the legislators as you purchase any other item in the market place? If Narendra Modi, the butcher of thousands of Muslims in Gujrat can win elections and get reelected as the chief minister. If criminals, dacoits, and most notoriously corrupt politicians can get elected; and if votes can be obtained at gun-point and through booth capturing and rigging then do you really think that there is any meaning in this so-called democracy?

That is why our party has complete clarity on the nature of legislative system unlike some other parties that swear to be revolutionary in parliamentary politics in practice. We are firm in our belief that it is only through struggle that people can solve their problems and the parliamentary institutions can do nothing good except creating illusions. Parliament is a safety valve to let out the pent-up anger of the masses lest the system blow to piece. You think raising issues in the parliament is the democratic way through organized protests. We shall always be at the head of such struggles and not step into the mire of the undemocratically elected powerless talking shop called Parliament that serves as the instrument of the big business and the feudal forces and is subordinate to imperialist dictates.

Q: Do you fear that if you go to Parliament, the party can become corrupt?

Ans: The answer to this question is already covered in my earlier elaboration. To say in one word, more than being corrupted after entering Parliament, which is also true in the case of the ML parties, it is the corrupt parties and individuals that can really become part of the parliamentary system. Our party firmly believes that as against the money power of the Parliament the real alternative before the people is the establishment of genuine people's democratic power. We had built such organs of people's power in some parts of the country such as Janthana sarkar in Dandakaranya. These revolutionary organs of power show how real power is exercised as compared to the impotent, corrupt and criminal parliamentary institutions.

Q: What do you mean by people's power—we have seen in a communist state in West Bengal what communists do when they come to power. How would you ensure you will be able to give power to people?

A: It is not surprising that like most people, you too are confused by the names. Just because a Party calls itself Communist does not make it communist just as a party calling itself Bharatya Janata Party does not make it an Indian people's Party or a Samajbadi Party into a socialist party. The stark fact is that the CPI (M) had long back abandoned the communist project and Marxist ideology though it calls itself a Marxist Party. It had become a social fascist party from the time of the outbreak of Naxalbari armed peasant uprising in 1967 when thousands of revolutionaries were massacred upon the orders of the then Home minister Jyoti Basu in West Bengal during the late 1960s and early 1970s. The recent massacre of scores of people in Nandigram on March 14, the brutal suppression of the people's struggle in Singur, and its open declaration to allow the MNCs and big comprador houses to set up SEZs and transform the state into a heaven for these sharks had shown how the Buddhadebs Marxist Party is acting at the behest of the Tatas, Salems, and imperialist MNCs. The pre-hatched systematic execution of the massacre in Nandigram by the police-CPI(M) goons combine, in particular, has revealed their social fascist character to the new generation of the Indian people. So what you are referring to in West Bengal is nothing but social fascist rule.

Now coming to your question about people's power—we call it people's power only when real power is exercised by the people themselves. You can see it in parts of Dandarakanya, Bihar and Jharkhanda. We had developed it in some villages in AP but these were destroyed due to the weakness of our armed strength which could not counter the massive offensive by the central and state's special forces. Wherever we had established organs of people's power in embryonic form, there you can see the initiative and energy of the masses being released and coming into full play, active participation of masses in administrating their own lives, collectively developing their villages through construction of schools, tanks, hospitals, etc and increasing production, resolving the local disputes by themselves without ever any need to go to the bourgeois feudal courts, in short shaping their own destiny. Where our people's army and people's militia are relatively strong and succeeded in destroying the state's assertion has also kept the big industrial sharks and the imperialists MNCs at bay. Women enjoy relatively greater freedom than their counterparts in the rest of the country.

We have to develop this people's power that the lower to higher levels by strengthening the people's army and transforming it into a mighty force, destroying the enemy power by intensifying the people's war and establishing the base areas. It is in the base areas that this power becomes relatively more consolidated. However, until the final capture of state power on a country wide scale there will be severe constraints to the exercise of the people's power at the village and area levels. You have to look at the power the people are exercising in these areas of struggle keeping these limitations in mind.

Q: Developments are taking place at a rapid pace in both international and national arena. How do you see the role for your Party in this turmoil?

Ans: Our Party has a great role to play in the contemporary international and domestic situation. Our Congress has analyzed the present political situation and issued calls to the Party and the people. It drew up the necessary immediate tactics and tasks to utilize the situation and achieve advances and leaps in the ongoing people's war in India. The new Central Committee had further concretized these in the form of time-bound programmes and plans. Several resolutions were adopted by the Congress on the issues confronting the people in our country as well as the world. We hope to actively intervene in these issues and build a broad based militant political mass movement.

The next ten to twenty years will witness massive political and social upheavals all over the world and our country is going to witness mass upheavals in several states against the onslaught of imperialism, anti-people policies of the Indian ruling classes such as carving our neo-colonial enclaves called SEZs, massive displacement of the poor in both urban and rural areas, against draconian laws, state repression, unemployment, corruption, inflation, neglect of social welfare, and so on. Military confrontation between the people and the state will become a general feature throughout the country and I am sure our Party will be at the head of these movements. It will grow to the status of providing leadership, to the vast majority of the oppressed masses of our country. Imposing ban on our Party and the mass organizations, murdering our comrades, unleashing cruel repression on the people, intimidating and harassing all those associated with the revolutionary movement and all their repressive measures cannot prevent this inevitable establishment of our Party's leadership over the vast masses. The reactionary and revisionist parties, the Parliamentary system are very much discredited in the eye of the people and they cannot but see our party as the only alternative before them to achieve their real liberation.

Q: And finally do you feel it is a very crucial moment in history of India's Maoist struggle? If so, why?

Ans: I do not know what exactly is in your mind when you placed the question. But I would say yes, for several reasons. When for the first time you see the emergence of a single directing centre for the Indian revolution after the merger of the two major Maoist streams in the Indian communist movement, when you hold a Congress—the highest authority in the Party—after over three and half decades, 37 years to be precise, it indeed becomes a crucial moment in the history of India's Maoist struggle. And it is more than that. Holding the Unity Congress itself has been the greatest challenge to our party in recent times. The reactionary ruling classes, of course with the advice of the imperialists, had tried by all means at their disposal to disrupt the Congress. However, with meticulous planning by our Central Committee and various leading committees of our Party, with the protection provided by the heroic fighters of our PLGA, and the ever-vigilant people's militia and revolutionary masses, we could complete this gigantic democratic exercise that was initiated two years ago. It is a matter of pride that we could give a fitting rebuff to the enemy by successfully holding the Congress for over a fortnight.

It is crucial moment for another reason too. Today the Maoist movement is facing the great challenge of building a strong PLA and establishing the base area in the remote countryside as an immediate task. The reactionary ruling classes are sparing no stone unturned to prevent the emergence of such Red bases (democratic government of the people) in India's heartland as that would mean the emergence of a real alternative to the rotten, Parliamentary system and the criminal, communal, fascist, comprador parliamentary parties. Hence we see the massive deployment not only of the central forces, state's special forces but also setting up huge armed force from the local population, arming and training them, and pitting them against the revolutionary movement organizing massacres that remind us of the pogroms of the Black Hundred in pre-revolutionary Russia, and Nazi gangs of fascist Hitler. Such is the scenario enacted in Dandakaranya in the name of salwa judum and to a lesser extent in Bihar-Jharkhand in the name of Sendra. They would not hesitate to send the Indian army to create more bloodbaths and, the Maoist movement can advance only by smashing these attacks by the enemy forces. That is how we see the present moment as a crucial moment in the history of the Maoist struggle in India.

And the last reason why we should call the present moment a crucial moment is that we, the Maoists, are confronted with the great task of providing revolutionary leadership to over a billion people at a time when the entire country is being transformed into a neo-colony, when the country is being sold away to the imperialists and the big business is in the name of SEZs, when workers, peasants, employees, students, sections of the intelligentsia, dalits, women adivasis, nationalities, religious minorities and others are seething with revolt.

The Worker, #11, July 2007, pp. 68-76.

***

Interview with Azad, Spokesperson, Central Committee, CPI (Maoist) - II

Reproduced below is an interview with Cherikuri Raj Kumar alias Uday alias Azad, who was the spokesperson of the CPI (Maoist) at the time. Azad, a B Tech in Chemical Engineering is widely acknowledged as the best ideologue of the the CPI (Maoist). He rose from the ranks, grew-up as a leader of the students'-wing of the rebels in Andhra Pradesh, the Revolutionary Students Organization (RSU), which he had joined in 1974.

According to a renowned authority on the CPI (Maoist), Mr K Srinivas Reddy, "Azad, around 58 years old, belonged to Krishna district, Andhra Pradesh. He went underground in 1979. He was arrested in 1975 and 1978 and jumped bail. He carried a reward of Rs. 12 lakh on his head. He is acknowledged as an ideologue and an expert in field-level tactics." He founded and led the movement in Karnataka for a number of years, and was fisrst elected to the Central Committee in 1995. Later he became a member of the Polit Bureau. He also once headed South Western Regional Bureau (SWRB) of the Maoists, in whose jurisdiction fall the States of Kerala, Karnataka, Maharashtra and Gujarat. Also, he was a member of the Urban Sub-Committee (USCO) which spearheads the urban movement/activities of the rebels.

Azad was killed in an encounter with the police in the forests in Andhra Pradesh's Adilabad district, on July 2, 2010.

Azad defends his comrades for their chilling massacres and much as any other Maoist leader claims that theirs is merely counter-violence and in defense of the exploited and harassed people. He admits that the beheading of Inspector Francis Induvar was a mistake.

EXCERPTS

Q: Maoists killed 20 policemen, most of them C-60 commandos, in Gadchiroli district. Is it not due to incidents like this which is provoking government to deploy huge forces in these areas?

It is the other way round. It is because of indescribable atrocities perpetrated by specially-trained anti-naxal forces that we are compelled to carry out such attacks. If they do not harass the poor, unarmed adivasis, torture, murder and rape them, then why will our forces undertake such attacks? Every act of ours is in defence of the poor adivasis... Our attack in Laheri (Gadchiroli) should be seen as part of our fight against state terrorism.

Q: The growing opinion is that Maoists are resorting to senseless violence, innocent people are falling victims. The beheading of Special Branch inspector recently in Jharkhand... was it not a cruel act?

It is hypocrisy on the part of those making such a big fuss about the plight of one Francis Induvar. They never speak of the thousands who had died in secret torture chambers maintained by the state flouting constitutional provisions. I assert that the case of Francis Induvar is an exception and not the rule. As for the act itself, we do not encourage such beheadings even if police carry out such brutalities. We will punish the enemy but there is no necessity for using cruel methods.

When our guerrillas capture a cruel police officer, especially one who has been responsible for the murder of several of our comrades, there is bound to be serious reaction due to pent-up anger... We will educate our cadre so that such beheadings do not occur in future.

We are aware that it is poor people who are forced to join the police force and we do not wish their families to be left grief-stricken. We too share the grief of Sunita Induvar and her children. But the rulers have compelled us to take up such actions for self-defence.

Q: How do you explain media reports that 6,000 people were killed in Maoist-related violence in six years?

This is a part of the propaganda war and psychological war unleashed by the reactionary rulers.

Times of India, November 6, 2009
http://timesofindia.indiatimes.com/india/We-regret-beheading-Induvar-Maoist-leader/articleshow/5201439.cms

****

INTERVIEW WITH AZAD, SPOKESPERSON, CPI (MAOIST) - II

In another interview in May 2009, after the General elections were completed Azad rejects that people's faith is parliamentary democracy is growing. He alleges that several crores of rupees were spent on canvassing alone. Even as he justifies his outfits call for boycott of the elections, he hits out at all political parties and leaders as hungry power seekers and terms the Communists as self-seeking opportunists and hypocrites.

CRORES ON PROPAGANDA SHOWS RULERS DESPERATE: AZAD, CPI (MAOIST)

Comrade Azad, spokesperson, central committee, CPI (Maoist), talks about why his party has called for an election boycott, how it plans to implement it, why Left-led Third Front government is out of the question as they are trying to brand themselves secular only to grab power. Azad spares no one, whether it is L K Advani, Congress, Mayawati or Prakash Karat, calling them opportunists.

Q: This is one of the biggest elections with about a billion voters participating. Don't you see it as people's growing faith in parliamentary democracy?

Certainly not. Every day, media, central and state governments and all contesting parties are dinning into the ears of people to exercise their vote. This shows the desperation of the ruling classes. Crores are being spent on propaganda alone. They are so scared that they cannot imagine allowing voters the minimum democratic right to reject parties and candidates contesting the elections.

Q: Your party has called for poll boycott. But involvement of people in elections seems to be growing.

There is neither any interest nor involvement of people in the elections. Even the narrow base of some parties has taken a beating this time. Contrary to images you see on TV, the involvement of people has declined compared to earlier elections. Hence, the desperate attempt by rulers to rope in film stars, cricketers and popular personalities into publicity campaigns to educate people regarding the virtues of parliamentary democracy, and about the great responsibility of citizens in casting their votes.

Q: Left parties are trying to build a non-BJP, non-Congress alternative at the Centre. What is your view on the Third Front?

The Third Front forged by CPI and CPM as a secular democratic front comprising non-Congress, non-BJP forces is actually a congregation of self-seeking discredited opportunists, all of whom have proved to be hypocrites and double-dealers in their respective states. Who needs to be taught about the infamous history of a Chandrababu Naidu, a Jayalalitha, a Mayawati, a Deve Gowda, a Naveen Patnaik? These leaders and their parties, who had, at one time or the other, shared power with the Hindu chauvinist BJP, are being given secular-democratic image by the Left.

The Karats, Yechuris and other power brokers of the so-called Left had churned out the slogan of anti-communalism to justify their alignment with the most loyal agent of imperialists, Congress, during the 2004 elections. Now, these opportunists see anti-communalism in parties like TDP, BSP, AAIDMK, JD(U) and BJD, all of whom had never really demarcated themselves from communal BJP, and have no compunction in striking an alliance with it if it gave them a share in power. For our Marxist ideologues, all these forces have suddenly become secular. One should not be surprised if they once again become the tail of Congress after the election.

Q: Why do you say that?

Just see. They found secularism, anti-imperialism and democratic moorings among parties such as TDP, a party which was first to transform a state into a laboratory of the World Bank and is responsible for the murder of over 2,000 Maoist revolutionaries besides the high-level of corruption of the regime led by Chandrababu Naidu. There are other opportunists such as Jayalalitha's AIADMK that had become infamous for the scale of corruption, abuse of power and fascist suppression of people's struggles in TN; Naveen Patnaik's BJD has sold the state to imperialists and proved itself to be executioner for the imperialists by massacring adivasis in Kaliga Nagar, POSCO, etc, besides protecting saffron hoodlums as they went about killing, raping and persecuting Christians. Deve Gowda's JD(S) shared power with BJP and broke with it only when the latter wanted a greater share of power; you have Mayawati who would do anything to grab power whether it be power-sharing with the BJP on rotational basis, or striking an alliance with Brahmins and subordinating Dalits to upper-caste Hindus, besides crushing all opponents ruthlessly.

The Third Front has certainly weakened the two major alliances, NDA and UPA, and has led to further fragmentation of Indian polity.

Q: How will you take your boycott campaign to the people?

We began after EC declared the poll schedule. Our stand has been made clear to people through circulars, press statements, interviews, leaflets, posters, wall writings. Cultural teams stage performances among the people. We will carry this out till the last phase of elections. It also includes questioning candidates and party members, gheraoing them, making them confess their misdeeds before the people.

Then there is active boycott where we prevent candidates from carrying out their campaigns in villages and smaller urban centres in our areas. We warn the parties not to venture out into our areas. When they do not heed our warnings, we stop their campaign, beat them up if they are notorious elements, burn their vehicles, conduct people's courts where possible and make the party representatives confess the misdeeds of their respective parties and seek apology from the people. They are let off after they agree not to come to the villages again. We carry out counter-offensive actions against police and central forces who are used by the reactionary rulers to enforce elections at gun-point. Basically our active boycott too is a political campaign though we undertake some actions aimed at destroying enemy forces.

Q: What about the growing impact of regional parties?

The elections this time are the most complex, most crisis-ridden and most fragmented. Extreme instability and contradictions plague every party and candidate. No party or candidate seems to be certain of the poll outcome. Hence they are resorting to all sorts of gimmicks to attract the apathetic voter. The desertion by the Left, Lalu's RJD, Mulayam's SP, Paswan's LJP, Ramdoss's PMK have left Congress and the UPA in a pathetic condition. Likewise, BJP and its NDA allies have lost support of strong allies like BJD, AIADMK and several smaller parties. Neither BJP nor Congress is in a position to hold their respective alliances together and centrifugal tendencies will continue to weaken these further.

Q: What is the alternative Maoists are offering to parliamentary democracy?

The alternative is people's democracy where it is the people, and not a few moneybags, who decide the destiny of the country and their own lives. It is genuine democracy as seen from the grassroots level to the top and not vice versa. You can see e grassroots democracy at work in the vast tracts of Dandakaranya where Maoists are running a parallel government. There, people are supreme and decisions are made through gram sabhas, assemblies of the people and not by invisible hands. The people's courts, of course, will be refined further but the content remains the same, deliverance of real and speedy justice by taking the side of the oppressed, persecuted people.

Times of India, May 2, 2009

***

Interview with Kishenji, Politburo Member, CPI (Maoist)

Popularly known as Kishanji, Mallojula Koteswara Rao was a member of the Polit Bureau of the Communist Party of India (Maoist). Born in Nachpalli Village, Karimnagar district, Andhra Pradesh (AP), he was a native of Peaddapalli town, Karimnagar district. At the time of his death in an encounter with the security forces, in the Burisole forest area, West Midnapore district, West Bengal, he was 56 years old. He graduated in Mathematics in 1973 and, subsequently, moved to Hyderabad to pursue a Bachelor's degree in Law (LLB). He was quite technology savvy and used laptop and data cards.

His father Venkataiah, now deceased, was Vice President of the Andhra Pradesh Congress Committee. His brother, Mallojula Venugopal alias Sonu alias Bhupathi, is Polit Bureau (PB) member and PB in-charge of the Dandakaranya Special Zone Committee (DKSZC).

Kishanji guided Maoist activities in West Bengal and Delhi. He also headed the Sub Committee on Political Education (SCOPE). He was the first Secretary of the

AP State Committee from 1980-85. Thereafter, he was demoted and made a member of the Forest Committee in Dandakaranya, which later evolved into the DKSZC. In 1993 he was asked by the Maoist leadership to move to West Bengal and build the movement there.

He founded the Radical Students Union (RSU) in AP in 1974 and was actively involved with the Telengana Regional Conference that was launched in 1977 by the rebels. The Conference was held basically to review the growing Telangana movement and to elect a leadership. In this conference three major decisions were taken: (i) to broaden the outfit's base amongst the masses (ii) to hold a series of political classes to train the large influx of new cadre and (iii) to send squads into the forest for launching armed struggle.

He had started and led a peasant movement in 1977 in Karimnagar-Adilabad districts, under the aegis of the AP State Committee of the CPI (M-L), in which 60,000 peasants participated. This movement evolved into what is popularly and famously known as the Sircilla-Jagityal Peasant Struggle (Sircilla-Jagityal Rytanga Poratam), and culminated in a massive rally of 35,000 people who marched into Jagitya town, on September 7, 1978. Police clamp-down started immediately thereafter and the awakening of the peasantry led to the next stage—formation of the PWG in 1980.

It is said that, in the Maoist outfit he is the founder of, and master at, the practice of organising/ infiltrating mass movements and later converting them into violent struggles. It is also said that he has done this successfully in many places in West Bengal. The experience gained in the Sircilla-Jagitya Peasant Struggle had stood him in good stead.

'TO ESTABLISH A LIBERATED AREA'

Koteswar Rao, alias Kishenji, is a politburo member of the banned CPI (Maoist) and is in charge of the party's operations in West Bengal, Jharkhand, Bihar and Orissa. He was drawn into the revolutionary movement when he was doing his B.Sc. (Mathematics) in Karimnagar, Andhra Pradesh. He became a full-time member of the CPI-ML (People's War) in 1974.

"We plan to spread our movement to north Bengal, the plains of Bihar, the central districts of Orissa and eastern Chhattisgarh," he told *Frontline* in an exclusive telephonic interview in which he talked about the Lalgarh movement, the Maoist programme of individual killings and future plans of the Maoist movement.

Excerpts

Q: Do you think the movement in Lalgarh is the fallout of the Singur and Nandigram movements rather than a heritage of the Naxalbari movement?

The movement in Lalgarh is the fallout of the Naxalbari movement, but the movements in Nandigram and Singur also had an impact on the Lalgarh movement and the people of Lalgarh. Such a long and sustained movement on a political issue has never taken place in the history of independent India. The main reason for this is the increase in political awareness among the masses.

At the same time, there is, on the one hand, a worldwide economic crisis and, on the other, Indian multinationals seizing the land and property of the common people. These, too, had a role to play in the eruption in Lalgarh.

And of course the Nandigram and Singur agitations, in which we were also present, are certainly big factors. At present, it is not possible to carry out just a peaceful agitation in West Bengal; along with peaceful agitations there must be huge rallies and meetings involving the direct participation of thousands of people.

Q: There is a view that the Lalgarh movement is a spontaneous tribal movement that became so big that the CPI (Maoist) had to get on to it or be left behind. Your comments.

It is not as if we started doing our groundwork in the region yesterday; we have been doing our groundwork for a long time. The Maoist role and leadership in the area has been a continuous process. But, at the same time, the PCPA [People's Committee against Police Atrocities] and the Maoist movement are not the same, and it would be incorrect to say that the people of the region have been influenced only by Maoists; they have been very much influenced by the PCPA, too.

Q: But if there were no arrests following the assassination attempt on Chief Minister Buddhadeb Bhattacharjee on November 2 last year, would you have been able to build such a strong movement?

Not something like this. It would have developed in a slow process. But the reaction of the people worked to our advantage – much more than it did in Nandigram or Singur. We didn't have any demand other than that the police apologise to the people, but the State government did not agree to it. We were left with few options.

Q: Did you at any point think that the movement might not need you?

Yes, I did. We expected a movement after November 2, but nothing so big. I expected the strength of the movement to be around 50 per cent of what it eventually became. But the movement itself has undergone a qualitative change over the months. Earlier, when the villagers protested, they assembled in large numbers with their traditional bows and arrows. Then the combined forces entered the region and many villagers fled.

Subsequently, they all returned and now they are not fleeing anywhere. They are standing their own ground and collecting weapons to strike back. So tell me, where do you think this spirit to retaliate is coming from? Whom do you think the villagers are supporting now?

Q: In 2007, it was decided that the CPI (Maoist) would broad-base its activities and not focus only on individual killings like the earlier naxalite movement.

But Maoist killings are being reported almost every other day. So in what way is it different from the old programme?

At that time, annihilation of the class enemy was the only form adopted to bring about the revolution. We have changed that. We say that annihilation is one of the forms. This was not invented by Maoists; we have seen in history that the masses have always allowed it. To us, annihilation is one aspect of our total movement.

It was not a regular feature earlier as you claim. It became a regular feature only after the combined forces entered the region. If you recollect, before the deployment of Central forces, we held a Jana Adalat [people's court] for 30 CPI(M) people in Madhupur [near Lalgarh].

More than 12,000 villagers attended the trial. The public wanted the death sentence for 13 of those under trial. But Bikas [the Maoist commander of operations in Lalgarh], after hours of persuasion, finally managed to convince the public that the time was not right to mete out such a punishment. Finally, the public agreed that those 13 people be just made to wear garlands of chappals and apologise. The other killings took place only after continued disregard of repeated warnings that were sent to the victims both by us and by the people of the region.

The victims were not just police informers, they practically marched with the combined forces. It is not that we killed only CPI(M) people, we killed members of the Jharkhand Party, too, for helping the combined forces and for joining the Gana Pratirodh [People's Resistance] Committee; and I would also like to add that there is no difference between the Salwa Judum and the Gana Pratirodh Committee.

We killed the main leaders of the committee. Of the six main leaders of the Gana Pratirodh Committee, three were from the CPI(M) and three from the Jharkhand Party. Here again, we killed them after repeatedly requesting them to desist from forming such a committee. They did not listen to us and we had no other alternative.

The annihilation policy of old and what we do today are not the same. Along with individual assassinations, there are also other forms of actions that we undertake – different kinds of mass movements, social boycotts of culprits, and various developmental works.

In fact, recently, in Shankabanga village [in Purbo Medhinipur], we dug a seven-kilometre canal for irrigation. We have done similar work in many villages.

Q: The CPI (Maoist) had announced that it will spread the movement to new areas following the general elections this year. Which are the areas that have been identified?

North Bengal, the plains of Bihar, the central districts of Orissa and eastern Chhattisgarh. All these are backward areas where multinational companies are trying to penetrate, and the State governments are signing memorandums of understanding with them. The strategic location of these areas will also help us in our movements.

The movement in Orissa is one of the most upcoming movements by our party and it will facilitate a combined consolidation of our movements in the neighbouring States of Jharkhand, West Bengal and Andhra Pradesh, bringing as many as 15 districts under our control.

Q: Tell us something about your plans in West Bengal.

Very simply, to establish a liberated area. We decided in 2007 that this [the Jangalmahal] would be a guerilla area. Since then we have progressed a lot, we have already reached out to more than half the population of the region and made it politically aware. I can tell you only so much. Our politburo does not allow us to divulge the tactical aspects of our programmes.

Q: But is there widespread recruitment into your movement from the region?

There has to be recruitment, or else how will the movement grow?

Q: There are reports of fresh plans by your party to try and assassinate the Chief Minister, and even storm Writers Buildings. Your comments.

The media need sensational news, and the police need to justify their fat salaries. Do I really need to elaborate? As I have repeatedly said, to kill Buddhadeb Bhattacharjee was not my decision. It was the decision of the people of Nandigram, the people of West Bengal, and even sections of the liberal bourgeoisie.

Q: Railway Minister Mamata Banerjee, who earlier extended her support to the PCPA's movement, seems to have distanced herself from it. Your comments.

I have been asking Mamata Banerjee for the last three months to make her stand clear. After the general elections her fortune has soared, but what about the fortune of the "Ma, Mati, Manush" [Mamata's political slogan of Mother, Earth, and People]? Their situation remains the same. What Mamata Banerjee is doing is indulging in opportunistic politics.

Q: With the State and the Centre now planning to launch a much stronger attack, do you not think that your movement, as it stands today will endanger the lives of thousands of innocent and apolitical villagers?

The state should think about that. People like Manmohan Singh, [P.] Chidambaram and Buddhababu are responsible for the situation as it stands today. Ultimately, they are the ones responsible for the killings. We still want peace, it is the government that does not.

Q: So are you willing to sit for dialogue with the government for the sake of peace?

You are probably the 210th person to ask me this question. Chidambaram and Buddhababu have clearly said there will not be any dialogue; they have already arrayed their forces for war, and still you people from the media keep harping, 'You will all not survive this'. This is clearly to break the spirit of the common people. I do not understand why you all are continuously asking me this question. It really is not possible for me to provide routine answers to such routine questions. I am standing in a battlefield here.

Frontline, Vol. 26, Issue 22, October 24 - November 6, 2009.
Accessible at http://frontlineonnet.com/stories/20091106262202200.htm

SECTION III

UNITY CONGRESS/9TH CONGRESS

The CPI (Maoist) styles itself as a political outfit. But, it is a proscribed organization under the Unlawful Activities Prevention Act, 1967, as amended in 2008, of the Government of India. Much as the other legitimate Communist parties conduct their Congress, once every three years, the CPI (Maoist) also conducts its Congress. The last such Congress was held in January 2007 in the Beembundh forest reserve, in Mungher district, Bihar. 100 delegates from 16 States attended this Congress, where it was decided that, from then on, unlike in the past, it would be held every five years.

The Congress has a very special and significant role in the Maoists' scheme of things. The all-powerful Central Committee (CC) is elected by the Congress. It is from within this CC that the Polit Bureau (PB) and the Central Military Commission (CMC) are constituted. Besides, the various decisions taken by the PP/CC, significant activities undertaken, an assessment of progress of the movement since the last Congress and its current state, etc are all put together in a document known as the Political Organisational Review (POR). Besides, the proposed agenda until the next Congress is held is also outlined here. The POR needs to be ratified by a majority of the Congress delegates, failing which the CC has to resign en masse *and a new CC is elected. Moreover, significant decisions that have been deferred by the PB/CC for various reasons (essentially, due to lack of unanimity among PB/CC members) or those that are proposed to be taken, are all discussed in the Congress and final decisions are, thus, made through majority vote.*

***

PRESS RELEASE

On February 19, 2007, Muppala Lakshmana Rao alias Ganapathy the general secretary and supremo of the CPI (Maoist), issued a press release declaring the first-ever Congress of the CPI (Maoist) after its founding, following the amalgamation of the PWG and MCCI, was successfully held. Though he desisted from mentioning, media reports later said that it was held in the Beembandh forest reserve—a bird sanctuary—in Mungher district of Bihar. He termed the holding of the Congress as an "event of historic significance".

PRESS RELEASE

CPI (MAOIST) COMPLETES ITS MUCH-AWAITED HISTORIC UNITY CONGRESS-9TH CONGRESS—A TURNING-POINT IN INDIAN REVOLUTION

The successful completion of the Unity Congress-9th Congress of the CPI(Maoist) in January-February 2007 is an event of historic significance for the oppressed masses of India and the world people at large. It achieved a higher level of unity throughout the Party and marked the completion of the unity of the two great streams of the Indian revolution—the CPI(ML) and the MCCI—that took place on September 21, 2004.

It resolved the disputed political issues in the Party through lively, democratic and comradely debate and discussion. The present Congress, held after a period of 36 years since the 8th Congress in 1970, stands out as another milestone in the long history of the Communist movement in India and has great significance in the history of the Maoist movement in India.

The Unity Congress-9th Congress of the Communist Party of India (Maoist) was held deep in the forests of one of the several Guerrilla Zones in the country. Under the protective umbrella provided by three Companies of the PLGA, with several sentry posts keeping round-the-clock vigil around the venue of the Congress—Comrades CM-KC Commune—with Patrolling Teams continuously scouring for enemy movements, and with the people in the surrounding villages acting as the eyes and ears of the Party, the Congress was completed successfully foiling all the attempts of the reactionary ruling classes to obstruct it. A few days prior to the Congress, Comrade Chandramouli alias Naveen, a member of the Central Committee and the Central Military Commission of the CPI(Maoist), his life-partner and Divisional Committee member comrade Karuna, were arrested, tortured cruelly and murdered by the APSIB goons. These two comrades stood steadfast in the torture chambers and gave up their lives placing the interests of the people and the Party above all else thereby contributing to the success of the Congress.

The Congress Hall was aptly christened as comrades Karam Singh-Chandramouli Hall after comrade Chandramouli and another martyr comrade and PB member, comrade Shamshersingh Sheri alias Karam Singh, who passed away in October 2005.

The Congress was held amidst massive enemy encirclement with the government setting up a special cell to foil the Congress. All the Guerrilla Zone areas were placed under the intelligence scanner with special surveillance on unusual movements in and around these zones. The media had even speculated on the probable dates of the Congress. Yet, amidst this extensive encirclement, over one hundred delegates from 16 States, comprising the core of the Maoist leadership of India, wound their way to the venue.

The inauguration of the Congress was done by the outgoing general secretary of the Party, Com Ganapathi. Com Kishan welcomed the entire gathering; wreaths were laid at the Martyr's Memorial column and glowing tributes were paid to the great martyrs comrades who had laid down their lives in the period since the 8th Congress. This was followed by a procession that converged at the Karam Singh-Chandramouli Congress Hall where the delegation began the deliberations.

This historic Congress adopted the five basic documents of the unified Party—Hold High the Bright Red Banner of Marxism-Leninism-Maoism; the Programme of the Party; the Constitution; the Strategy and Tactics of the Indian Revolution; and the Political Resolution on the current International and Domestic situation—after thoroughgoing and intense discussions in a free and frank manner.

It also focused its attention on a review of the past practice of the two erstwhile Maoist parties since their formation in 1969, the three-year post-Congress review of the erstwhile PW from 2001 to 2004 and also the 2-year practice of the newly formed party. Besides, it passed resolutions on the important political issues of the day—both international and domestic—made the necessary organisational changes and elected a new central committee. The Congress was the culmination of the process that has been going on throughout the Party over the last two years where the documents were discussed in depth and Conferences were held at the area, district, regional and the State level and hundreds of amendments were sent to the Congress from below.

The Unity Congress reaffirmed the general line of the new democratic revolution with agrarian revolution as its axis and protracted people's war as the path of the Indian revolution that had first come into the agenda with the Naxalbari upsurge. It further enriched the politico-military line of the Party. It set several new tasks for the party with the main focus on establishment of base areas as the immediate, basic and central task before the entire party. It also resolved to advance the people's war throughout the country, further strengthen the people's army, deepen the mass base of the party and wage a broad-based militant mass movement against the neo-liberal policies of globalization, liberalization, privatization pursued by the reactionary ruling classes under the dictates of imperialism.

The significant additions/development to the party documents were: the pin-pointing of the specific character of Indian feudalism/semi-feudalism as being deeply interwoven with the caste system and Brahaminical ideology; an assessment of the changes taking place in the agrarian situation especially in Punjab within the semi-feudal framework and its impact on our tactics; more clarity on the Comprador Bureaucrat Bourgeoisie (CBB) in the Indian context; a deeper understanding of the concepts of Guerrilla Base, Base Area, Dual Power, etc particularly in the Indian context; advancing the people's war and turning the PLGA into PLA, guerrilla war into mobile war, and the Guerrilla Zones into Base Areas; the importance and significance of work in the working-class, the United Front and other such important issues.

The Congress also passed a number of political resolutions on numerous current events like: world people's struggles, support to the nationality struggles, against Indian expansionism, on post-Khairlanji Dalit upsurge and against caste oppression, against Hindu fascism, against SEZs and displacement, etc.

Resolutions were also passed on the strengthening of the three magic weapons of the Party, People's Army and the United Front. The two-year financial balance sheet of the unified Party was presented to the House. After that the outgoing CC presented its collective self-criticism, pin-pointing the main areas of its weakness and invited the Congress delegates to present their criticisms. After this process a new CC was elected, which then re-elected Com Ganapathi as the General Secretary of the Party.

The Congress was completed amongst great euphoria with a Call to the world people:

Rise up as a tide to smash Imperialism and all its running dogs! Advance the Revolutionary war throughout the world!!

The Unity Congress-9th Congress of the CPI(Maoist) finally called on the people of India to come forward in large numbers to support the ongoing people's war in the country and the embryonic power emerging, to build a truly democratic society built on justice, equality, free from the chains of imperialism and semifeudal bondage.

Ganapathi,
General Secretary,
CPI(Maoist)
Feb 19, 2007

***

Call of the Unity Congress

This document summarises the assessment of the Maoists of the social, economic and political conditions then obtaining in the country, highlights the position of the rebels on various issues and gives direction to its sympathizers on what it expected them to do. It also brings out in a nut shell the various larger issues that were debated in the Congress and the Resolutions passed on them. The full text(s) of these Resolutions are being presented immediately after this document.

CALL OF THE UNITY CONGRESS

Oppressed people of India and the world! Rise up as a tide to smash Imperialism!

Advance the Revolutionary war throughout the world!!

The imperialist-sponsored policies being pursued by the ruling classes are devastating the lives of the already impoverished masses of the country on a scale unheard of in post-1947 India. No matter which party is in power at the Centre or in the States, all are aggressively pushing these policies of LPG in all spheres of the economy and social life of the country.

The grip of the imperialists, particularly of the US, is tightening, with each passing day, over every aspect of the life of the country. This is the result of the growing and deepening crisis of imperialism which has particularly hit the number one imperialist, the US. Bogged down in the wars in Iraq and Afghanistan, and an economic crisis in its economy, the US imperialists are facing serious problems. Facing worldwide opposition to their terroristic and warmongering policies and greater contention from rival imperialist powers, the US imperialists are getting more and more desperate. The crisis is intensifying all the contradictions worldwide, including India.

The people of India and the World are not taking these attacks lightly; they are fiercely resisting these attacks on their lives. But, their resistance is being crushed with fascist brutality and ruthlessness, where all countries have equipped themselves with terroristic laws. Due to the weakness of the genuine communist forces, the Maoists, to lead these struggles, the people's resistance faces problems of further intensification and tends to go around in circles. But the outbursts continue to intensify as seen with the massive revolts witnessed over Khairlanji in Maharashtra and the revolts in France. Where the Maoists movements have taken roots, as in India, Nepal, Philippines, Turkey, Peru, etc the revolts have taken the form of systematic armed resistance.

In India the policies of the rulers have affected the lives of every section of the masses while giving gigantic wealth to big business, TNCs the big semi-feudal elements and all their agents in the country. The worst affected are the poorest in the country.

The peasantry and landless poor have been the worst affected due to these policies pushing over one lakh to suicide and lakhs more to deeper and deeper hunger. The depth of the crisis is due to all the WTO, IMF, World Bank dictated policies that has badly hit also the middle peasants and even a section of the rich peasantry. The Unity Congress (9th Congress) of the CPI(Maoist) calls upon the vast oppressed peasantry to rise as a storm against these policies to sweep away their oppressors and establish their own people's power from village to village.

Together with the polices of liberalisation, privatisation and globalisation have come massive attacks on the working class and vicious attempts to bind labour hand-and-foot, which has facilitated a massive loot by big business. Massive contracturalisation of labour, wage freeze, VRS, dismissals, curbs on recruitment, anti-labour Court Judgments, de-facto ban on strikes, etc. are leading to greater and greater impoverisation of the entire working class. Rural destitution is resulting in lakhs of migrant labour floating around the urban pockets eking out a hand-to-mouth existence in a state of semi-starvation. The Congress calls on the working class to throw off the chains of the revisionists, reformists, and reactionary trade unionists and take to militants struggles against the attacks on their living standards and democratic rights.

The present policies have led to the further marginalisation of tribals and all forest dwellers, with huge projects leading to massive displacements. Mining and dam projects like Posco, Kalinganagar, bauxite mines etc in Orissa; Chargaon and Raoghat in Chhattisgarh, bauxite mines and Polavaram project in AP, massive iron mines, and uranium projects in Jharkhand; and other such projects throughout the country. The 9th Congress of the CPI(Maoist) calls on all forest dwellers to resist till the end the massive displacement taking place and protect their land and forests from the robbers and looters that seek to seize them.

The 300 planned SEZs (Special Economic Zones) are all set to create defacto foreign enclaves within our country by grabbing lakhs of acres of prime agricultural land by the foreign and local sharks. Together with this, to turn urban centres into elite enclaves and pave the way for big business retail chains, ruthless demolitions and eviction of lakhs of people are taking place demolishing slums and even permanent housing. The Unity Congress of the CPI(Maoist) calls on the people to resist the seizure of their lands and houses and beat back the demolition hordes by whatever means possible.

The big growth of imperialist capital in the country and that of the CBB has increased the expansionist designs of the Indian ruling classes which are resorting to greater and greater domination of the countries of South Asia. The Unity Congress supports the struggles of the people of South Asia against Indian expansionism and calls on the Indian people to be in the forefront of the struggle against Indian expansionism.

The heroic struggles of the nationalities particularly those of the Kashmiri and North East people, are continuing for decades against the oppressive Indian state. The Unity Congress of the CPI(Maoist) supports the struggles of the oppressed nationalities for their right to self-determination, including secession; and calls on the people of India not to fall prey to the hysterical Indian propaganda and lend support to these struggles. Imperialist and feudal culture has increased the exploitation and patriarchal oppression of women on a massive scale. So-called dowry deaths, increased sexual exploitation, and growing violence and discrimination by the state, feudal and male chauvinist forces, on women, has led to the massive increase on women's oppression. The 9th Congress of the CPI(Maoist) calls on women to rise against this crude exploitation/oppression, assert their rights, and stand up and fight all forms of oppression and discrimination by organising powerful women movements.

With greater dalit assertion there has been a big increase in attacks on dalits, together with the continuation of existing discrimination due to the disgusting practice of untouchability. The 9th Congress of the CPI(Maoist) calls on all dalits to rally under the revolutionary banner to militantly resist these growing attacks and discrimination on them and mobilise all the oppressed to continue the struggle to root out the caste system from its roots.

The Imperialist/CBB offensive together with the continuing stagnant semi-feudal relations has created a nightmare-like situation for the students and youth of the country who are facing a bleak future of unemployment, under-employment, cultural degeneration, careerism and desperation. The 9th Congress of the CPI(Maoist) calls on the student and youth of the country to resist these attacks and join the revolutionary movement on a huge scale to create a truely new democratic society, which alone can sole the problems they face.

The massive imperialist/TNC/CBB offensive have pushed lakhs of small industries and traders to bankruptcy and continues to do so. The 9th Congress of the CPI(Maoist) calls on all such small business to lend whatever possible support to the on-going people's war as it is only through the democratic transformation of society they will be able to break free from imperialist/CBB strangulation and semi-feudal restriction of their markets.

The big imperialist offensive, continuing deep stagnation in the rural economy, the cruel hindu fascist attacks and the brutal State authority is affecting all aspects of the life of the country creating great disillusionment and frustration amongst the progressive and democratic intellectuals throughout the country. The 9th Congress of the CPI(Maoist) calls on all the progressive and democratic intellectuals to raise their voice against all forms of injustice and state repression and thereby become a part of the overall democratic and revolutionary stream in the country.

Finally, the Indian anti-imperialist movement is part and parcel of the worldwide movement against imperialism, particularly US imperialism. Particularly the heroic armed resistance of the Iraqi people and Afghan people are in the forefront of these great battles. Together with this growing movements in the backward countries and the mass upsurges in the imperialist countries, particularly those led by the Maoist parties, is an important part of the worldwide anti-imperialist movement. The 9th Congress of the CPI(Maoist) lends full support to these anti-imperialist movements and calls on the Indian people to strongly condemn the aggressive war-mongering policies US imperialism throughout the world and supports the people's resistance, particularly those of Iraq, Afghanistan, Lebanon and Palestine.

Citizens of India

The 9th Congress of the CPI(Maoist) finally calls on the people of Indian to come forward in large numbers to support the ongoing people's war in the country and the embryonic power emerging, to build a truely democratic society built on justice, equality, free from the chains of imperialism and semi-feudal bondage.

Unity Congress-9th Congress,
CPI(Maoist)
February 1st 2007

***

RESOLUTION ON CONFLICTS ACROSS THE GLOBE

Essentially lambasting what it calls American, particularly, and British, partially, imperialism and hegemony, the CPI (Maoist) extends its moral support to non-fraternal groups fighting against the Unites States of America (USA) in their respective countries. It further lists out the ongoing conflicts/movements in various countries where each of the groups is fighting/opposing, or has fought/opposed, the state actor. These include Afghanistan, Iraq, Lebanon, Poland, France. It also lists out the countries where the state actor is opposed to the USA.

RESOLUTION ON PEOPLES' STRUGGLES THE WORLD OVER

The Unity Congress – 9th Congress of the CPI (Maoist) is being held at such a time when imperialists, particularly the US-UK imperialists, have in the name of "war against terrorism" launched an all-round attack on the exploited-oppressed nationalities, classes, minorities and against the peoples' wars being waged under the leadership of Maoist forces. In the wake of the 9/11 attacks, they attacked Afghanistan first and then Iraq. Their own trusted West Asian military bull, Zionist Israel, repeatedly attacked the liberation fighters of Palestine and also launched an attack on Lebanon. Afghanistan and Iraq were devastated with several million tons of explosives hurled upon them. Now they have set their eyes upon Iran, Syria, Cuba, North Korea and others. Some comprador rulers who were propped up as appendages in the past by the US imperialists, having tried to shift loyalties, are now sought to be replaced through military action, so that they may continue to plunder the resources of the oppressed-exploited countries of Asia, Africa and Latin America and exercise domination over the whole world.

The people of Afghanistan, Iraq and Lebanon, especially those of Iraq have stood up to these all-round imperialist attacks. The entire Arab world is seething with anti-American rage. Iraq has become yet another Vietnam for the imperialists. The people of Europe held massive protests over the unjust war. 70% people in the US itself are demanding withdrawal of the armed forces from Iraq. The US is weakening not only economically and politically, but also militarily.

The uprising in Poland, then in France and the struggles in West Europe, Japan and Russia indicate how shocks caused by the crisis are being felt even in the imperialist countries. In a nutshell, the struggles of the proletariat in capitalist, imperialist countries are getting sharper. The ground is being prepared for the socialist revolution.

This Unity Congress declares that the oppressed-exploited countries continue to be the 'storm centres' of revolution. Even while facing numerous problems, the people of India, Nepal, Peru, the Philippines and Turkey are advancing on the path of protracted peoples' war. This current of peoples' liberation shows the way for the emancipation of all peoples the world over even as it unmasks all slander against Marxism-Leninism-Maoism.

This Unity Congress believes that struggles against the policies of imperialist globalization-liberalization-privatization are becoming increasingly sharpened all over the world. This is so not only in Asia, Africa and Latin America, and the imperialist countries, but such struggles are stirring up even in revisionist centres of the Dengist variety. The peoples' struggles that emerged in China in 2006 are testimony enough.

This Unity Congress calls upon the genuine Maoist Parties working in suppressed countries and capitalist, imperialist countries to unite on a world scale and lead these struggles. The Unity Congress upholds all the just struggles of the world people. This Unity Congress calls upon the oppressed-exploited nationalities, classes and minorities to step up the revolutionary struggles against imperialism, particularly US-UK imperialism and the domestic reactionaries.

***

Resolution on Death Sentence

In principle, the CPI (Maoist) is opposed to the death sentence. It is quite ironical that a revolutionary group that swears by the gun, launches chilling massacres of security forces, as well as awards and executes capital punishment—at its illegitimate jan adalats*—to those it terms as its class enemies, should oppose the death sentence. Thus, clearly, the Maoists have chosen to oppose the death sentence in order to save the lives of their cadres who have been convicted through a legitimate process of the law by a duly constituted Court*

In a series of massacres and counter-massacres in Bihar—though it is difficult to determine who the agent provocateur *was in the first place, or what actually triggered the whole thing—four Maoist cadres were awarded the sentence by the Gaya Sessions Court in Bihar, on June 8, 2001. In the immediate context, opposing the death sentence awarded to these cadres the Maoists passed the following resolution, while also citing other instances. The Maoists noted in this Resolution: "Death sentence actually serves as a weapon in the hands of the ruling classes to suppress the exploited and oppressed classes."*

OPPOSE DEATH SENTENCE

On June 8, 2001 four innocent peasants were served the death sentence in Bara village incident under Tekari Police Station of Gaya district in Bihar. These four brave peasants are: (i) Krishna Mochi, (ii) Nanhelal Mochi, (iii) Vir Kunwar Paswan and (iv) Dharu Singh. It may be recalled that on February 12, 1992 the revolutionary masses had made a retaliatory attack on those linked to the private army of feudal lords, Sawarna Liberation Front. 37 people having connections with this private army were killed in the incident. This Bara incident was, in fact, a retaliatory mass action against the Main-Barasimha genocide in which 10 landless poor peasantsand dalit people were slaughtered. In Main-Barasimha village a struggle had then been going on for minimum wages under the leadership of Krantikari Kisan Committee. The genocide was a conspiracy by the feudal lords to teach the struggling masses a lesson.

From Rupaspur-Chandwa to Miyanpur, Bihar has been witness to dozens of such mass murders perpetrated by landlords and their private armies. Even so, not a single culprit responsible for these genocides was ever served the death sentence. On the contrary, they have been acquitted with honour and dignity. The acquittal of main accused in the Rupaspur-Chandwa genocide, the former Speaker of the Bihar Vidhan Sabha, Laxmi Narain Sudhanshu was one such example. However, it was after the revolutionary masses carried out retaliatory actions against these genocides that eight and four peasants, respectively were served the death sentence in the incidents at Dalelchak-Baghaura and Bara villages.

The death sentence served to eight brave peasants in the Dalelchak-Baghaura incident was converted to life-term imprisonment, while the death sentence in the Bara incident to four of them was confirmed by the Supreme Court. They may be hanged at the gallows any day.

Especially so in this phase of liberalization-privatisation-globalisation, the Supreme Court of India has increasingly been ruling against workers, peasants, dalits, adivasis and minorities. Ever since the so-called independence, over 90 percent of those served the death sentence so far were from landless, poor, dalit, adivasi and minority communities. This, in fact, reflects "court injustice." This in the name of the "rule of law" is nothing but a "farce of justice" perpetrated by the feudal and comprador bureaucrat capitalist classes. Death sentence actually serves as a weapon in the hands of the ruling classes to suppress the exploited and oppressed classes.

The Unity Congress – 9th Congress of CPI(Maoist) opposes the death sentence to four brave peasants and condemns it. This Congress considers this death sentence as an assault on the peoples' right of self-defence, and also that such a punishment would amount to nothing but collective murder of innocent peasants as an act of political vengeance. Death sentence is in fact a cold-blooded murder and such murders are an instrument for the suppression of class struggle.

Therefore, this Unity Congress – 9th Congress appeals to the broad masses of our country to oppose this death sentence and step up the countrywide mass movement for their release.

***

RESOLUTION ON FARMERS' SUICIDES

Since the past few years, there have been a number of suicides by farmers owing to crop failure in the Telengana region of Andhra Pradesh and the Vidarbha region of Maharashtra; these are essentially those who cultivated cotton crops. Also, some more suicide deaths have been reported from Punjab. The farmers borrow money from usurous characters at the start of the season right from the time of buying seeds through the entire cycle of the crop to purchase fertilizer, pesticides, etc. Nevertheless, for a variety of reasons the yield, and, hence, the returns were pretty low, which had the left the farmer in penury. Some of the distraught farmers, either because of one-time borrowing, or successive borrowings leading to mounting deaths, had committed suicide. Blaming the Union and State governments for all this and for everything that went wrong with some of the farmers, the Maoists had passed the following resolution at the 9th Congress.

They demanded that (a) debts of peasantry be waived, (b) agricultural subsidies restored, (c) investments in irrigation and other needs be enhanced, (d) declaration of proper prices for agricultural products (the government has, in any case, been issuing a Minimum Support Price [MSP] for agricultural produce), (e) ban MNCs like Monsanto and (e) halt liberalisation, privatisation and globalization (LPG).

RESOLUTION ON FARMERS' SUICIDES

The number of peasants committing suicides has increased phenomenally. This is particularly so in Vidarbha, AP & Punjab. In past 10 years several thousand peasants all over the country have committed suicide. In Maharashtra alone the number is almost 7000. From June 2006 to end of December, 900 peasants had committed suicide. Cotton cultivators have been particularly affected.

The Central and State Governments are diverting attention by placing the blame on loans for wasteful expenditure, poor crop/output, family and other psychological tensions. The financial package announced by PM Manmohan Singh is nothing but a cunning attempt of the finance department to befool the masses. While the peasants did not get a paisa the money went to cooperative banks. Hence rate of suicides has increased.

The real cause for these suicides is the pro-imperialist globalisation, liberalisation and privatisation policies pursued by the governments. These policies have led to the reduction of subsidies for agricultural inputs and low prices for agricultural products. Facing losses, peasants were forced to take loans, first from banks. When banks stopped giving loans they turned to money-lenders. More than 60% of loans are from private money lenders. Failure of MNC Monsanto's BT Cotton Seeds was the final straw. A section of farmers' leaders like Sharad Joshi had already betrayed the peasants by supporting globalisation. Disheartened farmers have turned to suicides. These are in reality killings by a government acting in the interests of the imperialists.

Unity Congress-9th Congress of CPI (Maoist) strongly opposes the pro-imperialist policies of the government and expresses its heartful sympathies with the peasants and appeals to them not to resort to self-destruction but to wage militant struggle, to organise and refuse to repay all debts and to join the ongoing revolutionary peasant war.

This Congress calls upon peasants to demand that all debts of peasantry be waived, agricultural subsidies be restored, investments in irrigation and other agricultural needs be increased, proper prices for agricultural products and ban on MNCs like Monsanto and their GM Seeds, and opposes the policies of liberalisation, privatisation and globalisation.

Only New Democratic Revolution will solve the problems of the peasantry. While struggling on immediate demands we pledge to organise the vast masses of the peasantry to intensify the armed struggle to overthrow this semi-colonial, semi-feudal system.

***

KHAIRLANJI DALIT MASSACRE

In caste-related violence, four members of a Dalit family were killed by upper caste Hindus in Khairlanji village in Maharashtra in September 2006, a few months before the 9th/ Unity Congress of the CPI (Maoist) was held in January 2007. Immediately after the killings large scle protests and rallies were conducted at a few places in Maharashtra. It was suspected that the Maoists had inspired these protests. Condemning the killings and refuting the allegations of their involvement in the protests, the Maoists passed a resolution at the 9th Congress.

In the resolution, the Maoists reiterated their opposition to all forms of caste-based oppression and discrimination and extended their un-equivocal support to the struggle by the Dalits for 'dignity and equality'. Moreover, they held that armed struggle, which would herald a New Democratic Revolution, was the only panacea for all such happenings.

RESOLUTION AGAINST DALIT KILLINGS IN KHAIRLANJI

On 29th September 2006 upper caste forces with a feudal outlook brutally killed four members of a Dalit family in Khairlanjhi village (Mohadi Taluka, Bhandara district) in Maharashtra. Bhaiyala Bhotmange is the sole survivor in this family. The family tilled their own land for subsistence. His wife Surekha, daughter Prujanta, sons Roshan and Sudhir were beaten to death. Surekha and Priyanka were stripped, gang raped and paraded before the village and their private parts injured. The atrocities are a shame for humanity. The local BJP and NCP politicians are involved and helped them in suppressing the entire incident by using the police, administration and hospital officials.

That is why the Dalit masses all over the state came out on the streets spontaneously against these cruel killings and militantly protested. The desecration of the Ambedkar statue in Kanpur enflamed the masses even more and a series of bandhs were called and even two trains set on fire. The Congress and NCP led Maharashtra government, instead of acting against the culprits and giving justice to Bhotmanges', launched police repression against the agitators. They used Lathi charge, curfews, firings and widespread arrests to crush the masses. Four Dalits died in these firings.

They exaggerated and propagated that Naxalites are involved in the agitation only in order to justify their repression. But the Dalit masses knew that Maoists have always stood with the oppressed. The masses took inspiration from this and intensified their agitation. The parliamentary Dalit politicians are using this mass agitation to bargain with the ruling parties. The anti-Dalit orientation of the Maharashtra Government stands completely exposed. Maharashtra government is a casteist fascist government of upper castes which seeks to maintain the feudal base so that imperialist exploitation can intensify.

The Unity Congress - 9th Congress of CPI (Maoist) strongly condemns the Khairlanjhi killings and stands firmly with the struggling Dalit masses. We uphold the struggle of Dalits for dignity and equality and call upon PLGA and masses to counter this killing. This Congress resolves to continuously struggle against Brahminical, casteist oppression and all forms of discrimination and untouchability. Dalits cannot gain liberation without armed struggle against the feudal order. Hence this Congress pledges to organuse mobilise Dalits for caste eradication as an integral part of New Democratic Revolution.

This Congress calls upon peasants to demand that all debts of peasantry be waived, agricultural subsidies be restored, investments in irrigation and other agricultural needs be increased, proper prices for agricultural products and ban on MNCs like Monsanto and their GM Seeds, and opposes the policies of liberalisation, privatisation and globalisation.

Only New Democratic Revolution will solve the problems of the peasantry. While struggling on immediate demands we pledge to organise the vast masses of the peasantry to intensify the armed struggle to overthrow this semi-colonial, semi-feudal system.

***

Resolution on Hindu Fascism

The CPI (Maoist) is atheist. The rebels are of the perception that the Indian ruling classes are perpetuating their dominance over the masses and continue to exploit them, besides following the "Imeprialist-dictated policies under the "patriotic garb of Hundutva." They consider the Indian ruling classes as part of the Hindu bandwagon and brand them as 'Hindu Fascists'.

According to the CPI (Maoist) "the main vehicle of the Hindu fascist onslaught has been the BJP-RSS combine", and outfits such as VHP, Bajarang Dal, Shiv Sena, etc. They consider these forces as "particularly dangerous since they have the support of the most important arms of the state in all their activities." Thus, in this Resolution, while terming the ruling classes as Hindu fascist forces, the Maoists are essentially referring to the Hindutva brigade *or the* Sangh Parivar *and not the entire ruling class.*

At the same time, in order to project themselves as the only saviours of the minorities the Maoists discredit all other political formations in the country. They do not include these political organizations as part of the Hindutva *bandwagon, but lampoon them in a different manner. They hold the now ruling Congress-I as the chief element responsible for communal riots and allege that it has been spreading "malicious propaganda" against all minority communities; the Communists are accused of helping in perpetuating "domination by the Hindu fascists; the regional parties are termed as "apologists for the Hindu fascists". In an attempt to project themselves as the only 'deliverers' the Maoists have been spreading such venom at will.*

RESOLUTION AGAINST HINDU FASCISM

The crisis of the Indian ruling classes is all round affecting not only the economic sphere, but also the social and political spheres. This is resulting in growing anger and revulsion of the masses of the people against the reactionary ruling classes. They are finding it increasingly difficult to continue their oppressive rule in the old forms. Consequently the ruling classes have developed fascist social forces with the aim of establishing full fledged fascist rule. Through this they hope not only to overcome this crisis but also establish rule with consent, and facilitate the intensification of imperialist exploitation. Under the "patriotic garb" of Hindutva policies, they are meekly implementing the imperialist-dictated policies of liberalization-privatisation-globalisation, especially after the 80's. For this they are conducting a Hindu fascist campaign, on the basis of which they will try to establish open terrorist forms of rule.

Since the early 1980s, the ruling classes have been promoting Hindu communalism, targeting religious minorities, with the hope of uniting the Hindu majority behind themselves. The Babri Masjid demolition in 1992 was a devious act committed with this very hope. The main vehicle of the Hindu fascist onslaught has been the BJP-RSS combine with its storm trooper organisations like the VHP, Bajrang Dal, etc. The Shiv Sena in Maharashtra too has been propped up to achieve this end. The Hindu fascists are particularly dangerous since they have the support of the most important arms of the state in all their activities.

Feb 2002 was a high point when the Hindu fascist forces in their laboratory, the BJP-ruled state of Gujarat, organized the worst-ever communal genocide since 1947. Thousands of muslims were brutally killed, thousands burnt alive or maimed. Hundreds of muslim women were gang-raped and murdered. Muslim property was targeted with absolute precision and destroyed by Hindu state organized goons of VHP, RSS and Bajrang Dal in connivance with state armed forces. Even after four years, many of them have not been able to return to their native places because of the threat of Hindu fascists.

While Gujarat was their own laboratory, similar hate campaigns against muslims were taken in Karnataka at Baba Budanagiri mazar, in Madhya Pradesh at Jhabua, in Rajasthan, in Maharashtra at Malegaon, and at various other places. They use the smallest opportunity to flare up the sentiments against muslims, like with the singing of *vande mataram.*

The Indian state too has targeted muslims, branding them "terrorist." After the 9/11 incident and the Parliament Attack Case muslims were targeted once again. Every muslim is supposed to prove his patriotism time and again. Indian state forces are even capturing and annihilating innocent muslims now and then, in the name of nabbing terrorists. Evidences implicating state and hindutva forces in "attacks" are being willfully suppressed, as can be seen in the Afzal Guru case and the attack on RSS headquarters at Nagpur.

The Cong-led UPA came to power projecting itself as a secular force, but it is the Congress party itself that has been mainly responsible for most of the communal riots ever since the transfer of power. Congress party is even more pernicious. It projects itself as a *messiah* of muslims, but in real practice it leaves no stone unturned to spread malicious propaganda against muslims and other minorities. The anti-Sikh pogroms of 1984 were one such example. In the name of equally opposing all types of fundamentalism, CPI and CPI[M] have actually helped in maintaining the status-quo of domination by the Hindu fascists. Various regional parties have made alliances with the Hindu fascists for the sake of votes and have become apologists for the Hindu fascists.

These Hindu fascists are trying to impose a hegemonistic Hindu culture on the various culturally diverse people of India. While their attacks are mainly concentrated against muslims, they are also targeting Christians, especially in the tribal areas, aggressively converting tribals to Hinduism. Similarly, they also attack dalits.

The Unity Congress - 9th congress of the CPI(Maoist) calls upon the revolutionary masses, all democratic forces and the oppressed religious minorities to unite in a struggle against the Hindu fascists. The worldwide experience of the struggle against fascism teaches that the fascists can be defeated only by militant class struggle in the streets, factories and in the rest of the countryside. The fascists can be defeated only by isolating them from the people and smashing their organizational forces, and by developing and intensifying protracted peoples' war with the aim of new democratic revolution, then socialism and ultimately establishing communism.

The CPI(Maoist) pledges to fight resolutely against each and every instance of the trampling on the democratic rights of the oppressed minorities and others by the Hindu fascists. It pledges to do its best to defend the sections of the population targeted by the Hindu fascists. Our party is willing to unite in a broad front with all the genuine democratic forces which would be willing to fight back the Hindu fascist offensive.

***

Resolution on Political Prisoners

The CPI (Maoist) has all along contended that all its leaders and cadres who have been arrested by the police and sent to jail are, indeed, political prisoners. Therefore, they demand that they should all be granted all rights that are due to a political prisoner.

Even as it lists out the names of various Maoist leaders and cadres, the document alleges that their democratic rights are being suppressed by the government. It also extols the detained Maoists to organize themselves and be active.

Indeed, the Maoists have formed such organizations; for instance, Committee for the Release of Political Prisoners and Indian Association of People's Lawyers.

RESOLUTION ON PRISONERS' STRUGGLES

A movement of various classes and sections is breaking out against the imperialist-dictated policies of globalization, liberalization and privatization and other anti-people policies being implemented by the ruling classes of India. In a bid to suppress these movements, the Indian Government has increasingly carried out repressive policies and become increasingly fascist. Several draconian laws have come about and are already in force. The main target of this repression campaign has been the struggles being waged against imperialism, feudalism and comprador bureaucrat capitalism under communist revolutionary leadership. Among these revolutionaries, particularly the leadership comrades, those who escape the inevitable fake encounters somehow or the other, find themselves thrown behind bars with numerous false charges heaped upon them.

Six comrades in AP, 26 in Tamil Nadu are detained under POTA, and 16 in Karnataka, and about 25 comrades in North Chhattisgarh have been languishing in jails. In many other states also the situation is not different. Hundreds of women comrades have also been incarcerated in different jails in the country. Besides them, thousands of other comrades and people have also been thrown into jails. Arrested comrades are not produced in court for days on end in stark violation of civil rights; any kind of protest by prison inmates is prohibited while depriving them of all their rights; lathi-charges are conducted to suppress any organized protest; leadership comrades are banished to distant jails; locked up in cells or harassed in other ways; visitors are denied permission to meet the inmates; they are not provided with medical treatment; bribes are extracted too often than not; false charges are framed against imprisoned comrades in instalments; "fast-track trials" are conducted to serve sentences without much ado even by the dint of false supporting evidence. These and other nefarious means have become common occurrence.

Besides comrade Tapas, Central Committee member of our Party and another important comrade Pratul, five comrades from Asagarh area, five from Bhamragarh and five from Tipragarh areas in of Gadchiroli division and five peasants of Gondia division (Maharashtra), five comrades from Chhattisgarh, four comrades each from Orissa and Andhra Pradesh, and some comrades from Bihar and Jharkhand have been served with life imprisonment. Some ordinary villagers from Bihar, languishing in jail on charges related to Bara (Gaya) and Meral (Garhwa) incidents, have been served life sentences.

In spite of tremendous torture, our comrades languishing behind bars have kept alive the ever-inspiring revolutionary legacy of resistance and struggle against repression and oppression in jails. The struggle of 1995 that broke out in various AP jails all at once and the solidarity struggle from outside were indeed historic in terms of their impact and spread. Our comrades in West Bengal, Karnataka and Tamil Nadu jails have also launched movements in demand of the rights of political prisoners and against various repressive measures of the authorities. We earnestly believe that even while bearing with the most inhuman, tough and hapless conditions in these torture chambers, our comrades shall leave no stone unturned to forge unyielding unity among themselves and to carry ahead the revolutionary legacy of roaring aloud, as caged lions would do.

The Congress urges you to:

Form secret Party units even in prison and carry on the task of running them regularly through secret methods.

Build action committees such as '*Jail Bandi Sanghursh Samiti*' behind bars. In case comrades are kept in separate prison barracks, then form barrack committees, and press with demands to keep all revolutionaries in the same barrack depending upon the concrete situation. Such action committees are quite helpful in further enhancement of the spirit of unity and sacrifice, and in identifying vacillators and coverts.

Transform the prisons into political universities.

In order to enhance your own theoretical-ideological and political levels, continue holding a series of study and political classes as far as possible.

Arouse and mobilize common prison inmates, forming cultural teams, aid committees and various types of organizations.

Develop the prisons as centres of struggle against the ongoing widespread extortion, corruption and atrocities as well as against the attacks on democratic rights. At the same time, unite and create a huge outcry in support of the revolutionary struggles being waged on the world scale, and against the repression campaigns aimed at them.

This Congress hereby adopts a resolution to take up every possible programme so as to express solidarity with the 'struggles of prison inmates;' to lend strength to their struggles; and to form suitable organizations. The Congress resolves to:

Form organizations, such as 'Committee to Release Prisoners' along with intellectuals, democracy-lovers and members of the families of imprisoned comrades, in solidarity with prisoners' struggles and to lend them strength. Such an organization shall conduct struggles on various demands related to the jail by establishing coordination between various Prisoners' Action Committees. Employing different means, such committees shall help create public opinion about the assault upon the civil rights of the prison inmates. In this direction efforts are already underway.

Organize progressive lawyers to provide legal support to the prisoners. Some efforts have been made in this direction. Yet we shall lay stress upon forming such organizations in different cities. These organizations shall provide legal support to imprisoned comrades as well as generate public opinion against draconian laws.

Mobilize 'Committees to Release Prisoners,' lawyers organizations, civil liberty organizations and the common masses against 'Fast Track Trials' and such other outright anti-people provisions.

Pay special attention to raise protest against and organize resistance to atrocities perpetrated upon women prisoners.

Rope in various means of propaganda in order to highlight the inhuman conditions in prisons.

Conduct signature campaigns on various demands of the prisoners and in support of their struggles issues in order to arouse and mobilize the masses.

Strive to punish the prison officials who carry out atrocities upon the prisoners.

Constitute a Prisoners' Fund to help secure their release.

This Congress resolves to strive to carry out every possible means to free our comrades from the jails besides waging different forms of struggle within constitutional limits. With support from the masses, we had carried out historic actions such as the Jehanabad and R Udaigiri Jailbreaks. The Congress calls upon the entire Party ranks and the mass organization rank and file to prepare in this direction and educate the masses.

***

Resolution on Secessionist/Insurgent Movements

The CPI (Maoist) has, all along, extended moral support to the various terrorist/secessionist/insurgent movements being waged in different States of India. The rebels term these as 'freedom struggle'. In this resolution, the Maoists lend 'unequivocal support' to these secessionist movements and hold that they have the right to secede from the Indian Union. They also contend that the attempt by the government to find a negotiated settlement to the various movements is a conspiracy to 'dilute' their demand.

Moreover, in this resolution, they also club the demand for separate Statehood in the various sub-regions of the country with the secessionist demand of the different insurgent groups, and extend and vow to fight for all these demands. The Maoists state, "According to the time and circumstances, it may be necessary to form a separate organization to take up the nationality issue, and we should form such organizations in accordance with the concrete situation."

This entire ploy by the Maoists should be viewed from the prism of the 'United Front Tactics'. Through the United Front the Maoists seek to form opportunistic alliances with any group/organization that is opposed to the Indian state for one reason or the other. For the Maoists these are 'partial struggles' and need to be undertaken alongside armed struggle. The objective of forming United Front is tactical and opportunistic. It is meant to politically corner the Indian state.

RESOLUTION ON NATIONALITY STRUGGLES

India is a country of many nationalities at various phases of development. They have been struggling in different forms against the repressive and expansionist policies of the Indian ruling classes. Kashmiris and different nationalities of North-East India such as the Assamese, Nagas, Manipuris, Tripuris, etc., have been long since waging armed struggle against the Indian Government for their right to self-determination, including the right to secede from the so-called Union of India. The Indian ruling classes and their imperialist masters, particularly US imperialism, have been suppressing these struggles mercilessly. They are being crushed under the boots of the Indian Army stationed in various states of the north-east and in Kashmir. In Kashmir alone, the Indian military and paramilitary forces have murdered over 70, 000 people in the last 16 years. A year ago, the Indian Army along with the Bhutanese Army killed hundreds of activists and supporters of the ULFA, Bodos and the KLO. However, even these most cruel repressive actions by the Indian Government could not stifle the voice of the struggling masses of these nationalities. They still continue to wage armed struggle and carry out their attacks, striking blows at the Indian armed forces.

Of late, the Indian ruling classes have deviously begun a phase of talks with organizations leading the nationality struggles in a bid to douse the fire of these struggles with false promises and to co-opt their leadership into the existing system. They are trying to win over a section of the leadership of the struggling organizations of these nationalities and conspiring to have them oppose the struggling sections. However, their ploy does not seem to succeed. The ULFA has become active once again. With the Indian Government's rejection of the Naga proposal to form a Union of Nagaland or 'Greater Nagaland,' the talks between NSCN and Government of India appear to be in dicey waters. Last year, the people of Manipur, especially the women waged a valiant struggle against the 'Armed Forces (Special Powers) Act.' The PLA too has stepped up its attacks in Manipur. The struggle of the Kashmiri people with the Indian forces, which hacontinued unabated, has generated fresh mass resentment in the wake of the Centre's designs to hang Afzal Guru. The Kashmiri people, along with the enlightened democratic sections all over India, have raised the just demand to desist from hanging the innocent Afzal Guru. Meanwhile, the demand for separate statehood in Telengana has again gathered momentum and the Vidarbha issue too seems to be emerging. Through the carving out of Jharkhand state, not only was the Jharkhandi nationality splintered up, but their aspirations too have been crushed.

This Unity Congress – 9th Congress unequivocally supports the right of self-determination of all the oppressed nationalities, including their right to secede from the autocratic Indian state (which they were forced to join). The Congress condemns the ongoing state repression of nationality movements and vows to carry out a joint movement against the Indian ruling classes along with the people of different nationalities. According to the time and circumstances, it may be necessary to form a separate organization to take up the nationality issue, and we should form such organizations in accordance with the concrete situation. This Congress believes asserts that the various nationalities are independent, equal and sovereign, and that they are free to form a voluntary union by basing themselves upon based on the principle of the right to self-determination and equality. The Congress also supports the just struggles of those nationalities and sub-nationalities that demand a separate state for their development. Moreover, it also reiterates its resolve to extend all possible support to their just and democratic struggle.

SECTION IV

CENTRAL COMMITTEE/POLITBURO CIRCULARS/STATEMENTS

The Central Committee of the CPI (Maoist) acts as the apex, all-India spokesperson of the rebels and issues press releases/statements from time-to-time. Until July 2010, the statements of the Central Committee were issued in the name of Azad. Thereafter, these are being issued in the name of Abhay.

At least in the past, there was no single person who was the official spokesperson of the rebels. Cherukuri Raj Kumar alias Uday also used the alias 'Azad', and was believed to be its spokesperson. But, a few others were also 'authoroised' to issue statements on behalf of the Central Committee. They, however, issued them in the name of Azad.

The Central Committee is the apex and all-powerful decision making body of the Maoists. At the 2007 Congress, 34 members were elected to the Central Committee. Of these, one has surrendered to the authorities, a few were arrested and some more were killed in encounters with the security forces. Presently the strength of the Central Committee is 17.

There is yet another body known as the Politburo. Its present strength is seven. The Politburo meets twice a year and is in-charge of the day-to-day activities of the rebels at the all-India level. However, any decision made by the Politburo has to be necessarily approved by the Central Committee. In case of lack of consensus between the Politburo and the Central Committee, the matter is deferred for wide debate at the Congress after which a policy direction is arrived at.

The following are a few circulars/statements issued by the Central Committee of the CPI (Maoist). These are not exhaustive, but selective and indicative.

***

Basaguda Exchange of Fire

In an operation based on intelligence inputs, security personnel led by the Central Reserve Police Force (CRPF) reached a village in Central India's Bastar and engaged a Maoist squad in an exchange of fire (EoF). The Maoists claimed that no armed squad was present there and that the security personnel opened indiscriminate fire and killed innocent villagers, including children. They further accused the security personnel of committing atrocities. On the other hand, even while they maintained that they had precise intelligence input on the presence of a Maoist squad in the village, the security personnel alleged that the fleeing squad used innocent civilians as human shield.

Following is the statement issued by the Central Committee of the CPI (Maoist) on the Basaguda encounter in Bastar.

COMMUNIST PARTY OF INDIA (MAOIST) CENTRAL COMMITTEE

PRESS RELEASE JULY 10, 2012

Punish the perpetrators of Basaguda Massacre! Demand the immediate withdrawal of all paramilitary and military forces from Bastar!

On 28-6-2012 in one of the most brutal massacres till date in Chhattisgarh's Bastar region 17 innocent, ordinary, unarmed villagers were killed by about a thousand blood-thirsty CRPF-CoBRA, state police forces and Koya Commandos and SPOs. These mercenary forces surrounded a gathering of villagers discussing about their harvest and related festivals in Sarkinguda on that night and killed several people in an indiscriminate, one-sided cold-blooded firing reminding one of the Jallianwalabagh massacre. Many more villagers were injured. Nine of the dead were juveniles between 12 and 16 years of age. There were children, women and elderly persons among the injured too. The mercenary forces wreaked havoc the whole night and shot dead some more villagers, looted their homes and resorted to sexual abuses on women. They threatened the villagers who tried to help the injured that they too would face the same fate. On the same day two more Adivasi peasants were murdered by the same fascist government armed forces in Simlipenta, a nearby village taking the toll to 19.

This massacre was perpetrated by the mercenary forces as part of the second phase of Operation Green Hunt (OGH) launched by the Indian ruling classes with the full support and aid of the imperialists, particularly the US imperialists since mid-2009. The blue-print for this well-planned massacre was prepared under the auspices of the notorious ruling clique of Sonia-Manmohan-Chidambaram-Jairam Ramesh and their 'reliable lieutenants' at the centre and in Chhattisgarh (CG) – secretary for Home RK Singh, CRPF DG Vijaya Kumar-Raman Singh-Nankiram Kanwar-Longkumer-Anil Navani-Ramnivas et al., who are carrying on this country-wide, multi-pronged, counter-revolutionary massive military offensive on the Maoist movement areas in the most atrocious manner and where massacres of ordinary villagers has come to be one of the most common forms of repression in this "War on the People". The statements by Raman Singh and Nankiram Kanwar about a massive offensive on Maoists to be launched in June in CG forewarned about what was in store because as any keen observer of these 'offensives on Maoists" is well aware – it is most common for ordinary people to become victims in fake encounters, lock-up deaths and massacres in such 'offensives on Maoists'.

In Dandakaranya (DK) starting from Singaram massacre in January 2009 several massacres of Adivasis have been carried on by the state and central mercenary forces like in Vechapad, Singanamadugu, Palachelima, Gompad, Gumiapal, Kokavada, Takilod, Ongnar and massive destruction and murders as in Tadimetla-Morpalli-Chintalnar etc., and none of the perpetrators – neither the 'Generals' like Sonia, Manmohan, Chidambaram, Raman Singh, Nankiram Kanwar, Vijay Kumar, Longkumer or a Kalluri nor the actual police-paramilitary officers and 'foot soldiers' who carried out their orders - of these massacres have been booked or punished till date. All the culprits are roaming scot-free in the corridors of power in New Delhi and Raipur and the off the hook police-paramilitary forces are ruthlessly going about their daily routine of mayhem, murder, loot, destruction, arson and rapes in the heart of India.

The Basaguda massacre is all the more bizarre for the utter lies, distortions, twisting of facts and the lower depths the ruling classes could stoop to justify their unscrupulous deed. Firstly, they for the umpteenth time repeated the routine story that armed Maoists had attacked them and that these 'Maoists' were killed when they retaliated. They even lied that they had seized weapons and explosives from the site. Six injured jawans were shown as 'proof' of the fact that an exchange of fire took place. Herr Chidambaram could not hide his glee at the death of 'twenty Maoists' and in a moment of truth announced that 'this was a pre-planned attack' based on information. Later this Indian avatar of Goebbels had to eat his foul lexis as every fact pointed out to a cold-blooded massacre and even the Congress in CG was forced to form a committee on this after the people of the village and neighboring villages came on the roads and stated the facts for the entire world to hear. In spite of the facts put forward by the entire people of the village and his own party, Chidambaram conveniently and shamelessly 'passed the buck' to the Raman Singh government saying that it is for the state government to decide if an enquiry is needed or not and that the central government had nothing to do with this. Shedding crocodile tears he had the audacity to say that he regretted if innocent people had died even while self contradicting himself that this was a 'transparent and upfront' attack. Raman Singh not even caring if any sane person believed him, once again spun the same old bull-shit theory that Maoists used the ordinary people as human shields and so they died! Like a pet dog more faithful than the master Nankiram Kanwar went to the end of saying that whoever is with the Maoists is also a Maoist implying that those villagers could be (or deserved to be) killed as 'they were with Maoists'.

The stark fact is that there were no Maoists with the villagers and no exchange of fire had taken place. The mercenary forces just surrounded the villagers from all sides and fired upon them and some were pulled out of their homes and shot dead. Even the so-called injuries of the jawans must have been a hoax as in some earlier instances or they might have been injured in their own cross-fire.

This massacre happened in the backdrop of the deployment of Indian Army in Bastar in the name of training and the attacks already being launched by the Air Force in the pretext of logistical support and self-defense. It is like a curtain-raiser to the things in store and let nobody make the mistake of seeing this massacre as a mistake of the government forces in the field. As every concerned democratic citizen in this country is increasingly realizing and as our party has stated several times, this "War on People" is being perpetuated with the sole aim of the plunder of the rich natural resources of our country and to crush every kind of force that proves to be a hurdle to it. The people led by the CPI (Maoist) and the party are perceived by the imperialists and the Indian ruling classes as the most formidable 'hurdle' (read biggest threat to the 'internal security' of the plunderers) to the loot of our country and particularly that of Adivasi areas by the imperialists, comprador bureaucratic bourgeoisie and the big landlords of our country which explains this massive military offensive on our movement areas. In the name of crushing Maoists the ruling classes are crushing all kinds of democratic and patriotic forces in this country and we once again appeal to the people to realize that this is not just an offensive on the Maoists but a "War on the People". This is what lies behind massacres like the one at Basaguda.

The lives of ordinary citizens and Adivasis of this country hold no value for the ruling classes is something that has been proven hundreds of times in police firings and such massacres. The only new thing is that now they are shouting this fact from the roof-tops openly. The convoluted logic that whoever is with the Maoists deserved to be killed or could be killed should be thoroughly exposed and condemned as this is nothing but a thinly veiled threat to the lives of the citizens of this country and particularly the Adivasis in the Maoist movement areas. The full scale preparations for drone attacks and the future deaths of Adivasis in these attacks would also be justified with the same logic of 'collateral damage' as in Afghanistan or a Pakistan. Already in Peda Kedwal and Chinna Kedwal villages of Bastar the government forces conducted an aerial operation in December 2011 using more than a dozen helicopters for deployment of forces. In all the massive military operations conducted recently in Dandakaranya, Bihar, Jharkhand, Chhattisgarh-Odisha Border and Andhra-Odisha Border areas involving Brigade level of forces, UAVs were used. They had openly declared that this is how future attacks would be conducted in Maoist areas.

We appeal to all citizens of this country, democrats, patriots, well-wishers of Adivasis and all civil liberties organizations to condemn the Basaguda brutal massacre in no uncertain terms and demand severe punishment for the perpetrators. Demand the immediate withdrawal of all paramilitary and military forces from Bastar. We particularly appeal to the media persons to bring the facts about this massacre into light as some pro-government corporate media persons are trying to hide the facts and falsely portray this massacre as 'people being crushed between government forces and Maoists'. We appeal to one and all to build a vast and united agitation all over the country with these demands. We appeal to all revolutionary and democratic forces in the country and the world to condemn this massacre, to oppose the deployment of UAVs to crush the Maoist movement in India and to demand an end to "War on People" – the Operation Green Hunt.

(Abhay)
Spokesperson,
Central Committee,
CPI (Maoist)

***

AGENDA, POST-2009 ELECTIONS

The CPI (Maoist) has consistently and avowedly held that parliamentary politics is a sham and has therefore kept itself away from the electoral processes. Moreover, they have routinely been issuing boycott calls during elections to the various tiers of government.

Following the 2009 General Elections the Politburo issued a circular. In it, they termed the elections as a "meaningless, pseudo-democratic exercise" in which several crores of rupees were spent on electioneering and argued that none of the political parties made 'the real people's issues' a part of its election plank or manifesto.

In this circular, further, the Maoists also identified their military and political agenda/tasks in the aftermath of the elections. In the section entitled "Immediate Tasks", the Maoists noted, prominently, the following:

Rouse the masses throughout the country;

Support struggles in all parts of the country and in the states where they have marked a presence and build a broad-based mass movement;

Conduct political campaigns i.e., partial struggles, in Maoist parlance;

Form Tactical United Front, i.e., forge unity with various over-ground organizations on various issues to politically fight the state;

Protect the leadership and preserve the guerrilla bases (GB);

Expand the underground strength of the outfit;

Mobilise the masses to launch militant mass struggles;

Undertake massive propaganda exercise against the state/security forces to put them on the defensive;

Given that there is an upper limit to the total number of security forces that can be deployed at any point in time in any one state, expand the guerrilla war to new areas, as well as intensify the attacks on the security forces, in order that the security forces are dispersed thinly across the country in various states;

Conduct rectification campaign;

Desist from causing damage to public property in order that the people are not put to inconvenience; and

Resolutely oppose and resist the deployment/advance of the security forces in Abuj Maad, which the Maoists refer to as Maad area.

POST-ELECTION SITUATION—OUR TASKS

The so-called people's mandate for stability and neo-liberal reforms is meant to legitimize the brutal state terror and economic oppression on the people!

Prepare the Party, PLGA and the people for the new brutal offensive being unleashed by the UPA government!!

The drama of elections to the 15th Lok Sabha and three state Assemblies of Andhra Pradesh, Sikkim and Orissa, enacted at a massive cost of over Rs. 15,000 crores, had been the dominant event in the country for almost four months of the current year. An artificial atmosphere was built up by the media and the reactionary rulers by projecting this farcical drama as the biggest democratic exercise in the world with 714 million voters said to be choosing the next government.

In many ways, Election-2009 had been a record of sorts. Never before had India witnessed such a degree of apathy, aversion and disgust among the voters towards the Parliamentary elections as during Election-2009. Never before had the reactionary ruling classes and the media indulged in such a massive propaganda campaign spending hundreds of crores of rupees just to convince the voters that their votes "decide" the destiny of the country and that they should not stay away from the polls. Never before had elections been so much fragmented and unpredictable regarding the outcome. And never before had an election seen such mind-boggling non-stop publicity blitz in the electronic media and meaningless chatter that is completely devoid of any real issue facing the country and people. The Parties and the media were totally silent on the real issues facing the people and the country. To the vast majority of the people of India the elections were a meaningless, irrelevant, pseudo-democratic exercise that had only aggravated the casteist, communal, regional and factional strife and tensions across the length and breadth of the country.

None of the Parties had touched upon any issue of importance. The electronic media went on howling and speculating round-the-clock on irrelevant questions such as: Who will become the Prime Minister? Which party will emerge as the single largest Party? Which Party will get how many seats? Which coalition of parties will form the government? Who will align with whom during the elections? And how will be the shift in the allegiances after the declaration of results on May 16? And so on. The media channels had deliberately avoided going into the burning issues of the people for that would have meant calling into question the irrelevance of the very system in the daily lives of the people. This fact also showed how divorced and disconnected has the so-called democratic election become from the lives of the people. The poll boycott by the majority of the Indian people itself is an indicator of this truth.

In such a situation the reactionary rulers naturally became panicky with our Party's call for the boycott of elections. They tried by all means to foil our call and to recreate illusions about the sanctity of the vote and the virtues of parliamentary democracy: bollywood actors, cricket stars, industrialists, and other popular personalities were mobilized into this campaign to refurbish the image of parliamentary democracy; several NGOs were engaged to raise the "awareness" among the people and to convince the skeptics; websites and blogs were used to spread the lies. And to make the campaign look more credible some NGOs and media channels called on the people not to vote for criminal and corrupt elements but to choose sincere candidates who worked for the country's progress and so on. What the voter should do when all the candidates are corrupt or criminal, which usually is the case, is not answered.

The day the first phase of elections to the Lok Sabha was completed on April 16, the media tried to show how democracy had won against anarchy, how ballot proved to be superior to bullet, how people defied the Maoists and came forth to exercise their franchise braving the bullet, and such endless rhetoric. "**Bullet vs ballot: Voters give mandate on Maoist-hit LS seats**" wrote a paper. "***Maoist warnings fail to deter voters in Red zone***" claimed another pointing to the 45 per cent votes polled in Gaya district. "***Despite red terror 50 % polling in Jharkhand***" crowed another paper. "***Ballot wins against Bullet***" ran another headline. There is no limit to such hollow claims and empty phrases to prove that so-called democracy got the upper-hand in this sham drama. Chief Election Commissioner-designate Navin Chawla howled that "***democracy triumphed over naxalism on April 16.***"

Election-2009 has earned the distinction of being the most discredited election held so far in the country. People everywhere, and not merely in the areas under the influence of our Party, resorted to boycott as a form of protest and struggle. Overall, the majority of the Indian people showed a higher level of consciousness this time by rejecting the contesting candidates, the political parties, and the pseudo-democratic parliamentary system. They gave the rulers sleepless nights, and all the tricks played by the reactionary rulers and their propaganda blitz and appeals to voters to exercise their "fundamental right" to vote, came to nought. **More people stayed away from the polling booths than those who went to cast their votes.** And even among those who voted the majority had little trust in the candidate or the party who can change loyalties after the votes are cast.

Of the 714 million total registered voters, hardly 50% had actually cast their votes whether it was out of coercion, or monetary and material incentives, or caste, community, ethnic, regional considerations, or for other reasons. Of the total votes that were actually cast, the Congress, which obtained 206 seats and emerged as the single largest Party, had obtained a vote share of just about 29.67 per cent with an increase of 61 seats from the 2004 elections. The BJP lost 22 seats and received 19.29 per cent of vote share. BSP came third with its vote share of 6.27 per cent followed by the CPI(M) with 5.52 per cent. Thus the Congress, with just over a hundred million votes or roughly 15 per cent of the total votes, has formed the government with a few other Parties all of which had a combined share of not more than 5 to 6 per cent or another 20 million votes. Yet, our rulers want us to believe that it is a government of the majority. But can one call this process democracy when 85 per cent voters had rejected the so-called single largest party and yet have to put up with a government that is formed on a minority of votes? This stark fact has to be propagated widely to expose the myth of rule by majority.

The reactionaries always hush up the actual truth that the majority of the population has hardly any faith in the parliamentary system or the political parties that contest the election. The fact is those who reject this so-called parliamentary system, whether consciously or unconsciously, always constitute the majority. But recognition of this fact and propagating this would jeopardize the legitimacy of the ruling class to rule. Hence the entire political spectrum is united in underplaying this crucial fact and sings in chorus about the success of "parliamentary democracy" in India. Such a lie is indispensable for the survival of these political parties and the reactionary rulers they represent.

In our propaganda and education on the "victory of democracy" claimed by the rulers, we have to focus on how the very election exercise is an undemocratic exercise held under semi-feudal conditions where it is more the caste, communal, regional, ethnic, gender factors along with money power and muscle power that play the principal role in ensuring the victory of a candidate. The fact that 300 of the 543 MPs are declared crorepatis shows the role of money power in elections. We must show how notorious criminals and communal fascists had won the elections by utilizing these. The elections this time saw more number of criminals as MPs than any time in the past with 150 MPs having criminal cases and 73 having serious charges. The dissolved Parliament had 128 MPs with criminal cases and 55 of them facing serious charges. BJP and Congress vied with each other in the number of criminal MPs with 42 and 41 respectively.

Election Results and the Myth of a Decisive Mandate

With the declaration of election results on May 16 and the UPA securing a majority in Parliament a big hype is being created that people had given a "decisive mandate" for stability and economic reform i.e., liberalization, privatization and globalisation or LPG. Some election analysts and commentators as well as leaders like LK Advani had even gone as far as to predict that these elections marked the beginning of the end to the phenomenon of regional parties and that they foreshadowed a two-party system. The number of seats secured by the two biggest coalitions—

the UPA and NDA—are shown as proof of this so-called emerging trend. However, nothing can be farther from truth. The election results prove neither their claims of stability and pro-LPG sentiment among the people nor the demise of the regional parties. An analysis of the voting pattern in the 15th Lok Sabha elections shows that the two biggest All India parties—the Congress and the BJP—are only relatively bigger regional parties than others. In several states these parties have a nominal presence while regional parties dominate the political scene.

The Congress and the BJP together received just 47 percent of the votes polled while the regional parties and the Left together obtained more than 50 per cent of the votes. The Congress had a ten per cent lead over the BJP compared to 4 per cent last time thereby giving it 206 seats. But the overall increase of vote share for the Congress from that of 2004 elections was just 3 per cent and the decline of BJP's vote share was 2.9 per cent. This marginal gain on one side and loss on the other sides is being interpreted by election pundits and experts as a decisive mandate. The vote share of the Congress is almost the same as in 1996 and 1999 and nearly 8 per cent less than in 1991. The myth gets more exposed when we analyse the showing of the so-called big parties in individual states.

Much hype was created about the revival of the Congress in the Hindi belt with its seat share in UP increasing from 9 seats in 2004 to 21 this time, and its voting percentage increasing from 12 to 18 per cent. The BSP which has been played down by the experts for getting just 20 seats had actually received 2.7 per cent more than last time with its vote share going up to 27.4 per cent in UP. In Bihar, another state in the Hindi heartland, the Congress obtained just two seats; in Chhattisgarh and Jharkhand just one seat each; and 6 each in West Bengal, Orissa and Karnataka. In Maharashtra the Congress got 17 out of 48 but this gain too was on account of the MNS eating into the vote share of Shiv Sena; and in Andhra Pradesh the Chiranjeevi factor helped the Congress gain 33 out of 42 Lok Sabha seats and to get a majority in the Assembly though its vote share had fallen from 41.6 in 2004 to 39 per cent this time. In West Bengal it was the Trinamul which gained most from anti-Left sentiment while the Congress only played a second fiddle. The states where the Congress made significant gains were Punjab, Haryana, Kerala and Rajasthan while its performance was better than expected in BJP-ruled states of MP and Gujarat.

In fact, it was factors such as the entry of PRP into electoral politics in Andhra Pradesh and MNS in Maharashtra which had altered the balance in favour of the Congress by splitting the votes of TDP and Shiv Sena in the two states where the Congress had won almost a quarter of its seats. In AP, the Congress got just 1.75 per cent more votes than the Grand Alliance. Much of the 16.22 per cent vote share of the PRP and 1.8 per cent of vote share of Lok Satta was said to have been the traditional vote base of the TDP thus giving the Congress an advantage. To describe this as a positive vote for the performance of the Congress is as deceptive as saying the re-election of Narendra Modi in Gujarat was a positive vote for his development work as claimed by the BJP.

It is clear that the Congress and the BJP are only like two big regional parties. Regional parties like the JD(U) and BJD gained in Bihar and Orissa; BSP had increased its vote share; Trinamul gained in West Bengal. The BJD which got only 61 seats in the 2004 Assembly elections in alliance with the BJP which obtained 32 seats, fared better this time by contesting alone and won 103 seats. The BJP got just 6 seats in the Assembly elections. Naveen Patnaik's BJD made the gains only after it had dissociated itself from the BJP and its communal attacks in Khandamal.

The so-called Left Parties were the biggest losers. The CPI(M) faced a rout in West Bengal and Kerala where it obtained only 16 Lok Sabha seats against the 41 it had earlier thus losing 25 sitting MPs. In West Bengal the CPI(M) won only 9 out of the 32 seats it had contested in the state, its worst showing in the 32 years since it first rode to power in the state with other Left partners. The post-election analysis and conclusions drawn by the CPI and CPI(M) also endorse the logic of political pundits that the people had voted for stability.

The Third Front fell apart with the TRS first shifting allegiance to the BJP-led NDA soon after the last phase of elections and the BSP and JD(S) declaring unconditional support to the UPA after the declaration of results. The dream of Karat ad Yechuri of playing the role of a king-maker (broker) if not the king were dashed to the ground. In fact, so confident was the CPI(M) of playing a crucial role in the formation of a new government at the Centre that their leaders repeatedly asserted that no government can be formed without the support of the Third Front. The CPI(M) leader Sitharam Yechuri admitted that it was a mistake on the part of his Party to have formed the Third Front as a "cut & paste" alliance without testing the commitment of these parties. He termed the Parties of the Third Front as neither credible nor viable. The experiment with the so-called anti-BJP, anti-Congress secular forces conducted by the bankrupt Left collapsed like a pack of cards.

No single Party could mange to obtain a majority by itself. While the Congress received 206 seats out of the total 543, the BJP got 116 seats. As has been the dominant trend for over two decades it was only through a coalition of several Parties that a government could be formed at the Centre. And even the formation of the Union Cabinet has been a dog-fight among the various constituents of the UPA. There was a scramble for the cabinet posts with the DMK staying away sulking that its demands for five cabinet berths and four Ministers of state were not conceded. Mamata Banerjee had a hard bargaining and finally got the posts it wanted. The UPA is clearly a divided lot and has managed to show a semblance of unity after much bargaining and accommodation of its constituents in the posts they coveted. On May 22 the Prime Minister along with 18 other Ministers were sworn in. It was only on May 28 when the names of another 59 Ministers were announced that the DMK came around after it was given three Cabinet posts.

The results led to an intensification of wrangling and dog-fights within every Party and alliance including the UPA. The BJP chief LK Advani resigned as the

Leader of the Opposition in Parliament taking responsibility for the debacle but was convinced within 24 hours to continue thus ending the drama. The pro-Narendra Modi lobby in BJP consisting of senior leaders like Arun Shourie, Arun Jaitley and Yashwant Sinha began recounting the prime ministerial qualities of Modi during the election campaign notwithstanding the fact that just a few days before the Supreme Court had asked the SIT to investigate into the involvement of Modi in the 2002 Gujarat genocide and to submit a report. Now there is a strong section in BJP which thinks it was wrong to have projected Advani as PM candidate or to have endorsed Varun's inflammatory communal speech against Muslim community. With the line of non-BJP, non-Congress secular Third Front—the brainchild of Prakash Karat—taking a severe beating there has been a virtual revolt against him in the Party and demand for his replacement as the chief of the Party.

While it is a fact that the Congress acquired more seats than it had earlier and the UPA received a majority in the 15th Lok Sabha more out of default than support for its policies as claimed by them, it is also an equally important fact that the Congress is now in a better position as it is not as desperately dependent on the allies as before. With the BSP, RJD and SP extending support even if they are not part of the UPA government, thereby taking the total MPs supporting the Manmohan Singh government to 322, the Congress will be more assertive vis-à-vis its allies, more authoritarian and repressive in its policies.

The so-called decisive mandate is meant to justify the cruel state repression and the imperialist-dictated LPG

As regards the claim of some election pundits that it was a vote for economic reform (a euphemism for selling away the natural and human resources of the country to the imperialist MNCs and the corporate big business), we can say it is a figment of their imagination or a deliberate distortion of the facts. Is the BJP lagging behind Congress in carrying out the so-called economic reforms at the behest of the imperialists and the CBB? Is a LK Advani, Arun Jaitley or a Narendra Modi any less trustworthy in the eyes of the imperialists and the CBB than a Manmohan Singh or Chidambaram or YS Reddy? If so one would not find all the top comprador business houses in the country and the MNCs praising Hindu fascist Modi and queuing up to open up their companies in Gujarat or rushing to exploit the natural resources in Raman Singh's police state of Chhattisgarh. In West Bengal, ironically, it was Mamata's Trinamul Congress which, for its own reasons, had bitterly opposed the "economic reforms" initiated by the Left Front government led by the CPI(M). Tatas had to shift their car factory from Singur and the Left Front government had to withdraw its plans to hand over the land to the big business houses in Nandigram.

One cannot differentiate Buddhadeb's government in West Bengal with a Congress or a BJP government in any other state in the matter of the neo-liberal reforms. In fact, the CPI(M)-led government had gone a step ahead by acquiring land for industrialists like Tatas, Jindals, etc and granting it free or for a nominal price. Then how did Trinamul gain in West Bengal if the people had voted for "economic reform"? Anyone with minimum common sense would not venture to draw such ridiculous and hilarious conclusions as our election pundits, media commentators and political leaders have been doing.

The media is carrying on a non-stop hype regarding the decisive mandate for reform and asserting with glee that Manmohan Singh government, in its second stint in office, has a free hand to carry out reforms without any hindrance whatsoever, unlike last time when it had to cow down before the demands of the Left.

The logic of decisive mandate for economic reform is deliberately put forth according to a pre-hatched conspiracy of the reactionary ruling classes and international capital. By placing this logic and repeating it *ad nauseum*, these exploiters want to justify and legitimize their agenda of globalization, liberalisation and complete privatization which had become unpopular and drew militant mass resistance in many areas. Showing the logic of decisive mandate for "reform", they are clamouring for carrying out the agenda of economic reforms at a faster pace.

Hence it is very much necessary to effectively counter the argument that it was a mandate for stability and economic reform. The real cruel essence of this argument has to be exposed; and all attempts to step up repression in the form of state terror and state-sponsored terror with the claim of bringing stability have to be unitedly opposed and militantly resisted. Likewise, its attempts to implement the traitorous, anti-people, imperialist-dictated economic reforms have to be bitterly opposed and militantly resisted. A broad-based mass movement has to be built against privatization, against handing over land and resources to the MNCs and CBB in the name of SEZs, against displacement of the peasants and other sections of people through so-called development projects that benefit the imperialists and big business, and so on. Through such militant mass movements we have to show how the people of our country are bitterly and totally opposed to the imperialist-dictated economic reforms.

Emergence of election boycott as a significant trend

Boycott of polls has emerged as a dominant form of struggle in the elections held in April-May 2009. And our Party has led this struggle in several states in the country. All the antics to refurbish the image of a system that had lost all credibility in the eyes of the vast majority of the Indian population and to pour new life into a rotten, stinking institution called Parliament had failed to create any interest whatsoever in the voter. The most publicized campaign by the NGOs, film actors, industrialists and eminent personalities in Mumbai saw only 43.52 per cent of the voters turning up, the lowest ever in the city.

Overall, the majority of the voters this time showed a greater awareness by staying away from the polls despite the 24-hour non-stop appeals by the media to the voters to exercise their franchise. In Chhattisgarh, Bihar, Jharkhand, Maharashtra, MP, Orissa, and Kashmir, polling has been quite low with more than 50 per cent of the voters rejecting the elections. If elections were held without the shadow of the gun, the percentage of votes polled would have been much lower everywhere. The presence of the police, para-military and army does make a difference for it creates a sense of fear and apprehension among the voters that if they did not vote they would be singled out and victimized. There are several cases of people being herded together and driven to the polling booths to cast their votes. In Kashmir, with a population of just over 80 lakhs and six seats to the Parliament, election was held in five phases! Just to ensure that the security forces overwhelm the voters and thereby ensuring a greater percentage of votes. Every visual of the elections in Kashmir Valley showed a sea of security personnel with a few civilian voters here and there. And hardly any of the faces lined up at the polling booths exhibited a feeling of enthusiasm or interest. The feeling on their faces was clearly one of fear and apathy. It is not difficult to understand as to how and why they came to the polling booths if one knows the ground reality in Kashmir which is a territory under Indian Army occupation just as Iraq.

Our Boycott Campaign

The reactionary rulers had tried by every means at their disposal to foil the call for boycott of elections given by our Party. They made elaborate plans to counter our campaign: elections in most of the areas in our guerrilla zones and main areas of armed struggle were held in the first phase itself. Two dozen choppers were pressed into service in Maoist-dominated States for surveillance and to provide operational support to the security forces in countering the Maoist revolutionaries who had given a call for boycott of the poll.

The aim of the ruling classes in holding the elections in our areas in the very first phase was to deploy the central forces several weeks prior to the elections and create an atmosphere of terror among the population so that polling is enforced in the areas of Maoist dominance thereby proving the victory of democracy over terrorism. Thus the plan of the EC was: deploy all the available central forces for at least three weeks in the areas under the influence of Maoists; stage as many fake encounters as possible in order to eliminate Maoist cadres prior to the election justifying these in the name of maintaining a free and fair atmosphere for the voters; establish area domination and achieve better coordination with the anti-Naxal commando units and special forces in various states; and enforce voting under the shadow of the gun thereby ensuring a higher percentage of polling and a higher score for democracy in India.

Notwithstanding the presence of a huge contingent of central and state police forces for over three weeks in the areas under Maoist influence and their attempts at area domination, our Party, PLGA, revolutionary organs of people's power in the countryside, and mass organsiations carried out a mass political propaganda campaign besides undertaking several tactical counter-offensives against the gun-toting enemy forces who were desperately trying to coerce people to vote. Our propaganda campaign was so effective that there was hardly any electioneering by the political parties in most parts of the countryside in Dandakaranya (Dantewada, Bijapur, Narayanpur, Bastar and Kanker districts, and some parts of Rajandgaon district); in many districts of Bihar and Jharkhand where the polling percentage had come down drastically from that in 2004; in West Midnapore, Bankura and Purulia and near-total boycott in Lalgarh area in West Bengal; in Malkangiri, Koraput, Gajapathi, Ganjam, Rayagada and other districts in Orissa; and other places.

Heroic tactical counter-offensives by our PLGA unnerves the reactionary rulers

The ten days that ended in the first phase of election on April 16 witnessed one of the biggest and most successful campaigns by Maoists in the electoral history of the country. They saw massive strikes by PLGA guerrillas across the states of Chhattisgarh, Jharkhand, Bihar, West Bengal, Orissa and Maharashtra. The period also saw mass political propaganda across the length and breadth of the country by our Party calling upon the people to boycott the elections and to establish their own revolutionary-democratic organs of political power as in the vast tracts of Dandakaranya. The ten days became a virtual nightmare for the reactionary rulers of India and the media commented that the violent attacks by Maoists prior to, and on the day of, the first phase of the polls showed that it was "*one of the bloodiest elections in recent times*". "*They (Maoists) are doing everything to disrupt elections,*" howled the home minister P Chidambaram in a Press meet.

The Election Commission, under the guidance of the Union Home Ministry, drew up an elaborate plan especially for the guerrilla zones and other areas under Maoist influence. It decided to concentrate all the central forces in these areas right from the day of announcement of notification of election dates i.e., at least three to four weeks in advance, in what it described as a **plan to achieve area domination** by the police and central forces prior to polling. It meant carrying out as many fake encounters as possible in order to eliminate Maoist cadres prior to the election and justifying these in the name of maintaining a free and fair atmosphere for the voters to cast their votes freely. Hence polling was conducted in most of these areas in the first phase itself. Due to this, the state's repressive forces had ample time to create terror in the areas whereas in other areas where polls were held in the subsequent phases they could be deployed for hardly a week.

Despite the massive deployment of the central forces and concentration of the entire police force in the states in the Maoist-dominated areas, and their desperate attempts to create an atmosphere of terror among the people, they could not achieve their objective. The people led by the CPI(Maoist) and PLGA resisted the onslaught by the central-state police forces, carried out daring attacks on these mercenary forces, and foiled their Operation Area Domination. No candidate or Party representative dared to venture into these areas for electioneering. Only Maoist posters, banners and leaflets were seen in vast tracts of Bihar, Jharkhand, Chhattisgarh, Orissa, West Bengal and Maharashtra besides parts of other states in the country. In the Maoist guerrilla attacks during the period starting from April 6 when three C-60 commandos were wiped out in Maharashtra to the annihilation of a BSF jawan near Kone village in Latehar after the completion of the polling on April 16, a total of 43 central-state forces were wiped out in Maoist counter-offensives. By the time the last phase of polling was completed on May 13, our PLGA carried out several more attacks on the enemy forces annihilating a total of over 70 enemy troops. As on June 12, when the present circular of our Politbureau is being released, a total of 112 police personnel, most of them central forces, were wiped out in the heroic actions carried out by our PLGA guerrillas.

Some of the major counter-offensives during the election period were: the Mugner ambush in Dhanora tehsil of Gadchiroli on April 6 wiping out three C-60 commandos; land-mine explosion near Bijapur on April 7 n which the district SP narrowly escaped while two policemen died; the daring attack on the CRPF-police force near Minta village under Chintagufa PS in Dantewada on April 10 in which 11 CRPF personnel including one Deputy Commandant and a Sub-Inspector were wiped out; the ambush in Khunti in Bihar eliminating 5 jawans on April 11 on the day of the visit of Sonia Gandhi to the district; wiping out 11 CISF jawans in a daring attack by our guerrillas on a well-guarded armoury in South Asia's biggest bauxite mines of NALCO in Damanjodi in Orissa's Koraput district on April 12; the daring attack by PLGA on a BSF camp in Rohtas district of Bihar in the intervening night of April 14/15; the April 15 attack on the CRPF personnel in Badhania Ghati in Latehar district of Jharkhand which wiped out two jawans and injured several others; attack on a bus carrying BSF personnel in Latehar when they were returning after the first phase of polling on April 16 wiping out six BSF jawans; annihilation of another BSF jawan in a mine explosion in the same district on April 16; annihilation of a homeguard and a policeman in Sighpur under Banke Bazaaar PS in Gaya; annihilation of the candidate of regional '*Samruddha Odisha*' party for the Assembly elections in Malkangiri on April 9 coinciding with the visit of Chief Minister Naveen Patnaik to the district.

In the second phase of polling to the Lok Sabha elections on April 23 our guerrillas triggered a landmine blast in Muzaffarpur district of North Bihar wiping out four policemen, including a sub-inspector; in Dantewada seven policemen were wiped out in an ambush near Vinjaram base camp on May 6; annihilation of two leaders of BJP, Darbara Singh Mandavi in Rajnandgaon district and another Narayan Haldar in Koilbeda; annihilation of Farasgaon SI in a daring day-light attack in the Farasgaon market in Narayanpur district on May 7; wiping out of 12 CRPF jawans on May 10th in a daring attack in Dhamtari district in Chhattisgarh; and several more actions on a smaller scale. Over a hundred policemen were injured in all these incidents carried out during the period of election.

There were some unfortunate incidents too such as the death of five polling officials also along with two policemen in Rajnandgaon district of Chhattisgarh, three in West Bengal, and also in Jharkhand. We lose the sympathy of the people through such incidents and the enemy will try to utilize these mistakes to turn the people against us and to justify his brutal offensive against Maoist revolutionaries. Hence the serious mistakes committed by our comrades due to which innocent lives were lost should be thoroughly reviewed and the comrades responsible for this should be warned and if it is proved to be gross negligence disciplinary action should be initiated against those responsible.

Centre's priorities: A brutal Fascist military and economic offensive

As soon as he assumed office as Prime Minster, Manmohan Singh declared that the foremost priorities before his new government at the Centre were: tackling terrorism and Left-wing extremism; and bringing the ailing economy on to right track. Home Minister Chidambaram was even more forthright. He declared that the Centre was determined to deal with Left-wing extremism with an iron hand. Without mincing words he made clear his government's goals: *first carry out police action to flush out Naxalites; then follow it up with development measures.* This is a very important point to take note of as the entire stress is on police action or military solution. So-called development is sought to be carried out only after carrying out massacres and establishing peace of the graveyard. Chidambaram also said that para-military forces would only play a secondary role in Kashmir which means some of these central forces would be withdrawn from Kashmir and redeployed in our areas of armed struggle. Terrorism and "Left-wing extremism" are used by the reactionary ruling classes as a pretext to step up their fascist offensive on the people at large. This is necessary for the reactionary rulers in order to enforce their imperialist-dictated anti-people market fundamentalist policies on a reluctant population.

We have to understand that our revolutionary war is a cruel class war. The reactionary rulers will show no mercy in suppressing the revolutionaries and the masses of people who support them. The principal instrument in their hands is the oppressive state machine—police, para-military, military, jails, torture chambers and so on. They aim to contain the Maoist movement and all struggles of the masses principally through military means and go to any extent committing mass murders, tortures, arrests, abductions and illegal detentions, mass rape of women, use of private armed militias or vigilante squads, destroying entire villages and rendering lakhs of people homeless, carrying out psychological war, etc. And, assisted by the imperialists, they have been refining their counter-insurgency tactics as part of their LIC strategy, continuously increasing and modernizing the police, para-military and other armed forces, deploying more and more battalions in the areas of armed struggle, spending huge sums for setting up and further strengthening the intelligence machinery and informer network, setting up scores of private gangs, and so on. The experience of LTTE's setback in Sri Lanka is very important for us to study and take lessons. The mistake of LTTE lay in its lack of study of the changes in the enemy tactics, capabilities, international support and open assistance by imperialist powers, etc i.e., an underestimation of the enemy along with an overestimation of its own forces and capabilities.

The baton of terrorism—whether it is branded as Islamic terrorism or Left-wing terrorism—is very much necessary for the rulers to unleash the worst forms of state terror and state-sponsored terror. Just as a George Bush tried to justify the inhuman atrocities by his CIA and mercenary troops in Guantanamo, Abu Ghraib and several torture chambers in the name of containing terrorism and his 'global war on terror' which itself is a product of the criminal brains of the military-industrial elites ruling the US, our Manmohan Singhs and Chidambarams too justify, in the name of containing the "*threat of terrorism and Left-wing extremism*", their savage, unconstitutional *salwa judum* in Chhattisgarh, Sendra in Jharkhand, various mercenary senas in Bihar, and the limitless atrocities by the CRPF, ITBP, BSF, ERF, and other central para-military forces jointly with Greyhounds, SOG, STF, C-60 commandos, and local police of various states. Burning of adivasi hamlets, displacement of lakhs of adivasis from their traditional lands and homes, mass murders of youth, torture and rape of women, destruction of houses, crops and other property of the poor adivasis, forced closure of the weekly bazaars, are all justified as collateral damage in the so-called "determined fight" against terrorism.

On April 28 the fascist Raman Singh regime in Chhattisgarh imposed a ban on the CPI(Maoist) and six other mass organizations in the state. These are: *Kisan Mazdoor Sangh, Krantikari Mahila Sangh, Krantikari Kisan Committee, Janathan Sarkar, Mahila Mukti Manch, Krantikari Balak Sangh*. The ban was imposed for one year by invoking the Public Security Act. While fake encounters, mass murders and arrests of innocent adivasis have been going on without a let up irrespective of whether there exists a ban or not, the imposition of the ban is meant to scare away the democratic and civil rights organizations and individuals from condemning the state and state-sponsored atrocities on Maoist revolutionaries and innocent adivasis in the name of sympathising with the banned organizations.

Thus the unfolding state terror and state-sponsored terror under Sonia-Manmohan-Chidambaram combine will be far more brutal, deadly and savage than under any other regime hitherto witnessed. Just as the reactionary fascist rulers everywhere carry out such savagery by imposing curfews, not permitting media personnel and feeding information and police version selectively, the criminals who have been re-elected to power at the Centre are conspiring to carry out the same in the forests of *Maad* (or *Abhujmaad* as is known to outside world). All the preparations are nearing completion on a war-footing.

Let us prepare the entire Party, PLGA and the masses at large to defeat the criminal plan of the central-state governments to launch a massive brutal fascist offensive against Maad

In the past few months, particularly from its re-election in November 2008 elections to state assembly in Chhattisgarh, Raman Singh government had intensified its attack on the revolutionary movement. Abducting militia and mass organization members and even ordinary youth from the villages, torturing and murdering them, raping adivasi women, have become a common feature in Chhattisgarh. Singaram massacre of 18 adivasis by Raman Singh-Manmohan Singh's mercenary police on January 8, 2009 stands out as an example of the brutal face of the state and central governments that have the least regard for the Indian Constitution and provisions of law. Abducting and murdering people is the meaning of 'rule of law' in Raman Singh-Manmohan Singh's dictionary. Several more mass killings and indiscriminate attacks on adivasi villages such as the murder of five militia members in Dondem Paara hamlet in Indravati area on January 24 revealed how brutal the reactionary rulers can become when faced with a threat to their exploitative, oppressive rule.

After the daring ambush and wiping out of 12 policemen near Risgaon in Dhamtari, Home Minister Nankiram Kanwar assured the media that he would suppress the Maoists within one year or else will resign from his post. Raman Singh declared that there is no scope of holding talks with the Maoists and that his government is prepared to take on the Maoists in a straight fight. DGP Vishwaranjan, who was asked to cut short his long leave and take charge, boasted off that he would suppress the Naxal movement in Bastar within six months if the Centre provided him with 55 battalions. Joint meetings between the top police brass of the states of Chhattisgarh, Andhra Pradesh, Jharkhand, Orissa and Maharashtra are taking place more frequently to co-ordinate their attacks.

At around the time of our successful counter-offensive in Dhamtari, a delegation from the American consulate had arrived in Raipur and had consultations with the chief minister, representatives of the government as well as the opposition congress. The American officials enquired regarding the steps taken by the government in suppressing the Naxals and also on the potentialities of making capital investments in Chhattisgarh. It is not a mere coincidence that soon after these secret discussions with the US delegation the plans of launching an attack on Maad region have come out in the open.

A blue-print for a massive military offensive was prepared by the Centre for gaining an upper-hand over the Maoists. A senior officer was appointed in Chhattisgarh by the Centre for coordination of the CRPF forces and local police. All-round preparations are in the final stage for launching the massive brutal offensive on the guerrilla zones and guerrilla bases. The Governor of Chhattisgarh, ESL Narasimhan—a former top official of the IB— has been busily carrying out secret parleys with the Union Home Minister, Army and para-military officials and bureaucrats in Delhi in the second week of June. He has been impressing upon the Centre for the immediate dispatch of several battalions of CRPF and other central forces to Maad. The scanning of the entire area by satellites is almost on the verge of completion and the satellite images and the concrete topographical map of entire Maad will be ready in another month. Based on this map complete with all hamlets, forest tracks, water points, etc the police and central forces will carry out their operations. They are also claiming that preparations are also on to check the retreat of Maoist guerrillas into neighbouring areas in Jharkhand and Orissa.

Maad is home to one of the oldest indigenous tribes known as Madia gonds who have survived to this day preserving their way of life, culture, customs etc. The UPA govt at the Centre and Raman Singh govt in the state have drawn up a plan to create a reign of terror in this area, burn and destroy tribal hamlets, and drive them out of the area to govt-organised camps as it had done in Dantewara and Bijapur. It is thus conspiring to vacate the Madia adivasis from the area thereby endangering the way of life, culture, customs and resources of one of the oldest surviving tribes of India.

Encompassing roughly an area of around 4,000 sq kms Maad is one division of Dandakaranya. Adivasis residing in this region have a heroic history of militant armed resistance against British and other exploiters. The spirit of Gundadur still prevails and every year madia gonds celebrate the martyrdom of Gundadur and the anniversary of *Bhumkal* rebellion which he led against British imperialism in 1910.

To justify its proposed attack on Maad the BJP government is propagating that Maad has become the military HQ of the Maoists. The fascist Raman Singh government in the state, with the active assistance of the Congress-led UPA government at the Centre, had unleashed the notorious salwa judum by arming vigilante gangs since June 2005. And now it is itching to directly send the police and central forces into Maad and unleash similar terror in accordance with its policy of "**Loot all! Kill all! Destroy all!**"

As our CC had pointed out several times in the past the reactionary rulers are having their greedy eyes on the mineral wealth of the adivasi areas right from Bankura-Purulia-Midnapur to Vishakha-Srikakulam Agency in north Andhra. That is why they have been crying hoarse that they are losing control over the natural resources of the country due to Maoist presence in the adivasi areas which the Centre had named as the "***Red Corridor***".

Prime Minister himself focused on this real aim of the reactionary rulers in launching the brutal offensive against adivasi population. Commenting on the danger posed by "Left-wing extremism" he said on June 7 that Naxals are controlling the mineral wealth and other resources of vast backward regions in the country. Mittals, Tats, Jindals, Essars and the like are offering huge funds for the suppression of the Maoists so as to swallow the entire resources of the region without any hindrance. That is the rationale behind the proposed attack on Maad and the decision to create a blood-bath. To justify this brutal offensive the rulers have also been playing up their fabricated lies that Naxals are against development. Just as development (or rather the obstruction to development by Maoists) was made into an issue when the notorious salwa judum was launched by Mahendra Karma of the Congress and the Raman Singh government in June 2005, they are trying to show that Maoists are destroying schools, roads, industries, etc and keeping the region in backwardness.

We have to once again prepare the people of the area to resist the marauders and mercenaries sent by Sonia-Manmohan-Chidambaram combine to subdue them, destroy their culture, and loot the resources of the region for the benefit of a handful of exploiters. This time the fight will be more long-drawn and more bitter than the one against the British imperialist armies.

Every proposal placed by BJP's Raman Singh government in Chhattisgarh before the Centre is readily accepted by the Congress-led UPA government. So much is the cooperation between the two sides that some reporters commented that it was very difficult to see that there were two different parties in the state and Centre. The Congress and BJP became indistinguishable in the tone, tenor and war against the Maoists. Never before was such a degree of coordination and cooperation achieved between the Centre and state on the Naxal issue.

Post-Election situation and its relation to our tactics

The fact that the Congress-led UPA has been re-elected, with the Congress improving its seat tally and in a position to play a more decisive role compared to its last stint in office, has given the UPA, and its biggest constituent Congress, greater scope for unleashing a more brutal and bigger military offensive against our Party and movement. In the last government, where it had a smaller number of seats, the Congress was totally dependent on its various allies in order to continue in power, and the Left too exerted some amount of pressure on Manmohan Singh government for almost four years. But today Manmohan Singh's government has acquired a majority with the support of just four other Parties. And other Parties like BSP, SP and RJD have expressed support to the government from outside. They will act as reserves if any of the existing partners in the UPA opt out. Thus overall, we can say that the present government will remain relatively more stable than the preceding one and will be in a position to carry out the pro-imperialist policies and suppression of the revolutionary-democratic movements more ruthlessly. **We have to keep in mind that the results have given scope for the UPA government to enact more draconian legislation, and implement more fascist measures and suppression of the people's struggles.**

Besides, the current political situation in South Asia arising out of the geo-strategic needs of US imperialism is also likely to provide some flexibility to the rulers to use the state's forces for carrying out fascist repression on revolutionary struggles, nationality movements and other people's movements. The situation in Afghanistan has been deteriorating rapidly in spite of deploying more US troops after Barack Obama took charge. The number of casualties suffered by

NATO troops is growing higher and higher like a spiral with every passing week. There is virtually no government in Afghanistan in the real sense of the term and most of it is under Taliban's control. The supply routes for NATO troops are continuously disrupted by the Taliban which has close coordination with the Pakistani Taliban. In Pakistan too the Taliban has control over large tracts of Northwest frontier Province and Swat Valley with extensive network throughout the country. Hence the US imperialists have been exerting pressure on Pakistan to concentrate all its forces on the western border to finish off the Taliban. The US cannot think of losing Afghanistan which is the gateway to the oil-rich Central Asian region. It is also essential for the US to keep South Asia under its thumb as part of its designs for global hegemony and its rivalry with China, the newly emerging global competitor to the US.

It is trying to mediate between India and Pakistan to reduce the tensions between the two countries so that both can free their forces from the borders and concentrate on what the US imperialists think are the real threat—the Taliban and other Islamic fundamentalist forces, Maoist revolutionaries, anti-American movements and other people's movements. If the Americans succeed, and most likely they would, then the Indian ruling classes will have some flexibility on the western front and in Kashmir. It can relieve some of the central forces from Kashmir and re-deploy them in our guerrilla zones and other areas of armed struggle. The setback suffered by the LTTE and the Tamil liberation struggle in Sri Lanka also has a negative effect on the revolutionary movement in India as well as South Asia and the world at large.

We have to correctly grasp this objective situation in the post-election period in order to evolve correct tactics and tasks.

Immediate Tasks

In order to defeat the new offensive by the enemy and to protect the gains of our people's war it is very essential to rouse the masses throughout the country, stand up in support of the struggles in Dandakaranya, Bihar-Jharkhand, Orissa, Andhra Pradesh, West Bengal, Maharashtra, Karnataka and other places, and build a broad-based countrywide mass movement against the fascist offensive by the reactionary rulers with the active assistance and guidance of the imperialists. To defend our guerrilla bases in Dandakaranya and BJ and to advance the armed struggle in the guerrilla zones we have to carry out the following immediate tasks:

Prepare the people, the Party and the PLGA politically to confront the brutal enemy onslaught; educate the people regarding the scale and intensity of the enemy offensive, its cruel nature and the need for enormous sacrifices on the part of the Party, PLGA and the masses; take initiative to unite with other struggling organizations and forces to forge strong united fronts on every issue and at every level possible; enthuse them with the daring counter-offensives carried out by our forces in various parts of the country and prepare them to undertake similar operations; enhance the initiative and involvement of the masses in fighting and defeating the superior enemy forces. The manner in which we had defeated the salwa judum should be projected as a model to be emulated elsewhere.

Prepare and mobilize the entire Party, PLGA and the people for carrying out tactical counter-offensives and various forms of armed resistance and inflict severe losses to the enemy forces; attacks should be organized with meticulous planning against the state's khaki and olive-clad terrorist forces, SPOs, police informants, and other counter-revolutionaries and enemies of the people; these attacks should be carried out in close coordination with, and in support of, the armed resistance of the masses; these should be linked to the seizure of political power and establishment of base areas; it is the combined attacks by all the three wings of the PLGA and the people at large that can ensure the defeat of the enemy offensive;

Purge the non-proletarian trends prevailing in our Party and the movement by conducting Rectification Campaign in an effective manner so as to provide capable proletarian leadership to the Indian revolution;

Protect the leadership and preserve the Party cadres and PLGA fighters by avoiding unnecessary losses; expand our Party by recruiting new members and train up comrades at every level to build new leadership; rectify the weaknesses in the existing mechanism and strengthen it by avoiding everything that is likely to be exposed to the enemy through betrayers, arrested persons and our Party records;

The aim of the enemy will be to isolate us from the broad masses engaging us in continuous military engagements, then to pin us down militarily using his superior armed force and other infrastructure; we have to foil this tactic of the enemy by taking up the basic issues of the people, mobilising them into militant mass struggles, taking up wide propaganda exposing state terror and state-sponsored terror and making serious attempts to build broad-based united fronts with all those forces who oppose the state's brutal offensive;

Though the enemy is itching to suppress our Party and movement by deploying a huge force in all our areas, he has severe difficulties in implementing this at present; he has plans to increase the number of central forces in the next few years, to set up and train special forces like the Cobras, but in the immediate context it is quite difficult for the Centre to send the forces required by each state to control our movement. Keeping this in mind, we have to further aggravate the situation and create more difficulties to the enemy forces by expanding our guerrilla war to new areas on the one hand and intensifying the mass resistance in the existing areas so as to disperse the enemy forces over a sufficiently wider area; hence the foremost task in every state is to intensify the war in their respective states while in areas of intense enemy repression there is need to expand the area of struggle by proper planning by the concerned committees; tactical counter-offensives should be stepped up and also taken up in new areas so as to divert a section of the enemy forces from attacking our guerrilla bases and organs of political power.

Any mistake on our part will be utilized by the enemy to isolate us, rally a section of the masses, and also justify his attacks on us by pointing to our mistakes, magnifying them and branding them as anti-people and terroristic; hence we should take extra precautions not to take up reckless actions, not to cause damage to people's property or cause inconvenience to the people by our actions, and to apologize for our mistakes promptly assuring the people that such mistakes will not be repeated in future;

As far as the offensive on Maad is concerned we have to mobiise all adivasi organizations throughout the country to protest against the destruction of one of the oldest tribes of India; we have to mobilize all forces cutting across all political and other lines to save Maad region;

The conspiracy of the ruling classes in planning their attack on Maad should be exposed thoroughly and its real intentions and motives should be laid bare. The link between Raoghat mines and the attack on Maad should be explained and the people should be educated as to how the entire region is being handed over to the comprador big business houses like the Tatas in Lohandiguda, Essar in Dhurli, NMDC's proposed steel plants in Nagarnaar and Dilimili, Raoghat mines and Bodhghat project. The bigger conspiracy of the reactionary rulers to extend mining from Raoghat to the innumerable hills in Maad and to loot the natural mineral wealth of the region should be exposed and a broad-based movement should be built against displacement.

Comrades!

Today we are facing an extraordinary situation.

Immense possibilities are unfolding in front of our eyes to advance the revolution at a rapid pace. The entire world is caught in neck-deep crisis and there seems to be no let up particularly since the past one year after the US was engulfed in the worst-ever economic crisis in its history. Industry after industry is closing down throwing out millions of workers onto the streets. Poverty and homelessness, starvation and destitution have become a global phenomenon providing an excellent condition for advancing the people's struggles and revolutions everywhere. National liberation struggles are erupting in various regions.

On the other hand, the reactionaries led by US imperialism have unleashed the most brutal fascist offensive in the economic, social, cultural and political spheres using brute force. In West Asia, the focal point of national liberation struggle in the contemporary world, the situation continues to resemble a burning volcano with Iraq, Afghanistan and Palestine engulfed in flames of national liberation. The fighters in Iraq and Afghanistan are inflicting heavy blows on the imperialist invaders and their armies of occupation. The Palestinian fighters led by Hamas in Gaza Strip and Hizbollah in Lebanon have shown enormous courage, put up bold resistance to the Israeli Zionist aggression and bombardment of their territories.

In South Asia, the second focal point of national liberation struggles in the contemporary world, the situation has continued to be explosive with militant uprisings in several parts of Pakistan such as the Swat Valley, North West Provinces, FATA, and other regions. In Sri Lanka, non-stop aerial bombardment of civilian areas has created graveyard in the Tamil-inhabited areas of Eelam. Lakhs of people are displaced from their homes and thousands of LTTE fighters including its leader Prabhakaran were killed. In Nepal, the Indian expansionists with the backing of US imperialists, have interfered to overthrow the government headed by the CPN(M).

In India, the Philippines, Bangladesh, Turkey and elsewhere deadly attacks are launched on revolutionary struggles. Thousands of people, national liberation fighters, and Maoist revolutionaries are massacred by the reactionary fascist forces. As the crisis deepens and people's dissatisfaction is rising at an unheard of pace, the reactionary offensive too is being stepped up at an unprecedented pace. Such is the situation in the contemporary world that is unfolding before our eyes.

Let us utilize the excellent situation arising out of the ever-deepening crisis in the world economy, overcome the negative factors like the setback in Sri Lanka, lull in Nepal, massive offensive on Islamic jihadist forces in Pakistan.

Let us prepare the entire Party, PLGA and mass organizations to face the brutal offensive the enemy is planning to launch on a massive scale in our areas of armed struggle! Let us mobilize the people politically and militarily to face this new offensive, strengthen and expand our military formations, consolidate and expand our areas of struggle and build strong solidarity movements throughout the country.

Politburo
CPI (Maoist)
June 12, 2009

***

Assessment of Political Conditions

In this document the Maoists make an assessment of the international and domestic situation and, on that basis, set out their goals.

They speak about the sub prime crisis in the Unites States, fluctuations in crude oil prices, shortage of food grain, plummeting of stock market prices, etc. They blame the United States and argue that the various forms of financial speculation have led to the economic crisis in many countries of the world. Taking a dig at China, the Maoists contend that it has shut down a number of export-oriented industries owing its excessive dependence on the United States and European Union for exports.

Similarly, they examine the global situation in different parts of the world. On South Asia, the rebels contend that the situation has become explosive.

On the domestic situation within India, the Maoists hold that the world economic crisis has impacted the country, too. In any case, in various documents the Maoists have always opposed the LPG policies of the country. By LPG they mean 'liberalisation, privatization and globalisation'. Much as they have passed a resolution opposing SEZs during the Unity Congress, in this document, too, they are critical of giving away land for the establishment of SEZs, and argue that fertile land was being given away at low prices and, as a result, the peasantry was being displaced from their lands.

The rebels quite vocally criticize the Indo-US Civilian Nuclear Deal and state that the 'country's interests have been sold away to the American imperialists'. Not sparing the Left parties either, the Maoists lambast them for inviting big private industry to open industries in West Bengal. They also take a ring-side view of the political situation and agitations in the various states of the country.

In the end, the rebels arrive at the conclusion that the "overall social and political crisis is deepening" in India. In this they see a lot of opportunity to carry forward their agenda. Even as they do not enumerate the tasks at hand in a lucid manner, these are mentioned at different places within the text of this document. The more important ones include:

a. Thorough investigation into all incidents of bomb explosions in the country;
b. Proscribe "saffron terrorist organizations";
c. Expose the dangers of Muslim fundamentalism";
d. Bring together the have-nots among Muslims and Hindus; and
e. Establish alliances with individuals and entities that oppose American imperialism and Indian expansionism

PRESENT POLITICAL SITUATION - OUR TASKS

"Utilise the Excellent crisis situation!"
"Intervene and carry on each and every struggle of people!"
—A call by Indian Maoists

International Situation

During the past one year the crisis in the world capitalist-imperialist systema has grown to levels unprecedented since the Great Depression of the 1930s. Manifested initially in the form of bursting of the sub-prime mortgage bubble in the US, it soon became the deepest financial crisis mainly in the US and then spread to EU, Japan and other parts of the world. By November 2008 it assumed the form of world recession after the US, 15-member Euro Zone and Japan officially declared their economies had entered a period of recession. Panic over the ever-deepening financial crisis soon gripped the real economy; exports fell and production had to be slowed down due to decrease in consumer spending in the US and Europe. The ongoing global crisis is not merely a financial crisis but a crisis encompassing all sectors of economy, social and political spheres in all countries.

The past year had seen many fluctuations in the prices of crude oil and commodities rising steeply in the first half and declining in the second half of the year. Reduction of area under food grains production led to acute shortages of food grains worldwide and high prices persisted for most part of the year. Food crisis has now become a worldwide phenomenon which will worsen further throwing a greater proportion of the world population into the clutches of poverty and hunger. In 2008 another 40 million people had joined the ranks of the hungry. Prices of oil ruled at record highs during the first eight months reaching a peak of $147 a barrel in August and then suddenly plummeting to more than half by September and reaching $40 a barrel by the third week of November due to drastic decline in automobile sales, lack of demand for land, air and sea transport. Not only oil prices but prices of many commodities like platinum, copper, steel and zinc have fallen by 35-40 per cent between July-September and agricultural commodities like soya and corn by over 50 per cent due to the fall in demand resulting from steep declines in purchasing power of the people, industrial closures due to credit crunch and falling demand, and overall economic downturn. Widespread speculation in these commodities is also an important reason for the extreme fluctuation in their prices. Fall in prices of agricultural commodities has affected commodity-producing countries like Australia, Argentina, India and several countries of Asia, Africa and Latin America. Partial or complete closure of industrial giants and lay-offs of millions of workers has become a world-wide phenomenon in 2008. 17 out of 29 steel mill blast furnaces in the L S closed down due to lack of demand. Sales in automobiles, steel, software, electronics, retailing, transport had gone down steeply. Big Three in automobile Industry, which were the icons of American industrial supremacy until a few years ago, are now on the verge of collapse. House prices are the lowest since 1991. In Germany, G.M's Opel plant was closed down. BMW and Diamler had ceased production for some months. Thus gloomy scenes of Depression are looming large on the scenario with continuing fall in demand for capital and consumer goods and even food grains. Agriculture too is badly affected due to non-availability of loans from banks.

The stock markets saw continuous shocks for most part of the year. The Black Monday of September 15 and the crisis-ridden third week of September witnessed the biggest failures of the financial institutions. Lehman Brothers, Merill Lynch. AIG Bear Stearns, Freddie Mac and Fannie Mae, and a host of other bankruptcies shook the US and world economy In spite of huge bailout; announced by the Rush administration, big hank, and companies continued to fail not to speak of smaller fry. The case of Citigroup, the pride of America, failing in mid-November showed the depths of the crisis. The so-called rallies of stock markets for a while in October proved fleeting moments in the ever-deepening crisis. Stock market: continued to crash even after massive financial assistance by the various governments. Interest rates were cut several times by the Central in the US, Germany, Japan and several countries including India but all to no avail. In the third week of October Japan's Nikkei 225 plunged by 24.5 per cent in five days-the worst weekly performance in Nikkei's 50-year history. Japan initially sanctioned $18 billion to stave off the crisis but w hen this did not prevent its economy from sliding into recession by mid-November, it had to announce a huge package of $265 billion to bail out the financial speculators. Losses in Asia in eight top markets during the third week of October totalled $870 billion.

The epi-centre of the world crisis lies in the US economy and is rooted in the unbridled growth of various forms of financial speculation such as securitization of debt, sub-prime lending, forward contracts etc., all of which are completely divorced from the real productive economy. Financial parasitism and the rise of a coupon-clipping, financial aristocracy, which com Lenin described as the essence of moribund capitalism had assumed the most vulgar and rapacious forms in the US at the cost of industry and trade. It is the unprecedented crisis in the US economy that had exacerbated the crisis in the world economy due to heavy dependence of the world on the US dollar and markets.

The Bush administration, representing the corporate-financial parasitical elite ruling America is desperately striving to push the burden of the everdeepening crisis onto the backs of the toiling people of the country and on the people of semi-colonial, neo-colonial countries of the world. It had already spent over $2.5 trillion of taxpayers' money to bail-out the bankrupt financial institutions. The allotment of huge funds to the financial sharks is meant to further fatten them by promoting a wave of take-overs and buy-outs of the smaller sharks leading to further concentration and centralization of wealth. Bail-out plan of Bush had facilitated the take-over of Bear Stearns and Washington Mutual by JP Morgan Chase, Merill Lynch by Bank of America. Wachovia by Wells Fargo and National City by PNC. Tax-breaks and write-offs were announced for the big banks that took over the relatively smaller ones. The ultimate outcome of the 'rescue plan' of Bush will be financial parasitism at its peak by way of further consolidation of the US banking system and domination of the entire economy by a few mega-banks. Only a small, negligible fraction of the funds will be spent to help the productive sphere and the masses of working people, such is the reactionary essence of the bailouts which are vehemently opposed by the vast majority of the toiling masses of America. Hence Republican Bush and Democratic Obama have the same solution for the crisis in the US-militarism, war (mainly in the form of regional wars or proxy wars), intervention in other countries in the name of 'war against terror', economic bullying of countries of Asia-Africa and Latin America, and ruthless conquests and plunder of the world resources and people. US imperialism is trying to offset its economic decline by military means. War is also used as a weapon to divert people's attention the deep internal all-round crisis by placing the blame on external factors.

In the November, 4 Presidential election, the ruling financial aristocracy in the US brought Democratic Party's Barack Obama to power to placate the mass of the American people who are totally disenchanted and furious with the policies of republican Bush that led to mass impoverishment at home and anti-Americanism abroad. The American ruling class think') that Obama's African-American descent and his relatively clean image and young age will help refurbish the battered image of American imperialism abroad and that they can more smoothly and efficiently carry out the interests of the corporate-financial elite than under a Republican candidate. But Obama can do precious little to improve the image of America abroad or resurrect the US economy which is bogged down in a perennial crisis. Obama's policies, both internal and foreign, are not different in anyway than those of Bush. Obama's slogan of helping the Main Street is a shield to hand over tax-payers' money to the Wall Street. And his war-mongering will be even more aggressive than that of Bush. The gravest crisis of American imperialism logically leads it to unleash more wars which, in turn, create greater crisis and social explosion at home and isolation abroad. Moreover, the so-called war on terror is strengthening the religious fundamentalist forces worldwide leading to further proliferation of terrorist attacks.

Today the situation is even more fragile and unstable than during the years of the Great Depression, for the simple reason that unlike the earlier period. when the epi-centre of world crisis lay in Europe and US imperialism could bring relative stability owing to its industrial supremacy and huge financial resources, today it has lost its economic supremacy, became transformed into the largest debtor nation, and. thriving on financial speculation, has no ability whatsoever to ensure stability in the world. On the contrary, today it is American imperialism itself that has become the greatest source of instability and crisis in the world. It has decided to increase its public debt from $10 trillion to $113 trillion by next year which is done through heavy borrowings from China and other countries. If China and other countries demand that its loans be paid back it will have a disastrous impact on the US economy. EU and Japan, being themselves crisis-ridden, have no resources or wherewithal to bring any soil of order in the present-day world. Moreover, every, country will try to grab a share of the shrinking markets at the expense of others through protectionism leading to wars of aggression and collapse of some countries. Keynesianism and monetarism had completely failed and, unable to understand the causes for the present stagflation, even mainstream economists are turning to Marx's Capital to understand the phenomenon. After decades of rhetoric about free enterprise, non-intervention of the state in the economy, total privatization of industrial and service sectors, and market being the regulator, there is a massive intervention of governments in a bid to rescue a tiny corporate-financial elite in every country. Besides giving out huge fund to this parasitic class, stock of major banks and financial institutions are bought over by governments, what the media has been depicting as 'partial nationalization'. Hence no talk of Bretton Woods II or any international regulating body in place of the World Bank. IMF and other US-led Agencies can bring any order despite the boasts of G-20 countries during their meeting in November.

In fact, huge sums of FII money are leaving the countries of Asia, Africa and Latin America. From China alone, sums ranging from $10 to 25 billion were said to have fled the country until September 2008 itself.

China, the fourth biggest economy in the world, which has been hailed as an engine of growth in the Asia-Pacific region, is also ridden with grave crisis and has closed down thousands of export-oriented industries as it is heavily dependent on the US and EU for export of its goods. For instance, more than half of the toy-exporting industries in China closed for most part of 2008. In turn, this has a deep impact on the economies of Japan and South Korea which are the biggest exporters of capital goods to China. To overcome its crisis China announced a $590 billion stimulus package. It is more likely that China and other Asian economies will strive to become less dependent on the US and EU and promote more intra-Asian trade and investments which will push the US and EU deeper into crisis.

The gravest global economic crisis since the 1930s has led to an accentuation of all the fundamental contradictions in contemporary world-between imperialism and oppressed nations and people; between the various imperialist powers; and between capital and labour and is leading to political and social crisis of unparalleled dimensions.

The global economic crisis has intensified the inter-imperialist contradictions further. Particularly the contradictions between the US and Russia have grown sharper over oil-rich Caucasian region and NATO's Missile Defence system in Europe. Russia threatened to destroy the European Missile Defence system if US-led NATO goes ahead with its plan to place the missiles in Poland. US recognized Kosovo in February. It pushed Georgia to occupy Tbilisi, the Capital of South Ossetia. In retaliation Russia declared war on Georgia and seized not only South Ossetia but also parts of Georgian territory. After the cease-fire, Russia and SCO (Shanghai Cooperation Organisation) recognized South Ossetia and Abkhazia (which was until then an autonomous republic in Georgia) as independent countries. Submerged in its own crisis American imperialism chose not to confront Russia at this point of time. Possessing the second largest oil reserves in the world and less dependent on exports, Russia's economy is relatively less vulnerable to the ongoing world economic crisis. It also improved ties with several European countries, China, Iran, North Korea, Venezuela and other countries. Of particular significance is the growing strategic relationship between Russia and China which can have far-reaching consequences in global power equations. The crisis has also created cracks in the European monetary system and has promoted nationalism and xenophobia among some countries.

China has emerged as a big competitor in the world market to the US and other imperialist powers. It has been the fastest-growing economy in the world with over 12 per cent growth rates for several years. Although it has been badly affected by the present world crisis, its growth rate continues to be around 9 per cent. It is trying to develop trade relations with countries of Africa. Asia and Latin America besides political and military alliances in order to extricate itself from over-dependence on US and EU and to eat into their spheres of influence. The recent official visits of top-level Chinese delegation to African and Latin American countries, its growing clout in the APEC (Asia-Pacific Economic Cooperation) Summit, and development of bilateral ties with several countries of the world should be seen as part of this move to seek alternative sources for its exports and investments. China is already the biggest trading partner of Japan replacing the US. It is also striving to stimulate its domestic consumption through massive investments in infrastructure, construction of housing, social welfare programmes and massive defence outlays. It is increasing its military might and is building its first aircraft carrier. Countries of BRIC (Brazil-Russia-India-China) have been playing an increasingly important role in world affairs.

The outcome of the current crisis will witness a realignment of various powers in the world which would inevitably weaken US imperialism further. Hence American imperialism is desperately trying to rope in India to its side to use it as a bulwark against the growing clout and might of China which it thinks will be the chief rival to US in future. India has become a willing strategic partner of American imperialism in order to fulfil its own expansionist interests not only in South Asia but also in Asia as a whole.

Iraq and Afghanistan continue to deliver deadly blows against US occupation forces thereby aggravating the economic, political and social crises in America. The Taliban has gained control of almost 40 per cent of Afghanistan, has presence in most parts of the country and is now within reach of Capital Kabul. 2008 witnessed the highest number of casualties of US and NATO troops in Afghanistan ever since the fighting commenced in late 2001. Hence American imperialism is planning to increase its troops in Afghanistan by another 30,000 by mid-2009. The anti-US sentiment is so great due to indiscriminate bombing of civilians with a large number of women and children becoming victims, and Taliban has become such a strong force. that even the US puppet Karzai is compelled to propose talks with Taliban. Obama's assurance that US occupation forces would be withdrawn from Iraq is a sheer ploy to pacify the growing anti-war sentiment of the people in the US and elsewhere in the world. Moreover, American imperialism stands isolated in Iraq as one country after another had pulled out its troops. Despite US pressure. Britain was compelled to announce its plans to pull out its last soldier from Iraq by May 2009. Although American imperialism tried through back-door methods to keep its forces for another three years in Iraq under the fig-leaf of a decision by the Iraqi cabinet. It was flatly rejected by the people of Iraq. Israeli Zionist terrorists had stepped up attacks on the Palestinian territories virtually razing down Palestinian residential areas in Gaza Strip. Hamas has put up brave resistance against the Israeli state attacks.

In South Asia the situation has become explosive. In Nepal, monarchy was overthrown in the elections to the Constituent Assembly and CPN (Maoist) had come to power in coalition with other parties of the exploiting classes. The position of Maoists is quite delicate and unstable as it is dependent on the mercy of the other comprador-feudal parties to continue in power. The abandonment of base areas, demobilization of PLA and participation in elections is a blow to the revolutionary movement in South Asia. However, inner-party struggle within CPN (M) is likely to break out in future as it hogs down deeper into the morass of bourgeois democracy and revisionism.

In Sri Lanka the fighting between the LTTE and the government's Sinhala chauvinist armed forces has increased in intensity in the past one year after Rajapakse broke the cease-fire in 2007. With the aid of several imperialist powers and the Indian expansionists, Rajapakse government had acquired helicopter gunships, bombers, naval fleet, and a huge arsenal of deadly munitions, and has unleashed a war of attrition. Sinhala troops have bombed civilian areas creating a humanitarian crisis with thousands becoming refugees. This has generated considerable reaction in Tamil Nadu. Indian government is assisting the Sri Lankan government by all means though outwardly it is posing as a neutral player to avoid adverse reactions from the people of Tamil Nadu. The LTTE seems to have much weakened and has been pushed into a defensive position but is putting up stiff resistance against the combined forces of Sri Lankan Army, Navy and Air Force. Considering the fact that the Sri Lankan Army is seen as a foreign chauvinist occupation force by the Tamils, it becomes clear that people of tile Tamil nation in Sri Lanka will continue their war against the forces of occupation. It is impossible to suppress the demand for Tamil Eelam and the national struggle for independence is bound to emerge stronger even if it suffers a temporary setback.

In Pakistan the situation has become extremely explosive. Prime Ministerial candidate Benazir Bhutto was assassinated. Musharraf was forced to abandon power, and President Zardari has become an object of despise in the eyes of the Muslim masses as he turned out to be a greater stooge of US imperialism than even Musharraf. The incessant bombing on FATA and Baluchis by US helicopter gunships and missiles killing hundreds of civilians is creating massive opposition internally and more and more people are taking up arms against the US client regime. Bush had signed a secret order in July authorizing the use of US ground troops in Pakistan. Obama was even more aggressive than Bush in his attitude towards Pakistan and he declared his policy of extending the fight against Al-Qaeda onto Pakistani soil. Due to pressure from American imperialism, the stooge government of Zardari has amassed his troops along the Afghan border and is indulging in a blood-bath. Taliban has intensified its attacks on NATO's transport trucks proceeding from Pakistan thereby disrupting the supplies of arms and other materials to the NATO troops in Afghanistan. Engulfed in severe economic crisis and high inflation, Pakistan begged the IMF and obtained a huge loan in October in return for total servility to US and other imperialist powers. The economicpolitical-social crisis in Pakistan is giving rise to massive people's movements, fundamentalist attacks and separatist movements.

The global economic crisis has led to terrible deterioration of the standards of living of the vast masses throughout the world. Job losses due to closures and lay-offs are unprecedented: unemployment figures have reached record levels in most of the imperialist countries with over 3 million in Britain and 8 million in Germany. Temporary and partial employment in low-paid jobs has increased greatly reaching 26.4 per cent of total work force in Germany. The ILO has estimated that 20 million jobs will be destroyed worldwide during 2008. 10.6 per cent of the 30-member OECD's population lives in poverty.

A recent report of OECD pointed out: "the average growth of recent decades has benefited the rich more than the poor." It also ranked the US the third worst in inequality and poverty among the Group's 30 member states. Only Mexico and Turkey fared better. Due to home foreclosures, more than 17 lakh families will be losing their homes in 2008 and the figure is expected to reach 50 lakh by 2012. In the US, top 10 per cent of the population possesses 71 per cent the national wealth; top one per cent own between 25-33 per cent.

No wonder, in the Nov 4 Presidential elections in the US, there was massive rejection of the regressive policies of Bush at home and aggressive wars and militarism abroad. Obama is projected by the ruling elite of the US to create an acceptable image to the American people and the rest of the world who have nothing but despise for the criminal acts of Bush. In the despotic two-Party system in the US people have no choice but to elect what they felt as the lesser evil Barack Obama. Obama has assured the parasitic 'financial aristocracy that he would continue the policies of militarism and war abroad with some cosmetic changes. He openly declared that he would step up the war of occupation in Afghanistan and extend it to Pakistan until the destruction of Al-Qaeda and its leader Osama Bin Laden. His stands with regard to Iran, Sudan, Russia. Afghanistan and the so-called war on terror point to the increasing prospects of wars just as under Bush. The danger of a resurgence of right-wing forces basing on people's discontent is looming large on the political horizon due to the weakness of the revolutionary forces.

Thus, overall, globalisation has created a volatile situation for the economies of all countries of the world. The crisis is bound to extend in space and time giving rise to massive movements of the working class and various sections of people against the reactionary ruling classes and imperialism. The job losses, wage cuts and mass lay-offs have created an objective situation for the rise of militant working class movements. The recent eruptions of mass violence all over Greece lasting for almost a fortnight point to the pent-up anger, frustration and hatred towards the exploitative system that is weighing down the majority of the people in the capitalist world. Such violent social eruptions as a manifestation of the intensification of the contradiction between capital and labour, are likely to increase in the capitalist countries as the crisis deepens.

Imperialist powers and their puppets and compradors in various countries will resort to the most savage methods of suppression of people's struggles; trample underfoot the basic human and democratic rights; set up Latin American-type death squads to murder leader; and activists of democratic movements and trade unions; snatch away the right to life of the vast majority of the people; and enforce the most brutal forms of fascist rule. They will increase their war preparations and undertake wars of aggression besides imposing fascist rule at home which is the only solution imperialists can think of to come out of severe crisis.

Economic crisis leads to militarism, war and revolutionary upsurge. And war leads to greater social-political crisis and to a new wave of revolutions. This is a historically proved truth. Hence it is the task of revolutionaries worldwide to consolidate and strengthen the subjective forces of revolution and prepare themselves to seize the tremendous opportunities arising from the current global economic crisis and the resultant political and social crises. By utilizing the excellent situation worldwide the Maoist parties can grow significantly and become a formidable force to challenge imperialism and international capital. If appropriate tactics are adopted, and the vast toiling masses, groaning under the heavy burden of the all-pervading global crisis, are mobilized into militant revolutionary struggles against the capitalist-imperialist system, we can surely make significant advances in the world socialist revolution.

Domestic Situation

In India, the world economic crisis has affected all spheres due to the rapid rate of its Integration into world economy and its implementation of imperialist-dictated globalisation policies. The growth rates had dropped to 7.6 per cent in the third quarter against 9.3 per cent in the same period last year. The BSE Sensex had touched a record 21.000 points in January 2008 which the Congress-led UPA government had boasted as indicating the soundness of the Indian economy. But soon the Sensex began to plunge reaching 15,000 points in March, 10.000 points in September and a record low of less than 8,000 by November. The government tried to counter the falling demand and downturn in production by decreasing the interest rate; decreasing the cash reserve ratio held by banks, and tried to promote borrowings and consumption all to no avail. Consumption continued to fall drastically. Due to the dearth in cash flow and bankruptcies of the major financial institutions in the US and Europe, FIIS withdrew their funds from the markets at a rapid pace to the tune of $9.6 billion in the first nine months of 2008. This outflow is a reversal of the record inflow of $17.2 billion into the economy last year. It is estimated that the total outflow by the end of the year could reach $13.5 billion. The cumulative market capitalisation of Indian shares, which was $1.8 trillion in January has slumped to less than $700 billion by November with the devaluation of the rupee adding to the woes. This resulted in rapid decline in dollar reserves and depreciated the rupee to a record level of Rs. 50 a dollar in November compared to Rs. 39 a dollar in January 2008.

Inflation Riled at two digits for most part of the year. Prices of food grains and vegetables had reached unaffordable levels. And with the global slow-down, even demand for consumer durables has reduced drastically. In a desperate move, Finance Minister called on the companies, hotels and traders to reduce the prices so as to increase consumption but it was flatly rejected by the big business sharks. In spite of tile seemingly-confident statements of the Prime Minister and Finance Minister that the world recession will not have any impact on the Indian economy, the terrible consequences are felt by every citizen. Thousands of industries have closed down; the BPO (Business Process Outsourcing) and KPO (Knowledge Process Outsourcing) sectors, airways and construction projects, etc., have retrenched workers in hundreds of thousands: the software industry is in a big due to dependence on US (61 per cent of BPO-KPO exports) and Europe for its exports. Obama had assured the people of US that he would stop outsourcing of lobs and bring back jobs outsourced to other countries. This will throw lakhs of people out of jobs. The so-called export-oriented industry which contributes a substantial share of the country's GDP is getting completely destroyed due to fall in demand. The crisis will worsen in the days to come as prospects of an early recovery of the world economy are ruled out by world economists.

The crisis is further accentuating all the contradictions in Indian society. It is leading to a redistribution of wealth from the poor to the filthy rich. In tile past few years there is staggering increase in the assets held by a handful of families: just one lakh families hold assets worth $350 billion (Rs. 17.5 lakh crores) or a little less than half the country's GDP. India boasts of 53 billionaires whose combined wealth amounts to 31 per cent of India's GDP. At the same time 83.6 crores of Indian people or 77% of the population live on less than Rs.20 a day. According to the Global Hunger Index of 2007, India ranks 94 out of 118 countries tailing behind even countries like Pakistan and Ethiopia. In Spite of such glaring inequalities, the reactionary rulers are continuing their regressive policies of tax breaks and write-offs to the corporate-financial houses while taxing the poor and resorting to cuts in social welfare spending. The current world crisis and crisis in Indian economy will lead to further pauperization of the poor and even a sizeable section of the middle classes on the one hand and a further jump in the number of billionaires and millionaires on the other. India is undoubtedly heading towards a grave social explosion.

During this period the Indian ruling classes have gone further into the grip of the US imperialists. By signing the civilian-nuclear deal the Manmohan Singh government has sold out the Country's interest, completely to the American imperialists. In the name of SEZs it has continued to displace people, particularly peasantry, from fertile lands and hand over the same to the real estate mafia. Corporate retail trade is driving lakhs of small retailers into bankruptcy.

The political crisis has further aggravated during the past year. The governments in Karnataka, Jharkhand and Mizoram collapsed due to internal dog tights. The UPA government itself was on the verge of collapse after the withdrawal of support by the so-called Left over the civilian-nuclear deal with the US. The Manmohan Singh government managed to survive through horse trading, support by Samajwadis and spending huge sums for bribing MPs. In what has become infamously known as for Votes scandal. In the elections to some state Assemblies in February-March. BJP won a majority of seats in Gujarat, Himachal Pradesh, Uttarakhand and later in Karnataka.

The so-called Left stands nakedly exposed after it sold out the interests of the people of West Bengal to the Tatas, Jindals, Salem, and imperialist capital. Tatas had to pull out of Singur after sustained agitation by the people and parties Iike Trinamool Congress. The role of the revisionists in endorsing several of the anti-people policies of Manmohan Singh's government and standing so] idly behind the government even when it was going against every promise it made in the Common Minimum Programme, earned the wrath of the people. Hence, not to get isolated and rejected in the parliamentary elections next year, it decided to withdraw its support to the UPA government after four years of hob-nobbing with it.

The crisis is reflected mainly in the form of outbursts of people's anger like those of the Gujjars in Rajasthan, mass upheaval in Kashmir. strikes by banks and public sector employees, doctors and teachers in several states, massive people's protests against rising prices of essential commodities and petrol-diesel price hikes, protests by small retail traders against the monopolisation of retail trade by a handful of the comprador big business houses and MNCs. the militant struggle of adivasis and peasantry against their displacement by mining projects, so-called mega development projects, SEZs, etc.

Under the pretext of fighting terrorism following the bomb blasts in Jaipur, Bangalore, Ahmedabad and Delhi. Muslim youth are arrested and tortured in thousands and many are incarcerated in jails. Some are murdered in the name of encounters as in Jamianagar in Delhi. The persecution and hounding of Muslim community is taking place irrespective of whoever is in power. While the BJP is using its various saffron outfits with the aid of the state machinery wherever it is in power, the Congress too has unleashed an equally ferocious offensive in Maharashtra, Delhi, AP where it is in power by using the Intelligence Bureau (IB) and state machinery. Myths regarding organisations like Indian Mujahideen are floated by the IB to divert the people and step up fascist rule. The involvement of saffron terrorists has at last come out in the open after the blasts in Muslim-majority Malegaon in end September and Samjhautha Express.

The state's complicity in the bomb blasts and the attacks on tile religious minorities is nakedly exposed before the people at large. The government has done nothing even after the involvement of the Bajrang Dal was proved in Kanpur blasts in May and the brutal carnage on Christians in Orissa, and state-sponsored attacks on Christian community in Karnataka and MP. Now it has become clear that most of the bomb blasts, particularly the blasts in Masjids and Muslim residential areas, that had taken place in the country, are the handiwork of the saffron terrorists with an eye on the elections. The RSS-VHP-Bajrang Dal-Shiv Sena and other saffron terrorist gangs are allowed to roam scot-free and unleash attacks on the religious minorities. We should demand a re-investigation of all incidents of bomb blasts that had taken place in the country and to ban the saffron terrorist organizations. While concentrating our attack on the saffron terrorists, we should also ideologically expose the danger of Muslim fundamentalism which diverts the Muslim masses from finding the real solution to their problems. Indiscriminate acts of killing of civilians and terrorist acts such as the November 26 attacks in Mumbai and in Assam on October, 31 in which civilians were killed in big number should also be condemned irrespective of who had committed these. We should strive to build the class unity of the people of Muslim minority and the Hindu majority and wage united struggle against the common enemies. We should explain to the people that such bomb blasts are not a solution to the problems faced by the religious minorities and expose the conspiracies of the ruling classes to utilize such incidents to enact fascist legislation and brutal reign of terror on all revolutionary, democratic, national liberation movements. The reactionary classes are also propping up organizations like MNS in Maharashtra to fan Marathi national chauvinism and launch attacks on North Indians. The Congress Government in the state has been acting as a passive onlooker in order to pander to Marathi chauvinists.

Overall, social and political crisis is deepening and the ruling classes are conspiring to bring in more draconian measures and unleash brutal suppression of people s struggles. File religious divide and communal passions are deliberately roused in a conspiratorial manner by the reactionary ruling classes so as to create a sense of insecurity and helplessness among the people : it large and thus use this to pin legitimacy to their fascist black laws and to brutally drown the people's struggles, particularly the revolutionary movement in rivers of blood. Anti-Pak war hysteria is also consciously incited in a systematic way by the reactionary rulers to divert people's attention from the internal crisis and actual problems confronted by the people, Utlising the bomb blasts, particularly the November 26 attacks in Mumbai, a series of measures were announced by the government to strengththen the state machinery, such as setting up four NSG centres, a national investigation agency, anti-terror act, beefing up coastal security, unified commands, strengthening the intelligence machinery, increasing the strength of the police, para-military and the Indian armed forces etc. Plans are also afoot to enact legislation to bring some aspects of law & order in the states into the central list, Indo-Pak war and the so-called war against terror are also promoted by the imperialists and the Indian comprador big business houses in order to find a way out of the current economic crisis. Such measures will only accentuate the crisis further. The strain on financial resources due to the severity of the current global economic crisis will have an adverse impact on the plans of the Imperialists and the reactionary ruling classes of India to further sharpen the fascist fangs of the state and intensify their offensive against the revolutionary, democratic and national liberation movements in the Country. Moreover, wasteful expenditures on defence, state machinery and war preparations places limits on the ability of the ruling classes to allot funds for social welfare which will lead to grave social and political crises.

During the past year the offensive against our Party and ongoing people's war has been stepped up to an unprecedented level. The mechanisms and methods of the enemy are being constantly refined ever since the merger and particularly since the successful completion of the Party Congress. The Prime Minister has stressed upon the need to improve the intelligence mechanism in various states, intelligence sharing and coordination between states, modernisation of the police forces, increase in fire-power, imparting special training in counter-insurgency warfare, setting up nodal centres, and joint coordinated offensives against the Maoist revolutionaries, besides initiating reforms as part of the policy of LIC. Ten Cobra Battalions with personnel selected from the CRPF are being raised in the next two years. Two companies are already sent to DK. The government also announced plans to set up twenty jungle warfare schools over the next three years to train the police forces of various states and the central forces in jungle warfare to counter Maoist guerrillas. Coordinated joint offensives are undertaken by the police in AP-Chhattisgarh-Orissa-Jharkhand-Bihar-West Bengal in all border regions. Setting up intelligence network in various states has been more or less completed by the beginning of this year. The focus of enemy attack and his main concentration has been to destroy our movement in DK and BJ as well as to eliminate the central and state leaderships of our Party. As we did not change our former methods despite the above changes on the part of the enemy, we suffered serious losses in the past year. Two PB members were arrested along with several members of other Party committees. Around 240 comrades, including several members of the Party committees, commanders, fighters and members of organs of revolutionary people's power and revolutionary mass organisations became martyrs.

The past one year had witnessed heroic counter-offensive operations by PLGA such as the historic Nayagarh multiple raid in Orissa that shook the reactionary rulers, Balimela (Chitrakonda) ambush in AOB wiping out 38 AP Grey Hounds personnel which shattered the myth of Invincibility built around this elite mercenary commando force,

MV-126 ambush eliminating 17 Orissa policemen and SOG personnel, Gollapally (Battigudem), Dantewada Jailbreak, Tadikel, Kursanar, Chhindpal, Vakulavayi, Battum (Orchha), Cheribeda, Mardoom ambushes, attack on the district collector and SP of Kanker, Narayanpur ambush wiping out 7 CRPF men, Kongupalli ambush in Bijapur wiping out 12 CRPF personnel, Mahamaya mine area ambush in Dalli Rajahara, Korepalli ambush in Gadchiroli district in Maharashtra, Jhajha raid in which 44 arms were seized, Ranigunj Bazaar ambush in Gaya, Parasnath ambush, Ranchi Pundidhin ambush, Galobad ambush in Hazaribagh. Tamar ambush wiping out Bundu DySP and two other policemen,

Burudih Dam ambush in East Singhbhum Wiping out 11 policemen, Purulia and Midnapur ambushes, Samri Pat ambush in North Chhattisgarh and attack on the IG of Ambikapur range and so on. All these counter-offensives have demonstrated the potential of the PLGA to transform into PLA and guerrilla war into mobile war. Some of these operations were carried out by Battalion-size formations which fought the enemy forces for hours and succeeded in seizing arms and wiping out the enemy forces in big numbers. Besides the attacks on the policemen and central forces PLGA had also carried out attacks on several reactionary political leaders and counterrevolutionaries such Laxmananda Saraswati of the VHP, former minister of Jharkhand Ramesh Munda of JD(U), BJP's Baliram Kashyap in Dandakaranya, and recently West Bengal's social-fascist Chief Minister Buddhadeb Bhatacharjee in Midnapur. We also carried out a systematic campaign to root out the enemy's informer network in several areas thereby cutting off his eyes and ears.

All these heroic actions against the class enemies of the oppressed people had enthused the entire people's camp and sent shivers down the spines of the rulers. Seeing the ever-growing strength of their own army, people of our country have become more confident of victory in the Indian revolution. The most significant victory of tile PLGA is over the Salwa Judum-state joint offensive in Dandakaranya. It had not only defeated the savage offensive but also played a key role in setting up and defending the revolutionary organs of people's power in various parts of Dandakaranya.

The present excellent revolutionary situation arising from the ever-growing economic-social-political crisis at the global and domestic level throws up immense possibilities for building broad-based fronts against imperialism, particularly American imperialism and in South Asia, against Indian expansionism. It throws up great possibilities for waging united militant struggles of the working class worldwide and in India against retrenchments, wage cuts, wage freeze, casualisation and infermalisation of labour, cuts in social benefits. and against class exploitation in various forms. It throws up favourable conditions for uniting the vast masses of toiling people the working class peasantry, adivasis, women, dalit masses, middle classes, sections of national bourgeoisie against price rise, plunder by MNCs and comprador big business houses, against increasing famine and food shortages, against tax cuts for the rich and tax hikes for the poor, against massive displacement of people by SEZs, mining projects and so-called mega development projects, and so on. It throws up (Treat opportunities to unite the religious minorities and the secular-democratic forces among the Hindu majority to fight state terror and state-sponsored terror, and Hindu fascist terror of the BJP-RSS-VHP-Bajrang Dal-Shiv Sena-Hindu Munnani-Rashtriya Jagaran Manch-Abhinav Bharat etc. It matures the conditions for the naked exposure of the social-fascists such as the revisionist CPI, CPI(M) which, despite their anti-capitalist rhetoric, increasingly become apologists of capitalism and collude with the monopoly capitalist class in their offensive against the working class in the period of crisis.

Overall, the present world crisis provides immense possibilities for advancing the world socialist revolution to its ultimate victory. Its terrible consequences in India will accelerate the pace of the ongoing revolutionary war and provide excellent opportunities for making big gains politicallymilitarily-organisationally thereby hastening the onward march of people's war to its ultimate goal. Our Party has to rise to the occasion, seize the opportunity, and steadfastly advance with unflinching determination and spirit of self-sacrifice to carry forward the responsibility placed on us by history. Towards this end, we must work out the correct tactics, deploy our subjective forces in accordance with the needs of the present situation and execute the tactics with Bolshevik spirit.

Utilise the excellent objective situation created by the world economic crisis and the all-round domestic crisis to initiate a wave of militant mass struggles countrywide! Leave no stone unturned to intervene and participate in every type of people's struggle on just demands!

Polit Bureau
CPI (Maoist)
December 20, 2008

***

STATEMENT ON THE EXPULSION OF LANKA PAPI REDDY

Lanka Papi Reddy alias Lachanna, a Central Committee member of the CPI (Maoist) was expelled from the organization a few dayds after he surrendered to the authorioties in Andhra Pradesh. He was alleged to have 'misbehaved' with a female Maoist cadre and was, thus, expelled for his misdemanour.

Lachanna went underground in 1981 and rose up the ranks from being a squad member to heading the Dandakaranya Special Zone Committee (DKSZC), currently the fiercest battle zone, and becoming a Central Committee member in 2001.

COMMUNIST PART OF INDIA (MAOIST) CENTRAL COMMITTEE

PRESS RELEASE: JANUARY 4, 2008

CC, CPI (Maoist) condemns the outright degeneration and betrayal of revolution by Lanka Papireddy and expels him from the Party!

On January 2nd, Lanka Papiraddy alias Latchanna alias Naresh, a member of our Central Committee, had deserted the Party and the movement and surrendered before the enemy citing ill-health as a reason. It is indeed shocking to all Party members and the revolutionary masses to see such degenerate behavior and extreme political weakness from a member of the highest committee of our Party. However, if one looks at the history of our Party one will not be surprised to see some leaders getting degenerated in course of the development of the revolutionary war. This happens when they are not able to mould themselves to the needs of the movement and place their personal interests above the interests of the Party and people. Papireddy, in spite of being in the CC, has not displayed the consciousness of even a primary Party member. He behaved in the most irresponsible way, firstly, by committing a mistake of a very serious nature, and then, deserting the movement instead of undertaking sincere self-criticism and striving by all means to come out of his weaknesses. Ill-health is only a plea to hide his degeneration and betrayal of the revolution. The CC condemns this arrogant behavior and degeneration of Papireddy and expels him from the Party.

The CC, after analyzing the weaknesses and deviations in Papireddy in the wake of his misbehavior with a woman comrade, passed a resolution in December 2007 demoting him to ZC level and transferring him out of the state where he had been working. It hoped that given his seniority he will display maturity and seriously rectify his mistakes by immersing himself in the class struggle. The CC has tried to save him by retaining him in the Party provided he realizes his serious weaknesses and strives to come out of these and take measures to transform himself into a genuine revolutionary. But instead of undertaking deep self-criticism of his weakness and assuring the CC and the entire Party that he would make all efforts to rectify and come out of the weakness, he placed conditions for continuing in the Party and the movement. He also cited some reasons such as problems with his wife to justify his degeneration.

What are the main reasons for his immediate desertion and betrayal?

Firstly, in spite of being in the revolutionary movement for a long period, he has not transformed and moulded himself into a proletarian revolutionary. Petty-bourgeois and feudal values and attitudes continued to remain strong. His behavior towards woman comrades reflected the strong patriarchal trend in him. In mid-2004 he was issued a serious warning about his patriarchal attitude, irresponsible and provocative behavior with a woman comrade.

Secondly, even though he was fully aware of his mistakes and weaknesses he did not make any attempts to come out of these. His pretty-bourgeois false prestige became a hurdle for undertaking sincere self-criticism and get rid of his weaknesses. This false prestige had quite often come to the fore during his earlier work in Dandakaranya and was criticized by comrades many a time.

Thirdly, his ego and individualism, lack of respect for collective committee functioning, putting on airs about his general knowledge and political depth, his sectarian approach towards others, bureaucratic style of functioning, etc had increased in recent years. He has infatuation for his own capabilities while underplaying the better capabilities of other comrades.

Fourthly, due to the above-mentioned weaknesses he began to lose confidence on revolution especially after seeing the series of losses suffered by the Party in recent years. He was not confident of playing his role in overcoming the present unfavourable situation and countering the countrywide coordinated cruel counter-offensive of the enemy. Defeatism overtook his mindset and being self-centred and individualist he had lost faith in the capacity of the Party and masses in defeating the enemy offensive.

Due to above-mentioned reasons it is not surprising that Papireddy, after serving as a revolutionary and also as a leader for a long period, has surrendered to the enemy, betrayed the revolution and turned into a counter-revolutionary. The weaknesses and mistakes which were once a secondary aspect of his revolutionary life have changed qualitatively and become principal aspect while the revolutionary character transformed into a secondary aspect; thus a revolutionary and a revolutionary leader has turned in to non-revolutionary and also a counter-revolutionary. No revolutionary, however exemplary be his/her past history, can last for long without intense internal struggle against his/her non-proletarian ideas and weaknesses. To continue as a life-long revolutionary one has to transform oneself to suit the needs of the revolution; it is the law of revolutionary dialects which operates in society and individuals including revolutionaries and a revolutionary party. Those self-seeking, careerist leaders who put themselves above the party, revolution and oppressed masses and gloat over their self-claimed intellectual talents and individual capabilities will be consigned to the scrap-heap of history. Through his surrender, Papireddy has become another addition to the list of betrayers and self-seeking opportunists in our party history such as Sathyamurthy, Murali, Bharath, etc.

Papireddy will serve as a negative teacher to the entire rank and file of the Party and the revolutionary masses. The internal struggle within oneself is far crueler, arduous and daunting than class struggle against the enemy class. It needs great courage and determination. And most important of all, it needs deep conviction on the ideology of MLM, faith on the oppressed masses and the Party.

Let us show utmost contempt and hatred towards renegades who run away from the people's cause for their own selfish interest. Let us advance along the bright red path blazed by the sacrifices of our beloved martyrs who had laid down their lives by upholding Communist values and practice until their last breath.

Spokesperson,
Central Committee
CPI (Maoist)

SECTION V

SYNCHRONISED/LARGE-SCALE ATTACKS

KORAPUT ARMOURY RAID (FEBRUARY 6, 2004)

Creating history, the Maoists, in their earlier avatar as the People's War Group (PWG), staged the maiden synchronized attack on multiple targets, involving a large number of cadres (estimated to be around 500), on the district headquarters town of Koraput, in Odisha. They lay seize to the town for a few hours, looted the district armoury and attacked various other government offices in the town. In the raid, weapons, ammunition and grenades worth Rs. 50 crore were seized. These included 528 weapons—.303 rifles, LMGs, SLRs, mortars, sten guns, revolvers and pistols—and over-30,000 rounds of ammunition, a number of mortar shells and grenades. There were two similar raids in the later years in other towns. Significantly, after the Chittagong Armoury Raid during the Independence Movement (circa 1930), this was said to be the largest raid on an armoury in the sub-continent.

The objective of the raid was, obviously, to loot weapons to arm the 'underground'. They, thus, seek to build the People's Liberation Guerrilla Army in order to overthrow the Indian state and advance their New Democratic Revolution. Further, through such daring raids the rebels seek to send a 'political message', 'create an electrifying effect', and use it as a propaganda tool in other parts of the country in which they envisage establishing their presence.

The rebels were of the view that the raid had the following effects: (a) displayed the military capabilities of the guerrilla units, (b) added grist to the idea that the merger between the PWG and the MCCI was in the offing, and (c) boosted the morale of a vast number of sympathisers and gave them the confidence that the 'revolutionary, movement would receive a fillip. In effect, the raid, the rebels, averred, was a high-impact action.

Koraput Campaign in Orissa is a Milestone in the Annals of Indian Agrarian Revolution !

To Arm the People with State Arms to Defeat its Offensive War !

At the time of colonial rule revolutionaries of India attacked the Chittagong police head quarters in East Bengal in 1930. Again almost 75 years later Maoist revolutionaries attacked Orissa's Koraput district police Head Quarters (HQ) in India, with a different aim. At the time of the Chittagang attack they had the task to overthrow colonialism. This time around Maoists had the task to arm their People's Guerrilla Army (PGA) to transform it into Peoples' Liberation Army (PLA) and to establish liberated areas, where the neo-colonial type of exploitation in the semi-colonial and semi-feudal system will be overthrown.

Koraput, an oldest district HQ, in Orissa has seen many a people's movement. Since two decades back the CPI(ML)[PW] has been active in large parts of the district. It has been mobilizing the tribal people in various revolutionary movements. The 9th Congress of the CPI(ML)[PW], which was held in 2001, had taken a task to transform the Andhra-Orissa border region (AOB) as Liberated Zone. It has been putting in its efforts in a consolidated manner in that area to achieve its task. After the Party Congress the PW Party took the "Tactical Counter Offensive Campaign" (TCOC) to arm its PGA and to destroy the morale and advancement of state Special Forces and Para-Military forces in 8 Guerrilla Zones spread across AP, Chhattisgarh, Maharashtra, Orissa, Jharkhand and Bihar. In its TCOC a good number of attacks on police and paramilitary forces were conducted in the entire above Zone in the last 3 years. But the attack which they executed on 6th February was a well-planned and meticulously executed one by mobilizing various PGA units, which was the first of its nature and type in the last 3 decades old revolutionary movement or to say second in the last 75 years history of the Indian new democratic revolution, which has given a nerve-breaking jolt to the entire ruling classes of the country, irrespective of their political identities.

Koraput A Seized City by People's Guerrillas

The massive attack took place on the night of 6th Feb. synchronising with similar attacks on various targets in the city. To excute their well-calculated plan Naxalites made reconnaissance (recce) for several days and assessed the police HQ's weaknesses and strong points to virtually seize the armoury. Their target was to sieze the weaponry with minimum human loss and bloodshed, to arm the people to strengthen the PGA fighters. The national and regional news papers which started to write on the attack from 7 Feb. onwards to the end of this month accept two things in general i.e. the morale of the police is almost lost and Naxalites put the state on tenter hooks, which now needs a fresh look into the security of police HQs in all most all the 12 states in the country.

According to the newspapers 200-armed Naxalites were engaged in the well-executed plan to overpower the targets. On the Friday night (quoted by the state as black Friday and a good revolutionary Friday Naxalites) systematically occupied all the vital points in the city to seize the Armoury of police HQ. It seems that they planned to neutralise all the armed forces present in the city and in the vicinity of the city. For this they struck on the District Superintendent's office, two police stations (rural and urban), district Jail, Treasury office and their main target i.e. police HQ and its Armoury.

To keep engaged other forces, which were camping near the city such as 3rd battalion of the Orissa Special Armed Police (OSAP), India Reserve Battalion (IRB) including CRPF contingents in housed OSAP and IRB head quarters they had planned a mock attack on the 3rd BN, HQ of the OSAP and engaged the force in a gun battle to stop their advancement to help the forces of the district HQ. Apart from this they laid powerful land mines at various points to stop new deployment, which could cordon off the combatants of the PGA of the PW party. According to media reports, to avoid such a trap or encounter with extra new forces the PGA took all the precautions. Apart from this they seized all the main roads, which lead to Koraput town.

Without any significant resistance one after another target surrendered to the Naxalites. A Jawan guarding the district armoury N.Nayak was shot dead first to seize the Armoury. Another assault batch, which attacked the jail premises, faced some mild resistance, according to the news reaching till now, in which the Jail Superintendent and a few constables were injured and 20 rifles captured by the Naxalites from the Jail police. The Jawans in the two police stations surrendered and handed over their weapons. And at the SP office also there was no resistance, and the Naxalites did not give any scope for the demoralised forces to regroup. Not only this, the news items that appeared so far in the media have written in black and white that all the higher officialdom of the administration was so much panicked by the stunning attack that they went underground till the fresh battalions of CRPF arrived and positioned themselves in the city. Every corrupt official waited with abated breath apprehending that Naxals might target him or her. Actually Naxals targeted particularly the HQ Armoury. When they attacked the SBI's ATM counter and the district treasury, they did not touch the lockers, but picked the weapons in the persons of the guards on duty. This shows the commitment of the guerrillas to stick to the task.

According to government reports, weapons, ammunition, grenades valued at Rs. 50 crore were seized by the Naxalites of the People's War. Among them there were 500 sophisticated weapons of different types (.303, LMG, SLR, Mortars, Stens, Revolvers, Pistols), along with more than 30,000 rounds of ammunition, number of Mortar shells and Grenades. Whatever be the exact number, the PGA has achieved its task for the time being. To carry all this huge quantity of arms and ammunition to the jungles the PGA guerrillas picked some vehicles of govts, health department and others.

To avoid any interception by the police, a meticulous plan was chalked out for their retreat according to news item appeared in the local media. On their retreat the daredevil guerrillas attacked 3 police stations at Laxmipur, Narayanpatna and Kakiriguma and a Dy. Superintendent of Police's office at Laxmipur. In order to pre-empt retaliation from these police stations, separate assault batches were deployed and they took control immediately after the temporary seizure of Koraput.

The five police stations, jail and the district HQ of the police are the centres and edifices for the loot of the people's wealth and repression on Adivasies of this ancient land, where from colonial rulers to the current rulers rule with the symbol of khaki power. To avenge the centuries old draconian repression, the police buildings were exploded, their vehicles burnt and weapons seized by the peoples' guerrillas to arm the people, who were in acute need of them to resist the repression of the state.

The three roads which lead to Koraput were also blockaded by other guerrilla units to challenge the central forces which could have been rushed from Rayagada, Vijayanagaram or from nearby IRB HQ, Kolab, where IRB and CRPF forces were stationed. The anticipation of the guerrillas proved correct. A truckload of CRPF and IRB forces were rushed from Kolab, which were ambushed at Dhadapadar village off Koraput at 11:30 PM. In retaliation 3 CRPF jawans died and half a dozen were injured. Altogether 4 jawans died and 10 were injured in the total operation and there were no losses from the side of the PGA. Finally the PGA guerrillas torched 7-8 vehicles at Balipeta on their retreat, apart from ½ a dozen police vehicles damaged by them at various spots.

Aftermath of the Attack

The shuddering dimension of the lightning attacks threw the entire state administration in to a state of helplessness. After hearing the news of the attacks state and central governments gradually tried to rush the extra forces. But they were stunned after hearing the news of attacks on 3 PSs and land mine blasts near Koraput. All these forestalled deployment of the forces at night. On the 7th morning the DGP N.C. Padli, Home Secretary Santosh Kumar, Director of Intelligence Man Mohan Praharaj, IG (Intelligence) R.P. Singh dashed to Koraput and appealed to the Centre to send extra forces within hours to cordon off the forests to trace out the guerrillas and their seized weapons. A good number of para-military companies were rushed from different points of the para-military battalion HQs. Apart from this, the Eastern Naval Command which is based in Vishakapatnam was also pressed into service particularly its helicopters to coordinate the ground forces in the border region of Andhra Pradesh and Orissa spanning the districts of Koraput, Malkangiri, Rayagada, Gajapathi and Ganjam of Orissa and East Godavary, Vishakapatnam, Vijayanagaram and Srikakulam districts of Andhra Pradesh i.e. Eastern Ghats as a whole due to its topography.

Greyhounds of Andhra under air cover too were deployed in large numbers to track down the guerrillas. A Red alert was sounded in Andhra, Orissa and Chhattisgarh. Even the Jharkhand and West Bengal governments were alerted and asked to mobilise their forces in its borders with Orissa. The Koraput SP Arun Kumar Bothra and collector Usha Padhee and other officials and political leaders started to issue different statements, which never matched with the ground realities. For example, on 8th February the CM of Orissa Naveen Patnaik said he was prepared for talks; the DGP Padhi said that all police stations would be given more security cover to combat Naxalites. Koraput collector Usha Padhee suggested a compact package of welfare work in all Naxal influenced areas. Congress President J.B. Patnaik demanded president rule and another Congress leader Dilip Roy demanded Army deployment to check the Naxalite violence.

When these statements came pouring in, the regional press and news, the country-wide electronic and print media almost blacked out the news of such monumental dimensions and did not dare to put the details of the massive and stunning Naxalite campaigns where 13 targets were attacked simultaneously and some more daring ambushes were successfully laid. The stirring military campaign by the Maoists in India has boosted the morale of the oppressed masses of these areas. This unprecedented attack on the states armed HQ sent cheers to the revolutionary camp of India and the world. When one after another news item came pouring out from the battlefront the entire revolutionary camp acknowledged Koraput as a model to arm the people and to resist the offensive of the state and central governments.

Other guerrilla units in AOB and Dandakaranya, initiated counter attacks on some police stations throwing the concerned state government strategists into a tizzy. The guerrillas who planted some more mines on the way among which one mine was exploded on 13 February around noon. One IAS probationer, incharge of Narayanpatna Block was hit badly and 13 jawans of the CRPF and OSAP were too critically injured at Dandabati village near Narayanpatna. The Andhra-Orissa Border Special Zonal Committee (AOBSZC), a provincial level committee of the CPI(ML)[PW] which is the leading committee of the AOB peoples' movement owned responsibility in a press release and at the time of laying seize to the Koraput armed head quarters, loud speakers were used to openly thunder out threats to the armed forces, for surrender as well as to declare to the people the objective of the CPI(ML)[PW] and the need for such campaigns. Wall posters were scribbled out to educate and convince the masses to support their act. This massive campaign was never possible without the enthusiastic support of the masses of the population.

Why this Attack

The Orissa government is a member state in the Joint Operational Command (JOC), which was formed a few years back under the leadership of the central Home Ministry, to curb Naxal activities in 12 states of India. In summer 2003 a joint operation led by para Military, OSAP and Greyhounds forces were conducted in Malkangiri, Koraput and Rayagada districts. Hundreds of supporters and members of the revolutionary mass organisations were picked up and numberless false cases were filed against them. At the time of the operation some encounters took place. Due to the white terror let loose in a large scale some surrendered to the police. In Rayagada district the government pitted Dalits and other castes against the Adivasis and tried to capitalise on the contradictions among the masses. The State government stepped up repression in Malkangiri in a planned manner since the last two years. The state governments deliberately spread the news that the backbone of the Naxalite movement was broken in the joint combing operations of 2003. Actually the Andhra Pradesh government is also part and parcel in the operations from the very beginning to the end, because it also needed the repression campaigns to gain the upper hand against the movements of North Andhra. To concentrate its greyhound forces in the AOB region the AP state govt. sanctioned Rs. 100 crore to establish a Greyhounds HQ, on warpath at Vishakapatnam, to supervise and coordinate its North Andhra deployment.

In the AOB region the revolutionary movement is advancing by leaps and bounds in the midst of the severe state repression earlier by the AP state—which is still continuing in large scale—and later by the Orissa government. The CPI(ML)[PW] is spearheading the movement by mobilising the masses the in political, military fronts including the day to day partial struggles in which people were consolidated. In some selected pockets of the AOB zone the PW Party has been establishing guerrilla bases (GB) as part of the liberated zones. To build the GB or Liberated area the destruction of the enemy's political power is a vital aspect. Already in large pockets feudal and tribal chiefs' power has been smashed. The sate administration is defunct in these areas, especially where the revolutionary people's committees were established. An alternative people's political power in its embryonic form is formed and the political, military consciousness of the people keeps developing at a certain level. In the cooperation and participation by the masses in the Koraput attack such new-elevated consciousness is visible. This stupendous achievement is a befitting homage to the sacrifices of innumerable party cadres, guerrilla fighters including the vast masses. The JOC wants to curb this people's power, by liquidating the Maoist vanguard party of the movement i.e. CPI(ML)[PW] by hook or by crook. So, all the democratic rights of the masses were curbed and a police raj established

So to counter the state violence and the role of the state armed forces the CPI(ML)[PW] is initiating tactical offensive on the military front. If the state offensive is unchecked militarily, peoples' movements can never advance in history. To wield political power people need their own armed forces and the destruction of enemy power is imperative to achieve the goal. So, the Koraput campaign was led by the military commission of the CPI(ML)[PW].

Arming the Masses is the Historic Need

Generally, all the Maoists accept the adages of Mao such as, "political power flows from the barrel of the gun", "without a peoples' Army people have nothing", "arm the masses" etc. Apart from this, every Maoist party accepts that to lead the revolution for victory three magic weapons are needed. They are: 1. Party, 2. Army, 3. United Front. Accepting the theory is one thing, to put it in practice is another. But to judge any group/party one has to observe their theory and practice on these questions to decide which camp they belong.

In India after the setback of Naxalbari many ML groups accept Maoism in general but when it to transformed it into practice numerous webs of arguments will be woven from a safe distance. Some may express purely left jargon without any practice; some may stick on always to their forefathers' right opportunistic line without any review of the past or concrete application of the three magic weapons. When the question of arming the masses comes onto the agenda the leadership of the so-called ML parties will start lectures and write piles of articles to prove the time is not mature enough for taking a plunge into the real life activities challenging the enemy. It cries hoarse that people are not prepared, arming the few advanced activists is sectarianism, MCCI-PW parties are adopting sectarian, anarchic polices which Mao never said, etc., etc.

To say frankly, the party, army and UF, the three components are inseparable and will influence one another and by wielding the army and UF, Party will be made to initiate the war and if once war is initiated all the fronts will be subordinate to the advancement of the war. So, one needs the army from the very beginning of the preparation. If the peasant-agricultural labour association is formed at the village level simultaneously the village defence squad is also to be formed to protect the village masses from the landlords their henchmen and police attacks. If the associations are formed at block, tahasil or district level then military formations above the VDS is needed at the same time. In the urban revolutionary mass movement also, open and underground defence squads are needed from the very beginning in the workers, student, youth, women, slum dwellers and other fronts to face onslaught of the reactionary forces. These defence corps will become part of the people's militia. In the history of the revolutionary movement none will win the war purely with militias. To lead the militia and to smash the state's regular forces, a well-trained and politically steeled people's regular army is essential. So, the PGA/PLGA needs to be transformed into a full-fledged liberation army in the course of development of the guerrilla war.

Of course, the liberal bourgeois intellectuals and the leadership of right opportunistic and revisionist ML parties never accept this. However, they will start to condemn the Koraput campaign. The leadership of the CPI(ML) [Liberation] Orissa, already took this inglorious task on their shoulders, some more may join with them by writing 'before and after Koraput' type articles. Kanubabu type leaders may form another 'genuine' ML party to purge the evils of the history of ML formation or the ghost of armed uprising of the great Naxalbari.

War is after all the continuation of politics by other means. Political, economic, social and cultural relations are interlinked with the politics and policies of war. Feudalism, capitalism, imperialism, semi-colonial, semi-feudal, whatever the system may be, to fight and overthrow it people need to arm themselves. It is a historical generalisation of law of the transformation of societies. In India after the spring thunder the onerous need came upon us as an imminent factor to transform the Maoist principles of war into practice. No doubt there are a lot of changes took place if we compare today's India with the old china. Basically all these transformations happened in the super-structure not in the base. So, imperialism has been more nakdly issuing threats to the world people. It is an old colonialist method and an alibi to unleash wars of aggression on the masses, which we can see in Afghanistan, Iraq, and earlier Vietnam etc. To put up resistance against the rule of reactionaries and their armed units people need arms. To advance the protracted people's war by building the People's Army is one of the fundamental conditions.

Glimpses of the PGA

2 December 2000 witnessed a historic day in the on going people's war in India i.e. the formation of the people's guerrilla army (PGA) as a separate military wing under the leadership of the CPI(ML)[PW]. For almost two decades of its agrarian struggle the people's war party organised its armed units in different names. It resisted the enemy onslaught from Andhra to Bihar and in the course of development all the guerrilla units were organised as the PGA. It had three types of forces such as the main, secondary and base forces. The Main forces were developed for mainly combatant task, secondary forces mainly for organisational task (along with combatant as secondary task) and in the base force village defence squads and other militia units were organised.

To lead the PGA, the PW party also formed separate command structures to specialise in the military front. The PGA units are spread across the country in 10 states and their experience and combatant skills are also developing. Whenever the PGA strikes on major targets—civilian or military—in and around the guerrilla zones, always it impacted the political and military scenario of the particular state or at the country level. Say for example: Last October; it punished the World Bank and imperialist pet dog Andhra Pradesh CM, Chandrababu Naidu, creating repercussion not only in AP but also in the entire country and the world, even though he survived. Enquiry commissions were formed and the security to all the 'VVIP, VIPs' was beefed-up in India.

When the PGA units ambush or raided state and central armed forces a major reshuffling and rearrangement of police camps, personnel and police stations were executed. Special forces were formed, special welfare projects were announced. Modernisation of forces is continuously taking place in all the states under the strong influence of Naxalism. Till now thousands of crores of rupees was spent to crush the PGA units, which were engaged in a revolutionary war to check state violence and to push back enemy contingents falling on guerrilla bases and guerrilla units.

Orissa, Andhra Pradesh, Maharashtra, Madhya Pradesh, Chhattisgarh, Jharkhand, Bihar, Uttar Pradesh and West Bengal state armed forces and para-military forces were attacked by PGA and PLGA many times in the past 3 years. Targets were selected by assessing their role against the mass movements. In 2001-2003 roughly more than 250 targets were attacked by the PGA forces, which checked the advancement of the government forces. Today the PGA is a dedicated, well disciplined, courageous daring force to checkmate enemy brutality on the oppressed masses. Tele-communication net-work, rail-roads, government buildings which house for armed forces of states and central armed forces naturally become the targets of the PGA on various occasions. All these targets are generally military targets and the destruction of these targets is justified. The struggles send warning message, particularly whenever, brave resistance is put up by the PGA/PLGA forces. It also carries a clear political message like big campaigns among the country people, where earlier they did not hear about Naxalism. There too politics of war i.e. armed agrarian revolutionary politics creates an electrifying impact.

Today in the battlefield when the main force, which may be in platoon formation or in higher forms, enters an area, there enemy Special Forces stop their movements. From the district HQ, massages will flash in VHF walkie-talkies that the PGA platoons entering in the area may strike somewhere, do not move from the barracks. Police bosses will spend sleepless nights in the area.

Action teams (a small specialised units of the main forces) are much more daredevil units, and the officials and reactionaries get nervous if they hear an AT is moving in the areas. SMS will be passed on over all the mobile phones from the SP office, regarding the AT and precautions taken for saving the supposed targeted persons or installation.

A good number of villages will inform the party committees and military commands to keep the main forces in their area, which will protect them form the attacks and the cruelty which the para-military and state special forces will unleash.

'Gram Rakhsa Dal', 'Area Rakhsa Dal' and other formations belong to the base force as per the categorisation decided by of party. These units will work always with the main, secondary forces and keep an eye on the reactionaries and government forces. They will strike at the enemy if it is possible, or the message of enemy contingents moving to the main or secondary forces be sent out. Immediately opportunity of ambushes or other form of attacks will be planed. Now the slogan of the PGA is, "Don't leave the enemy forces unhurt, once it enters in our area".

Enormous Effect of the Koraput Campaign on the Political Scenario of the Country

The political and military message of the Koraput Campaign has already spread and to the four corners of the country. In the annals of the undivided communist party and in today's revolutionary history if the first time that such a major action has taken place. Since last October to the end of this February almost for five months the CPI(ML)[PW] and MCCI are in the daily news. The news has come up not only on the military strike power of these two Maoist parties but also the possible merger of there two parties into a single party. All this spreads like wildfire in the country. All such pieces of news themselves create a big political campaign among the vast majority of masses of India and abroad, which gave confidence to them to fight and resist firmly the three big mountains i.e. imperialism-comprador bureaucratic bourgeoisie and feudalism. And the hearts of the ruling classes shrink like a earthquake jolt on them.

In the last, quarter of 2003 the Home minister and BJP 'lohapursh' iron man Advani started a hulaballoh about left extremism as the main danger for the country's security (read danger for the rule of three big mountains). Social fascist Buddha and Anil babu started whining that in comparison to the N-E rebels and the KLO the PW-MCCI combine appear to be more dangerous because they have their ideology. Yes, it is true the PW-MCCI forces have a strong ideological base i.e. Marxism-Leninism-Maoism, which is etching history.

Ideology is, after all, the basis of any truly revolutionary communist party which acts as the guide to all political and military activities. The ruling classes and also some bankrupt 'left' groups/parties, try and portray this as "mindless violence". These apologists of the status quo fear real revolutionary struggle more than anything else. But the freedom of our country is unthinkable without it.

Fearing the impact of such a major action the big-business/political media sought a complete blackout of this action. Though it was the biggest such action since the Chittagong Armoury raid in 1930, the news was virtually ignored by the "free Press". But truth cannot be suppressed for ever. It has already begun to filter through to the entire country and world, to enspire an entire generation to action.

Today, after the action, all the district HQ have been beefed up with additional security cover. Para-military forces have been deployed in the four southern districts of Orissa and another four districts have also been provided such forces. Separate intelligence units under the IG level have been sanctioned. Another Indian Reserve Battalion is being sent. After the elections a major offensive is planned. But all this will come to nought due to the growing tide of the revolutionary in the region. It is time for all democrats to welcome this new awakening for a new future of the country and its oppressed masses. Let us all welcome the new dawn.

***

GIRIDIH HOME GUARDS ARMOURY RAID (NOVEMBER 11, 2005)

On November 11, 2005, two days before the Jehanabad Jailbreak (Operation Jailbreak), cadres of the People's Liberation Guerrilla Army (PLGA), raided the Home Guards Training Centre in Giridih, Jakrkhand, and looted 193 weapons and two revolvers. The raid was conducted under the direct command of the Zonal Command of the Jharkhand Regional Military Commission, for which leadership was provided by the Bihar-Jharkhand Special Area Military Commission. The objective of the raid was to arm various units of the PLGA, with the aim of eventually turning the PLGA into the regular PLA.

PRESS STATEMENT: DECEMBER 20, 2005

On The Heroic Raid on Girdhi Armoury of Home Guards

On the historic occasion of 150th anniversary of Great Santhal Hul revolt, on 11th November, 2005 the heroic raid and seizure of exploitative rulling class's armory (Armoury of Home Guards) took place. This was conducted by the brave sons of Jharkhand – the fighters of the People's Liberation Guerrilla Army (PLGA) in the land of Jharkhand, irrigated with the blood of brave fighters like Sidhu-Kanhu, Tilka Majhi and Veer Birsa Munda. The people of Jharkhand having dreams of establishing an exploitation free Jharkhand state were highly enthused by this raid, strengthening the hope of realization of their dream. This courageous act spread hopes not only amongst the people of the Jharkhandi Nationality but also amongst the struggling people of various nationalities in entire India.

On the other hand, the exploitative rulling class once again trembled with fear at this action. With the news of the raid on the Girdhi Armoury, not only the fascist BJP-Nitish government of Jharkhand, together with their bureaucrats, administration and police machinery, but also the higher officers of Delhi and the Central Govt. lost their sleep.

This action is an indication of the strengthening of the PLGA towards the transformation from the PLGA into a PLA and thereby advancing the struggle to a higher stage.

The brave fighters of the PLGA stormed into the district headquarters of Girdhi on 11th November, 2005 to raid the Armoury of the Home Guards and fled unhurt seizing with them 193 rifles and 2 revolvers. The police and administration were stunned with the surprise attack. The senior officers of police and administration were so terrorized that they locked themselves up in their room even on getting information of the raid.

Under the direction of the Central Military Commission and under the leadership of the Bihar-Jharkhand Special Area Military Commission, the PLGA fighters under the leadership of Zonal command of the Jharkhand Regional

Military Commission undertook this heroic action, which was aimed at equipping the cadres, company, platoons, LGS and peoples militia squads with these arms to establish a powerful Peoples Liberation Army. This action was conducted in the present scenario, where the class enemy has been equipping its paramilitary armed forces with sophisticated arms such as AK-47, AK-56, Insas rifles etc., providing them with night vision equipment, mine-proof & bullet proof vehicles and army helicopters, sophisticated communication gadgets, global positioning systems and connecting up the police mobiles in order to counter the guerrilla war. Every police station in the struggle area has been fortified. For all these funds are flowing in hundreds of crores of rupees. In addition, to counter the guerrilla war the rulling class is training its armed forces under the direct supervision of US Army experts in counter-insurgency and Jungle warfare in the hills of Manipur, Hyderabad and in the Army training school at Kanker in Chhattisgarh. Apart from this, new para-armed forces are being raised recruiting local adivasi youth such as the Sengel battalion (in Santhali and Mundari language this means fire).

Besides this, in Jharkhand too, the govt. is dividing the people to suppress the revolutionary movement, making the poor people fight each other in the name of Adivasi/non-Adivasi or in the name of Jharkhandi Adivasis versus other Adivasis. The rulling class is also organizing reactionary elements to build a lumpen gang – the Nagrik Suraksha Samiti. They are forcing ordinary people to join the Samiti against the revolutionaries and indulging in killing of revolutionaries, activists and their sympathizers. They are adopting brutal methods, after killing the people they poke arrows into their bodies and term this 'sendara' which means in Santhali language – hunted. This is just like the Salwa Judum in Chhatisgarh. Here, in Jharkhand this is going on under the leadership of the former CM and national Vice President of the BJP, Babu Lal Maradi.

To cope up this situation the fighters of the PLGA have to seize sophisticated arms, apparatus and gadgets from the enemy's armoury to arm the vast militant masses and in this way strengthen the PLGA to form a powerful PLA. This army alone will be the genuine people's army, which will protect the people's rights and dignity and will serve the people. Through building the PLA it will be possible to establish base areas by fighting the well equipped police force of class enemy and smashing its local administrative organs. Then only will it be possible for the peasants-workers to build their own revolutionary people's government. That would be the fulfillment of the call to "transform the guerrilla zones into base areas and the PLGA in the PLA" given by the CC (Provisional) CPI (Maoist). And the Girdhi armoury raid is the first step in the direction of achieving this goal.

Special Area Military Commission
Communist Party of India (Maoist)
Date: 20.12.2005

JEHANABAD JAIL BREAK (NOVEMBER 13, 2005)

Jehanabad Jail Break attracted wide publicity and massive attention. It was following this raid that analysts began writing about the participation of the People's Militia (Jan militia), *a very important component of the People's Liberation Guerrilla Army, realise its scale of membership, estimate its potency and visualise the impact it could create in future.*

The Maoists have termed it a "successful politico-military campaign". They have also averred that such attacks were a "rehearsal" for their People's Militia. Further, they noted that 'as more such attacks happen, the People's Liberation Guerrilla Army shall turn into a regular People's Liberation Army'.

The objectives of the jail break, the Maoist noted, were: (a) set free Maoist leaders and cadres and other prisoners, (b) capture and kill leaders and cadres (who they hold are their/people's enemies) of the Ranveer Sena, who have been imprisoned there, and (c) loot hundreds of rifles and thousands of rounds of ammunition.

PRESS RELEASE, NOVEMBER 14, 2005

COMMUNIST PARTY OF INDIA (MAOIST)

Hail the historic politico-military campaign in Jehanabad by the PLGA led by the CPI (Maoist)!

Mobilise the masses in a big way to intensify and expand the people's war in India!

One thousand guerrillas of the People's Liberation Guerrilla Army led by the Central Military Commission and the Bihar-Jharkhand Special Area Military Commission of the CPI (Maoist) laid siege to the town of Jehanabad in Bihar for almost two and half hours from 9 PM on November 13 and conducted simultaneous raids and attacks on the district jail, district Court, police lines, police quarters, district armoury, and police stations in the town and successfully carried out the Operation Jail-break. The biggest operation in Bihar's history was a complete success and the CPI-Maoist was able to achieve its three objectives. Firstly, it was able to secure the release of its leaders, activists and ordinary prisoners who have been languishing in the jail for many years; secondly, it carried out the people's verdict against the reactionary state-sponsored Ranveer Sena by annihilating its leaders and capturing several of is activists; and, thirdly, it seized hundreds of rifles and thousands of rounds of ammunition.

The Central Committee of the CPI (Maoist) hails the heroic guerrillas of the PLGA by successfully carrying out the series of death-defying military actions through the meticulous planning by the Central Military Commission and the Party and the call given out by the Central Committee to carry out tactical counter offensive campaign. It pays its Red Salutes to the comrades who laid down their precious lives in the historic campaign for liberating the oppressed masses. These daring actions are not only significant from the military point of view but have a wide political significance and the demonstrate to the entire world the justness of the cause for which the Maoists have been fighting. The punishment to the Ranveer Sena leaders is long overdue and has inspired the entire oppressed masses in the country, particularly the Dalit and other oppressed caste masses, who had suffered terribly at the hands of these lumpen feudal gangsters.

Jehanabad politico-military campaign is an answer to the countrywide counter-revolutionary campaign of the reactionary Congress-led UPA government in the Centre and the state governments led by various parties. The successive Central governments, whether the BJP-led NDA in the past or the Congress-led UPA at present, and the governments in various states such as the BJP governments in Jharkhand and Chathisgarh and MP, or the Congress governments in AP, Maharashtra, Karnataka and Uttaranchal, CPI (M)-led Left Front government in West Bengal, BJD government in Orissa, Samajwadi Party's government in UP, AIADMK government in Tamil Nadu, have unleashed a brutal campaign of killing leaders, activists and sympathisers of the CPI (Maoist) and the revolutionary mass organisations; arresting and implicating cases against thousands of revolutionaries and the common people and suppressing even the nominal fundamental rights guaranteed by the Indian Constitution.

In just 14 months since the formation of the new Party of the Indian proletariat, CPI (Maoist), over 200 revolutionaries were killed by the police, most of these in fake encounters. Apart from this state terror, the reactionary ruling classes of India have unleashed an even more gruesome and obnoxious plan of massacring the people living in the areas of Maoist influence through so-called Jan Jagaran Abhiyan's Salwa Judum in Chhattisgarh, Sendra in Jharkhand, and setting up lumpen gangs like the Narsa Cobras, Nallamala Cobras, Kakatiya Cobras etc in AP, Nagarik Suraksha Samiti and Gana Suraksha Samiti in Jharkhand and West Bengal, Shanthi Sena in Orissa, Ranveer Sena in Bihar, and so on. In Chathisgarh, this diabolic game-plan of attacking entire villages, burning them, killing adivasis not sparing even women, children and old aged people has been continuing since last June which took a toll of over 70 adivasi lives. Untold atrocities are committed by these lumpen gangs and the central para-military forces, such as beheading men, women and children, raping women activists of the mass organisations and sympathisers of CPI (Maoist) and the entire media has been conniving with the police and administration in suppressing these facts, and publishing lies and falsehoods against the movement led by the CPI (Maoist). As if this were not enough, the various state governments have begun to acquire Unmanned Aerial Vehicles (UAVs), helicopters, MPVs, and sophisticated arms. Mine-proof police stations are being constructed in all the areas of armed struggle. Cover agents are deployed in a big way by the intelligence department and the police officials are trying such dirty methods like mixing poison in food and water to kill the Party leaders and PLGA forces.

The Jehanabad operation is an answer to his brutal campaign unleashed by the Central and state governments led by the recently set-up Joint Task Force. It is a turning point in the ongoing people's war in the country. Jehanabad district administration and its police forces, the central para-military forces, the reactionary upper-caste landlord private armies such as the Ranveer Sena, Sunlight Sena, Bhumarshi Sena etc., have a notorious history of unleashing blood-baths in the paste two decades like Arwal and Laxmapur Bathe. Through such massacres the reactionary rules dream of suppressing the people's war and the democratic struggles of the oppressed people. Moreover, hundreds pf people have been languishing in jails for years without an trial under the most miserable conditions inside the prisons in violation of the provisions stipulated in the Jail Manuals. No wonder, the people were overjoyed by the Operation Jail-break by the Maoists that saw at least 431 prisoners escape from the dark dungeons of the Jehanabad jail. This daring action has also inspired the masses all over the country who see how innocent people are placed behind bars even as the bigger criminals, blood-sucking and tax-evading businessmen, money-lenders, traders and industrialists, corrupt officials and political leaders hold reins of powers ad roam freely.

The Jehanabad politico-military campaign, like the Koraput campaign in February last year in which over 500 arms were captured from ten different locations in the district, show the superiority of guerrilla tactics based ion the military line enunciated by Com. Mao for waging war in situations where the enemy has a vastly superior force. It shows that the well-equipped, well-trained, and numerically superior mercenary forces can be dealt heavy blows by a numerically weaker but determined, fearless and politically motivated armed force of the people through concrete survey of the weak points of the enemy force, meticulous planning and effective execution based on the principle of taking on the enemy through surprise and lightening speed.

The recent tactical counter-offensives carried out by the PLGA guerrillas such as daring raid on a Home Guards Training Centre in Giridih district in Jharkhand and capture of 185 arms and 25,000 rounds of ammunition on November 11; the killing of the SP of Mungher district of Bihar; the daring series of actions in Madhuban town of east Champaran district in North Bihar; the seizure of arms through raids on a police outpost near Sambhalpur and the armed outpost of the Minister Dali in Malkangiri district of Orissa last month; the annihilation of over 20 CRPF and injuring over 70 in the tactical counter-offensive campaign during April-June, blasting of the MPV and killing 24 CRPF personnel in Dantewara district and the seizure of LMG and Insas rifle from the CRPF by the people's militia and the PLGA guerrillas in North Bastar in Dandakarnya in the past two months, the seizure of arms from the STF in Gadchiroli and Gondia districts, the attempt on the life of the SP of Prakasam district in AP, and the politico-military campaign in Jehanabad on November13, and several such daring actions have inspired the masses all over the country and show the path for the liberation of our country from the stranglehold of imperialism, feudalism and the comprador bureaucratic capital. All these tactical offensives were conducted by countering the increasing encirclement-suppression campaigns by the central para-military forces, the STF, Grey Hounds and special police forces, with the active support of the revolutionary masses.

The CPI (Maoist) once again pledges that the heroic PLGA guerrillas under the CMC will secure the release of the hundreds of comrades languishing in various jails such as the Bewoor jail of Patna, Gaya, Buxar, Bhagalpur, Muzafarpur, Hazaribagh, Ranchi, Bethia and Bagia jails of Bihar and Jharkhand; the scores of comrades imprisoned by the fascist YSR government AP, Jayalalitha government in Tamil Nadu, Dharam Singh's government in Karnataka; the comrades lodged in Banpada, Sambhalpr, Koraput, Jeypore, Raigada, Koraput jails in Orissa; Jagdalpur, Dantewara, Kanker, Ambikapur in Chhattisgarh; Gdchiroli, Chandrapur, Gondia, Nagpur in Maharashtra; Balaghat in MP, and in various poisons all over the country, just as they had freed the prisoners in Jehanabad. The CC of our Party calls upon the oppressed masses to join the PLGA in thousands upon thousands to transform it into the People's Liberation Army (PLA) and achieve the objective of establishing a new society free from all forms of exploitation and oppression by overthrowing the enemies of the Indian people.

The oppressed masses in Jehanabad and other parts of the country are overjoyed at the humiliating defeat of the enemy forces who harass them daily and perpetuate untold atrocities. The politico-military campaign in Jehanabad reflects the aspirations of the oppressed masses who had lent active support to the guerrillas during the preparation and execution of the actions.

The CC of the CPI (Maoist) once again sends its heartfelt revolutionary greetings to the heroic guerrillas of the PLGA who had carried out the series of simultaneous tactical counter-offensives in Jehanabad, Giridih and elsewhere with unflinching Bolshevik determination, revolutionary mettle and death-defying valour and heroism. We also send our Red Greetings to the revolutionary masses who had extended their full cooperation in various forms to the guerrillas in order to successfully carry out the operation.

We call upon the people to be vigilant against possible brutal attacks by the mercenary police forces who, like cowards, attack unarmed people being scared to confront the armed guerrillas. The intensified suppression campaign by the enemy forces should be countered by creating more Jehanabads and sending nightmares to the enemy even in his own headquarters.

There is no alternative before the people but to arm themselves with the arms snatched from the enemy in order to carry out the people's war till final victory. The guerrilla forces of our party as well as the revolutionary masses of our country have to undertake more and more such actions in a big way so as to strengthen the guerrilla armies and to transform them into the People's Liberation Army in due course. Vast masses have to be mobilised to expand and deepen the ongoing people's war in our country.

AZAD
All India Spokesperson
Central Committee (Provisional)
CPI (Maoist)

***

NAYAGARH ARMOURY RAID (FEBRUARY 15, 2008)

On February 15, 2008, the Maoists laid siege to the district headquarters town of Nayagarh, Odisha, and looted the district armoury. In all, 12,000 weapons of various make and 2000,000 (two lakh) rounds) of ammunitrion were reportedlty looted. This was the last syncronised, large-sclae attack on multiple taregets within a given location by the rebels. It is believed that approximately 500 people participated in this raid.

Nayagarh, when this researcher visited the place in November 2009, had a population of 14,000 and could be best described as a major Panchyat. Sabyasachi Panda, who was the Odisha State Organisiung Committee Secretary at the time of the raid, is a native of Nayagarh.

COMMUNIST PARTY OF INDIA (MAOIST) CENTRAL COMMITTEE

PRESS RELEASE: FEBRUARY 19, 2008

Hail the daring Nayagarh raids—the biggest ever in Indian history—by PLGA guerrillas!

The fascist ruling classes of India can never douse the fire of revolution by intensifying fascist repression on the masses!!

On the 15th of February, the gallant guerrillas of PLGA led by the CPI (Maoist), with the active participation and support of the masses, had carried out the biggest tactical counteroffensive in the history of India. The magnitude and scale of the counteroffensive operation by the Maoists and the quantity of arms confiscated by them is also perhaps a record in world history. They laid siege to the town of Nayagarh in Orissa, simultaneously carried out raids on three police stations, district armoury, a police training school and a police outpost; seized over 1100 arms, including sophisticated ones such as AK-47, LMG, SLR etc., along with over one hundred thousand rounds of ammunition. They carried away the arms and ammunition in two trucks after fighting the police forces for almost four hours. The Maoist guerrillas did not suffer a single casualty. 14 police personnel and a civilian were annihilated as they did not lay down their arms but persisted in firing at the Maoist guerrillas despite repeated warnings. The CC, CPI (Maoist), hails the heroic counteroffensive carried out by the PLGA under the direct leadership of its Central Military Commission with complete success. The multiple raids in Nayagarh expose the hollowness of the claims of the government that Maoist movement is in decline due to the arrest or murder of several of its leaders in the past few years.

The panic-struck reactionary ruling classes had immediately deployed a huge contingent of their mercenary police forces, para-military forces, Grey Hounds and other anti-Naxal forces set up and trained by the governments of Orissa, AP, Chhattisgarh and the Central government. The spokespersons of the governments at the Centre and Orissa claim that they had killed over 20 Maoists but are not able to produce a single dead body. They also claim that a huge quantity of arms and ammunition seized from Nayagarh was recovered from the Maoists. All this is sheer humbug and Goebelsian propaganda to boost the morale of their mercenary forces. Our PLGA guerrillas had successfully retreated into the guerrilla bases with the active help of the masses while heroically pushing back the security forces which had been trying to encircle the retreating guerilla forces and even to bomb them by using IAF helicopters. A small portion of the weapons seized was left behind as it became difficult and extremely trying to carry such a huge haul of weapons over long distances. Even our forces had not expected such a huge quantity of arms and ammunition from the multiple raids in Nayagarh and hence they took away all the sophisticated ones. The inferior variety o arms left behind by the Maoists were shown to the media and claimed as a big success by the government. Our PLGA has completed its mission successfully contrary to the false claims of the police top brass and other government spokespersons. The massive combing operations undertaken jointly by the police forces of various states and the central para-military forces had totally failed in achieving any success over the Maoist guerrillas.

Manmohan Singh and Shivraj Patil at the Centre, who remained mere spectators when Mumbai was paralysed by Raj Thakeray's goons and poor labourers from north India were beaten up, found no problem in sending huge contingent of CRPF and other para-military forces within hours to attack the Maoists. And Naveen Patnaik, the blue-eyed boy of the imperialist MNCs and the comprador big business houses of India, who watched for days without end as lawlessness ruled Khandamal, had promptly mobilized the police forces of Orissa against the Maoists to please his imperialist masters. The centre has assured the states to assist fully in raising another 35 India Reserve Battalions in addition to the 35 CRPF battalions already deployed against the Maoist movement. The atrocities of these para-military forces and specially trained anti-Naxal mercenary forces like the elite Grey Hounds had so much alienated the people from the Indian state that the new move to deploy such a huge force will bring the masses intothe revolutionary movement on far greater scale. The campaign of fascist suppression by the reactionary ruling classes of India, with the active backing of the imperialists, will only further strengthen the ongoing people's war. As more and more people join the PLGA the day is not far off when the PLGA will be transformed into People's Liberation Army (PLA) and mobile war will be the order of the day creating several Nayagarhs, Koraputs, Giridihs, Jehanabads, R Udayagiris and Dantewaras. The people will arm themselves with the arms seized from the enemy.

As long as there is repression there will be resistance. And as long as there is exploitation and oppression there will be revolution.

Azad,
Spokesperson,
Central Committee,
CPI (Maoist)

***

BALIMELA ATTACK (JUNE 29, 2008)

This attack by the Maoists on the elite Grey Hounds anti-Maoist force of Andhra Pradesh does not, in the strict sense, fall under the category of synchronised attacks, but is, nevertheless, significant because of the highest number of fatalities suffered ever by this elite force. Hence, it has been included in this section.

On June 29, 2008, guerrillas of the CPI (Maoist) lay in ambush and attacked the Greyhounds personnel who were returning after a combing operation along the Andhra-Odisha border and inside Odisha. They were returning in a steamer when they were attacked in the Balimela reservoir that lies between Andhra and Odisha. 36 personnel were martyred in this chilling and gruesome attack, in which at least one of them was inflicted multiple body wounds with a sharp edge weapon.

Terming it a "Red letter day" for the Maoists, the Central Committee and the Central Military Commission said, "The daring day-light attack on two platoons of anti-Naxal specially-trained Greyhounds by a Company of our PLGA … fulfills the long-cherished desire of the revolutionary people all over the country, particularly the people of Andhra Pradesh, to deal severe blows on this fascist, terrorist, cunning force... The CC and CMC of CPI (Maoist) send their revolutionary greetings to the heroic fighters of PLGA … and calls upon the PLGA forces all over the country to emulate the heroism, meticulous planning and daring execution displayed by our forces".

COMMUNIST PARTY OF INDIA (MAOIST)
CENTRAL COMMITTEE
CENTRAL MILITARY COMMISSION

PRESS RELEASE: JULY 1, 2008

Hail the historic attack by the PLGA warriors in Andhra-Orissa Border on the anti-people blood-thirsty Greyhound forces that had unleashed a reign of terror in Andhra Pradesh!

Our PLGA and revolutionary masses will punish the Congress leaders and the police officials if they indulge in attacks on innocent people and revolutionary sympathizers in the name of retaliation!!

June 29, 2008 shall remain a historic red-letter day in the annals of the revolutionary movement of Andhra Pradesh and India as a whole. It marks a leap in the growing armed resistance of the masses and tactical counter-offensives of the People's Liberation Guerrilla Army. The daring day-light attack on two platoons of anti-Naxal specially-trained Greyhounds by a Company of our PLGA near Alempaka on Sileru river in Andhra-Orissa border wiping out three dozen commandos fulfills the long-cherished desire of the revolutionary people all over the country, particularly the people of Andhra Pradesh, to deal severe blows on this fascist, terrorist, cunning force that had transformed the state into a veritable hell for the vast oppressed masses. The CC and CMC of CPI (Maoist) send their revolutionary greetings to the heroic fighters of PLGA who had carried out this daring day-light lightning counter-offensive and calls upon the PLGA forces all over the country to emulate the heroism, meticulous planning and daring execution displayed by our forces in this counter-offensive that will remain a glorious example to all fighters in our ever-advancing people's war.

YS Reddy and Janareddy—the two big terrorist bandits who are running a virtual police raj in AP since end of 2004 after they had conspiratorially broke off the talks—have been crying hoarse that violence has no place in democracy. Like the devil himself citing scriptures! These hypocrites and imperialist stooges had overseen the cold-blooded murder of several hundred Maoist revolutionaries, sympathizers and people at large. And today they are citing scriptures like the devil. And the Greyhounds, along with its twin, the notorious, lawless and sadistic APSIB, had committed indescribable atrocities and cold-blooded massacres of the revolutionaries and their well-wishers ever since these were set up during the 1980s. The catalogue of crimes committed by these lawless goons on the people and revolutionaries in the past two decades sends shivers down one's spine and brings into one's memory the brutalities of the Nazis under Hitler. The PLGA, on behalf of the vast majority of the people whom it represents, carried out this retaliatory action on this bunch of thugs in accordance with its pledge to the people of Andhra Pradesh and the country as a whole.

After suffering the most serious loss to its mercenary elite force YS-Jana clique along with the top police brass have been crying for revenge and have openly declared that they will draw blood. Janareddy, who is supposed to oversee law & order had himself declared like a street ruffian that his government would kill ten times the number suffered by the Greyhounds. We warn the fascist YS-Jana regime and the police officials that if they indulge in killing the innocent people and revolutionary sympathizers they will have to pay a heavy price. All Congress leaders will be held responsible and punished in due course of time if the YSR police raj unleashes attacks on people.

Our Party and PLGA will never indulge in violence on the people and we resort to revolutionary counterviolence only to stop the brutal state terrorist violence on the struggling masses and the revolutionaries who lead them. Some are mistakenly interpreting our attacks against the greyhounds, police forces and informers as a deviation from the goal of fighting for people's demands. Our revolutionary violence is only meant to advance the struggle of the people for achieving their basic socio-economic demands, to liberate them from all types of exploitation and to lead a life of dignity and self-respect. And undemocratic fascist forces like the APSIB and Greyhounds have become the biggest hurdle to the people's struggles and have become cold-blooded murderers. They had murdered great leaders of the Indian revolution like comrades Shyam, Mahesh, Murali, Vadkapur Chandramouli, Sande Rajamouli, Madhav, Matta Ravi Kumar, Pamula Venkatesh, Raghavulu and uncountable comrades. Of late they have unleashed brutal terror on the adivasis of Andhra-Orissa border region, raped 11 adivasi women in Vakapalli and murdered comrades Komma, Sudheer, Ranadheer, Santosh, Jhansi and others. They have been conducting joint operations with their counterparts in Orissa and Chhattisgarh and terrorizing the adivasis in all the three states. Hence we appeal to all sections of the people to understand the justness of our revolutionary counter-violence and call upon them to extend support to the selfless efforts of the Maoist revolutionaries. We warn the Greyhounds that if they venture into neighbouring Orissa and Chhattisgarh again to conduct joint terror campaigns the same fate awaits them. Our PLGA forces too will carry out joint counter-campaigns and deal effective blows to these khaki-clad terrorists.

Azad,
Central Committee,
CPI(Maoist).

Basavaraj,
Spokesperson, Central Military Commission
CPI(Maoist).

SECTION VI

STATEMENTS ON OTHER ORGANIZATIONS

For a Communist Party to succeed, according to classical understanding, it has to have 'three magic weapons'. These are strong Party (the organizational wing), strong Army (the underground, or People's Liberation Guerrilla Army) and United Front.

United Front is of two types: Tactical and Strategic. The latter is nothing but a conglomeration or alliance of a number of underground/secret mass organizations of the CPI (Maoist). The former is an alliance with organizations that need not necessarily agree with the 'revolutionary agenda' of the Maoists

In this wake, the Maoists have formed alliances with different organizations, have established fraternal as well as entirely opportunistic linkages with various outfits. Also, they have been seeking to extend support to various elements with a view to garnering their support.

Thus, this section contains statements issued by the Maoists on the proscription of Students Islamic Movement of India (SIMI), their moral support to the terrorist movement in Jammu and Kashmir, and a joint-declaration with the People's Liberation Army/Revolutionary People's Front (PLA/RPF) of Manipur with whom they have a three-point MoU.

The section also contains a document on the Indian Maoists, view-point on their Nepalese counterparts (Unified Communist Party of Nepal – Maoist) coming over-ground, joining the political mainstream and participating in democratic processes. They condemn their Nepalese counterparts for joining the mainstream and lodging the PLA in designated camps. The Maoists hold the view that the people have nothing without the revolutionary PLA and, thus, find fault with the Nepalese Maoist leadership. Further, they also state that the debate is an ongoing one between the two organizations on the correct direction of the revolutionary movement and, thus, leave some scope for vagueness on their stand vis-à-vis *the Nepalese Maoists.*

***

COMMUNIST PARTY OF INDIA (MAOIST) CENTRAL COMMITTEE

PRESS RELEASE: AUGUST 17, 2008

Re-imposition of ban on SIMI is reiteration of UPA government's intention to continue its brutal war on Muslims!

Secular and democratic forces of India! Let us unite to fight back the assaults by the reactionary ruling classes on the fundamental rights of the people!!

When the special tribunal headed by Justice Geeta Mittal announced that there were no sufficient grounds for re-imposing ban on the Student Islamic Movement of India (SIMI), the ruling lasses of India, particularly the Hindu fascist forces, received a severe jolt. They immediately moved the Supreme Court, which, as a loyal servant of the exploiting classes and inherent bias towards the Muslims, like every government institution in our country, ordered a stay on the Tribunal's decision. The irresponsibility of the judiciary is seen from the fact that the petitioner on behalf of SIMI was not even intimated about the Tribunal's order. One would not, of course, have expected anything less from the pro-Hindu, anti-Muslim fascist rulers of India. Whether they are in the guise of the BJP or Congress or any other parliamentary party, (the ban on SIMI was first imposed by the BJP government in 2001 and later continued by the Congress government) or in the form of the legislative, judiciary, executive, the police and other security forces, the bias against the Muslim community is crystal-clear. That is why, in the past several decades, not a single Hindu chauvinist organization was banned (barring the Emergency period when all democratic and revolutionary organizations too were banned) and not a single Hindu terrorist has been awarded any punishment, no matter if he had burnt alive scores of Muslims, dalits, adivasis and women. Mass murderers of the Muslims like Narendra Modi of the BJP or butchers of Sikhs like HKL Bhagath of the Congress were even adorned with titles of honour. Vajapayees and Advanis, who should have been hanged for their crimes of inflaming communal passions leading to the demolition of Babari Masjid and causing death and destruction on an unprecedented scale in the country. The real terrorists, whether communal-fascist, or state-sponsored, roam scot-free while national liberation fighters, revolutionaries and Muslim youth are killed every day by the state and state-sponsored gangs. They are even denied the right to association, right to speech and movement. Such is the real face of democracy in our country.

It is, in fact, the Parliament that has the greatest number of the top terrorists, gangsters, criminals and scamsters of our country. These criminal gangsters are in leading positions in every parliamentary party and they enter the Parliament and Assemblies, and this has now become a granted thing. There are scamsters who occupy the highest seats of power despite swindling hundreds of crores of people's heard-earned money through kickbacks and commissions. These traitors have no compunction in selling the motherland to the videshi masters for a few crumbs. Yet all these anti-national, anti-people continue to hold the lifelines of the country, posing a grave threat to the security of the country. The BJP, whose hands are stained with the blood of thousands of Muslim people, and whose bestiality and sadism was displayed in full colours during the Gujarat genocide, has been shamelessly clamouring loudly for imposing ban on every Muslim organisation and re-introducing POTA for harassing the Muslim community without any hindrance. Rabidly anti-Muslim Narendra Modi's government in Gujarat had incarcerated thousands of Muslim youth in prisons and eliminated hundreds in the name of encounters.

Today it is trying to enact a drama by arresting some SIMI activists and trying to implicate them in Bangalore, Ahmedabad bomb blasts. It has been "unearthing" every day bombs planted by its own men in Surat and elsewhere in order to defame the Muslims and to justify its genocide of Muslims. Every charge made by the Hindu fascists and the Indian state against Muslims will turn to be false if proper investigation is conducted. The blasts in Bangalore, Ahmedabad themselves could be the handiwork of the Hindu communal forces in the two BJP-rule states in order to whip up communal tension, justify their brutal assaults on the fundamental rights of the people and genocide of Muslims, and gain seats in the coming elections with inspiration derived from Modi's Gujarat.

The CPI (Maoist) calls upon the people not to get diverted by the malicious propaganda made by the ruling classes and their media which portrays all the militant struggles waged by the oppressed masses and oppressed nationalities as terrorist violence. The struggling people resort to revolutionary violence as a response to the white terror/state terror unleashed by the big landlord big bourgeois ruling classes and their armed forces in order to put down their legitimate struggles. It is the ploy of the imperialists and their running dogs all over the world in their 'war against terrorism' to utilize the killing of innocent people to ruthlessly crush the people's struggles under the 'sacred' banner of "war on terror". It is these gangsters who are the real culprits causing death of millions of people not only through direct aggression over the sovereign states, killing millions of children, women and aged through economic sanctions but also through their policies of Liberalization, Privatization, and Globalization. The CC calls upon the workers, peasants, women, youths, and all other oppressed people to fight unitedly against the growing assaults by the rulers on the fundamental rights of the people, against the draconian policies imposed by the imperialists and the Indian ruling classes in the name of 'war on terror'. Our slogan should be to wage a united "war on state terror".

Lift the ban on SIMI, CPI(Maoist) and other organisations!

Punish the criminals who had unleashed attacks and committed atrocities on Muslims and other religious minorities!

Azad,
Spokesperson,
Central Committee,
CPI(Maoist)

***

COMMUNIST PARTY OF INDIA (MAOIST) CENTRAL COMMITTEE

PRESS RELEASE: AUGUST 27, 2008

Azad Kashmir is the birth-right of every Kashmiri! Arrests and massacres cannot crush the right to national self-determination!

People of India! Rise up in support of the just and democratic struggle of the people of Kashmir!!

Fight back the brutal onslaught of the Indian fascist state!!

The political scene in Kashmir today brings into one's memory the people's uprising in East Europe and the various Russian republics against the Russian imperialist stranglehold during the late 1980s. Even the mighty Russian state—its armed forces, KGB, mental asylums and concentration camps—could not cow down the will of the people. It had to ultimately bow down before the national aspirations of the people oppressed under its jackboots. Today, more determined than ever before, the people of Kashmir have boldly risen up asserting their nation's right to self-determination in the most unambiguous manner. The strong-arm tactics of the Indian fascist state which had deployed over six lakh-strong army and several battalions of para-military and special police forces to brutally crush a genuine people's struggle for their liberation from the yoke of foreign rule has failed to subdue the people's aspirations for freedom and independence. The imposition of endless curfews in the entire Kashmir Valley to thwart peaceful protest marches by the people, detention of the leaders of Huriyat and others to render the people leaderless, the killings of peaceful protestors, and the brutal reign of state terror in the entire Kashmir Valley are a re-enactment of the British colonial savagery against the struggling people of India for azadi. The present rulers, true heirs to their then British imperialist masters, haven't learnt any lesson from history. It is the peace-loving people of Kashmir with the support of the vast masses of India who have to teach these plunderers a fitting lesson. The CC, CPI(Maoist), hails the glorious role of the people of Kashmir in their just struggle for national self-determination. It calls upon the people of India to rise up in support of this just and democratic struggle of our brothers and sisters of Kashmir and to fight against the high-handedness and brutal suppression of their struggle by the expansionist Indian state.

Today no citizen of India can call himself or herself a real democrat unless he/she extends unconditional support to the demand for azad Kashmir. Manmohan Singhs and Advanis, like every colonialist in history, go to any extent in retaining territory even if it means exterminating an entire population. It is only such greedy sharks, who conspire to loot and plunder the wealth of other's land, that oppose the aspirations of the people. These die-hards refuse to learn from history and continue to suppress people's struggles in rivers of blood for the sake of their narrow class interests. However, history had demonstrated repeatedly that no nation, however small and weak, can be kept enslaved forever by another, however strong and mighty the latter may be. History has shown that it is the people, and people alone, who can decide their destiny. The mightiest superpower was kicked out of Vietnam and entire Indo-China. Their napalm bombs and My Lai massacres could not subdue the fiercely peace-loving Vietnamese nation. The other erstwhile superpower, Soviet social imperialism too, had to bite the dust before the might of the people in Afghanistan and its own republics. The fate of the reactionary Indian ruling classes can never be anything different. Even if they cling on to Kashmir through brute force for another few years they will ultimately be consigned to the dust-bin of history.

The CC, CPI(Maoist), unequivocally supports Kashmiri people's struggle for azadi and believes that one who does not support the people's aspirations for freedom and independence can never be a democrat. It calls upon its Party members and the People's Liberation Guerrilla Army fighters to mobilize the people in support of the Kashmiri people's struggle for azadi. It appeals to every peace-loving, democratic-minded citizen of India to rise up boldly in support of the just and democratic struggle of the Kashmiri nation and to condemn the brutal suppression and reign of state terror unleashed by the Indian ruling classes on the people of Kashmir. It also warns the people to beware of the conspiracies of the reactionary rulers to bring in the ghost of Pakistan to justify their brutal suppression of Kashmiri people's struggle and their sinister designs to whip up anti-Pak hysteria and even a war with Pakistan in order to divert the people from the issue of azadi. The people of Kashmir should come out clearly with the slogan: "Neither India nor Pakistan, but a sovereign, independent Kashmir!"

Azad,
Spokesperson,
Central Committee,
CPI(Maoist)

***

PRESS RELEASE: OCTOBER 22, 2008

Joint Declaration between the CPI (Maoist) and the Revolutionary People's Front

A two days joint meeting was held between the CPI (Maoist) and the Revolutionary People's Front (RPF) at the Council Head Quarters of the Revolutionary People's Front on 21-22 October 2008. At that meeting, both sides have unanimously condemned the hegemonic capitalist design of the Indian regime and have agreed to consolidate the mutual understanding and friendship, further more agreed firmly to stand hand in hand to overthrow the common enemy, the present Indian reactionary regime and to gain political goals of the respective two Parties.

The CPI (Maoist) strongly condemned the annexation of Manipur by the Dominion of India, which was done under the instigation of reactionary Indian Congress led by Gandhi, Nehru and Sardar Patel and their hegemonic and colonial designed. The so-called Merger Agreement of Manipur with the Dominion of India was, indeed, illegal and unconstitutional. The very verdict was given by the two days convention on Manipur Merger Agreement held at GM Hall, Imphal, on 22-29 October 1993. Now it becomes the voice of the people of Manipur.

A revolutionary movement was born under the leadership of Comrade Hijam Irabot to liberate Manipur from the yoke of the British remnant India style Black Raj. As a continuation of liberation struggle and a total revolution, the Revolutionary People's Front has been struggling for their political rights to self-determination. Therefore, the CPI (Maoist) upholds the true nature of the revolutionary movement in Manipur and support the liberation struggle recognizing the sovereignty of Manipur.

Moreover, the Revolutionary People's Front stands and supports the revolutionary movement of the CPI (Maoist) as well. The downtrodden proletariat Peoples of all over India are facing the suppression and subjugation of the reactionary regime of India since the departure of the British Raj from the Indian soil. Under the new leadership of Comrade Charu Majumdar and Comrade Kanhai Chatterjee two streams of revolutionary movement was founded in 1969 to give the Indian people the rights to political emancipation. Comrade Charu Majumdar was assassinated by the repressive Indian regime in the police custody and Comrade Kanhai Chatterjee embraced martyrdom in 1982 suffering from kidney failure. In 2004, the two revolutionary streams, CPIML (People's War) and MCC (Maoist Communist Centre) merged and formed one new Party – The Communist Party of India (Maoist). Following the footsteps of the two founder leaders, the CPI (Maoist) is still struggling arms in hand to overthrow the Indian reactionary regime and to bring the victory of the Indian people.

The Revolutionary People's Front firmly believes that the general Indian peoples are not our enemy. In fact, they are under privileged and downtrodden people who are gravely suffering under the semi-feudal, semi-colonial regime of India.

Joint Declaration

Today, the 22nd day of October 2008, after having a thorough discussion, session for two consecutive days, in every aspect of the two organizations the Communist Party of India (Maoist) and the Revolutionary People's Front, unanimously declare the following agreement:

1. That, both sides will honour and support the Sovereignty of the two countries (the Sovereignty of India and the sovereignty of Manipur).
2. That, both sides will extend full morale and political support to each other in the liberation struggles to overthrow the common enemy, the Indian reactionary and oppressive regime, respectively.
3. That, both sides deem to recognize and honour the historically endorsed territorial integrity of the two countries viz. Manipur and India.

Signed by:

(Aloke)
Political Bureau Member
On behalf of CPI (Maoist)

(S Gunen)
General Secretary
On behalf of R P F

Annexures

State-wise Extent of Naxal Violence During 2008 to 2013

State	*2008*		*2009*		*2010*		*2011*		*2012*		*2013*	
	Incidents	*Deaths*	*Incidents*	*Deaths*	*Incidents*	*Deaths*	*Incidents*	*Deaths*	*Incidents*	*Deaths*	*Incidents*	*Deaths*
Andhra Pradesh	92	46	66	18	100	24	54	9	67	13	36	11
Bihar	164	73	232	72	307	97	316	63	166	44	176	69
Chhattisgarh	620	242	529	290	625	343	465	204	370	109	353	110
Jharkhand	484	207	742	208	501	157	517	182	480	163	383	150
M.P.	07	0	1	0	7	1	8	0	11	0	1	0
Maharashtra	68	22	154	93	94	45	109	54	134	41	71	19
Odisha	103	101	266	67	218	79	192	53	171	45	101	35
Uttar Pradesh	4	0	8	2	6	1	1	0	2	0	0	0
West Bengal	35	26	255	158	350	258	92	45	6	0	1	0
Others	14	4	5	0	5	0	6	1	8	0	7	0
TOTAL	1591	721	2258	908	2213	1005	1760	611	1415	415	1129	394

Source: Ministry of Home Affairs, New Delhi.

Comparative Important Parameters of Naxal Violence During 2008 to 2013

S.No.	Parameters	2008	2009	2010	2011	2012	2013
A.	No. of incidents	1591	2258	2213	1760	1415	1129
B.	Civilians killed	490	591	720	469	301	279
	(Out of which 'Police Informers' killed)	170	211	323	218	134	113
C.	No. of Security Forces killed	231	317	285	142	114	115
D.	No. of encounters with police	271	309	272	223	216	218
E.	No. of attacks on police (including landmines)	192	250	230	131	135	143
F.	No. of naxalites killed (during encounters as well as attacks on police)	199	220	172	99	74	99
G.	No. of naxalites arrested	1743	1981	2916	2030	1901	1397
H.	No. of naxalites surrendered	400	150	266	394	445	283
I.	Total no. of arms snatched	1219	217	256	67	55	77
J.	Total no. of arms recovered	1511	572	642	636	591	627
K.	Arms training camps held	52	61	94	84	53	28
L.	No of Jan Adalats held	71	50	75	97	62	54

Source: Ministry of Home Affairs, New Delhi.

State-wise Statistics of Naxal Violence of Various Indices for 2013 vis-a-vis 2012

Sl. No.	*State*	*No. of incidents*	*No. of civilians killed*	*'Police Informers' Killed (Out of total civilians killed)*	*No. of Security Forces killed*	*No. of encounters with police*	*No. of attacks on police (including landmines)*	*No. of naxalites killed (encounters and attacks)*	*No. of naxalites arrested*	*No. of naxalites surrendered*	*Total no. of arms snatched*	*Total no. of arms recovered*	*Arms training camps held*	*No. of Jan Adalats held*
		A	*B*	*B*	*C*	*D*	*E*	*F*	*G*	*H*	*I*	*J*	*K*	*L*
1	Andhra Pradesh	36 (67)	10 (12)	7 (10)	1 (1)	3 (4)	2 (2)	1 (3)	152 (312)	82 (301)	0 (2)	17 (42)	0 (0)	1 (1)
2	Bihar	176 (166)	42 (34)	7 (13)	27 (10)	6 (12)	10 (7)	0 (5)	311 (426)	3 (42)	38 (2)	88 (151)	1 (5)	2 (11)
3	Chhattisgarh	353 (370)	66 (63)	31 (35)	44 (46)	92 (87)	102 (77)	38 (38)	387 (404)	28 (26)	29 (17)	155 (91)	14 (26)	7 (14)
4	Jharkhand	383 (480)	120 (134)	35 (32)	30 (29)	55 (43)	14 (21)	12 (7)	332 (384)	15 (6)	8 (30)	173 (162)	9 (12)	41 (25)
5	M.P.	1 (11)	0 (0)	0 (0)	0 (0)	0 (2)	0 (0)	0 (1)	2 (2)	0 (0)	0 (0)	3 (3)	1 (0)	0 (0)
6	Maharashtra	71 (134)	13 (27)	8 (21)	6 (14)	36 (42)	12 (8)	26 (4)	39 (78)	53 (10)	0 (1)	43 (18)	1 (2)	0 (2)
7	Odisha	101 (171)	28 (31)	25 (23)	7 (14)	25 (15)	3 (19)	22 (10)	129 (187)	101 (34)	2 (3)	103 (59)	2 (8)	3 (9)
8	Uttar Pradesh	0 (2)	0 (0)	0 (0)	0 (0)	0 (1)	0 (0)	0 (0)	4 (6)	0 (0)	0 (0)	0 (2)	0 (0)	0 (0)
9	West Bengal	1 (6)	0 (0)	0 (0)	0 (0)	0 (3)	0 (1)	0 (1)	21 (76)	0 (26)	0 (0)	45 (51)	0 (0)	0 (0)
10	Others	7 (8)	0 (0)	0 (0)	0 (0)	1 (7)	0 (0)	0 (5)	20 (26)	1 (0)	0 (0)	0 (12)	0 (0)	0 (0)
	Total	1129 (1415)	279 (301)	113 (134)	115 (114)	218 (216)	143 (135)	99 (74)	1397 (1901)	283 (445)	77 (55)	627 (591)	28 (53)	54 (62)

*Figures in Brackets are of 2012. *Source:* Ministry of Home Affairs, New Delhi.

Incidents of Economic Targets by LWE Extremists All Over the Country

			2008		2009		2010		2011		2012		2013	
				Total		Total		Total		Total		Total		Total
Economic targets	Andhra Pradesh	Uranium Mines	0	5	0	17	0	24	0	18	0	11	0	22
		Essar steel	1		0		0		0		0		0	
		Gramin Sadak Nirman Yojana	0		0		0		0		1		1	
	Chhattisgarh	NMDC	0		2		11		2		3		7	
		Essar pipe lines	3		1		1		0		0		0	
		BRO	0		0		0		0		0		0	
		Gramin Sadak Nirman Yojana	1		4		3		4		1		3	
	Odisha	Essar pipe lines	0		5		1		2		1		0	
		Gramin Sadak Nirman Yojana	0		2		4		3		2		4	
	Maharashtra	BRO	0		0		1		1		0		0	
	Madhya Pradesh	Gramin Sadak Nirman Yojana	0		0		1		0		1		1	
	Bihar	Cement Plant	0		0		0		0		0		0	
		Solar Plate	0		2		0		0		0		0	
		Gramin Sadak Nirmal Yojana	0		1		1		2		1		5	
	Jharkhand	Gramin Sadak Nirmal Yojana	0		0		1		3		1		1	
		Essar Pipe lines	0		0		0		1		0		0	
Railway	Andhra Pradesh		2	27	0	46	1	54	0	31	0	12	0	12
	Bihar		11		8		16		3		1		4	
	Chhattisgarh		6		5		8		11		9		7	
	Jharkhand		7		17		13		10		2		1	
	Maharashtra		0		0		0		0		0		0	
	Odisha		0		10		7		7		0		0	
	West Bengal		1		6		7		0		0		0	
	Uttar Pradesh		0		0		2		0		0		0	

Telephone exchange/tower	Andhra Pradesh	1	46	0	67	4	45	2	51	2	24	0	12
	Bihar	14		24		14		25		10		4	
	Maharashtra	2		1		1		2		1		0	
	Chhattisgarh	15		10		2		3		0		0	
	Jharkhand	10		14		6		8		3		1	
	Odisha	4		18		17		11		7		7	
	West Bengal	0		0		1		0		0		0	
	Madhya Pradesh	-		-		-		0		1		0	
Power plant	Andhra Pradesh	0	1	0	2	1	3	0	0	0	0	0	1
	Chhattisgarh	0		0		0		0		0		0	
	West Bengal	0		0		1		0		0		0	
	Maharashtra	1		2		1		0		0		0	
	Bihar	0		0		0		0		0		I	
Mining	Odisha	0	6	1	3	1	9	1	6	0	1	0	1
	Jharkhand	4		2		6		2		0		0	
	Chhattisgarh	2		0		0		3		1		1	
	Andhra Pradesh	0		0		0		0		0		0	
	Maharashtra	0		0		1		0		0		0	
	West Bengal	0		0		1		0		0		0	
Pole/transmission	Chhattisgarh	23	24	7	7	1	2	4	4	0	0	0	0
	Odisha	01		0		0		0		0		0	
	Jharkhand	0		0		1		0		0		0	

(Contd.)

		2008		2009		2010		2011		2012		2013	
			Total		*Total*		*Total*		*Total*		*Total*		*Total*
Panchayat Bhawan	Chhattisgarh	2	7	0	23	3	31	0	10	2	5	1	8
	Jharkhand	0		7		4		0		1		2	
	Andhra Pradesh	0		0		0		0		0		0	
	Maharashtra	5		8		6		6		1		2	
	Bihar	0		3		0		1		0		2	
	Odisha	0		3		11		1		1		1	
	West Bengal	0		2		7		2		0		0	
School Building	Chhattisgarh	19	25	7	71	13	39	2	27	3	3	1	4
	Andhra Pradesh	0		0		1		0		0		0	
	Jharkhand	4		37		7		6		0		2	
	Bihar	0		21		10		18		0		1	
	Maharashtra	2		1		0		0		0		0	
	Odisha	0		5		8		1		0		0	
Forest road, culverts etc.		41	41	126	126	158	158	146	146	158	158	109	109
	TOTAL	182	182	362	362	365	365	293	293	214	214	169	169

Source: Ministry of Home Affairs, New Delhi.

Maoist Violence Profile, 2012

State	*2012 (up to August 15)*		
	Number of Encounters	*Naxals killed*	*Naxals arrested*
Andhra Pradesh	2	3	182
Bihar	9	5	292
Chhattisgarh	47	29	230
Jharkhand	32	5	249
Karnataka	3	0	2
Madhya Pradesh	2	1	1
Maharashtra	17	2	49
Odisha	10	4	87
West Bengal	3	1	54
Assam	2	4	11
Uttar Pradesh	1	0	6
Tamil Nadu	0	0	4
Delhi	0	0	1
TOTAL	128	54	1168

Source: Rajya Sabha, Unstarred Question No. 1914, answered on August 29, 2012.

Naxalites Arrested and Killed, 2009-2012

State	*2009*		*2010*		*2011*		*2012 (up to July 31)*	
	Naxals Arrested	*Naxals Killed*	*Naxals Arrested*	*Naxals Killed*	*Naxals Arrested*	*Naxals Killed*	*Naxals Arrested*	*Naxals Killed*
Andhra Pradesh	358	17	289	13	158	4	176	3
Bihar	341	2	364	5	428	14	278	5
Chhattisgarh	421	142	902	83	509	34	190	28
Delhi	1	0	5	0	01	0	1	0
Gujarat	0	0	17	0	0	0	0	0
Goa	0	0	2	0	0	0	0	0
Haryana	31	0	0	0	0	0	0	0
Jharkhand	367	31	359	15	380	16	219	5
Karnataka	29	0	6	1	01	0	2	0
Kerala	1	0	10	0	03	0	0	0
Madhya Pradesh	11	0	0	0	06	0	1	1
Maharashtra	50	4	76	3	94	3	48	2
Odisha	176	14	247	10	171	23	83	4
Punjab	3	0	4	0	01	0	0	0
Tamil Nadu	14	0	21	0	0	0	4	0
Uttar Pradesh	35	1	77	0	13	0	6	0
Uttrakhand	0	0	1	0	0	0	0	0
West Bengal	143	8	536	42	238	5	49	1
Assam	0	0	0	0	22	0	10	4
Arunachal Pradesh	0	0	0	0	05	0	0	0
Total	1981	219	2916	172	2030	99	1067	53

Source: Rajya Sabha, Unstarred Question No. 72, answered on August 8, 2012.

State-wise, District-wise Details of Incidents and Deaths Due to LWE Violence, 2009-2012

Andhra Pradesh

Districts	*2009*		*2010*		*2011*		*2012 (up to August 15)*	
	Incidents	*Deaths*	*Incidents*	*Deaths*	*Incidents*	*Deaths*	*Incidents*	*Deaths*
Adilabad	3	0	1	0	0	0	0	0
Cuddapah	1	0	0	0	0	0	0	0
East Godavari	2	1	2	1	1	0	2	0
Guntur	0	0	1	0	0	0	0	0
Karimnagar	3	2	1	1	2	1	2	0
Khammam	16	9	15	5	17	2	17	4
Prakasam	1	0	1	0	0	0	0	0
Rangareddy	0	0	0	0	1	0	0	0
Vishakhapatnam	22	3	67	15	30	5	21	2
Vijaynagaram	2	0	4	0	0	0	2	0
Warangal	16	3	8	2	3	1	0	0
Total	66	18	100	24	54	9	44	6

Bihar

Districts	*2009*		*2010*		*2011*		*2012 (up to August 15)*	
	Incidents	*Deaths*	*Incidents*	*Deaths*	*Incidents*	*Deaths*	*Incidents*	*Deaths*
Arwal	5	1	3	1	3	0	3	0
Aurangabad	43	5	30	15	31	4	23	1
Banka	1	0	4	5	6	3	4	0
Begusarai	2	0	4	2	4	2	2	0
Bhagalpur	0	0	1	0	0	0	0	0
Bhojpur	0	0	1	0	1	0	0	0
Buxar	0	0	1	0	0	0	0	0
Darbhanga	0	0	1	0	0	0	0	0
East Champaran	5	0	13	3	23	9	6	0
Gaya	81	13	92	15	94	5	26	4
Gopalganj	0	0	1	0	0	0	0	0
Jamui	16	8	27	19	36	18	26	9
Jehanabad	2	0	7	0	3	6	0	0
Kaimur	3	1	12	0	18	1	1	0
Katihar	0	0	3	0	0	0	0	0
Khagria	3	3	2	1	0	0	1	1
Lakhisarai	6	4	1	8	0	0	1	0
Munger	13	5	13	3	3	2	4	5
Muzaffarpur	7	9	17	1	18	1	4	1
Nalanda	0	0	3	0	0	0	0	0
Nawada	2	11	1	0	0	0	1	0
Patna	3	0	5	2	4	0	1	0

(*Contd.*)

Districts	*2009*		*2010*		*2011*		*2012 (up to August 15)*	
	Incidents	*Deaths*	*Incidents*	*Deaths*	*Incidents*	*Deaths*	*Incidents*	*Deaths*
Rohtas	14	0	28	6	51	9	5	0
Saran	3	4	7	1	3	0	1	0
Sharsa	1	0	0	0	0	0	1	0
Sheohar	9	7	12	12	9	1	1	1
Sitamarhi	7	0	11	3	8	2	4	0
Siwan	3	0	2	0	0	0	0	0
Vaishali	3	1	5	0	0	0	5	0
West Champaran	0	0	0	0	1	0	0	0
Total	232	72	307	97	316	63	120	22

Maharashtra

Districts	*2009*		*2010*		*2011*		*2012 (up to August 15)*	
	Incidents	*Deaths*	*Incidents*	*Deaths*	*Incidents*	*Deaths*	*Incidents*	*Deaths*
Gadchiroli	145	88	92	43	103	53	74	35
Gondia	9	5	2	2	6	1	14	2
Total	154	93	94	45	109	54	88	37

Madhya Pradesh

Districts	*2009*		*2010*		*2011*		*2012 (up to August 15)*	
	Incidents	*Deaths*	*Incidents*	*Deaths*	*Incidents*	*Deaths*	*Incidents*	*Deaths*
Balaghat	1	0	7	1	6	0	9	0
Singrauli	0	0	0	0	2	0	0	0
Total	1	0	7	1	8	0	9	0

Chhattisgarh

Districts	*2009*		*2010*		*2011*		*2012 (up to August 15)*	
	Incidents	*Deaths*	*Incidents*	*Deaths*	*Incidents*	*Deaths*	*Incidents*	*Deaths*
Bastar	32	6	36	8	30	20	6	0
Bijapur	177	79	203	81	133	65	59	30
Dantewada	128	92	200	138	139	50	34	13
Dhamtari	6	13	0	0	2	1	3	0
Durg	0	0	2	1	2	0	0	0
Jashpur	5	0	1	0	2	0	1	0
Kanker	69	31	64	31	50	24	16	6
Koriya	1	0	0	0	0	0	0	0

(*Contd.*)

Districts	2009		2010		2011		2012 (up to August 15)	
	Incidents	Deaths	Incidents	Deaths	Incidents	Deaths	Incidents	Deaths
Mahasamund	0	0	3	3	0	0	1	0
Narayanpur	52	8	74	52	47	19	31	8
Raigarh	1	1	0	0	1	0	1	0
Raipur	1	1	5	2	13	8	0	0
Rajnandgaon	39	56	30	27	26	16	17	4
Surguja	18	3	7	0	20	1	0	0
Balod	0	0	0	0	0	0	2	0
Balrampur	0	0	0	0	0	0	2	0
Gariabandh	0	0	0	0	0	0	14	4
Kondagaon	0	0	0	0	0	0	10	4
Sukma	0	0	0	0	0	0	55	16
Total	529	290	625	343	465	204	252	85

Jharkhand

Districts	2009		2010		2011		2012 (up to August 15)	
	Incidents	Deaths	Incidents	Deaths	Incidents	Deaths	Incidents	Deaths
Bokaro	29	15	16	3	36	5	18	2
Chatra	98	4	57	6	92	10	39	2
Deoghar	1	0	1	0	0	0	0	0
Dhanbad	9	3	4	0	3	0	5	2
Dumka	5	4	3	2	2	3	2	1
East Singhbhum	38	17	47	17	13	2	3	0
Garhwa	44	6	37	8	17	2	13	15
Giridih	25	8	18	12	19	3	21	9
Gumla	63	23	28	20	41	42	29	17
Hazaribagh	23	4	8	1	21	1	10	0
Jamtara	0	0	0	0	0	0	0	0
Khunti	31	15	39	26	42	24	27	23
Koderma	2	1	0	0	1	0	1	0
Latehar	95	28	80	19	61	29	47	5
Lohardaga	30	5	19	1	22	11	3	0
Pakur	1	2	0	0	3	1	2	1
Palamu	145	23	55	6	81	12	44	1
Ramgarh	5	2	3	0	1	0	3	0
Ranchi	39	21	30	9	12	9	13	6
Sahebganj	0	0	0	0	1	1	0	0
Saraikela- Kharswan	11	6	8	4	7	4	6	0
Simdega	12	4	18	11	21	13	25	18
West Singhbhum	36	17	30	12	21	10	17	6
Total	742	208	501	157	517	182	328	108

Karnataka

Districts	*2009*		*2010*		*2011*		*2012 (up to August 15)*	
	Incidents	*Deaths*	*Incidents*	*Deaths*	*Incidents*	*Deaths*	*Incidents*	*Deaths*
Chikmagalur	2	0	0	0	0	0	0	0
Shimoga	1	0	0	0	0	0	1	0
Udupi	1	0	1	0	1	1	0	0
Dakshina Kannada	0	0	0	0	0	0	2	0
Total	4	0	1	0	1	1	3	0

Kerala

Districts	*2009*		*2010*		*2011*		*2012 (up to August 15)*	
	Incidents	*Deaths*	*Incidents*	*Deaths*	*Incidents*	*Deaths*	*Incidents*	*Deaths*
Malappuram	0	0	1	0	0	0	0	0
Thrissur	0	0	2	0	1	0	0	0
Wynad	0	0	0	0	1	0	0	0
Total	0	0	3	0	2	0	0	0

Assam

Districts	*2009*		*2010*		*2011*		*2012 (up to August 15)*	
	Incidents	*Deaths*	*Incidents*	*Deaths*	*Incidents*	*Deaths*	*Incidents*	*Deaths*
Dibrugarh	0	0	1	0	0	0	0	0
Tinsukia	0	0	0	0	3	0	1	0
Dhemaji	0	0	0	0	0	0	2	0
Total	0	0	1	0	3	0	3	0

Haryana

Districts	*2009*		*2010*		*2011*		*2012 (up to August 15)*	
	Incidents	*Deaths*	*Incidents*	*Deaths*	*Incidents*	*Deaths*	*Incidents*	*Deaths*
Yamunanagar	1	0	0	0	0	0	0	0
Total	1	0	0	0	0	0	0	0

Odisha

Districts	2009		2010		2011		2012 (up to August 15)	
	Incidents	*Deaths*	*Incidents*	*Deaths*	*Incidents*	*Deaths*	*Incidents*	*Deaths*
Bargarh	0	0	1	0	3	1	9	2
Bolangir	0	0	0	0	5	2	30	1
Deogarh	1	0	0	0	0	0	1	0
Dhenkanal	1	0	0	0	0	0	0	0
Gajapati	9	0	12	5	3	0	0	0
Ganjam	1	0	8	1	18	0	5	0
Jajpur	0	0	2	0	1	0	0	0
Kalahandi	0	0	2	0	1	1	4	0
Kandhamal	11	2	8	6	10	5	5	3
Keonjhar	12	4	15	4	3	0	1	0
Koraput	52	26	57	31	59	15	40	11
Malkangiri	102	15	50	13	41	8	20	11
Mayurbhanj	17	4	4	2	1	0	0	0
Nawrangpur	0	0	4	5	3	2	1	0
Nuapada	4	2	5	1	11	14	8	2
Rayagada	14	8	12	1	11	3	5	1
Sambalpur	2	1	0	0	3	0	0	0
Sundergarh	40	5	38	10	19	2	4	2
Total	266	67	218	79	192	53	133	33

West Bengal

Districts	2009		2010		2011		2012 (up to August 15)	
	Incidents	*Deaths*	*Incidents*	*Deaths*	*Incidents*	*Deaths*	*Incidents*	*Deaths*
Bankura	12	14	29	20	3	1	0	0
Birbhum	0	0	6	5	0	0	0	0
Malda	1	1	0	0	0	0	0	0
Murshidabad	1	0	1	2	0	0	0	0
Purulia	36	15	50	37	10	6	0	0
West Midnapore	205	128	264	194	79	38	5	0
Total	255	158	350	258	92	45	5	0

Uttar Pradesh

Districts	2009		2010		2011		2012 (up to August 15)	
	Incidents	*Deaths*	*Incidents*	*Deaths*	*Incidents*	*Deaths*	*Incidents*	*Deaths*
Chandauli	1	0	1	1	0	0	0	0
Pilibhit	0	0	1	0	1	0	0	0
Sonebhadra	7	2	4	0	0	0	1	0
Total	8	2	6	1	1	0	1	0

Source: Rajya Sabha, Question No. 1935, answered on August 29, 2012.

Arms Looted by LWE Groups and Recovered by Security Forces

State	*2009 (June 1 to December 31)*		*2010*		*2011*		*2012 (up to July 31)*	
	Arms looted from SFs	*Arms recovered from naxalites*	*Arms looted from SFs*	*Arms recovered from naxalites*	*Arms looted from SFs*	*Arms recovered from naxalites*	*Arms looted from SFs*	*Arms recovered from naxalites*
Andhra Pradesh	0	65	0	48	0	24	0	35
Bihar	10	44	46	59	0	171	0	103
Jharkhand	4	96	11	217	15	165	19	91
Chhattisgarh	37	61	109	122	28	108	11	48
Madhya Pradesh	0	2	1	1	0	12	0	3
Maharashtra	21	13	0	27	1	12	1	8
Odisha	09	10	0	32	9	68	3	32
Uttar Pradesh	0	11	0	26	0	2	0	2
West Bengal	22	12	51	110	0	74	0	25
Karnataka	0	1	0	0	0	0	0	3
Kerala	0	0	0	0	0	0	0	0
Haryana	0	2	0	0	0	0	0	0
Tamil Nadu	0	0	0	0	0	0	0	5
Assam	0	0	3	0	1	0	0	0
Delhi	0	0	0	0	0	0	0	0
Gujarat	0	0	0	0	0	0	0	0
Goa	0	0	0	0	0	0	0	0
Punjab	0	0	0	0	0	0	0	0
Uttarakhand	0	0	0	0	0	0	0	0
TOTAL	103	317	221	642	54	636	34	355

Source: Rajya Sabha, Question No. 77, answered on August 8, 2012

Funds Relaeased under SRE, SIS and FPS Schemes, 2010-2012

(Figures in Rs. Crore)

State	*SRE Scheme*		*SIS*		*Scheme for Fortified Police Stations*	
	2010-11	*2011-12*	*2010-11*	*2011-12*	*2010-11*	*2011-12*
Andhra Pradesh	28.19	10.73	17.51	23.77	2.00	20.00
Bihar	29.41	13.65	17.39	34.66	2.00	44.75
Chhattisgarh	87.74	42.38	20.34	30.41	2.00	39.25
Jharkhand	59.40	75.35	20.08	35.61	2.00	39.25
Madhya Pradesh	1.56	0.27	2.32	7.48	1.00	5.60
Maharashtra	13.67	7.63	8.79	4.34	-	5.50
Odisha	56.62	21.57	20.36	40.47	1.00	37.50
Uttar Pradesh	3.56	2.00	11.22	4.41	-	8.25
West Bengal	18.91	13.90	11.99	4.67	-	9.90
Total	299.06	187.48	130.00	185.82	10.00	210.00

Source: Rajya Sabha, Unstarred Question No. 1922, answered on August 29, 2012.

LWE Violence-affected/ Under Influence Districts, 2011

Sl. No.	*State*	*Districts*	*Violence/ Under Influence*
1.	Andhra Pradesh	Khammam	Violence affected
2.		Karimnagar	Violence affected
3.		Rangareddy	Violence affected
4.		Vishakhapatnam	Violence affected
5.		Warangal	Violence affected
6.		East Godavari	Violence affected
7.		Adilabad	Under influence
8.		Ananthapur	Under influence
9.		Chittor	Under influence
10.		Guntur	Under influence
11.		Krishna	Under influence
12.		Nalgonda	Under influence
13.		Nellore	Under influence
14.		Nizamabad	Under influence
15.		Prakasam	Under influence
16.		Vizianagram	Under influence
17.		Srikalulam	Under influence
18.	Bihar	Arwal	Violence affected
19.		Aurangabad	Violence affected
20.		Banka	Violence affected
21.		Begusarai	Violence affected
22.		Bhojpur	Violence affected
23.		East Champaran	Violence affected
24.		Gaya	Violence affected
25.		Jamui	Violence affected
26.		Jehanabad	Violence affected
27.		Kaimur	Violence affected
28.		Munger	Violence affected
29.		Muzaffarpur	Violence affected
30.		Patna	Violence affected
31.		Rohtas	Violence affected
32.		Saran	Violence affected
33.		Sheohar	Violence affected
34.		Sitamarhi	Violence affected
35.		West Champaran	Violence affected
36.		Bhagalpur	Under influence
37.		Buxar	Under influence
38.		Darbangha	Under influence
39.		Gopalganj	Under influence
40.		Katihar	Under influence
41.		Khagaria	Under influence
42.		Lakhisarai	Under influence
43.		Nawada	Under influence
44.		Nalanda	Under influence
45.		Purnia	Under influence
46.		Samastipur	Under influence
47.		Siwan	Under influence

(*Contd.*)

Sl. No.	State	Districts	Violence/ Under Influence
48.		Vaishali	Under influence
49.	Chhattisgarh	Bastar	Violence affected
50.		Bijapur	Violence affected
51.		Dantewada	Violence affected
52.		Durg	Violence affected
53.		Dhamtari	Violence affected
54.		Jashpur	Violence affected
55.		Kanker	Violence affected
56.		Narayanpur	Violence affected
57.		Raipur	Violence affected
58.		Rajnandgaon	Violence affected
59.		Raigarh	Violence affected
60.		Surguja	Violence affected
61.		Bilaspur	Under influence
62.		Mahasamund	Under influence
63.	Delhi	Central Delhi	Under influence
64.		New Delhi	Under influence
65.		South Delhi	Under influence
66.		North West Delhi	Under influence
67.		South West Delhi	Under influence
68.		North	Under influence
69.		North East Delhi	Under influence
70.	Haryana	Jind	Under influence
71.		Fatehabad	Under influence
72.	Jharkhand	Bokaro	Violence affected
73.		Chatra	Violence affected
74.		Dumka	Violence affected
75.		Dhanbad	Violence affected
76.		East Singhbhum	Violence affected
77.		Garhwa	Violence affected
78.		Giridih	Violence affected
79.		Gumla	Violence affected
80.		Hazaribagh	Violence affected
81.		Khunti	Violence affected
82.		Koderma	Violence affected
83.		Latehar	Violence affected
84.		Lohardaga	Violence affected
85.		Palamu	Violence affected
86.		Pakur	Violence affected
87.		Ramgarh	Violence affected
88.		Ranchi	Violence affected
89.		Simdega	Violence affected
90.		Saraikela Kharswan	Violence affected
91.		Sahebganj	Violence affected
92.		West Singhbhum	Violence affected
93.		Deoghar	Under influence
94.		Jamtara	Under influence

(*Contd.*)

Sl. No.	State	Districts	Violence/ Under Influence
95.		Godda	Under influence
96.	Karnataka	Udupi	Violence affected
97.		Bangalore	Under influence
98.		Chikmanglur	Under influence
99.		Dakshina Kannada	Under influence
100.		Devanagere	Under influence
101.		Kopal	Under influence
102.		Kodagu	Under influence
103.		Mysore	Under influence
104.		Raichur	Under influence
105.		Shimoga	Under influence
106.	Kerala	Thrissur	Violence affected
107.		Alappuzha	Under influence
108.		Eranakulam	Under influence
109.		Idukki	Under influence
110.		Kasaragod	Under influence
111.		Kozhikode	Under influence
112.		Malapuram	Under influence
113.		Pathanamthitta	Under influence
114.		Palakkad	Under influence
115.		Trivandrum	Under influence
116.		Wayanad	Under influence
117.	Madhya Pradesh	Singroli	Violence affected
118.		Balaghat	Violence affected
119.		Bhind	Under influence
120.	Maharashtra	Gadchiroli	Violence affected
121.		Gondia	Violence affected
122.		Mumbai	Under influence
123.		Pune	Under influence
124.		Chandrapur	Under influence
125.		Nasik	Under influence
126.		Wardha	Under influence
127.	Odisha	Bargarh	Violence affected
128.		Bolangir	Violence affected
129.		Gajapati	Violence affected
130.		Ganjam	Violence affected
131.		Jajpur	Violence affected
132.		Kandhamal	Violence affected
133.		Keonjhar	Violence affected
134.		Kalahandi	Violence affected
135.		Koraput	Violence affected
136.		Malkangiri	Violence affected
137.		Mayurbhanj	Violence affected
138.		Nuapada	Violence affected
139.		Nabarangpur	Violence affected
140.		Rayagada	Violence affected

(*Contd.*)

Sl. No.	State	Districts	Violence/ Under Influence
141.		Sundergarh	Violence affected
142.		Sambhalpur	Violence affected
143.		Angul	Under influence
144.		Bhadrak	Under influence
145.		Deogarh	Under influence
146.		Sonepur	Under influence
147.		Cuttack	Under influence
148.		Khurda	Under influence
149.	Uttar Pradesh	Pilibhit	Violence affected
150.		Allahabad	Under influence
151.		Azamgarh	Under influence
152.		Balia	Under influence
153.		Chandauli	Under influence
154.		Kaushambi	Under influence
155.		Sonbhadra	Under influence
156.		Shravasti	Under influence
157.	West Bengal	Bankura	Violence affected
158.		Purulia	Violence affected
159.		West Midnapore	Violence affected
160.		Birbhim	Under influence
161.		Darjeeling	Under influence
162.		Jalpaiguri	Under influence
163.		Kolkata	Under influence
164.		Malda	Under influence
165.		Murshidabad	Under influence
166.		Nadia	Under influence
167.		North Dinajpur	Under influence
168.		South 24 Parganas	Under influence
169.	Tamil Nadu	Dharmapuri	Under influence
170.		Chennai	Under influence
171.		Krishnagiri	Under influence
172.		Madurai	Under influence
173.		Namakkul	Under influence
174.		Salem	Under influence
175.		Vellore	Under influence
176.	Uttrakhand	Nainital	Under influence
177.		U.S. Nagar	Under influence
178.		Pithoragarh	Under influence
179.		Pauri	Under influence
180.	Punjab	Amritsar	Under influence
181.		Bathinda	Under influence
182.		Ferozpur	Under influence
183.		Gurdaspur	Under influence
184.		Ludhiana	Under influence
185.		Mansa	Under influence
186.		Moga	Under influence

(*Contd.*)

Sl. No.	*State*	*Districts*	*Violence/ Under Influence*
187.		Nawanshahar	Under influence
188.		Patiala	Under influence
189.	Tripura	North Tripura	Under influence
190.		South Tripura	Under influence
191.	Assam	Tinsukia	Violence affected
192.		Karbi Anglong	Under influence
193.		Jorehat	Under influence
194.		Sonitpur	Under influence
195.		Shivsagar	Under influence
196.		Lakhimpur	Under influence
197.		Golaghat	Under influence
198.		Dhemaji	Under influence
199.		Dibrugarh	Under influence
200.		Darrang	Under influence
201.	Rajasthan	Jhunjhunu	Under influence
202.	Arunachal Pradesh	Dibang Valley	Under influence
203.		Lohit	Under influence

Source: Rajya Sabha Unstarred Question No. 1943, answered on August 29, 2012

States and Disricts under Schedule V Areas

State	*Districts that are fully under Schedule V*	*Districts that are partially under Schedule V*
Andhra Pradesh		1. Vishakhapatnam 2. East Godavari 3. West Godavari 4. Adilabad 5. Warangal
Jharkhand	1. Ranchi 2. Singhbhum	1. Palamu 2. Santhal Parganas
Gujarat	1. Dangs	1. Surat 2. Bharuch 3. Valsad 4. Panchmahals 5. Sadodara 6. Sabarkantha
Himachal Pradesh	1. Lahul and Spiti 2. Kinnaur	1. Chamba
Madhya Pradesh	1. Jhabua 2. Mandla 3. Dindori 4. Barwani	1. Dhar 2. West Nimar (Khargone) 3. East Nimar (Khandwa), 4. Ratlam 5. Betul 6. Seoni 7. Balaghat 8. Hoshangabad 9. Sidhi 10. Shahdol 11. Umariya 12. Sheopur 13. Chhindwara

(*Contd.*)

State	*Districts that are fully under Schedule V*	*Districts that are partially under Schedule V*
Chhattisgarh	1. Sarguja 2. Koriya 3. Jashpur 4. Kanker 5. Bastar 6. Dantewada 7. Korba	1. Raigarh 2. Bilaspur 3. Durg 4. Rajnandgaon 5. Raipur 6. Dhamtari
Maharashtra		1. Thane 2. Nasik 3. Dhule 4. Jalgaon 5. Ahmednagar 6. Pune 7. Nanded 8. Amravati 9. Yavatmal 10. Gadchiroli 11. Chandrapur
Odisha	1. Mayurbhanj 2. Sundargarh 3. Koraput	1. Sambalpur 2. Keonjhar 3. Khondmals 4. Ganjam 5. Kalahandi 6. Balasore
Rajasthan	1. Banswara 2. Dungarpur	1. Udaipur 2. Chhitaurgarh 3. Sirohi

Source: Rajya Sabha Unstarred Question No. 1943, answered on August 29, 2012.

Maoist Violence Profile, 2009-2012

State	*2009*			*2010*			*2011*			*2012 (up to July 31)*		
	Naxals killed	*Civilians killed*	*CAPFs killed*	*Naxals killed*	*Civilians killed*	*CAPFs killed*	*Naxals killed*	*Civilians killed*	*CAPFs killed*	*Naxals killed*	*Civilians killed*	*CAPFs killed*
Andhra Pradesh	17	0	0	13	0	0	4	0	0	3	0	0
Bihar	1	0	0	4	0	0	14	1	2	5	0	1
Chhattisgarh	120	0	10	82	2	0	34	1	6	26	0	1
Jharkhand	25	3	8	15	2	1	13	4	2	5	0	1
Karnataka	0	0	0	1	0	0	0	0	0	0	0	0
Madhya Pradesh	0	0	0	0	0	0	0	0	0	1	0	0
Maharashtra	4	0	0	2	0	0	3	0	4	2	0	0
Odisha	6	0	0	9	0	0	23	0	0	4	0	0
Uttar Pradesh	1	0	0	0	0	0	0	0	0	0	0	0
West Bengal	7	3	0	34	0	2	5	1	0	1	0	0
Assam	0	0	0	0	0	0	0	0	0	4	0	0
Total	181	6	18	160	4	3	96	7	14	51	0	3

CAPFs: Central Armed Police Forces

Source: Rajya Sabha, Question No. 64, answered on August 8, 2012.

Pan-India Economc Targets by LWE Extremists, 2009-2012

		2009	*2010*	*2011*	*2012 (up to 15 July)*
ECONOMIC TARGETS					
Andhra Pradesh	Uranium Mines	0	0	0	0 (0)
	Essar steel	0	0	0	0 (0)
Chhattisgarh	NMDC	2	11	2	0 (1)
	Essar pipe lines	1	1	0	0 (0)
	BRO	0	0	0	0 (0)
	Gramin Sadak Nirman Yojana	4	3	4	1 (4)
Odisha	Essar pipe lines	5	1	2	1 (0)
	Gramin Sadak Nirman Yojana	2	4	3	2 (2)
Maharashtra	BRO	0	1	1	0 (0)
Madhya Pradesh	Gramin Sadak Nirman Yojana	0	1	0	1 (0)
Bihar	Cement Plant	0	0	0	0 (0)
	Solar Plate	2	0	0	0 (0)
	Gramin Sadak Nirmal Yojana	1	1	2	0 (2)
Jharkhand	Gramin Sadak Nirmal Yojana	0	1	3	0 (0)
	Essar Pipe lines	0	0	1	0 (1)
	Total	17	24	18	5 (10)
RAILWAY					
Andhra Pradesh		0	1	0	0 (0)
Bihar		8	16	3	1 (3)
Chhattisgarh		5	8	11	6 (5)
Jharkhand		17	13	10	2 (7)
Maharashtra		0	0	0	0 (0)
Odisha		10	7	7	0 (7)
West Bengal		6	7	0	0 (0)
Uttar Pradesh		0	2	0	0 (0)
	Total	46	54	31	9 (22)
TELEPHONE EXCHANGE/TOWER					
Andhra Pradesh		0	4	2	1 (1)
Bihar		24	14	25	10 (16)
Maharashtra		1	1	2	1 (0)
Chhattisgarh		10	2	3	0 (2)
Jharkhand		14	6	8	3 (3)
Odisha		18	17	11	7 (3)
West Bengal		0	1	0	0 (0)
Madhya Pradesh		-	-	-	1 (0)
	Total	67	45	51	23 (25)
POWER PLANT					
Andhra Pradesh		0	1	0	0 (0)
Chhattisgarh		0	0	0	0 (0)
West Bengal		0	1	0	0 (0)
Maharashtra		2	1	0	0 (0)
	Total	2	3	0	0 (0)

(*Contd.*)

	2009	*2010*	*2011*	*2012 (up to 15 July)*
MINING				
Odisha	1	1	1	0 (1)
Jharkhand	2	6	2	0 (2)
Chhattisgarh	0	0	3	1 (3)
Andhra Pradesh	0	0	0	0 (0)
Maharashtra	0	1	0	0 (0)
West Bengal	0	1	0	0 (0)
Total	3	9	6	1 (6)
POLE/TRANSMISSION				
Chhattisgarh	7	1	3	0 (2)
Odisha	0	0	0	0 (0)
Jharkhand	0	1	0	0 (0)
Total	7	2	3	0 (2)
PANCHAYAT BHAWAN				
Chhattisgarh	0	3	0	0 (0)
Jharkhand	7	4	0	1 (0)
Andhra Pradsesh	0	0	0	0 (0)
Maharashtra	8	6	6	1 (0)
Bihar	3	0	1	0 (1)
Odisha	3	11	1	1 (1)
West Bengal	2	7	2	0 (2)
Total	23	31	10	3 (4)
SCHOOL BUILDING				
Chhattisgarh	7	13	2	3 (0)
Andhra Pradesh	0	1	0	0 (0)
Jharkhand	37	7	6	0 (3)
Bihar	21	10	18	0 (10)
Maharashtra	1	0	0	0 (0)
Odisha	5	8	1	0 (0)
Total	71	39	27	3 (13)
Forest road, culverts etc.	126	158	147	116 (96)
TOTAL	362	365	293	160 (178)

*Figures in Brackets are of corresponding period for 2011.

Source: Rajya Sabha Unstarred Question No. 72, answered on August 8, 2012.

Index